Working Memory and Academic Learning

Assessment and Intervention

By
Milton J. Dehn

WILEY

John Wiley & Sons, Inc.

Library of Congress Cataloging-in-Publication Data:

Dehn, Milton J.
   Working memory and academic learning : assessment and intervention / by Milton J. Dehn.
      p. cm.
   Includes bibliographical references and index.
   ISBN 978-0-470-14419-0 (pbk.)
1. Short-term memory. 2. Learning, Psychology of. I. Title.
   BF378.S54D44 2008
   370.15'22—dc22   2007041569

Printed in the United States of America

10 9 8 7 6 5 4 3 2 1

*To my parents, LeRoy Louis Dehn
and Norene C. Dehn, who
taught me the value of
honesty and hard work.*

CONTENTS

FOREWORD

Working memory (WM) is an important cortical construct that can be described in many ways. It has been identified as the translator between sensory input and long-term memory, the cognitive difference between a baby who is bound by external stimuli and a toddler who becomes dictatorial about his or her likes and dislikes. It is rehearsal, images, inner speech, emotion, attention, and the stuff of how an individual develops preferences.

Deficits in WM produce systemic and lifelong problems. Living a stressful life can diminish WM capacity and depression can radically alter its course, causing significant issues that will affect other aspects of behavior and memory. Deficits in the central executive component of WM create attentional problems that directly affect learning and behavior. Similarly, deficits in the phonological loop and visual sketchpad of WM are involved in most reading disabilities. Therefore, WM interacts with the world and becomes a buffer or conduit depending on the genetic makeup of the individual and his or her experiences in the environment.

The National Institutes of Health and the Centers for Disease Control and Prevention have recently placed great emphasis on the translation of research from the "bench to the bedside." While many of the federally funded translational research grants that have been recently created focus on medical research, the need for brain-behavior research that translates studies of the brain into practical interventions are also coming to fruition. In some respects, the recent call for accountability in clinical practice and school practice has also prompted translational efforts. Many researchers in neuroscience and neuropsychology are now extending their efforts from prior theory-to-analysis to theory-to-analysis-to-treatment efficacy. Interventions must be well grounded in theory and studied with multiple validation methods that do not stop short of or omit ecological validity concerns.

In terms of working memory, there is a great deal of federal interest and international discourse on its definition, localization, and functional reach. Studies have sought to define working memory parameters and constituent parts and, although all do not agree on those issues, there is a consensus that deficits in working memory wreak havoc on higher cortical processes such as reading, mathematics, and the organization of intentional behavior. Neuroimaging has sustained the localization of WM functions as generally outlined in theory by Baddeley and Hitch. Now we have images that, for the first time, validate what was hypothesized all along. The future holds much promise for supporting working memory interventions because recent brain imaging techniques have taken a quantum leap in efficiency, practicality, cost, and availability. Perhaps the future will support assessment and intervention with working memory in ways that we cannot attain or even imagine at the present time. Therefore, it is time to be practical and codify theoretical perspectives on working memory and utilize research studies that shed light on interventions that remediate and compensate for working memory deficits. It is time to translate theory into practice because we now know enough to affect positive changes and we are acutely aware of how important WM is to academic and behavioral success.

This *Working Memory* volume by Dr. Milton Dehn is going to be a timely and welcome addition to the resources available for psychology professionals assisting children in schools, private practice, and clinics. We have known about the importance of working memory for many years and neuroimaging has confirmed the localization of its main constituent parts, but very little practical information is written about how to identify and enhance working memory in children. In addition, very little is written about the practical aspects of assessing working memory components and relating the information into everyday learning activities in the classroom. There is so much raw information on WM available it is very difficult for the working professional to codify the existing research and theory about WM and then relate it to clinical practice; and here, Dr. Dehn has done the work for us.

In this volume, Dr. Dehn has taken the time to lay out the prodigious history of theory and research on WM. He provides a historical analysis of how working memory came to be defined and also describes the synergy of multiple theorists. The reader is left with an intuitive understanding of how working memory came to be deconstructed in the research literature and a summary of the extensive list of models of WM construction that have come into being. Probably the most important foundational support of this book is Dr. Dehn's presentation of an integrated model of WM. He presents a parsimonious model that easily translates into clinical practice. The model is a bridge between research and intervention and it accurately translates theory into practice.

Also of basic importance for a work of this type, Dr. Dehn stresses developmental aspects of WM that are integral for understanding WM in children and its relationship to other cognitive processes. How WM deficits play out in different disorders first identified in childhood is another area of focus that is important in this book.

Clinicians and teachers are directed to specific information about the most common disorders that have WM deficits as a part of the condition. Knowing how WM affects a learning disability, for example, paves the way to utilizing WM interventions with precision for children with reading disabilities or math disabilities. Dr. Dehn describes various types of cognitive and memory assessment instruments that tap into working memory and describes the contents, strengths, and weaknesses of each instrument. This valuable synopsis allows the clinical reader to easily find and adapt instruments already commonly used in assessment in schools, clinics, and inpatient facilities. Dr. Dehn does not leave it there, however, but he goes on to explain in very explicit terms how WM affects classroom performance and how the clinician or teacher should intervene in everyday learning activities.

It is very rare that an author can demonstrate a thorough understanding of the history and theory of a cognitive construct as complex as WM. It is even more rare to witness an author taking the benefit of history and theory and translating it into assessment, differential diagnosis, and interventions that can be easily administered by educational personnel in the classroom. We live in an age when laboratory research that seeks to infiltrate real life is encouraged and supported by the federal government—when theory and neuroimaging are combined to produce workable models of intervention for those who suffer from disorders that affect thinking and learning. Most of the time, it is up to us clinicians to assemble all of the historical and theoretical studies, digest the information at length, relate the information to fields of study outside of our own, maintain objectivity, build assessment batteries that will address differential diagnosis, develop interventions that directly relate to our efforts, and consult with other professionals who will actually carry out our recommendations. Realistically speaking, this is very difficult and time consuming for the average clinician to do, although we do it. In the case of working memory, however, Dr. Milt Dehn has completed it for us and with rigorous adherence to the scientist-practitioner model of inquiry. This is a book that demonstrates state-of-the-art brain-behavior relationships. This is a book we can rely on. This is a book that will help us help children. Many thanks to Dr. Dehn!

Elaine Fletcher-Janzen, Ed.D., NCSP

PREFACE

Working memory is one of the most important concepts to emerge from cognitive psychology in the past 35 years. What is known about working memory has significant implications for cognitive functioning and, in particular, for academic learning. For instance, knowledge of working memory functions can facilitate identification of learning disabilities. Yet many psychologists and educators do not fully appreciate the multidimensional nature of working memory and the critical roles it plays in cognitive functioning and learning. Also, they are not fully aware of the measurement options and evidence-based interventions for working memory deficiencies. Consequently, it is not surprising that psychologists seldom test memory in a direct or comprehensive manner when children and adolescents are referred for learning difficulties, despite the likelihood that a working memory deficit is underlying the child's learning problems. From my perspective, learners of all ages will benefit if educators, psychologists, and related professionals acquire a better understanding of working memory and its relationship with learning, as well as develop more expertise in working memory assessment and intervention. Thus, the primary purpose of this book is to provide professional development on this extremely important topic. This book is also intended for use as a course textbook and a professional reference book.

We have all experienced the limitations of a normal working memory. How many times have we forgotten a piece of information because the focus of our attention shifted to something else? For example, on countless occasions, we have not been able to remember what we were going to say or what someone else just said. Surely, we have all felt the frustration that occurs when we cannot retrieve information that we were processing just a moment ago. Now try to imagine what it would be like if you were a student with subaverage working memory capacity or a significant intra-individual weakness in working memory. Compound that with not knowing that you have such a deficiency, and for that matter, no one else knowing about it either. Then, imagine having the learning problem resulting from your working memory deficiency attributed to some irrelevant variable, such as motivation. Finally, imagine missing opportunities to learn strategies that could help you compensate for the working memory shortcoming. If you have dedicated your life to helping and teaching children and adolescents, you should now have some compelling reasons for reading this book. What you can learn from this book will increase your ability to help those with working memory problems.

Here's a preview of the chapters:

1. *Introduction and Overview* introduces the construct of working memory, along with some of the key topics and major themes. The response-to-intervention model is compared with the approach advocated in this book.

2. *Theories and Models of Working Memory* traces the history of the working memory construct and reviews several major theories. The preeminent model, Baddeley's four-part model, is discussed in depth. Neuropsychological evidence for the construct is summarized. The chapter concludes with an examination of the controversy surrounding the distribution of working memory resources.

3. *An Integrated Model of Working Memory* proposes an integrated model of working memory designed to facilitate working memory assessment. For the remainder of the book, the model is used to classify subtests according to the memory component they are thought to measure. The model's structure also forms the basis for analyzing working memory test results.

4. *Working Memory Development and Related Cognitive Processes* begins with an overview of working memory development, including the emersion of strategies and recoding during the early elementary years. The chapter concludes with descriptions of highly related cognitive processes and disorders that frequently include working memory deficits.

5. *Working Memory and Academic Learning* is a core chapter with an in-depth review of the literature on the relations between specific memory components and the specific academic skills of reading, mathematics, and written language.

6. *Working Memory Assessment Strategies* provides a structure for working memory assessment. Step-by-step methods that cover initial hypothesis generation to analysis and interpretation are described in detail. The heart of the recommended methodology is a cross-battery, selective testing approach. The informal methods section contains a comprehensive list of classroom behaviors that are indicative of working memory deficits.

7. *Using Cognitive Scales to Assess Working Memory* includes a table that identifies the short-term memory and working memory components measured by each of several major cognitive scales. For each scale, the memory subtests are described and interpretative suggestions are provided.

8. *Assessing Working Memory with Memory Scales* has a similar structure to that of Chapter 7, only this time broad memory scales are reviewed, followed by detailed introductions to three scales that are designed specifically for working memory assessment.

9. *Working Memory Interventions* is a core chapter that begins with general strategy training procedures. The chapter then proceeds to cite the empirical support for several working memory, several long-term memory, and a few related cognitive interventions. For most of the interventions, enough details are provided for basic implementation. Effective teaching practices that address working memory limitations are also included.

10. *Case Studies, Reporting Results, and Recommendations* discusses some assessment cases that illustrate typical profiles found in children and adolescents with disabilities. The chapter also contains recommendations for the oral explanation of test results, how to interpret cross-battery results in written reports, future research, and future test development.

ACKNOWLEDGMENTS

This project could not have been completed without the encouragement, support, and hard work of Paula A. Dehn. I also wish to thank Ryan Weigel for gathering the literature and reviewing the manuscript, and I am grateful to Aimee Zabrowski for providing feedback on chapters.

CHAPTER 1

Introduction and Overview

N early every aspect of human life depends on memory. Individuals who cannot encode, store, or retrieve information must rely on others for their survival. Even mild memory impairments can make daily activities challenging. Because learning depends on memory, deficiencies in any aspect of memory can prevent children and adolescents from acquiring the skills and knowledge necessary for success in life. As the research accumulates, it is becoming quite evident that memory problems are frequently the cause of learning problems. Even individuals with normal memory capacity must utilize their memory resources efficiently if they are to learn effectively. Successful teachers have recognized the limitations of human memory and have discovered how to facilitate the construction of strong memory representations in their students. Therefore, those engaged in supporting learning can be more effective when they have expertise in memory.

The recognition of memory's crucial role in life and learning can be traced back to the days of the ancient Greeks. With the advent of public education in the nineteenth century, American educators began to identify different types of memories and instructional methods designed to support memory. The young science of psychology was also quick to focus on memory models and measurement (James, 1890). For example, the classic digit span test goes back to the 1880s. However, it wasn't until the mid-twentieth century that psychologists were able to identify distinct memory dimensions and functions. More recently, the memory construct known as "working memory" has emerged and refinement of the construct continues to the present day. Currently, research on working memory is at the forefront of neuroscientific investigations. Also, the fields of education and psychology have demonstrated a high interest in learning more about working memory. In the first six months of 2007 alone, more than 150 articles on working memory were published in professional journals.

The scientific literature provides an opportunity to learn more about the functioning of memory and how to treat memory deficits. Acquiring more knowledge about working memory can make a significant contribution to our understanding of how students think, learn, and remember. Armed with such knowledge, we can better identify the probable causes of learning difficulties and suggest evidence-based interventions that address memory deficiencies.

What is Working Memory?

In the study of human cognitive functions over the past 35 years, working memory has been one of the most influential constructs. Traditionally, working memory has been conceptualized as an active memory system that is responsible for the temporary maintenance and simultaneous processing of information (Bayliss, Jarrold, Baddeley, Gunn, & Leigh, 2005). Alternatively, working memory has been defined as the use of temporarily stored information in the performance of more complex cognitive tasks (Hulme & Mackenzie, 1992), or as a mental workspace for manipulating activated long-term memory representations (Stoltzfus, Hasher, & Zacks, 1996). Overall, working memory is viewed as a comprehensive system that unites various short- and long-term memory subsystems and functions (Baddeley, 1986). Diverse working memory theories and models (see Chapter 2) have several structures and processes in common: (1) a division into verbal and visuospatial stores; (2) an encoding function; (3) involvement in effortful retrieval from long-term memory; (4) enactment of strategic processes; and (5) executive and attentional processes. In general, the combination of moment-to-moment awareness, efforts to maintain information in short-term memory, and the effortful retrieval of archived information constitutes working memory. Despite definitions limiting working memory to memory-related functions, many researchers and practitioners use the term broadly. From the perspective offered in this text, we must be cautious when considering the construct of working memory, lest everything that goes on in the mind is classified as working memory. If the construct is allowed to become too inclusive, then its usefulness will decline. Consequently, in this text, the definition of working memory is limited to the management, manipulation, and transformation of information drawn from either short-term or long-term memory (see Chapter 3).

However, it is difficult to delimit working memory and disentangle it from related cognitive processes, such as reasoning. From a broad perspective, working memory is a central cognitive process that is responsible for the active processing of information. It appears to be a fundamental capacity that underlies complex as well as elementary cognitive processes (Lepine, Barrouillet, & Camos, 2005). Working memory supports human cognitive processing by providing an interface between perception, short-term memory, long-term memory, and goal-directed actions. Working memory is particularly necessary for conscious cognitive processing because it permits internal representation of information to guide decision making and overt behavior. Fundamentally, working memory is one of the main cognitive processes underlying thinking and learning. By utilizing the contents of various memory-storage systems, working memory enables us to learn and to string together thoughts and ideas.

Working memory's relations with various aspects of academic learning (see Chapter 5) mainly arise from its limited capacity. Although there are individual differences, the capacity of working memory is quite restricted, even in individuals with normal working memory resources. For example, the typical individual can only manipulate about four pieces of information at a time (Cowan, 2001). And, unless information is being manipulated, it will only remain in working memory for a short interval, perhaps as little as 2 seconds. Thus, there has always been an emphasis on working memory's limited capacity to retain information while simultaneously processing the same or other information (Swanson, 2000). Because of the central role working memory plays in cognitive functioning and learning, successful learning is largely a function of the individual's working memory capacity. For instance, a child with a severe deficit in verbal working memory is likely to have a reading disability (see Chapter 5). Moreover, given the inherent limitations of working memory, efficient utilization of its resources is important for all individuals, not just those with working memory deficits.

In our daily activities, we are constantly dealing with demands and goals that compete for the limited processing capability of working memory. Luckily, the active participation of the working memory system is not needed for all cognitive operations or behavior. Many cognitive functions and behaviors can be carried out in a fairly automatic fashion with little or no reliance on working memory (Unsworth & Engle, 2007). However, working memory is necessary for the acquisition of skill mastery that leads to automatized processing. It is also necessary when dealing with novel information, problems, or situations; trying to inhibit irrelevant information; maintaining new information; and consciously retrieving information from long-term memory.

Working Memory versus Short-Term Memory

Many cognitive psychologists and memory experts view short-term and working memory as interchangeable or consider one to be a subtype of the other. Other theorists and researchers contend that working memory and short-term memory are distinguishable constructs (see Chapter 2)—a perspective promoted in this text (see Chapter 3). Regardless of which view the reader adopts, it is important for assessment and intervention purposes to recognize the contrasts between short-term memory (STM) and working memory (WM). The chief differences are:

- STM passively holds information; WM actively processes it.
- STM capacity is domain specific (verbal and visual); WM capacity is less domain specific.
- WM has stronger relationships with academic learning and with higher-level cognitive functions.
- STM automatically activates information stored in long-term memory; WM consciously directs retrieval of desired information from long-term memory.
- STM has no management functions; WM has some executive functions.
- STM can operate independently of long-term memory; WM operations rely heavily on long-term memory structures.
- STM retains information coming from the environment; WM retains products of various cognitive processes.

Short-term memory and working memory are separable, and short-term memory can function without working memory. Nonetheless, short-term memory and its measurement are included in this text, mainly because the predominant theories of working memory incorporate short-term memory as a subsidiary system. Accordingly, the majority of empirical investigations have included short-term memory, with many not discriminating well between short-term and working memory. Likewise, several assessment instruments are structured in ways that confound the measurement of short-term and working memory.

Controversies Surrounding Working Memory

Some psychologists question the working memory construct itself. Unlike short-term memory, it is more difficult to prove that working memory is a unique cognitive entity. For example, working memory has been viewed as essentially the same as focused attention, executive processing, and linguistic processing. Moreover, we have much to learn about some of the subprocesses that comprise the working memory system. For instance, the functioning of phonological short-term memory and verbal working memory is well documented but there remains considerable cloudiness regarding the executive functions of working memory. In addition to these uncertainties, there has been an ongoing dispute over the distribution of working memory resources. Some researchers argue that there is a single pool of resources shared by all short-term and working memory components, whereas others advocate for separate capacities for each component. Furthermore, the debate over the immutability of working memory capacity is far from settled. Some recent research (see Chapter 9) has indicated that capacity can be increased; however, most evidence-based interventions for working memory focus on increasing its efficiency. Regarding the relations between working memory and academic learning, overwhelming evidence has un-equivocally established learning's dependence on working memory (see Chapter 5). With learning, about the only dispute that remains is whether students with learning disabilities have diminished working memory capacity or are simply not using their working memory resources efficiently (see Chapter 5).

Working Memory Measurement

Since the early days of psychology, when more children began attending school for longer periods of time, the existence of individual differences in mental capabilities, including memory, has been apparent. In 1905, Binet and Simon included short-term memory subtests in their seminal intelligence scale. Wechsler did the same with the introduction of his first scale in 1939. Despite the early start, the development of broad-based memory scales did not occur until nearly the end of the Twentieth Century. Within the past 15 years, interest in the measurement of working memory has corresponded with several new options. For example, the most recent revisions of intellectual scales have incorporated "working memory" measures for the first time. Also, batteries designed for the comprehensive assessment of working memory have been introduced. Unfortunately, now that we have the measurement technology for working memory assessment, the usefulness of school-based cognitive testing is being challenged, especially in regards to assessment for learning disabilities.

The apparent decline in school-based cognitive testing is primarily the result of dissatisfaction with the ability-achievement discrepancy approach to identifying learning disabilities. However, some of the "blame" for the impending decline in cognitive testing can be placed on the structure of intellectual scales and an overemphasis on IQ scores. Although measures of general intelligence are strong predictors of academic learning and success in life, an IQ score leaves many questions unanswered. In particular, an IQ score fails to explain *why* some students with normal intelligence have extreme difficulties learning. Furthermore, IQ scores provide little direction regarding the selection of interventions that might benefit individual students.

At the forefront of working memory assessment are multiple-factor instruments that allow investigation of the subprocesses involved in short-term and working memory (see Chapter 8). If we could only obtain estimates of overall working memory functioning or only one component of short-term and working memory, there would be little need for this text. Although knowing that a working memory impairment exists is important information, it is even more helpful to know the underlying processing problem that accounts for the deficit. For example, a working memory deficit might be due to a phonological/verbal memory deficit, a visuospatial memory deficit, or an executive memory deficit. Depending on which memory processes or components are deficient, the learning implications and the best interventions differ dramatically. The application of the assessment methods recommended in this text, in conjunction with the use of existing test batteries (including intellectual and cognitive scales), will allow psychologists to parse and distinguish the various short-term memory and working memory components that are so indispensable for academic learning.

Despite the recent advances, assessment of working memory presents some challenges (see Chapter 6). The main obstacle is the paucity of test batteries designed for the comprehensive assessment of working memory and related memory functions. Moreover, there is inconsistent measurement across tests (partly because some of the batteries are atheoretical). Given the exact same task, different test authors will claim that it is measuring different constructs. For example, some authors claim that forward digit span is measuring attention, others say it is measuring short-term memory, and still others classify it as a working memory measure. Consequently, it is usually unclear as to which memory components the scales actually measure and how short-term and working memory are differentiated (see Chapter 6). Of the various working memory stores and processes, phonological short-term memory is the only one for which there are relatively pure measures. Even with adequate measurement tools, working memory performance is highly influenced by several factors, including attention, executive processes, processing speed, long-term memory, and the individual's level of expertise in particular domains, such as mathematics skills. Finally, the assessment of working memory is challenging because it is difficult to measure directly. Because working memory subtests typically measure short-term memory span, examiners can only draw inferences about working memory capacity and processes.

Compatibility with Response-to-Intervention

The Response-to-Intervention (RTI) movement now being adopted by many states and school districts emphasizes early, evidence-based interventions for all children who fail to meet grade-level benchmarks in academics. Proponents of RTI believe that a child's failure to respond to an evidence-based intervention is a strong indication of a learning disability. According to RTI advocates, the identification of a "processing deficit" (working memory is a type of processing) is an ineffective method of determining the existence of a learning disability. RTI proponents also consider processing and memory assessment irrelevant because they do not believe there are any effective interventions for processing and memory problems. Both of these claims are disputed in this text and an abundance of evidence is provided that will allow the reader to make an informed decision regarding this debate. First, there is overwhelming evidence that working memory and all types of academic achievement are highly related (see Chapter 5). Furthermore, a high percentage of children with learning disabilities are found to have working memory weaknesses and deficits. There should be little doubt that working memory difficulties are highly predictive of early school failure. Not only can working memory assessment inform the diagnosis of learning disabilities, but the early screening of working memory could identify children at risk for learning problems. Second, there are evidence-based interventions for memory impairments, and these interventions can produce more effective learning (see Chapter 9).

Assessment and intervention for working-memory problems are compatible with RTI. Even with an extremely effective RTI program, some students with learning challenges will continue to struggle academically. Following the RTI approach, these students will then receive more intense interventions and be considered for special education placement. An assessment, including cognitive testing, may be conducted when a child has failed to respond to regular education interventions. Inclusion of working memory testing can be justified because: (a) it might identify why the student is not responding to intervention (many students with disabilities are "resistant" to routine interventions because of a memory or processing impairment); and (b) identification of a working memory weakness or deficit is important information to consider when designing or selecting more intense interventions. (Not all academic interventions include practices that address working memory deficiencies.) To ignore the information a working memory assessment can provide is to make intervention selections with limited knowledge of the child's learning processes. Both RTI and the practices advocated in this text have the best interests of learners in mind. Current psychological measurement tools can provide invaluable information about the working memory strengths and weaknesses of students in need of academic assistance. Learners with working memory deficits might benefit from evidence-based interventions specifically designed to ameliorate memory weaknesses. It is also important that teachers recognize the student's working memory problems and provide appropriate accommodations. In addition, it is essential that the selected academic interventions incorporate methods that allow a student with working memory deficiencies to learn effectively.

Interventions for Working Memory

Most of the working memory interventions reviewed in this text are intended for school settings and can be performed by teachers and related professionals. Consistent with other types of educational interventions, these interventions are often compensatory in nature. The interventions are not intended to increase working memory capacity any more than interventions for students with mental retardation claim to increase intelligence. Rather, the bulk of the interventions are designed to improve performance. Most often, performance can be improved by increasing the efficiency of working memory processing. Increased efficiency allows for more effective utilization of working memory resources. Thus, many of the recommended interventions consist of strategies that enhance working memory processes.

It may surprise some readers to learn that some of the recommended interventions (see Chapter 9) are not specifically designed for working memory impairments. Because of the highly interactive nature of working memory, strengthening peripheral systems can improve working memory performance. For example, interventions that improve phonological processing may produce collateral improvement in phonological short-term memory. This principle also applies to mnemonics and other long-term memory interventions. That is, stronger long-term memory structures or representations reduce the load on working memory, thereby improving working memory performance. In addition, the interventions approach in this text adheres to a top-down model. The top-down philosophy is that improvements in higher-level functions will produce improvements in subsidiary systems. For example, when most of the working memory components are weak, the initial intervention should focus on executive working memory. Finally, this text will review effective teaching practices and instructional models that support the working memory deficiencies of challenged learners.

Learning Objectives

After reading, reviewing, and applying the information and practices discussed in this text, the reader will be able to:

1. Trace the history of the working memory construct, from its origins in the 1950s to contemporary factor structures.

2. Identify the four components of Baddeley's preeminent working memory model, as well as some of the supportive research.

3. Explain the interdependency between working memory and long-term memory, and state why the connection between the two is as important as the short-term memory and working memory relationship.

4. Recognize the limitations of working memory and short-term resources, and how these resources are distributed during different processing activities.

5. State some of the key differences between short-term memory and working memory.

6. Recognize the effects of expertise and automatization on working memory.

7. Differentiate between cognitive weaknesses and cognitive deficits.

8. Identify several cognitive processes that are closely related with working memory.

9. Identify some of the relationships that short-term memory and working memory components have with specific academic skills.

10. Differentiate between subtests that measure short-term memory and those that measure working memory.

11. Recognize several classroom behaviors that are indicative of working memory deficiencies.

12. Apply selective testing and cross-battery procedures to a comprehensive assessment of working memory.

13. Correctly complete the *Working Memory Analysis Worksheet.*

14. In regards to working memory assessment, state the relative advantages and disadvantages of several cognitive ability scales.

15. In regards to working memory assessment, state the relative advantages and disadvantages of several broad memory batteries.

16. Recognize the unique contributions of recently published tests that are designed for the comprehensive assessment of working memory.

17. Describe several strategy-training procedures that should be used when implementing working memory interventions.

18. Identify several evidence-based working memory interventions.

19. Identify several effective teaching practices that address working memory limitations.

20. Describe the unique aspects of interpreting working memory assessment results.

CHAPTER 2

Theories and Models of Working Memory

T he origins of the working memory construct can be traced to the early days of modern psychology. In fact, the concept of working memory, in one form or another, predates the advent of psychology. In 1690, the philosopher John Locke differentiated between *contemplation*—bringing an idea to mind—and *memory*. Later, William James (1890) would be the first American psychologist to propose two types of memory, which he labeled as *primary* and *secondary*. James defined primary memory as the trailing edge of the conscious present and secondary memory as the vast amount of information stored for a lifetime. Some contemporary psychologists still refer to working memory as *primary memory* and long-term memory as *secondary memory*. The terms *short-* and *long-term memory* were probably coined by Thorndike as early as 1910. However, during the first half of the Twentieth Century memory was generally viewed as a unified construct, with short-term memory subsumed by what we now consider long-term memory. By 1950 most psychologists recognized the need for some sort of special memory process that could account for recall of information in the short term. In 1949, Hebb proposed that the brain is divided into separate storage systems, one temporary and the other permanent. Hebb's division of memory was supported by case studies of acquired brain injury in which some subjects had quite normal short-term recall, coupled with very deficient long-term storage, whereas other subjects demonstrated the reverse profile. The introduction of information processing theory at midcentury sparked numerous investigations into working memory itself and several models of working memory soon emerged. Advances in technology, along with a growing interest in neuropsychology and neuroscience, have spurred on brain-based working memory research over the past 15 years.

An indication of the widespread appeal of working memory is the fact that more than 200 research articles on working memory were published in 2006 and 2007 alone.

The unabated empirical investigation of working memory has also been driven by evolving theories of working memory and several controversies surrounding contemporary models. From the beginning, there has been a consensus that working memory, or short-term memory as it was called prior to 1960, has limited capacity. The popular conception of working memory limitations was cemented by Miller's (1956) classic article on *The Magical Number Seven, Plus or Minus Two*, which proposed that individuals could retain approximately seven chunks of information in short-term memory. The limited capacity of working memory has been a contentious issue ever since. Attempts to measure and identify various capacities have been at the center of working memory research. In fact, many of the working memory theories postulated in the 1960s, 70s, 80s, and 90s differ mainly in how they portray working memory capacity.

In spite of the appeal of the working memory construct, some cognitive psychologists saw no need for dividing memory into separate entities. They continued to advance a theory of unified memory with one storage system and processor handling both short- and long-term functions (Broadbent, 1971). Advocates of the unified theory remain (for a review, see Cowan, 2005) despite compelling experimental and neuropsychological evidence that should have rendered the debate moot a long time ago. In response to their claims, there is rather convincing neuropsychological evidence for two broad types of memory.

The advancement of cognitive psychology, educational psychology, neuropsychology, and other related specialties has led to the propagation of several working memory theories and models over the past half-century. Experimental cognitive psychologists proposed the first processing model of working memory. Later, educational psychologists began to examine the role of working memory in academic learning. Currently, neuropsychologists seem to be at the forefront, as they apply working memory models to various brain dysfunctions. As research continues, working memory models have become more intricate, with the division of working memory into several components and processes. There have also been more attempts to apply the experimental laboratory research and neuroscience research to the world of education (e.g., Berninger & Richards, 2002; Swanson & Berninger, 1995, 1996).

Information Processing Model

In the 1960s, a cognitive model of human mental processing known as the *information processing model* gained wide acceptance. Using computer processing as a metaphor, the model describes the flow and processing of information from sensory input to storage and behavioral responses (see Fig. 2.1). According to the model, the cognitive processing system is comprised of a set of separate but interconnected

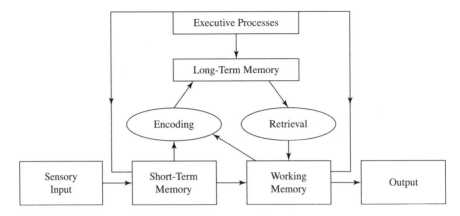

FIGURE 2.1 Example of an information processing model.

information processing subsystems, with memory components constituting the core of the system (Gagne, Yekovich, & Yekovich, 1993). The main types of processing in the model consist of selective perception, encoding, storage, retrieval, response organization, and system control. The original model was criticized as being too static and as lacking relevance for academic learning. Current conceptions of the model stress parallel processing and neural networks that are consistent with our understanding of brain functioning. From its inception, the information processing model has identified working memory as a central component of information processing. Those who discuss and apply working memory concepts, assessments, and treatments need to be aware that working memory is part of the *cognitive processing* approach to mental functioning.

The Atkinson-Shiffrin Model

From the plethora of memory models in the 1960s and 1970s, the Atkinson-Shiffrin model (Atkinson & Shiffrin, 1968) emerged as the most accepted and enduring. The Atkinson-Shiffrin model (see Fig. 2.2) is an elaboration of the information processing model originally proposed by Broadbent (1958). Atkinson and Shiffrin divide memory into three major types of storage: several peripheral sensory stores or buffers that each accept information from one sense modality; a short-term store that is fed by the sensory buffer stores; and a long-term store that exchanges incoming and outgoing information with the short-term store (Hulme & Mackenzie, 1992). Some sort of filtering device is assumed to allow only a certain amount of the unlimited information in the passive sensory store (held there for only a very brief interval) to pass to the short-term, limited store. After another brief interval, information proceeds from temporary short-term storage to more durable long-term memory. Atkinson and Shiffrin view short-term memory as the workspace for long-term learning. They were

FIGURE 2.2 Atkinson-Shiffrin (1968) modal memory model.

also the first to introduce the notion of *control processes* in memory, suggesting that these control processes flexibly divide limited capacity between storage and processing functions.

The first component in the Atkinson-Shiffrin information processing memory model is sensory memory or storage, also known as *immediate memory* or the *sensory register*. This form of memory is closely associated with visual and auditory perceptual processing. The brief retention of visual information is referred to as *iconic memory*, whereas brief auditory retention is referred to as *echoic memory* (Torgesen, 1996). Both types of storage last only for a matter of milliseconds, just long enough to create a trace or activate some form of representational code from long-term memory for further processing in short-term memory. The contents of sensory memory are supplied by external stimulation only; in contrast, the contents of short-term memory can be either externally supplied or can be derived from internally initiated processes.

Short-term memory is the central feature of the model. As described by Atkinson and Shiffrin (1968), short-term memory has very limited capacity. Information in short-term memory quickly fades unless it is maintained through rehearsal (subvocal repetition). Forgetting also occurs as new units of information displace old units. The encoding or transferring of information into long-term storage depends on short-term memory. Atkinson and Shiffrin propose that learning is dependent on the amount of time information resides in temporary storage. This model also assumes that short-term memory plays an important role in long-term retrieval. Despite the division of memory functions, Atkinson and Shiffrin believe that long-term memory and other cognitive processes are also involved in performance of immediate serial recall tasks (Hulme & Mackenzie, 1992).

As research continued, the Atkinson-Shiffrin model, which was referred to as the *modal model*, was found to be an oversimplification of memory and to place too much emphasis on structure while ignoring the processes. For example, little support has been found for the prediction that the probability of learning a piece of information is a function of how long that information resides in short-term storage. Experiments in which subjects use rote rehearsal to maintain items in short-term storage have failed to find this predicted relationship (Baddeley, 1996a). With the emergence of working memory theories, the modal model faded away. Nevertheless, Atkinson-Shiffrin's three-part division still provides a useful framework for interpreting memory performance, and it is consistent with the information processing model that persists to this day.

Levels-of-Processing Model

In the 1970s, as cognitive psychologists became more concerned with memory processes over structure, it was proposed that the level of processing affected the durability of the memory representation, with deeper and more elaborate processing and encoding leading to more long-term learning (Craig & Lockhart, 1972). Shallow encoding, such as judging acoustic similarity, was thought to result in weaker retention, whereas deeper encoding, such as making a semantic judgment, produced substantially better recall; thus, the deeper the processing, the better the learning. Even though the model emphasized processing over structure, it did retain the distinction between short-term and long-term memory. Despite its intuitive appeal, the levels-of-processing theory had a number of problems and did not hold up well under scrutiny (Baddeley, 1986; Logie, 1996). Research on the levels-of-processing model discovered the following inconsistencies: (a) even superficial encoding, such as rehearsal, can produce memory traces that persist over time; (b) the optimal method of encoding depends on the material and the retrieval cues; (c) retention may depend on mode of processing (verbal being stronger than visual); and (d) shallow processing does not necessarily take less time than deeper processing. The eventual consensus was that parallel distributed processing models describe memory functioning better than overly simplified sequential models, such as the modal and levels-of-processing views.

Baddeley's Model

By 1974, the time was ripe for a more elaborate theory of short-term memory that could account for emerging empirical findings. Considering the earlier models as overly simplistic, Baddeley and Hitch (1974) stepped forward to propose a multi-component model of short-term memory in which some components serve primarily as passive storage buffers while others process information. The two British psychologists developed the idea of a *working memory* within short-term memory. They defined *working memory* as "a system for the temporary holding and manipulation of information during the performance of a range of cognitive tasks such as comprehension, learning, and reasoning" (Baddeley, 1986, p. 34). As originally proposed, Baddeley and Hitch's multifaceted model comprised three aspects of working memory—a phonological loop, a visuospatial sketchpad, and a central executive that controlled the other two subsystems, referred to as *slave systems*. In effect, Baddeley's model is hierarchical, with the central executive as the top-level, domain-free factor that controls all the subcomponents. Apparently, Baddeley views the central executive as the essence of working memory; he usually refers to the two subsidiary systems as short-term memory components. Recently, Baddeley (2000) added another subcomponent—the episodic buffer (see Fig. 2.3). Over the past 3 decades a large number of studies have investigated Baddeley's model. Overwhelmingly, the

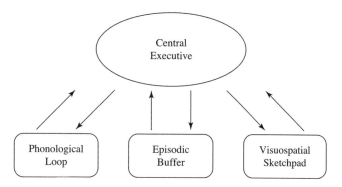

FIGURE 2.3 Baddeley's (2006) working memory model.

empirical evidence supports the division of working memory into modality-based short-term stores and a modality-free processing center where the *work* of working memory is conducted.

The Phonological Loop

The phonological loop, originally referred to as the *articulatory loop*, is a limited-capacity, speech-based store of verbal information (Baddeley, 1986, 2003a; Baddeley, Gathercole, & Papagno, 1998). Baddeley divides the loop into two subcomponents: a temporary, passive phonological input store and a subvocal, articulatory rehearsal process. Orally presented verbal information gains immediate, direct, and automatic access to the phonological loop, where it is briefly stored in phonological form (Hitch, 1990; Logie, 1996). The phonological loop is analogous to an audio tape recorder loop of specific length. Words or other auditory units are recorded in the order they are perceived, and they will quickly decay or be recorded over by new auditory units unless rehearsal re-records them onto the tape.

The phonological loop has a specific function and is limited in the type of information it stores. The phonological loop transforms perceptual stimuli into phonological codes that include the acoustic, temporal, and sequential properties of the verbal stimulus (Gilliam & van Kleeck, 1996). Phonological codes are then matched with existing codes (i.e., phonemes and words) stored in long-term memory and also linked with meaning representations. Higher level processing of the verbal information, such as putting the words together to form an idea, involves complex working memory functions that are conducted by the central executive.

Verbal Short-Term Memory Span and Articulatory Rehearsal

Unless action is taken to preserve the phonologically coded information, the phonological loop will hold information for only 2 seconds or less (Baddeley, 1986; Hulme & Mackenzie, 1992). The number of verbal items that can be fitted onto the phonological "tape" loop depends on the time taken to articulate them. This phenomenon explains why recall of short, one-syllable words is better than that for longer words; longer words take longer to articulate and therefore take up more space on the phonological tape loop. Adult recall of a five-word sequence of monosyllabic words is about 90%, whereas it drops to about 50% when the equivalent number of words consists of five syllables each (Baddeley, 2003a). Thus, the capacity of the phonological loop can be expressed as: words held in loop = the length of the loop × speech rate (Hulme & Mackenzie). Research has found the length of the normal phonological tape loop to be about 2 seconds, regardless of the individual's age. Subjects can recall as many words as they can articulate in that amount of time (Baddeley, 1986; Hulme & Mackenzie). For example, if an individual's speech rate is two words per second, his or her memory span will be about four words. The number of words recalled is not a function of how many items are presented within 2 seconds but rather the number of words the individual can articulate within 2 seconds. The implications are that any retention of verbal information in short-term memory beyond 2 seconds depends on rehearsal (repetition) and that the amount of information that can be rehearsed is also constrained by the 2-second loop. Subvocal rehearsal rate is thought to be equivalent to overt speech rate. This relationship accounts for the findings that verbal short-term memory span varies according to the length of the items and that span has a strong positive correlation with speech rate; individuals with faster articulation rates can maintain more items than individuals who are slow articulators (Hulme & Mackenzie).

For adults, normal phonological memory span has long been assumed to be approximately seven units (Miller, 1956). The span is typically measured with tasks such as digit or word span and is often referred to as *verbal short-term memory span* or *verbal working memory span*. The finding that memory span is highly related to the time it takes to articulate the stimulus words implies that working memory is not necessarily limited to seven, plus or minus two, units of information as is usually believed. With a few short words, individuals are able to subvocally rehearse the complete sequence in less time than it takes for the memory trace to decay, thereby extending maintenance of the sequence indefinitely. The immediate serial recall of word sequences decreases as the constituent words become longer (Baddeley, 1990). This phenomenon, known as the *word length effect*, has been attributed to the greater time it takes to subvocally rehearse items of longer articulatory duration (Gathercole & Martin, 1996). The crucial feature is the spoken duration of the word and not the number of syllables. When subvocal articulation of the sequence exceeds the decay time, errors begin to occur. Therefore, verbal memory span should be expressed as the number of words that can be articulated in approximately 2 seconds (Baddeley, 1990), rather than thinking of it as a specific number of spoken words. Even the classic digit-span task is subject to this rule. For instance, the digit span of Welsh-speaking children (Ellis & Hennelley, 1980) is substantially lower than that of English-speaking children because Welsh digits take longer to articulate than English digits. The word length effect has even been observed during reading, as reading rate decreases for longer words, so does recall (Gathercole & Baddeley, 1993). Prevention of rehearsal eliminates the word length effect; if the individual is not subvocally rehearsing, the length of individual words doesn't matter.

Despite the strong evidence that word length and articulatory rehearsal speed determine verbal short-term memory span, other influences also affect performance. Undoubtedly, some of the effect occurs because long words take longer to present and recall, leading to more forgetting as total elapsed time exceeds retention interval (Baddeley, 2003a). Another influence is prior knowledge; meaningful phonological information may activate relevant long-term memory structures, which may then facilitate short-term recall in the absence of rehearsal. That is why the average adult has a longer span for meaningful words than for nonsensical pseudowords and a verbatim serial span of 15 words when they are used in a sentence. The degree of chunking—the grouping of items into larger units—also affects span. For example, the separate digits "5" and "8" can be chunked as "58."

Nevertheless, subvocal rehearsal seems to largely determine verbal span. Whenever individuals are prevented from rehearsing verbal items, performance is markedly impaired (Baddeley, 1990). The typical interference task prevents rehearsal by requiring the participant to engage in concurrent speech (e.g., "the, the, the . . . "). Prevention of rehearsal allows researchers and examiners to assess pure phonological loop capacity. The impact of disrupting phonological short-term rehearsal provides evidence of the importance of rehearsal to the short-term retention of information, and it provides evidence for the subdivision of the phonological loop into a passive store and a rehearsal function.

Numerous studies have investigated verbal span and found it to be an incredibly robust phenomenon, with high predictive relationships with cognitive functioning, academic learning, and everyday tasks (see Chapter 5 for an in-depth discussion). For example, the phonological loop plays a crucial role in language processing, literacy, and learning. It is even hypothesized that the phonological loop may have evolved in order to facilitate the acquisition of language. Accordingly, individuals with longer phonological spans are better at vocabulary and language learning than those with shorter spans (Baddeley, 2003a).

In summary, phonological short-term memory span is primarily a joint function of rate of decay and rate of rehearsal. Articulation rate determines how much information can be repeated before it decays. Repeated subvocal rehearsal can extend the interval over which information can be recalled. When individuals are prevented from rehearsing information by introducing an interference task, such as repeating an irrelevant word, their short-term memory performance decreases dramatically, as well as the amount of information that is retained long term (Henry, 2001). Our verbal span is mainly limited by our ability to rehearse all the verbal stimuli rapidly enough to avoid losing one or more items due to decay (Baddeley, 2006). Therefore, the capacity of the phonological loop is not fully realized without the application of articulatory rehearsal strategies.

Phonological Similarity Effects

Another variable that affects the operation of the phonological loop, in particular the length of serial recall, is acoustic or phonological similarity. Individuals with normal phonological processing ability find it more difficult to remember lists of words that sound similar, such as *man*, *map*, and *mat*. The phenomenon most likely results from confusions that occur in the passive phonological input store and mis-identifications during rehearsal and later retrieval (Hulme & Mackenzie, 1992). Any loss of information due to decay leads to confusion between acoustically similar items. Phonological similarity can have profound effects on recall. For instance, in a study by Baddeley (1986), dissimilar words were recalled correctly 82.1% of the time while similar-sounding words were correctly recalled only 9.6% of the time. The effect of phonological similarity supports Baddeley's claim that short-term memory encoding for verbal information is phonetically based (Logie, 1996), whereas long-term encoding is based more on meaning. For example, phonological similarity has no effect on long-term retrieval, indicating that, while it is the basis for immediate encoding, it is not the basis for long-term encoding (McElree, 1998). More evidence for the phonological similarity effect comes from the study of how unattended background speech and noise impact short-term verbal span. Concurrent but irrelevant speech in the background can have a deleterious effect on word retention, especially when the words to be recalled are phonologically similar to the irrelevant material (Gathercole & Baddeley, 1993). Additional evidence that short-term verbal memory is based on phonological coding comes from the fact that orthographic (the visual representation of words) similarity has very little influence on word retention.

Phonological similarity effects may be only one aspect of a broader interference effect that arises whenever there is similarity between content being stored and content being operated on. For example, recall of digits is substantially lower when subjects are required to engage in arithmetic calculation while trying to maintain a string of digits, whereas processing the meaning of sentences during digit span causes less interference (Conlin & Gathercole, 2006). When exactly the interference is most disruptive is unclear. There are indications that the detrimental interference occurs mainly during retrieval when it is difficult to discriminate between phonologically similar items (Conlin & Gathercole).

Recency and Primacy Effects

The recency effect is often cited as further evidence for the existence of a temporary phonological store (Baddeley, 1990). Recency, one of the most persistent findings in memory research, is the tendency of the most recently presented oral items to be recalled better than prior items, especially items from the middle of a list. The recency-based phenomenon seems to result from the displacement or overwriting of earlier cues; recent items are remembered because they are still retained in the phonological store at the time of recall. As such, they are automatically recalled without rehearsal being necessary or without there having been time for rehearsal. The fact that little or no rehearsal occurred is borne out by the finding that subsequent long-term retrieval of items at the end of the list is poorer than for items at the beginning or middle (Cowan, 2005), indicating that earlier items were rehearsed and encoded into long-term storage. Apparently, the lack of rehearsal for the final items limits the encoding of the items into long-term memory—an effect that has implications for academic instruction. The recency effect also indicates that the last item or chunk heard still remains active in awareness or is still the focus of attention. Proactive interference, which is interference from previously learned similar information, has no impact on immediate recall, indicating that no retrieval processes are needed for items that are still maintained in active awareness (McElree, 1998), unless they have been lost and retrieval from long-term memory is necessary. Primacy, the superior recall of items from the beginning of a list compared to the middle items, is another memory constant. The effect is particularly strong when there is subvocal rehearsal, most likely because there is an opportunity to repeat these items more than subsequent items.

The Visuospatial Sketchpad

The visuospatial sketchpad is responsible for the short-term storage of visual and spatial information, such as memory for objects and their locations. It also plays a key role in the generation and manipulation of mental images (Baddeley, 2006). Like the phonological loop, it consists of a passive temporary store and an active rehearsal process. Decay in the temporary visuospatial store seems to be as rapid as phonological decay, taking place within a matter of seconds. The rate of forgetting seems to be a function of stimulus complexity and of how long the stimulus is viewed. Refreshment of the visual trace appears to result from eye movement, manipulation of the image, or some type of visual mnemonic (Baddeley, 1986). The sketchpad seems primarily designed to maintain spatial or patterned stimuli, which explains why it has been linked to the control and production of physical movement (Logie, 1996). The visuospatial sketchpad may also serve an important function during reading, as it visually encodes printed letters and words while maintaining a visuospatial frame of reference that allows the reader to backtrack and keep his or her place in the text (Baddeley, 1986).

Much of short-term visuospatial storage, rehearsal, and processing seems dependent on other working memory components. Although the phonological loop is designed for sequential processing and the visuospatial sketchpad is better suited to holistic processing, most normal individuals will verbally recode much of their visuospatial input. Furthermore, recent evidence suggests that visuospatial storage is more dependent on the central executive component than is phonological storage (Gathercole & Pickering, 2000b).

Visuospatial Storage

Although visuospatial sketchpad storage was originally described as a unified subcomponent, it was later divided into two storage subcomponents: visual and spatial (Baddeley, 2006; Pickering et al., 2001; Van Der Sluis, Van Der Leij, & De Jong, 2005). The visual subcomponent is responsible for the storage of static visual information (i.e., information about objects' shapes and colors), and the spatial subcomponent is responsible for the storage of dynamic spatial information (i.e., information about motion and direction). The visual subcomponent (also referred to as the *visual cache*) is a passive system that stores visual information in the form of static visual representations. In contrast, the spatial subcomponent (also referred to as the *inner scribe*) is an active spatial rehearsal system that maintains sequential locations and movements. According to Olive (2004), the spatial subcomponent necessarily employs rehearsal to continually update dynamic information, as well as to refresh decaying information in the visual cache. Visual short-term storage is limited in capacity, typically to about three or four objects for a matter of seconds. Because of the limitations, individuals may not notice when objects in a series move, change color, or disappear. Of course, in the real world, objects and their characteristics usually persist over time, making detailed visual retention and rehearsal unnecessary (Baddeley, 1996).

Complex patterns are not retained as well as simple patterns (Kemps, 1999). *Complexity* refers to the amount of variety in a stimulus. For example, blocks displayed in a matrix are easier to recall than a random display, and asymmetrical figures are more difficult to recall than symmetrical ones. These findings indicate that structured visuospatial information consumes less short-term storage capacity than unstructured (Kemps). However, better recall for structured images may also be facilitated by the conversion of visuospatial information into verbal information, which is more likely to occur when images are recognizable. The fact that visuospatial span is better for structured material also suggests that long-term memory representations of structured material are facilitating short-term visuospatial memory, much like long-term phonological representations contribute to phonological memory span.

Rehearsal and Recoding of Visuospatial Information

Although there has been an abundance of research on the phonological loop and visual imagery itself, direct research on the visuospatial sketchpad has been minimal. Consequently, less is known about the functioning of this aspect of working memory, especially the form of visuospatial rehearsal. Nevertheless, some form of visuospatial rehearsal seems necessary for the short-term retention of visuospatial information. Evidence of visuospatial rehearsal derives from studies demonstrating that engaging in concurrent visuospatial activity disrupts short-term visuospatial storage (Henry, 2001). However, there is also evidence to indicate that maintenance of short-term visuospatial information depends on more than visuospatial rehearsal processes. Although the visuospatial sketchpad can operate independently from the phonological loop (Kemps, 1999), visuospatial storage and rehearsal appears to depend a great deal on the phonological loop and articulatory rehearsal. Visuospatial information does not automatically access the phonological store. Access occurs through the deliberate process of recoding visuospatial information into verbal information, which occurs when the individual verbalizes the names of the objects and locations to be remembered (Richardson, 1996a). Not all visuospatial input is easily transformed; the individual has to be able to articulate the information in order for the transfer to occur. Visually presented patterns that are difficult to name must be encoded visually. Failure to create a verbal representation of visual material may prevent rehearsal and affect retention. While the conversion of visual information into verbal information usually results in better recall, some visual information is usually lost in the process (Baddeley, 2003b). The visual–verbal conversion process seems to be one of the functions of the phonological rehearsal component (Gathercole & Baddeley, 1993).

Despite the efficiency of this information transformation, individuals typically do not recode visually presented material into a speech-based form until about age 10. Children at 5 years of age appear limited to some form of visual storage and rehearsal for visually presented materials. Their recall is impaired by visual similarity (similar to phonological similarity effects in the phonological loop) but not verbal interference, whereas older children display the opposite effects (Hitch, 1990). Younger children's inability to use verbal rehearsal to store the names of visual materials may be because such a transformation is beyond their working memory processing capacity. As general capacity increases, children rely more on visual-to-verbal recoding. Consequently, by age 10, the visuospatial rehearsal process may amount to little more than verbal rehearsal (Hulme & Mackenzie, 1992), although there is evidence that individuals over 10 years of age continue to use some visuospatial storage. Adults' tendency to use verbal rehearsal for visually presented materials is demonstrated by their decreased retention when they are exposed to auditory interference (Hitch).

Visual Imagery

The generation, manipulation, and maintenance of visual imagery also appears to involve the visuospatial sketchpad (Gathercole & Baddeley, 1993). Recent research (De Beni, Pazzaglia, Meneghetti, & Mondoloni, 2007) has provided support for the claim that visuospatial working memory is involved in mental imagery and in the construction of spatial mental models. Maintenance and manipulation of visual images is highly demanding of working memory resources, probably beyond the capacity of the visuospatial sketchpad itself. Therefore, working memory's central executive must be involved whenever internally generated visual images are being consciously generated and manipulated (Pearson, Logie, & Gilhooly, 1999). The phonological loop may also lend some assistance during image processing by attaching labels to the shapes involved. In fact, subsequent reconstruction of the images during recall may depend heavily on verbal representations (Pearson et al.). The coordination of the verbal and visual subsystems and control of image manipulation are attributed to the central executive. Hence, manipulation of spatial information, such as images, appears to involve all aspects of the working memory system and to consume many of the resources as well.

The Central Executive

The central executive—what many consider the core of working memory (Baddeley, 2003b; Torgesen, 1996)—is responsible for controlling the other three subsystems and regulating and coordinating all of the cognitive processes involved in working memory performance, such as allocating limited attentional capacity. Controlling the flow of information through working memory, the central executive is involved anytime information is transformed or manipulated, such as during mental arithmetic. The central executive is analogous to an executive board that controls attention, selects strategies, and integrates information from several different sources. It is modality or domain free, acting as a link between subsystems that are dependent on auditory or visual processing. As described by Baddeley (1986, 1996b), the central executive, which may not have its own have storage capacity, draws on the overall limited capacity of working memory. Despite its important role, the functioning of the central executive is the least understood component of working memory. The lack of a clear construct is due to measurement challenges and to the multiple functions of the central executive (Richardson, 1996a). Nevertheless, there is a consensus among theorists on the central role of executive processing in working memory. Most agree that individual differences in working memory are primarily determined by central executive processes.

In general, the central executive is involved whenever an individual must simultaneously store and process information (Tronsky, 2005). Tasks that introduce interference or a secondary processing task while requiring the retention of information will necessarily involve the central executive. For example, the central executive is responsible for managing dual-task situations, which typically involve processing information while trying to retain the same or different information. While experimental researchers often portray this scenario as unique, it is actually the norm in daily life, especially in an academic learning environment. The added demands of coordinating two tasks may slow down and depress performance on the processing and memory tasks. Similarly, as short-term memory load increases, the demands made on the executive may increase. Overall, the primary role of the central executive is to coordinate information from a number of different sources and manage performance on separate, simultaneous tasks (Baddeley, 1996b). The central executive will be called into play whenever control functions are necessary, such as when an individual is trying to cope with cognitive multitasking or dual-processing tasks (Savage, Cornish, Manly, & Hollis, 2006).

The central executive has limited resources for storage and processing (Gathercole & Baddeley, 1993), creating the need to maintain short-term modality-specific stores and to incorporate long-term memory structures that can assist with storage and retrieval. Until recently, conducting a long-term memory search and recollecting episodic events has been one of the main functions ascribed to the central executive. However, such a responsibility seems inconsistent with the lack of specific storage space. The result has been the recent addition of an episodic buffer where central executive products can be temporarily stored and activated long-term memory representations can be held. The processing limitations of the central executive mean that the greater the competition for its available resources, the more its efficiency at completing particular functions will be reduced.

Central Executive Core Functions

Over the years, Baddeley (1986,1996b, 2003b, 2006) has described several core central executive functions: (a) selective attention, which is the ability to focus attention on relevant information while inhibiting the disruptive effects of irrelevant information; (b) switching, which is the capacity to coordinate multiple concurrent cognitive activities, such as timesharing during dual tasks; (c) selecting and executing plans and flexible strategies; (d) the capacity to allocate resources to other parts of the working memory system; and (e) the capacity to retrieve, hold, and manipulate temporarily activated information from long-term memory. Miyake, Friedman, Emerson, Witzki, and Howerter (2000) have examined Baddeley's structure and identified three focused and related central executive functions—inhibition, switching, and updating. *Inhibition*, perhaps the most crucial function of the central executive, is the ability to attend to one stimulus while screening out and suppressing the disruptive effects of automatically generated or retrieved information that is not pertinent to the task at hand. Inhibition also discards previously activated but no longer relevant information and suppresses incorrect responses. *Switching*, or shifting, refers to the ability to alternate between different tasks, sets, and operations, such as switching retrieval plans. *Updating*, which is similar to inhibition, is the ability to control and update information in working memory, such as when attempting to retain the last word of each presented sentence. Updating is a constant process of revision whereby newer, more relevant information replaces old, no longer relevant information (Swanson, Howard, & Saez, 2006). In general, the main functions of the central executive seem to be: coordinating performance on two separate tasks (e.g., simultaneous storage and processing of information); switching between tasks such as retrieval and encoding; attending selectively to specific information while inhibiting irrelevant information; and activating and retrieving information from long-term memory.

Control of Attention

According to Baddeley (1986), the central executive is not just controlling working memory. Rather, it is a supervisory attentional system responsible for the control, regulation, and monitoring of many complex cognitive processes, most of which are related to working memory. The regulatory functions of Baddeley's central executive component are similar to those of the Supervisory Attentional System (SAS) proposed by Norman and Shallice (1980). The SAS model proposes that action is controlled in two ways. Automated activities are guided by schemas that are triggered by environmental cues, such as a driver stepping on the vehicle's brake pedal when a red light appears (a schema is an organized memory network for a concept or procedure). However, when novel stimuli or activities are involved, a higher level SAS intervenes to consciously control behavior. At this level, SAS is portrayed as a conscious control mechanism that focuses attention on the most relevant memory representation and inhibits activation of irrelevant schemas, thus preventing interference. The SAS and central executive models are also concordant on the contention that processing demands decrease as tasks become more routine and automated (Gathercole & Baddeley, 1993). Although the central executive is referred to as an *attentional processor*, it should not be construed as interchangeable with the construct of attention (see Chapter 4 for further discussion on this distinction).

Automaticity

Central executive processing is necessary whenever there is a disruption or a failure in automatic processing. The central executive benefits from the development of skill automaticity (the ability to complete a task without conscious mental effort), such as speech and reading fluency, because mastered skills require less monitoring by the central executive, thereby allowing the central executive to attend to higher level processes such as reasoning. The extent to which the central executive is required is also dependent on the degree of automatization of working memory routines and strategies, such as rehearsal and chunking. For example, adults may require few central executive resources when reversing digits because it is a more automated process for them, whereas children need more central executive support for such a challenging task. The automated functioning of the phonological loop and visuospatial sketchpad also provide more capacity for the central executive to draw on.

Long-Term Memory Encoding and Retrieval

It is important to realize that the central executive is not uniquely dedicated to short-term and working memory management; it is also recruited in the service of long-term memory. In addition to strategy implementation and other management functions, the central executive is involved with the effortful activation, retrieval, and manipulation of long-term memory representations. Its primary interactions with long-term memory include activating and retrieving information from long-term storage, deciding which information is relevant, and forming associations between items—particularly novel information and previously acquired knowledge. In addition to retrieval, the central executive is responsible for the effortful, conscious encoding of new information, particularly semantic information, into long-term memory. As the theory evolved, Baddeley (1996b) placed more emphasis on the central executive's role in temporarily activating long-term memory representations, a view more in accord with American models of working memory. This expanded view of working memory probably led to his recent addition of the episodic working memory component.

The Episodic Buffer

To explain the influence of long-term memory on the contents of working memory, Baddeley (2000, 2006) recently added a fourth subcomponent—the episodic buffer—to his model. The *episodic buffer* is a limited-capacity subcomponent, consciously accessible, that interfaces with long-term episodic and semantic memory to construct integrated representations based on new information. The episodic buffer also provides direct encoding into long-term episodic memory (Pickering & Gathercole, 2004) and controls directed searches of long-term memory. The addition of the episodic component greatly increases the types of information, such as semantic information, that can be stored and processed in working memory.

The addition of the episodic buffer acknowledges some of the shortcomings of the original model (Cowan, 2005). In particular, the episodic component can account for temporary storage of large amounts of information that seem to exceed the capacities of the phonological and visuospatial storage systems, without relying on storage in the executive component or direct retrieval from long-term memory (Baddeley, 2003). It was added to Baddeley's model (Baddeley, 2006) after research (Hulme & Mackenzie, 1992; Logie, 1996) found that short-term memory span depends substantially on information from long-term memory. The episodic buffer is also a response to other models of working memory that claim that working memory is little more than activated regions of long-term memory. However, Baddeley (2006) rejects the notion that the episodic buffer is simply reflecting activated long-term memory representations. From Baddeley's perspective, the episodic buffer is seen as functioning in a way that is complimentary to a separate long-term store. The episodic buffer also addresses the reality that working memory processes abstract, conceptual knowledge, which is composed of more than the basic phonological and visuospatial codes found in the model's two short-term memory buffers (Cowan, Saults, & Morey, 2006). It is not that the episodic subcomponent introduces new functions to Baddeley's working memory model. Functions now assigned to the episodic buffer were always included, ascribed to the central executive. That is why Baddeley (2006) considers the episodic buffer a fractionation of the central executive.

The episodic buffer is important for learning because it uses multimodal codes to integrate representations from components of working memory and long-term memory into unitary representations. The episodic component combines visual and verbal codes and links them to multidimensional representations in long-term memory. The episodic buffer may be responsible for binding separate episodes or units of information into chunks, and it may even integrate elements into new coherent structures. Changes in long-term representations occur slowly, after many repeated exposures to the same information. In contrast, episodic working memory can quickly represent information for immediate learning and processing (Brown & Hulme, 1996).

Factor-Analytic Support for Baddeley's Model

Several investigations into working memory models have conducted factor-analytic studies to assess the validity of the construct. In general, results have been supportive of Baddeley's multicomponent working memory model, with two or three factors typically identified. Some studies (e.g., Engle, Tuholski, Laughlin, & Conway, 1999) have discovered two broad factors that divide tasks into short-term memory and working memory, whereas other factor analyses have pointed to three factors that are similar to Baddeley's (1986) original three components. Other factor-analytic studies (Swanson & Berninger, 1996) have reported that verbal and spatial working memory load on two different factors. Attempts to further separate memory functions have typically met with failure, such as Oberauer, Sub, Schulze, Wilhelm, and Wittman's (2000) attempt to identify a numerical short-term memory factor. Typically, the identified factors have high positive intercorrelations. These high intercorrelations, although they change somewhat with development (see Chapter 4), strongly support the construct validity of working memory as one general cognitive resource (Oberauer et al., 2000).

With the publication of a working memory test battery (see Chapter 8) based on Baddeley's model, traditional psychometric validity evidence is now available. Exploratory and confirmatory factor analyses of the Working Memory Test Battery for Children resulted in a factor structure supportive of Baddeley's tripartite model (Pickering & Gathercole, 2001b). Recently, Alloway, Gathercole, and Pickering (2006) completed a confirmatory factor-analytic study that produced a three-factor model, with related but separable verbal and visuospatial storage factors, along with an executive factor representing the shared variance between short-term verbal and visuospatial processing.

Contributions from Daneman and Carpenter

Daneman and Carpenter (1980) are credited with expanding the working memory construct, especially to higher level linguistic processing, and with developing the first direct measure of working memory's complex functioning. Daneman and Carpenter noticed that simple span tasks, such as digit span, have only low correlations with demanding cognitive tasks, such as reading comprehension. These weak relationships led them to conclude that existing memory measures (circa 1980) did not really tap processing, the essence of working memory. Consequently, they devised a measure, known as *reading span* (see details in Chapter 6), that required concurrent processing and storage. Their new measure correlated highly with complex cognitive tasks like reading comprehension (correlations ranging from .49 to .59) and has since become a mainstay of working memory assessment.

Daneman and Carpenter (1980) emphasize the processing dimension of working memory, arguing that what appears to be smaller storage capacity may actually be the result of inefficient processing, which reduces the resources available for retention of information. They contend that complex mental operations utilize working memory resources and the more efficient the mental processing, the more resources are available for short-term storage. Because processing efficiency varies by task, working memory capacity varies, depending on the task at the moment. From this perspective, individuals do not vary in available capacity but rather in processing efficiency. Developmentally, this means that storage and processing capacity remain constant; age-related changes in memory span result from increased operational efficiency. Therefore, working memory performance is determined by the demands of the task and the individual's processing efficiency.

Although the model views working memory as including both storage and processing functions (Just & Carpenter, 1992), the model reduces the need for modality-specific storage buffers. For Daneman and Carpenter (1980), working memory essentially corresponds to the central executive in Baddeley's theory. From their perspective, performance on complex span tasks is due primarily to central executive processing efficiency—a claim disputed by Bayliss, Jarrold, Baddeley, and Gunn (2003), who found that differences in storage capacity are an important determinant of complex span performance.

Kane and Engle's Executive Attention Model

Kane, Engle, and colleagues (Engle 1996, 2002; Kane et al., 2001) portray working memory as an executive attention function that is distinguishable from short-term memory. Kane and Engle make the case that working memory capacity is not about short-term span but rather about the ability to control attention in order to maintain information in an active, quickly retrievable state. They define executive attention, also referred to as *controlled attention*, as "an executive control capability; that is, an ability to effectively maintain stimulus, goal, or context information in an active, easily accessible state in the face of interference, to effectively inhibit goal-irrelevant stimuli or responses, or both" (Kane et al., 2001, p. 180). Executive attention not only allows switching between competing tasks but maintains desired information by suppressing and inhibiting unwanted, irrelevant information. Therefore, the capacity of working memory is a function of how well executive processes can focus attention on the relevant material and goals, not on the length of the interval or how much short-term storage is available.

Evidence for their model comes from studies in which high memory span participants demonstrate better attentional control than low span subjects. Particularly under normal conditions, high span individuals are more adept at resisting interference than low span subjects (Kane et al., 2001). Their ability to inhibit interference allows them to retain and process more information. Most of the interference is internally generated, often caused by associating current information with earlier information that is no longer relevant. Low working memory span individuals do not normally allocate attention to resisting interference (Kane & Engle, 2000). Thus, individuals with a high working memory span may not necessarily have a greater short-term storage capacity than those with a low span. Rather, working memory span is constrained by the executive capacity to control attention and resist interference (Hester & Garavan, 2005).

Kane and Engle (2000) currently emphasize the role of working memory in retrieving and actively maintaining information from long-term memory. Working memory is responsible for cue-dependent, focused searching that has a high probability of leading to correct recall. Cues are used at the beginning of the retrieval phase to delimit the search to the most likely targets. Furthermore, this cue-dependent process applies to retrieval of information just recently lost from short-term storage because of the removal of attention, extended time intervals, or distractions. Such information has often transferred to the recently activated pool of memory items found in long-term memory. The successful use of cues by working memory facilitates bringing this recently lost information back into working memory. Cues also allow working memory to retrieve the correct information in the presence of interference. According to Kane and Engle (2000), low working memory capacity individuals have more difficulty selecting and using correct cues to guide the long-term memory search process, resulting in too many irrelevant representations being retrieved and ultimately failure to retrieve the sought-after information. Thus, individual differences in working memory capacity are also related to individual differences in the ability to engage in a controlled, strategic search of long-term memory, not just differences in controlling attention (Unsworth & Engle, 2007).

In the most recent rendition of Kane and Engle's theory (Unsworth & Engle, 2007), working memory is viewed as a subset of activated memory units, some of which are highly active and can be considered in a limited-capacity short-term component, whereas others are contained in a larger pool that can be maintained for longer intervals. By continually focusing attention, working memory maintains a few representations (typically about four) for ongoing processing. As attentional resources increase with age, more long-term memory structures can be activated concurrently. (This view is very consistent with Cowan's model, which is discussed in the next section.) In addition to expanding on the relationship between working memory and long-term memory, Kane and Engle (2000) have also investigated the relationships working memory has with higher level cognitive functions. According to their theory, controlled attention is the factor that binds all of the cognitive processes, components, and functions together. Engle (2002) argues that domain-free executive attention is the underlying process that connects working memory with other high-level cognitive processes, such as fluid intelligence, whereas short-term memory is not significantly related to higher level cognition.

Kane and Engle's (2000) model is not inconsistent with Baddeley's. Baddeley also stresses the attentional and inhibitory aspects of the central executive. The distinction is more in regards to what determines working memory capacity. Whereas Baddeley emphasizes the span of the phonological loop, Kane and Engle consider it less relevant. From their perspective, the reason short-term span decreases when working memory load is increased is that the ability to exert inhibitory control over irrelevant items decreases.

In summary, Engle and colleagues are proposing that working memory consists of domain-general controlled attention, which is mainly applied to retrieving and maintaining activation of long-term memory structures. Individual differences in working memory reflect the degree to which distracters can be inhibited and relevant information can be actively maintained as the focus of attention (Kane et al., 2001). The theory makes inhibitory control the primary determinant of working memory capacity, a proposal supported by others as well (e.g., Hasher & Zacks, 1988). With inhibitory failure, working memory becomes overloaded with information that is not relevant to the task at hand.

Cowan's Embedded-Process Model

Cowan (2005) is another American psychologist who has greatly expanded the construct of working memory, altered the view of working memory capacity, and closely linked working memory with long-term memory. Cowan (1993, 1995, 1999, 2001, 2005) has advanced a theory of working memory that addresses some of the shortcomings of Baddeley's theory and responds to contemporary findings. His model (2005) emphasizes focus of attention, levels of activation, and expertise as essential properties of working memory. Cowan (1995) posits close interaction and mutual interdependence between working memory and long-term memory, originally suggesting that there is a single memory-storage system that consists of elements at various levels of activation. As the single memory-storage system is long-term memory, this theory embeds working memory within long-term memory (see later section on long-term working memory). While Cowan (2005) still recognizes the need for working memory and short-term memory constructs, he argues that, at the very least, long-term retrieval precedes short-term processing and that well-defined long-term structures and representations enhance working memory performance, including the retrieval of recently presented information that has been held briefly in short-term memory. Nevertheless, Cowan's theory proposes that working memory essentially refers to information in long-term memory that is activated above some threshold.

Cowan's (2005) model mainly distinguishes between the activated part of long-term memory and the focus of attention. There is also a large set of long-term memory elements that are mostly in an inactive state (see Fig. 2.4) Only the focus of attention is assumed to have limited capacity—typically a few highly activated

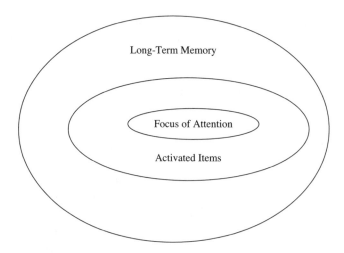

FIGURE 2.4 Cowan's (2005) embedded-process model.

elements at a time. The larger pool of activated items is not capacity limited, but items can be lost through decay or interference (Oberauer, 2002). This pool contains elements that are activated above a certain threshold but are outside the focus of attention. The degree of activation distinguishes between the three pools of information: (a) a vast pool of inactive long-term memory structures that are available for activation and retrieval; (b) a pool of long-term memory items that have been recently activated through unconscious automatic or conscious retrieval processes; and (c) a few items that are the focus of attention. Items in the activated pool quickly move in and out of the focus of attention, depending on what is needed at the moment. As originally proposed by Anderson (1983), activation is a limited resource that automatically spreads among related concepts. When the amount of activation reaches some critical threshold, the item moves into the activated pool and becomes easily accessible. The few highly activated items that are the focus of attention are embedded within the activated memory pool. The system functions efficiently because activated but unneeded items are inhibited, yet they are readily accessible.

The focus of attention replaces the multiple separate storage buffers and the central executive of Baddeley's model. Cowan posits that a limited focus of attention restricts working memory retention and processing, not storage capacity. The focus of attention can typically handle three to five chunks of activated information at a time, depending on the complexity of the task, whereas the broader pool of activated memory does not have such narrow limits. The readily accessible pool of activated long-term memory information accounts for our ability to seemingly handle much more information than is indicated by working memory span measures. Conscious processing of information relies on the ability to constantly shift and restrict attention to necessary information only. For example, semantic encoding requires activating and focusing on relevant schema. Studies of retrieval speed (e.g., McElree, 1998) provide support for Cowan's model by finding that items expected to be in the focus of attention are retrieved more quickly than recently activated items that are no longer the focus of attention. Accordingly, the capacity of the focus of attention can be measured by the number of items that are immediately accessible. Activated items that are outside the focus of attention require more time to access because a retrieval step is necessary (Verhaeghen, Cerella, & Basak, 2004).

In its interaction with long-term memory, working memory forms new episodic links between items activated in long-term memory and the new information that is being processed. Cowan (2005) suggests a high level of activation is associated with current working memory contents, which are the focus of attention, whereas a moderate level is associated with activated information that has recently been the focus or is closely associated with the current contents (Cowan, 1993). Because of moderate activation, information is readily available that is not actually in working memory. When this related information is called into working memory, it can be used to create new chunks or episodes for long-term storage. Cowan's (2005) view of working memory's role in forming new episodic links is consistent with Baddeley's episodic buffer.

Regarding working memory capacity, Cowan (2001) presents extensive convergent evidence in support of four, not seven, as the magic number. In his 2001 publication, Cowan provides a table listing 41 different studies from 17 research domains that all point to an adult working memory capacity of four chunks. Cowan views this capacity limit as somewhat universal, applying across individuals, across modalities, and across levels of expertise. In his view, what varies is the size of the chunks, not the number of chunks. Cowan's (2005) claim that four is the magic number applies to normal situations, in which individuals are passively attending to information and in which most of the working memory processing is automatic. When individuals use a rehearsal strategy to supplement the limited storage function, capacity can be extended to six or seven chunks. Despite Cowan's convincing evidence, some recent studies (reviewed by Verhaeghen et al., 2004) have indicated that the typical focus of attention is actually only one item, not four. For example, Oberauer (2002) contends that, at any one time, the focus of attention holds only the single item that is the object of the current or next cognitive operation.

Oberauer (2002) expanded on Cowan's model by dividing activated long-term memory structures into three functionally distinct regions instead of only two. Oberauer uses concentric circles to illustrate regions characterized by increasing availability to cognitive processes. The largest region contains a network of all the long-term memory representations that have been activated recently. A limited subset, perhaps as few as four of these items, is held in the region of direct access (this region corresponds to Cowan's focus of attention). Within the region of direct access, one item is selected for processing by the focus of attention. Whereas the focus of attention in Cowan's model corresponds to the region of direct access, Oberauer believes the focus of attention is limited to processing the one chunk of information that is the focus of the current or next cognitive operation. Oberauer's one-item hypothesis postulates that focus of attention capacity varies, depending on the demands of the task at hand. It consists of only one item when all resources must be committed to the processing of that particular item, and it expands up to four items when multiple items can be processed in parallel. Accordingly, the focus on one item is not a structural limitation but rather due to the capacity demands of the task (Verhaeghen et al., 2004). Keep in mind that the unit can be a chunk, not just a discrete item. Also, the number of items that can be processed concurrently is dependent on how much the task is automatized. When the processing of specific information is highly automatized, individuals have immediate access to more information, giving the impression of a larger working memory capacity.

Oberauer's Facet Theory

Another perspective with emphasis on the executive aspects of working memory is the facet model offered by Oberauer et al. (2000, 2003). Oberauer divides working memory into two broad dimensions—one is a content facet, which has two components, and the other is a functional dimension that consists of three general processes. In line with Baddeley's model, the content facet consists of two factors: (a) verbal and numerical; and (b) figural and spatial. The three functional factors are storage in the context of processing, coordination, and supervision. There is already consensus that storage in the context of processing, also referred to as *simultaneous storage and processing*, is the central function of working memory. *Coordination* is the ability to build new relations between elements and to integrate relations into structures. *Supervision* involves monitoring of ongoing processes, selective activation of relevant representations, and suppression of irrelevant, distracting representations. In an effort to better distinguish between short-term memory and working memory, Oberauer et al. (2003) define working memory processing as the transformation of information or the derivation of new information. Their narrow definition of working memory does not include short-term memory and its functions, such as rehearsal and grouping of items.

Whereas Baddeley and others have hypothesized several different executive functions, only a few investigators such as Oberauer have attempted to empirically identify specific functions. Studies by Buehner, Mangels, Krumm, and Ziegler (2005) and Oberauer et al. (2003) have provided support for Oberauer's model by identifying the three functional factors proposed by Oberauer. Oberauer contends that the evidence for his model points to a highly organized structure of information in working memory. Oberauer's explanation for why we have the capacity to both store and process information at the same time is that we are capable of retaining unneeded contents in the background without those contents interfering with the "working" part of working memory. He distinguishes between passive and active contents, with active contents directly accessible for ongoing processing. Holding too many items in an active state will slow down the speed of working memory operations.

Long-Term Working Memory

Given the close connection between working memory and long-term memory, it is not surprising that there are advocates (Ericsson & Kintsch, 1995) for a *long-term working memory*. According to this view, working memory is not structurally distinct from long-term memory. Essentially, working memory is the skillful utilization of information stored in long-term memory (Richardson, 1996a; Wagner, 1996). Although working memory may not be separable from long-term memory in this model, working memory still performs the same functions, such as processing select sensory input and encoding new information into long-term storage.

The notion of long-term working memory changes the perspective on storage capacity. Instead of how many chunks can be held in short-term storage, capacity entails how many nodes or long-term representations can be in a highly active state at any one time (Richardson, 1996a). As suggested by Cowan (2005), the typical individual can hold and manipulate about four pieces of information concurrently. Similar to decay in short-term memory models, activated portions of long-term memory must quickly return to an inactive state so that there is room for other long-term representations as they become activated (Wagner, 1996). If Ericsson and Kintsch are correct, then we may never be able to identify the modal working memory span. Furthermore, their perspective opens the door to the possibility that much of what is immediately retrieved is actually being retrieved from long-term, not short-term, storage. This leads to several educational implications, among them the benefits of long-term mnemonics on working memory functioning.

Ericsson and Kintsch suggest that the skillful use of information held in long-term memory depends on expertise and the use of mnemonics, both of which enable individuals to use long-term memory as an efficient extension of working memory. By employing a practiced mnemonic, individuals can quickly encode incoming information into long-term memory while attaching retrieval cues that are maintained in short-term memory. During recall the retrieval cues activate the relevant long-term information, which is usually stored in schematic form, giving the appearance of a working memory with super capacity. As evidence, Ericsson and Kintsch cite the performance of chess masters and other experts who seem to have tremendous working memory capacity, as well as subjects who were able to dramatically increase their short-term memory span. For example, two college students were able to attain a digit span of over 80 digits after hundreds of hours of practice. According to Ericsson and Kintsch, the superior immediate recall of these trained subjects resulted from storing the information in long-term memory. The evidence that what appears to be held solely in a short-term working memory is really stored in long-term memory comes from experiments in which an interruption of 30 seconds of more does not affect recall. Extended working memory seems to depend mainly on grouping items into chunks and then associating the chunks with familiar patterns, such as schemas, already stored in long-term memory (see Chapter 4 for more details on chunking). Encoding information into long-term memory needs to happen rapidly. Encoding also requires a large body of relevant knowledge and chunks for the particular type of information involved, which is why experts appear to have a greater working memory capacity. The schema the new information is attached to must be readily accessible from retrieval cues that have been practiced and deliberately attached. When these cuing procedures are successful, retrieval from long-term memory is as rapid as retrieval from short-term memory. Additional evidence for long-term working memory was reported by McNamara and Kintsch (1996), who compared retrieval intervals. Conscious retrieval from long-term memory typically takes 1 to 2 seconds, but an expert's direct retrieval from long-term memory takes only 400 milliseconds because the expert is able to bypass short-term memory limitations.

The long-term working memory model also seems applicable to more than chess experts. For example, the process of reading comprehension makes large, ongoing demands of working memory. Comprehension over extended parts of text would not be possible without long-term memory involvement. As the reader progresses through text, a representation is constructed in long-term memory. This structure is continually expanded to integrate new information from the text, with relevant parts remaining accessible during reading. Ericsson and Kintsch view the accessible portions of this structure as an extended working memory. Their argument is convincing, given that text comprehension increases dramatically from childhood to adulthood without concomitant increases in short-term and working memory capacity. Purportedly, the increased comprehension results from greater skill at immediately encoding information into long-term memory.

Although the idea of a long-term working memory is very similar to other proposals discussed in this chapter, most theorists believe that working memory is a separate cognitive process, even if it might be embedded within long-term memory. Most memory experts agree that working memory operates on knowledge units that have been activated or retrieved from long-term memory. Perhaps, Anderson (1983) was the first to theorize that working memory consists of currently activated knowledge units in long-term memory. Cowan (2005) and Oberauer (2002) are among others who have placed working memory squarely within the realm of long-term memory. Despite the close interaction between long-term and working memory, there is a current consensus (Gobet, 2000) that working memory is more than a long-term memory process. In regards to the examples of exceptional working memory used to support the long-term working memory model, exceptional working memory capacity seems to be limited to individuals who have made a directed effort to develop a successful mnemonic that attaches effective retrieval cues to the material. Furthermore, their large working memory spans are limited to their domain of expertise. For example, the large capacity chess masters have for recalling positions on a chessboard does not generalize to other types of information.

Even if working memory is viewed as structurally separate (with its own storage areas), it has become increasingly clear that working memory is deeply intertwined with long-term memory and that stimuli may activate relevant representations in long-term storage before any processing of the stimuli takes place in working memory. Logie's (1996) memory model emphasizes this interpretation, postulating that information must first be accessed in long-term storage before being processed within working memory. Logie argues that working memory could not function well without the instantaneous and automatic activation of auditory and visual long-term memory traces. Even subvocal auditory rehearsal strategies seem to rely on long-term phonologically stored information. When higher level processing is required, semantic information is activated for processing in working memory. Activated long-term memory representations may not decay as rapidly, allowing individuals to retain or access information for more than a few seconds. Even if long-term activation generally precedes working memory processing, it does not mean that working memory is inseparable from long-term memory. Working memory could still possess its own storage areas and processing capacities. What needs to be altered is our traditional belief that incoming information must pass through working memory before relevant long-term memory representations are activated.

Also, Conway and Engle (1994) point out that short-term memory retrieval processes are distinct from the processes involved in long-term retrieval. Short-term retrieval is a controlled process limited to a certain set size, whereas long-term retrieval is an automated process and not a function of set size. These qualitative distinctions mean that short-term memory is not just one end of a continuum of interaction, with long-term memory at the other end. For example, long-term retrieval speed is mostly independent of short-term span length. Consequently, working memory capacity and the amount of information that can be activated in long-term memory should not be equated. Nonetheless, working memory and long-term memory are highly interactive; for example, working memory uses its attentional resources to inhibit activation of irrelevant long-term memory structures.

Neuropsychological Evidence

Neuropsychological studies generally provide support for multicomponent working memory models, primarily Baddeley's. Of course, models of memory attempt to represent the functional, rather than the structural, properties. Therefore, the theoretical division of working memory into broad functions does not mean there are distinct brain locations corresponding to these different working memory processes. Nevertheless, recent neuroimaging research has found activation of distinct brain regions during different working memory activities. For example, the results of Hedden and

Table 2.1 Brain Regions with Reported Activation During Working Memory Processes

Working Memory Process	Hemisphere	Cortical Areas
Phonological	Left	
Storage	Left	Posterior parietal
		Inferior parietal
		Brodmann's area 40
		Supramarginal gyrus
Rehearsal	Left	Broca's area
		Anterior temporal frontal
Visuospatial	Right	Premotor cortex
		Occipital
		Inferior frontal
Visual	Right	Occipital
Spatial	Right	Parietal
Episodic	Left/Right	Left hippocampus
		Right middle temporal
Executive	Bilateral	Dorsolateral prefrontal
		Anterior cingulated

Yoon's (2006) study indicate that verbal, visuospatial, and executive working memory are each associated with distinct brain regions. Other neurological investigations (e.g., Prabhakaran et al., 2000) have also found evidence of separate neural circuitry for verbal and visuospatial subcomponents. In addition, several neuropsychological case studies of patients with acquired brain injury have established a large degree of independence in the brain mechanisms underlying Baddeley's original three components (reviewed in Gathercole & Baddeley, 1993). The research supports these conclusions about the neuroanatomy of working memory (see Table 2.1): (a) the phonological loop is located in the temporal lobes of the left hemisphere; (b) visuospatial memory is situated in the right hemisphere; and (c) central executive activities are primarily associated with the dorsolateral prefrontal cortex (Pickering & Gathercole, 2001b). The reader is referred to Berninger and Richards (2002) or Hale and Fiorello (2004) for explanations of brain anatomy terms used in this section.

Depending on the working memory task, several brain regions may be activated simultaneously, including locations in the frontal, parietal, and temporal lobes. Many studies (reviewed by Cowan, 2005) have shown the coactivation of frontal and posterior systems during working memory storage and processing. While the frontal lobes may allocate resources, the parietal areas are involved in further processing, and the perceptual processing areas are involved in the retention of modality-specific information (Cowan, 2005). Cowan (1995) suggested that the frontal lobes keep active the appropriate neural systems in other parts of the brain so as to maintain representation of the stimuli. These studies have also demonstrated that the prefrontal cortex prolongs posterior activation, including activation of long-term memory storage areas. This evidence indicates that working memory processing is not confined to the frontal lobes, and it also lends further support to the belief that long-term memory and working memory are highly interactive. From a neurological perspective, capacity might be an indication of how many brain areas the frontal lobes can simultaneously involve in working memory processing.

Despite wide-spread activation during working memory tasks, neuroimaging of short-term memory tasks (storage-only tasks) reveals brain activation primarily in areas related to the content of the material (Prabhakaran et al., 2000). Accordingly, verbal short-term storage is generally associated with left-hemisphere functioning, whereas visuospatial storage is generally associated with right-hemisphere functioning. Posterior activations are material related, with specific areas in parietal and temporal regions involved either in verbal or spatial working memory; for example, the right-hemisphere premotor cortex is activated for visuospatial material (Smith & Jonides, 1997). Thus, the different activation sites reflect the neural separation of short-term storage for verbal versus visuospatial information, as well as the neural separation of executive processes from the domain-specific subsystems.

To a lesser degree, the prefrontal regions are also involved with retention and processing of visuospatial and verbal material. The left prefrontal region (Broca's area) is activated when verbal material is being processed. In contrast, the right prefrontal region processes both verbal and visuospatial information (Prabhakaran et al., 2000). However, activation of the prefrontal cortex is more likely to occur when both verbal and visuospatial information are being processed. Hence, complex working memory activities (storage-plus-processing tasks) reveal content-specific activation but also activation of the dorsolateral prefrontal cortex and anterior cingulate (Fiez, 1996; Jonides et al., 1998). These latter two brain regions are also the sites of executive attention, fluid reasoning, and general intelligence (Kane & Engle, 2002).

Phonological Loop Evidence

Neuropsychological evidence (Baddeley, 1986, 1996a) is most clear-cut for the phonological loop. Neuroimaging indicates that the phonological loop and its rehearsal processes operate at a relatively deep, central level. According to Baddeley (2003b), phonological loop activity is associated with left-hemisphere activation, with Brodmann's area 40 associated with phonological storage and Broca's area associated with subvocal rehearsal. Gathercole et al. (2004) describe it somewhat differently. Phonological storage is served by a neural circuit in the left hemisphere spanning inferior parietal areas, and rehearsal is associated with anterior temporal frontal areas. Baldo and Dronkers (2006) recently reported that the supramarginal gyrus subserves the phonological store while Broca's area subserves articulatory rehearsal. Despite the somewhat different mapping, there is clearly neurological evidence supporting the division of the phonological loop into a passive storage component and a rehearsal component.

Visuospatial Sketchpad Evidence

Neuroimaging studies indicate that visuospatial working memory is principally, but not entirely, localized in the right hemisphere of the brain (Baddeley, 2003b), especially in the occipital and inferior frontal areas. Neuroimaging studies have also provided strong indications of separate neural systems serving the two visuospatial subcomponents of storage and rehearsal (Smith & Jonides, 1997). There is also evidence that the visuospatial sketchpad can be divided into visual and spatial components, with the visual component located in the occipital lobes, whereas the spatial component is more parietally based.

Central Executive Evidence and the Role of the Prefrontal Cortex

The functioning of core working memory processes, namely executive processes, are thought to reside in the prefrontal cortex (Engle, Kane, & Tuholski, 1999). Recent neuropsychological investigations have focused on the role of the frontal lobes in controlling working memory (see Kane & Engle, 2002, for a review). According to Kane and Engle (2002), the dorsolateral prefrontal cortex is responsible for resisting interference from a secondary processing task while trying to sustain information that is the focus of attention. Dorsolateral prefrontal activation is also observed whenever updating, shifting, and refreshing are needed, such as when engaged in dual-task performance (D'Esposito et al., 1995). Moreover, the prefrontal areas seem to have a special role in integrating different types of information in working memory, such as when retaining both verbal and visual-spatial information about a stimulus. As the demands on working memory increase, there is greater activation in the prefrontal cortex (Prabhakaran et al., 2000).

Despite these encouraging findings, brain-mapping of executive working memory will continue to be a challenge because the executive functions cannot be implemented by a single unitary brain network (Linden, 2007). Furthermore, the prefrontal cortex is a structurally and functionally heterogeneous brain region. Some neuroimaging studies reveal considerable variability across individuals in the distribution of activated regions during executive working memory tasks, with no specific frontal region predominant (D'Esposito et al., 1995). Perhaps this variability reflects the use of differing strategies to perform an executive processing task, or it could arise from differences in how demanding the task is for individuals. Also, the prefrontal cortex is not the only part of the brain involved in executive working memory functions (Baddeley, 1996b).

After an extensive review of the literature on the role of the prefrontal cortex in working memory capacity, Kane and Engle (2002) came to the following conclusions: (a) the evidence consistently underscores the role of the dorsolateral prefrontal cortex (dPFC) in executive working memory; (b) normal individual differences in working memory capacity are mediated by individual differences in the dPFC; (c) the dPFC is a necessary but insufficient structure for working memory functions— other neurological structures are also necessary; (d) the primary role of the dPFC is to actively maintain information in the presence of interference by blocking distractions and irrelevant information; (e) the neuroanatomic evidence supports a hierarchical view of working memory, with distinct working memory systems in the posterior regions networked to the dPFC; and (f) working memory capacity predicts other tasks that demand executive attention.

It has also been discovered that the same prefrontal regions are active during both working memory and long-term memory tasks (Ranganath, Johnson, & D'Esposito, 2003), lending support to the claim that the same executive processes located in the prefrontal regions support both working memory and long-term memory task performance. This finding does not negate the position that there are distinct working memory and long-term memory systems. Rather, it indicates that the same executive component processes are recruited during different goal-directed memory activities.

Episodic Buffer Evidence

In addition to neurological evidence for the phonological, visuospatial, and executive components of Baddeley's theory, there has also been support for episodic working memory. Prabhakaran et al. (2000) found evidence of a buffer that allows for the temporary retention of integrated information. Rudner, Fransson, Ingvar, Nyberg, and Ronnberg (2007) recently collected neuroimaging data supporting the existence of episodic buffer processing. In addition to engagement of the left hippocampus, posterior regions—including the right middle temporal lobe—are involved during episodic processing. Consistent with the fractionation of the episodic buffer from executive working memory processing, only a minor role was played by regions known to perform executive functions.

Additional Findings

The bulk of neuropsychological investigations have been based on Baddeley's working memory framework. Consequently, neuroimaging studies of working memory have provided only preliminary evidence for models other than Baddeley's. For example, Cowan's model has been supported by studies that have found a possible distinction between the focus of attention and a region of direct access (Rypma & D'Esposito, 1999). Working memory also depends on neurochemical balance in the brain. Dopamine is an important neurotransmitter that is known to regulate cell activity associated with working memory (Goldman-Rakic, 1992). A deficiency in dopamine in the prefrontal cortex can impair working memory performance.

The Controversy Over Working Memory Capacity

Although there is consensus that even normal working memory capacity is very limited and that all components of working memory are capacity limited, the exact nature of the constraints and the actual amount of working memory capacity remain very controversial. Cognitive psychologists and others specializing in working memory research have yet to reach agreement on how we retain information while occupied with processing other information. The main controversy over capacity centers on whether there is a single overall system capacity (a pool of resources from which all components and processes draw) or a separate capacity for each subsystem. The resource-sharing theory postulates that there is a trade-off between processing and storage, causing memory span to decline and processing to slow as more resources are allocated to demanding tasks. The separate-resources hypothesis says there are distinct resources that are only minimally affected by the overall demands on working memory. In part, the controversy stems from different conceptions of the working memory construct and of its processes and subcomponents. Many questions remain unanswered: (a) does a simple measure of memory span represent working memory capacity; (b) do the subcomponents, such as the phonological loop, each have a separate store that is unaffected by working memory processing; (c) is there a total capacity consisting of processes and stores added together; and (d) is capacity set by the limits of attention? The terminology and specifics vary depending on theoretical perspective, but at the heart of the controversy is the debate over shared resources versus separate resources.

Shared Resources: The General Capacity Hypothesis

Many working memory models represent working memory as a unitary, limited-capacity system where processing and storage demands compete for a limited, common pool of resources. Essentially, the shared-resources position, known as the *general capacity hypothesis* (Engle, Cantor, & Carullo, 1992), promotes the view that working memory (and short-term memory) performance is supported by shared resources that are flexibly divided between processing and storage. The gist of the hypothesis is that there is moment-to-moment trade-off between resources allocated for storage and resources allocated for processing, with processing demands receiving priority. When the processing demands of the task are high, less capacity will be available to meet storage requirements (Daneman & Carpenter, 1980), resulting in a decrement in short-term memory span (the main measure of capacity). The resource pool has a total capacity limit, which the combination of all engaged processes and activated buffers may not exceed. Executive control, which consumes some capacity itself, is thought to flexibly and automatically allocate resources from the common pool. As one process or buffer "demands" more resources, fewer are available for other components and processes. When the demands of the task are high, such as trying to solve a complex mental arithmetic problem, capacity cannot meet demand

and working memory becomes overloaded. The result is information loss, an inability to complete the task, or, at the very least, slower processing. Studies supportive of the general capacity hypothesis (Engle et al., 1992) have usually found that increased demands on working memory slow down processing and decrease short-term memory spans. In typical cognitive activities, the difficulty of the processing task is inversely related to memory span. Performance may be further impaired when the processing task has its own competing storage demands (Towse, Hitch, & Hutton, 2002).

Memory researchers who advance the general capacity hypothesis assume that working memory is a general-purpose system that can perform multiple functions, but unfortunately has a limited ability to perform different cognitive activities simultaneously (Towse, Hitch, & Hutton, 1998). These researchers also presume that working memory is domain general instead of task specific; for example, there is not a specific set of working memory processes for reading and another set for math. The same working memory processes and structures function across a diverse range of mental activities (Seigneuric et al., 2000). These general capacity assumptions lead to the conclusion that an individual's working memory capacity is a relatively stable characteristic that is not dependent on specific task demands or processing efficiency for a particular task (Engle et al., 1992; Turner & Engle, 1989). Therefore, the same resources are used to support working memory storage and processing activities, regardless of the nature of the task or the type of domain or modality (Gathercole & Pickering, 2000a).

Among proponents of the general capacity hypothesis, there is debate over the exact nature of the resources and the distribution process. Some researchers (Conlin, Gathercole, & Adams, 2005; Towse & Hitch, 1995) argue that the efficiency of task switching determines general capacity. That is, individuals are incapable of simultaneously storing and processing information. Consequently, they must continually and rapidly switch back and forth between storage and processing. During the storage phase they are rehearsing the material to prevent decay, and during the processing phase the items in storage are neglected. According to this perspective, span reduction results from limited, disrupted, infrequent, or too-late rehearsal opportunities. Advocates for the shared resources position emphasize that the limited resource is primarily general purpose attention. From this perspective, attention-demanding processes reduce the proportion of time that can be allocated to storage (Barrouillet et al., 2007). Those who adhere to the notion that there is a shared common resource also tend to view the resource as constant throughout childhood, attributing improved performance to increased processing efficiency (Case, Kurland, & Goldberg, 1982). According to this developmental account, more efficient processing releases additional resources for short-term storage, thereby increasing memory span.

Separate Resources Hypothesis

In contrast to the position that working memory has limited resources that are shared between storage and processing, some cognitive psychologists (e.g., Halford, Wilson,

& Phillips, 2001) postulate that there are separate capacity limits for storage (short-term memory components) and processing (the central executive). Storage limits are determined by the number of chunks that can be retained, and processing is limited by the number of ideas that can be operated on. This claim is in accord with the beliefs that storage and processing demands are quite different; therefore, different types of resources are required. From this viewpoint, the capacity of the central executive determines the rate of information processing, whereas short-term memory span reflects the storage capacity of the phonological loop or visuospatial sketchpad (Baddeley, 1990). Furthermore, each component of working memory is thought to possess its own pool of resources, with storage resources distinct from processing resources, implying that the central executive has its own storage capability. In essence, the separate resources position makes the case that short-term storage components, such as the phonological loop, have their own capacity limitations, which are distinct from working memory capacity.

The preponderance of empirical evidence supports the separate resources hypothesis. As expressed by Towse, Hitch, and Hutton (1998), "Storage is independent of concurrent processing load, and processing performance is independent of concurrent storage load. The relationship between processing and storage arises because the time spent in processing affects the amount of forgetting that accrues" (p. 219). They concluded that there is no support for resource-sharing models, given that the majority of studies have found no disruptive effect of concurrent storage load on processing operations. Also, there are numerous examples (reviewed by Oberauer, 2002) of short-term retention being unimpaired by concurrent secondary processing tasks. Moreover, the amount of storage seems unaffected by the degree of processing; even in demanding dual-task experimental designs, participants typically perform well on both storage and processing (Seigneuric et al., 2000). In instances where there is a decrement in storage (Duff & Logie, 2001), it is not the substantial drop predicted by the common resource model. Finally, factor-analytic studies of working memory (reviewed by Richardson, 1996b) consistently identify multiple working memory factors, a strong indication of separate capacities. Overall, contemporary research has pretty well established that working memory capacity is not limited to a common pool of general resources.

Efficiency Theories

The *specific processing hypothesis* posits that working memory capacity is task specific—that is, processing efficiency, not storage capacity, is the real determinant of individual differences in working memory (Daneman & Tardiff, 1987). For example, phonological loop span is dependent on the efficiency of phonological processing. More broadly, the efficiency with which people process language determines verbal working memory capacity. According to this hypothesis, originally proposed by Daneman and Carpenter (1980), working memory capacity will vary, depending on the task and the individual's processing proficiency at that task. For instance, individuals who display working memory deficiencies during reading may demonstrate perfectly normal working memory capacity for arithmetic. As task expertise, efficiency, and automaticity increase, the greater the apparent working memory capacity (Daneman & Carpenter). Despite the intuitive appeal of this hypothesis, direct empirical support for it is equivocal. Perhaps the best support for the hypothesis is the fact that experts appear to have much greater working memory capacity than novices (Ericsson & Kintsch, 1995).

A related alternative is the *general processing hypothesis*, which postulates that general processing efficiency determines working memory performance. Recent research (reviewed by Bayliss, Jarrold, Baddeley, Gunn, & Leigh, 2005) has reported convincing evidence that the capacity of working memory depends heavily on general processing efficiency. This hypothesis is consistent with the *general capacity hypothesis* in that the more efficiently the processing systems work, the more resources remain for temporary storage. The effective use of strategies may promote general processing efficiency. For instance, there is ample evidence (McNamara & Scott, 2001; Turley-Ames & Whitfield, 2003) that individuals with high working memory spans are more strategic than those with low spans.

Long-Term Memory Activation Theories

As discussed previously in this chapter, Cowan (2005), Engle (1996), and others view working memory as intimately connected with long-term memory. According to these theories, working memory capacity is essentially limited by attentional capacity combined with long-term memory activation capacity. Cowan proposed that about four activated long-term representations could be the focus of attention at any one point in time. When too much information is in an activated state, processing slows down. Thus, the rate of information processing is determined by how many long-term representations are currently activated (Richardson, 1996b). From this perspective, the amount of information that is currently active may be greater than indicated by the length of short-term memory span—that is, memory span may not provide an accurate appraisal of total working memory capacity (Richardson, 1996b).

As explained by Engle (1996), the contents of working memory consist of both temporary units and currently activated permanent units from long-term declarative memory. Accordingly, individual differences in working memory capacity are determined primarily by how much long-term information individuals can activate at one time. Activation and the spread of activation usually occur automatically without conscious effort. Thus, working memory capacity is essentially the number of ideas or units of information from long-term storage that can be held and manipulated simultaneously. This is in contrast to the traditional view that working memory capacity is essentially limited by short-term memory span. A similar perspective of higher level working memory capacity has been offered by Pascual-Leone (2001), a neo-Piagetian, who believes the essence of working memory capacity is the number of separate cognitive schemas that can be operated on simultaneously. Pascual-Leone contends that active schemas require mental energy and the amount of energy available increases during development. Thus, the number of schemas that can be maintained and manipulated concurrently increases during development.

A logical prediction that arises from the preeminence of long-term memory activation is that differences in working memory capacity are determined by how well individuals can activate and retrieve long-term information. When Engle (1996) tested this prediction, he found that differences in activation do not entirely account for differences in working memory capacity. In fact, amount of activation, especially automatic activation, does not differ much across individuals. What differs more is the amount of information that can be activated and retrieved during controlled, intentional processing. Engle attributed this finding to individual differences in inhibition or attentional resources—similar to the model proposed by Hasher and Zacks (1988), which stresses the ability to inhibit irrelevant information.

Attention and Inhibition

While most theorists focus on the allocation of working memory resources to processing and storage activities (Hitch, Towse, & Hutton, 2001), some take the position that capacity is really about controlled, sustained attention in the presence of interference or distraction (Conway & Engle, 1996). From this alternative perspective, loss of information from working memory is not entirely due to decay; rather, it is primarily due to interference and the disruption of attention (Nelson & Goodmon, 2003). In other words, working memory performance does not depend on the size of short-term span or on general processing efficiency. Instead, it depends on the ability to maintain focus on content that matches the goals of the current task (Hasher & Zachs, 1988). Therefore, controlled attention accounts for measured capacity. Specifically, selective attention allows relevant information to enter working memory while it inhibits irrelevant information, including information that was relevant just a moment ago. If irrelevant or marginally relevant information is selected or retained after it is useful, interference results. Interference slows down processing, reduces span, and diminishes encoding and retrieval efficiency. The irrelevant information can originate externally or be internally generated, such as when inappropriate long-term memory representations are activated. When inhibitory processes are deficient, such as in the elderly or those with Attention-Deficit/Hyperactivity Disorder (ADHD), there is increased distractibility and a consequent reduction in working memory performance that is independent of the individual's working memory capabilities. On the other hand, inhibition efficiency may be a consequence of capacity constraints—that is, individuals with limited working memory capacity may not have enough resources to suppress irrelevant information (Cantor & Engle, 1993).

The Processing Speed and Task Duration Hypotheses

Cognitive processing speed is another hypothesis that has been advanced to explain the relationship between processing and storage capacity and how forgetting occurs. Research has confirmed a linear relationship between working memory capacity and processing speed: as duration increases, span decreases. One explanation for the relationship is that faster processing speed allows quicker, more efficient completion of working memory tasks, thereby allowing more resources for storage (Towse, Hitch, & Hutton, 1998). An alternative, more parsimonious explanation is simply that items decay and are forgotten because of the extended retention interval created by slow processing. Thus, working memory span is a function of the total task-processing time. Furthermore, decay seems to be purely a function of duration, as difficulty and complexity of the processing task seem unrelated. Hitch, Towse, and Hutton (2001) documented the effect of task-completion time on retention. Because processing speed affects task-completion time, it influences working memory span indirectly by mediating the time period over which memory items may be forgotten (Bayliss et al., 2003). The longer it takes to complete a working memory processing task, the more items in short-term storage are forgotten. Nevertheless, neither processing speed nor time-based forgetting provides a complete account of working memory limitations.

Measurement of Capacity

Some of the arguments over working memory capacity might be eliminated if the measurement of working memory was more consistent and refined (see Chapter 6 for an in-depth discussion of measurement challenges). For example, working memory spans usually measure a combination (Leather & Henry, 1994) of domain-free (common resources) and domain-specific (separate resources) processes. To complicate matters further, general working memory capacity entails more than the auditory sequential recall of a list, the most common form of working memory measure. Spans and other operationalizations of capacity are only isolated snapshots of overall working memory capacity. For instance, we have no experimental paradigms or commercially available measures that isolate executive control functions, the core of working memory. Then there is the issue of experimental or test paradigms versus real-world performance. Tested span is usually sequential, but how often in daily life must an exact sequence be recalled? And to say that an individual can only retain or process a few words or items of information at a time is misleading. For example, during conversation we seldom have verbatim recall but we usually can comprehend and maintain several ideas over an extended period of time. Furthermore, many investigators believe that working memory capacity must be far greater than indicated by short-term memory span. How else could we account for our ability to maintain the subgoals and products of complex working memory operations, such as mental arithmetic, until the cognitive operation is complete?

Memory Span

The popular conception of short-term memory span began with Miller's (1956) classic article on the *The Magical Number Seven, Plus or Minus Two*. Miller, whose article was based more on speculation than empirical evidence, was referring to the immediate verbatim recall of auditory chunks of information, not separate stimuli such as discrete words. A *chunk* is defined as a memorable group of items that results from pairing or combining discrete pieces of information, such as creating a set from two or three adjacent words. The composition and size of a chunk varies depending on the individual's strategies, expertise, and age. Yet, instead of measuring the number of chunks, we typically count the number of individual items that are recalled. Thus, from the beginning of working memory research we have probably inflated the estimate of fundamental short-term and working memory capacity (Verhaeghen et al., 2004). This is ironic, given that Miller (1956) was referring to the number of chunks, not individual items.

At seven chunks (plus or minus two), the estimate of verbal working memory span is probably too large. The estimate was derived from the forward digit span of healthy adults. In testing situations, most adults will use a repetition or chunking strategy to extend their digit span. However, in daily, ongoing working memory processing, how often do we have the luxury of dealing only with discrete items like digits that we have time to chunk or rehearse? Thus, a more realistic estimate of working memory span is to use backward digit span, for which the typical adult span is four to five digits, or visuospatial span, which is typically three to four chunks.

In line with this proposal, Cowan (2005) recently proposed a working memory span of three to five chunks, when the grouping or chunking of the stimulus items is known. Based on numerous studies, Cowan argues for the "magic number four" as a working memory constant. Nonetheless, Cowan's magic number four may only apply when there is interference or when subvocal rehearsal and other strategies are prevented. In situations where the individual is using strategic processes to maximize retention, or in a situation where there is not a concurrent processing task, four chunks may be an underestimate. Cowan is not the only memory researcher to question the seven-chunk standard. Gobet and Clarkson (2004) contend that most theories have overestimated the number of chunks that can be maintained in working memory. They argue that the real number may be closer to two, that the capacity of short-term and working memory is really less than we thought, or that we have been underestimating the size of chunks. Oberauer (2002) has taken the discussion a step further by suggesting that working memory typically processes only one chunk of information at a time.

Retention Intervals

In addition to limits on the amount of information that can be retained and processed, working memory is constrained by elapsed time. One of the earliest claims in working memory research was that verbal memory traces quickly fade or decay, in as little as 2 seconds (Baddeley, 1986). It has also been suggested frequently that the typical retention interval for unrehearsed information is about 7 seconds. A popular misconception about short-term memory is that it lasts for minutes or hours. Despite the assumptions, there has been very little research that has identified a specific interval, probably because of confounds that are introduced by strategies or long-term retrieval. Despite the lack of quantification, we can assume that most information that enters short-term memory is highly degraded within 7 to 15 seconds and completely erased from the short-term store within 20 to 30 seconds (Cowan, 2005; Richardson, 1996b). Of course, the variable that most confounds determination of the modal interval is rehearsal and manipulation; as long as information is being acted upon, the retention interval can be extended indefinitely.

What appears to be a verbal item limit may actually be a temporal limit. Baddeley (1986) found that individuals can recall about as much as they can articulate, or repeat, in about 2 seconds. This early finding explains why we can recall more short words than long words. The finding also implies that verbal short-term memory persists for only 2 seconds unless it is maintained through covert articulatory rehearsal. While subvocal rehearsal extends the interval between presentation and recall, it does not necessarily extend the number of items that can be recalled. This occurs because the phonological loop is only about 2 seconds in duration; even with repetition, we might forget items outside the 2-second loop. Also, rehearsal itself is displacing other incoming items. However, these findings may apply more to simple phonological short-term memory than broader verbal working memory capacity. Through the assistance of more elaborate strategies, such as chunking, and the activation of related long-term memory structures, adults can typically recall a sequence of more than a few words, especially when the words form a sentence.

Whatever the length of the modal short-term retention interval, there is clearly an inverse relationship between length of interval and length of span. Longer intervals undoubtedly constrict the span (Bayliss et al., 2003). Short-term memory's restricted interval even limits the amount of information that can be rehearsed. Longer words extend both the stimulus presentation interval and the response interval to the point where decay will occur simply as a function of time. It appears that extending the duration of the retention interval probably accounts for most of the reduced span performance in complex working memory tasks (Conlin et al., 2005). Nevertheless, it is difficult to find direct evidence of decay strictly as a function of elapsed time (Cowan, 2005). Equivocal results have led some researchers (e.g., Nairne, 2002) to maintain that span capacity rather than time interval is the main factor in forgetting.

Distinguishing between short-term memory capacity and working memory capacity may clarify some of the discrepancies found across studies. Without rehearsal, passive retention in phonological short-term memory may be as little as 2 seconds. With rehearsal this interval can be extended, and with chunking the number of items can be increased. That is why it is important to assess different types of working memory capacity and to use measures that prevent strategies or take strategies into account.

Conclusions Regarding Capacity

There is now a general consensus among working memory theorists that no single factor determines complex working memory capacity and performance. To begin with, there are most likely separate resources, with separate limits for storage and processing, while at the same time some shared general resources. The degree to which resources are shared may be less significant than the hard fact that separate and combined resources are extremely limited. Furthermore, other cognitive factors clearly impact capacity. The ability to control attention and inhibit interference, as well as processing speed and the extent of long-term memory activation, all play a role. Finally, the influence of strategies and processing efficiency is acknowledged but largely undetermined. Clearly, working memory potential is not realized without the application of strategies, and most individuals recognize the effectiveness of strategies, as they normally rehearse without being prompted to do so (Cowan et al., 1998). Perhaps we will never be able to determine whether poor performance is due to real capacity limitations or insufficient use of strategies that allow for more retention and processing of material.

Although we often bemoan our working memory limitations, there may be adaptive benefits from the normal restricted capacity. One advantage of limited storage is that it prevents proactive interference by constantly removing previously encountered but no longer relevant information (Cowan, 2005). Imagine the outcomes for our prehistoric hunting ancestors if their behavior had been dominated by no-longer-relevant information instead of the immediate cues and information in an ever-changing environment. Capacity limits may be the necessary price of avoiding too much interference. Without working memory limitations it might be more difficult to process any information in sufficient depth. Moreover, the working memory system might be uncontrollable were it not limited to about four items at a time. Even the lower working memory capacity of young children may be advantageous, given that their attentional control is less well developed than that of older children.

Despite consensus on some aspects, the controversy over the nature and extent of working memory capacity is far from settled. Whether we shall ultimately determine the prototypical working memory span and processing capacity is primarily the concern of scientists. Without quantifying the exact capacity, the limitations of working memory are something that every educator, psychologist, and nearly every cognizant human being is well aware of. On countless occasions, we are overwhelmed by trying to handle too much information in too short an interval. So, in daily functioning and in a learning environment, the specific causes of our limitations may not be that important. What matters is that we, and those who are imparting information to us, know how to reduce the overload or manage it as effectively as possible, so that cognitive processing goals are accomplished and more information is encoded into long-term storage.

CHAPTER 3

An Integrated Model of Working Memory

Nearly a half-century of research on working memory has significantly increased our understanding of memory, learning, and cognitive functioning. Especially in the past 20 years there has been substantial progress in working memory research, measurement, applications, and interventions. However, the recent progress also illuminates just how much we do not know about working memory. Regardless of which theory, and its supporting research, you examine, none of the working memory models seems to paint a complete picture, especially one that is fully applicable to academic learning. These inadequacies not only create measurement challenges but also provide little clear direction for interventions. From this author's perspective, these are the main concerns about current working memory models:

1. There are no clear boundaries between working memory and short-term memory. Many researchers use the terms interchangeably, implying that short-term and working memory are equivalent. Others claim that one type of memory is subsumed by the other.

2. Working memory models that emphasize interaction with short-term memory have not fully conceptualized the interaction of working memory with long-term memory, largely ignoring the influence of long-term memory on working memory capacity and performance.

3. Contemporary researchers who emphasize the interaction of working memory with long-term memory tend to ignore the role of working memory in short-term memory. Moreover, while these models explicate activation and retrieval,

they are often remiss in describing how working memory encodes information into long-term memory.

4. Baddeley's episodic buffer emphasizes additions to episodic memory while omitting an explanation of how working memory modifies schemas in semantic memory.

5. Outside of working memory's reliance on short- and long-term memory stores, there is general disagreement about the form and extent of the temporary storage capability of working memory itself.

6. Some psychologists have so broadened the concept of working memory as to make it nearly meaningless. They have equated working memory with nearly all conscious cognitive processing, including executive processing, reasoning, attention, linguistic processing, and even general intelligence. Broad definitions of working memory such as "mental workspace" and "processing while trying to retain information" do little to refine the construct.

7. Some theorists classify all working memory functions as executive functions and vaguely refer to the actual nonexecutive processes conducted by working memory. There is a need to distinguish between working memory and executive functioning, as well as to delineate the specific nonexecutive operations working memory performs.

8. For models that emphasize the limitations of short-term and working memory, the estimated capacities of the storage systems are too small to account for all types of complex learning, comprehension, and cognitive performance in which much more information is processed and retrieved.

The Structure of the Integrated Model

Traditional theories have developed memory models that place short-term memory within working memory (Baddeley, 2003b; Daneman & Carpenter, 1980), whereas recently published models have included long-term memory functions and representations within working memory (Cowan, 2005) or have placed the locus of working memory within long-term memory (Ericsson & Kintsch, 1995). In the integrated model of working memory proposed here (see Fig. 3.1), short-term memory, working memory, and long-term memory are all distinct and independent types of memory. Working memory, which is often the interface between the two storage systems, *works* both with units temporarily retained in short-term memory and with activated permanent units from long-term memory. At any one point in time, the focus of working memory might be material from short-term storage, elements from long-term storage, or a combination of the two. Without assistance from working memory, short-term memory can automatically encode information into long-term memory, and long-term

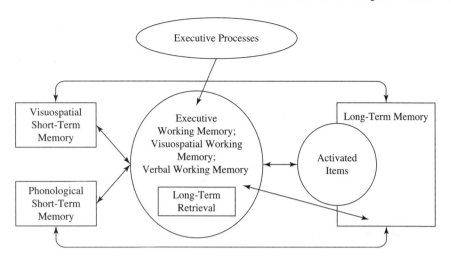

FIGURE 3.1 Integrated model of working memory.

memory can automatically activate and retrieve information. Information storage in both short- and long-term memory is *passive*, in that most information is directly encoded or retrieved without any manipulation or conscious processing.

Because both short- and long-term memory can function independently and automatically, neither should be considered a subsystem of working memory. Nonetheless, as previously stated, working memory *works* with material held in both stores. The *work* involves some type of effortful manipulation designed to more effectively utilize the available information. Although some of working memory's functions can be considered managerial or supervisory, it is misleading to consider short- or long-term memory as subsidiary systems. Likewise, working memory should not be considered a subsystem of either short- or long-term memory. To use an analogy, executive functions periodically manage and supervise every cognitive function; however, we do not consider every cognitive process to be nothing more than a subsystem of executive processing. The notion of three separate memory systems is supported by research showing a weak correlation between the capacity of short-term auditory memory and the capacity of the working memory central executive (Pennington et al., 1996; Swanson, 1994). Furthermore, there is a consensus among psychologists that short-term memory, working memory, and long-term memory are separable memory systems. Unfortunately, current measurement instruments often obscure the distinctions, as two or more different types of memory are often tapped by the same task (see Chapter 6 for a full discussion of measurement challenges).

Under the integrated model, working memory is more closely linked with long-term memory than with short-term memory. Consistent with several contemporary American models of working memory, the priorities for working memory are the activation, retrieval, maintenance, encoding, and restructuring of information drawn from long-term storage. From this perspective, working memory continues to interact with short-term memory but more of its resources are devoted to interaction with long-term memory. Perhaps this is why information is so easily lost from short-term storage and why short-term storage suffers somewhat when heavy demands (requiring more utilization of long-term representations) are placed on working memory. More importantly, a closer connection with long-term memory explains why we demonstrate a greater real-world working-memory capacity than can be accounted for by short-term memory measures of working memory, such as digit span. Given the likelihood that working memory is more interactive with and dependent on long-term memory, estimates of working memory capacity should not be based solely on short-term memory measures. For example, Anderson (1983) found that working memory can sometimes contain over 20 active long-term units at a time. The close connection with long-term memory might also explain working memory's strong relationships with complex processing and academic learning. The integrated model's emphasis on the interaction between long-term memory and working memory is consistent with the views of several contemporary psychologists who specialize in working memory research (e.g., Cowan, 2005; see Chapter 2 for more details).

Short-Term Memory Components and Functioning

Short-term memory, defined as the passive storage of verbal and visuospatial information, can bypass working memory and automatically encode information into long-term memory, as well as automatically activate long-term memory representations. Short-term memory structures and processes are limited to those that are passive, instantaneous, and fairly automatic. In this integrated model, short-term memory components consist of phonological short-term memory and visuospatial short-term memory, as described in Baddeley's model, but without the conscious rehearsal aspects that are the responsibility of working memory. Rehearsal or refreshment processes that do not reach awareness or require effortful strategies are within the realm of short-term memory. An example of automated rehearsal is the rereading of a word. Although the lines between short-term and working memory have been somewhat obscured by many advocates of the working memory construct, the main distinction between the two is that working memory primarily involves active, conscious processing of information, whereas short-term memory consists only of passive storage along with automated subconscious processes. Another distinction is that short-term memory is modality (phonological and visuospatial) specific and working memory is less so. Factor analysis of memory functioning has revealed that short-term memory and working memory operate fairly independent of one another (Engle, Tuholski, et al., 1999; Swanson & Howell, 2001). Factor analysis of memory tests also has supported the distinction between short-term memory and working memory (Passolunghi & Siegel, 2004). The separation of short-term and working memory means that working memory must have some temporary storage capacity of its own, a concept that is consistent with the separate resources hypothesis (see

Chapter 2 for details). In summary, simple, passive, and automated short-term memory tasks can be accomplished without supervision from working memory and without tapping working memory resources.

Interaction with Long-Term Memory

Similarly, long-term memory is mainly a passive storehouse of information; its independent functions primarily consist of automated processes. For example, when reading orally we automatically retrieve known words and convert them directly into a response without the involvement of working memory. The traditional information processing model promoted the idea that short-term memory information must pass through working memory in order to activate relevant long-term memory representations. This conventional wisdom now seems outmoded. It appears that much of the long-term content in working memory is brought into working memory as a result of automatic activation, initiated directly by short-term memory contents. Logie (1996) insists that working memory only becomes involved with processing information after long-term memory schemas have been activated and brought into working memory.

Working memory capacity and functioning is effected by the knowledge and skill base in long-term memory. As knowledge and skills become firmly entrenched in long-term memory, less processing is required of working memory, as automated responses and procedures occur. From this perspective, long-term memory *assists* working memory, assuming normal long-term retrieval speed. When automated activation, retrieval, and processing are insufficient for the task, working memory initiates and conducts effortful searches that deliberately retrieve information for active restructuring and encoding. One of the primary roles of working memory is to *work* on selected long-term memory units. Working memory works on all types of long-term memory structures and content, but in a learning situation, working memory is primarily operating on semantic memory structures, the details of which are suggested under the Working Memory Operations section later in this chapter.

In addition to being readily accessible for working memory processing and prompting automated responses and procedures, long-term memory representations may directly enhance short-term and working memory spans. When information enters short-term memory, short-term memory immediately encodes the items for long-term storage while simultaneously activating related long-term information. In turn, long-term memory immediately, automatically, and subconsciously sends cues to short-term memory that can be used to reconstruct partially decayed information, thereby extending short-term memory span (Nairne, 2002). This interaction explains why we are able to remember some information for longer than a few seconds.

Activated Long-Term Memory Units

During complex cognitive processing, most of the contents of working memory consist of long-term memory representations that have recently been activated or retrieved. In addition to the several units (probably around four) that working memory can process simultaneously, there is large pool of activated long-term memory items and structures (located within long-term memory) to which working memory has immediate access. This immediately available pool adds tremendously to total working memory capacity. The pool includes more than individual items when entire schemas and other working memory structures are activated. The activated units facilitate on-line processing, as well as conscious long-term encoding, and may even enhance short-term retrieval. For example, short-term recall of words is greater than that for nonwords, most likely because the nonwords are not available in long-term storage. The capacity of the activated pool is unknown, especially given that there may be varying degrees of activation. Nevertheless, the pool has limitations and the items it contains are constantly changing. Keeping the number of items selected from the pool manageable is one of working memory's functions. It does this by suppressing irrelevant memory items and structures while focusing on the information necessary for accomplishing the immediate goal. The addition of a pool of activated long-term memory units to the working memory construct, as well as prioritizing interaction with long-term memory, has several implications for education and interventions (see Chapter 9).

Several models (see Chapter 2) of working memory have investigated and validated the concept of an activated long-term memory pool that supports working memory operations. However, Baddeley (2000) continues to promote the idea of an episodic buffer in lieu of a long-term activated pool. Although the functions Baddeley ascribes to the episodic buffer are indisputably working memory operations, the idea of a *buffer* implies brief retention and periodic complete loss of information, whereas a large pool of activated items allows for greater capacity and ongoing activation. It seems there is no need for a buffer between working memory and long-term memory because the operations attributed to the buffer are core working memory functions, which are referred to as *working memory operations* in the integrated model.

Separating Executive Processing from Working Memory

From this author's perspective, general executive processes and working memory processes need to be disentangled, and there also needs to be a distinction between working memory functions that are executive in nature and those that are regular working memory operations. All information processing models include an executive processing system that monitors and controls other cognitive functions. Thus, working memory is only one of the cognitive processes controlled by a broader and higher level executive processing system. Much has been written about the importance and functioning of executive processing (e.g., Dawson & Guare, 2004), apart from its management of working memory. Yet some working memory theorists (e.g., Baddeley, 1996b) give the impression that the central executive of working memory and broad executive processing are the same construct, or, at the very least, some theorists provide us with little guidance on demarcation. Combining working memory and executive processes makes it difficult to establish the construct validity of working memory. Furthermore, maintaining the separation between working memory and general executive processing narrows the responsibilities of working memory and keeps the emphasis on working with the contents of memory. Failure to distinguish between broad executive processing and working memory creates measurement and diagnostic challenges and does little to enhance our understanding of disorders. For example, some theorists (e.g., Engle, 2002) place the executive management of attention within the working memory system. Yet there are many aspects of attention, such as arousal or inhibiting a behavioral response, that need not be under the purview of working memory. Despite the advantages of distinguishing between the two systems, executive processes do perform some hierarchical functions that assist working memory processing, such as coordinating working memory with other higher level cognitive processes.

Essentially, what Baddeley (1986) describes as the *central executive* is working memory itself. In fact, when most researchers refer to working memory, they are equating it with the central executive. Baddeley's labeling gives the impression that working memory functions are nothing more than executive in nature. In his model, the modality-based short-term memory stores are controlled by the central executive. Some memory researchers have disputed this claim. Goldman-Rakic (1995) argues that there is no need to postulate a central executive unit within working memory. She believes each short-term memory domain can perform its functions without executive management. Even if one grants the assumption that working memory has supervisory responsibility over short-term memory components, why should working memory's work with memory contents, such as modifying a schema, be considered an executive function? Nonetheless, working memory performs some functions that can be classified as executive control functions, such as inhibiting irrelevant information from long-term memory (see Chapter 2 for detailed discussion).

Some working memory operations are dependent on management from the broader executive processing system, such as a conscious decision to employ a particular memory strategy. Successful working memory functioning in the integrated model also depends on automatic executive control processes embedded within the working memory system—in particular, the ability to constantly shift the focus of attention while inhibiting irrelevant information. Inhibition of interference seems to be the central control function of working memory and one of the foundations of working memory capacity (Kane & Engle, 2002). For example, individuals with low working memory spans are more susceptible than those with high spans to interference from long-term memory. Inhibition, which ensures the maintenance of the most relevant information, usually occurs subconsciously. Perhaps level of awareness is one way to distinguish between higher level executive processes and those ongoing within working memory. Ongoing executive working memory control processes, such as shifting, are mostly automated and operate below the level of awareness. In contrast, working memory management processes brought into consciousness tend to elicit assistance from higher level executive management, which resides outside the working memory system. For instance, working memory operations automatically facilitate reading comprehension while relying on unconscious control functions embedded within working memory until a comprehension failure occurs, at which point the broader executive processing system is enlisted in a effort to solve the comprehension problem. Another perspective on the difference between working memory operations and higher level executive processes is that the distinction is similar to that made between cognition and metacognition (see Metacognitive section in Chapter 9).

In conclusion, it seems helpful to distinguish between executive controls that come from the higher level executive system and those specific management responsibilities located within working memory. Or perhaps it would be helpful to consider the control aspects of working memory as a subset of broader executive functions. Understanding the interplay between a higher level executive system and a working memory system that performs some executive functions of its own helps us to better understand and remediate working memory deficiencies. For example, some individuals, such as those with the hyperactive and impulsive subtype of ADHD, may demonstrate significant problems with broad executive processes but may possess normal functioning within working memory. Finally, portraying working memory as nothing more than storage and executive functions results in an incomplete depiction of working memory.

Working Memory Operations

Very little of what is written about working memory directly addresses nonexecutive working memory processes. Experimental and neuropsychological research has emphasized executive processes, such as inhibition, while ignoring how working memory actually operates on memory contents, even though most of working memory's processing of information might be considered nonexecutive. In many theories, the working memory executive component is an all-inclusive component, within which basic working memory functions have usually been referred to simply as *processing*. Even Baddeley (2000) recognizes this problem, which is why he recently fractionated episodic memory from the central executive. Thus, an account of the actual *work* conducted by working memory seems underdeveloped and poorly delineated in most models. Consequently, this author believes it is helpful to separate the *work* of working memory from its executive functions. In the integrated model, nonexecutive functions are referred to as *working memory operations*.

Working memory operations consist of several processes that utilize contents selected from both short- and long-term storage to accomplish a mental or behavioral goal. In general, these operations consist of some type of manipulation or transformation of information, including: (a) encoding information into long-term memory, such as encoding information semantically; (b) associating new information with existing long-term representations; (c) transforming information, such as verbal recoding of visually perceived material; (d) completing multistep computations; (e) holding the subproducts of computational procedures until the final product is reached; (f) conducting a conscious, directed search for information stored in long-term memory; (g) creating new memory representations; (h) chunking related items into groups or categories; and (i) any other procedures or strategies that involve manipulation of memory items or recombination of memory items. Encoding can be divided into two types: basic encoding and complex encoding. *Basic encoding* is defined as the conversion of perceptual input into a code suitable for short- or long-term storage, such as conversion of auditory stimuli into a phonological code. *Complex encoding* is defined as the process of associating meaningful information with related schemas in long-term storage.

Working memory operations are both conscious and unconscious. Working memory theories and research have focused mainly on reportable, conscious functioning. However, we must acknowledge that a myriad of unconscious specialized operations carry out detailed working memory functions (Baars & Franklin, 2003). Working memory functions are able to operate below the level of consciousness because they have become automated. Unconscious, automated processing is crucial to successful working memory performance because it is believed that automated processing does not draw on the measurable capacity of working memory. Automated processes operating below the level of awareness tend to be readily accessible, being called into consciousness whenever effortful processing is required. Operations that were once conscious but became unconscious as their function became automated are the most accessible. When working memory operations are brought into awareness, executive processes within and outside of working memory are usually called into play simultaneously.

In conclusion, the working memory operations component involves active processing of information, such as the transformation, manipulation, and restructuring of information from short- and long-term memory. The working memory operations component is where current goal-driven activity, short-term memory, and long-term memory interface. Baddeley's episodic component fits within working memory operations, as does Cowan's focus of attention. Working memory operations are controlled by two levels of executive processes but are not executive processes in and of themselves. Nevertheless, the theoretical and research emphasis has been on executive processes, such as how working memory selects information from different sources and keeps the focus on the most relevant information. Unfortunately, there has been less theoretical development of other core working memory functions, such as complex encoding. Perhaps one reason the research has been relatively silent on the specific operational processes involved in working memory is that there is a multiplicity of contributions from several other cognitive processes, such as phonological processing and fluid reasoning.

Definition of Working Memory

Working memory is customarily defined in a broad manner, such as the retention of information while processing the same or other information. It has also been described as an information processing workspace or a gateway between short-term and long-term memory. However, if the construct of working memory is to remain useful, it is important to maintain a narrow definition that can be operationalized for measurement and intervention purposes. In this text, *working memory* is defined as the management, manipulation, and transformation of information drawn from short-term and long-term memory. At its core, working memory consists of processes that work with material from short- and long-term working memory. Of course, most of our mental processing involves working with the contents of short- and long-term memory. Nonetheless, all mental processing should not be considered working memory. It is important to continue to differentiate between working memory and other related processes, such as executive, linguistic, phonological, reasoning, planning, and visuospatial. Working memory is not about the temporary or long-term storage of information; those are short-term and long-term memory functions. Rather, working memory is a cognitive process whose primary function is to facilitate and enhance the capacity of encoding, storage, and retrieval functions that are essential for learning and higher level processing of information.

Until research and measurement tools allow us to further delineate working memory processes, it might be safest to define working memory as what simple and complex working memory span tests measure. This somewhat circular definition is not an attempt to evade the challenge of delimiting the construct. The reality is that our understanding of working memory is built mainly on attempts to measure it. Furthermore, the "relationships" between working memory and academic learning are actually correlations between working memory test scores and measures of academic performance. Thus, the demands of the testing tasks inform us about the nature of the cognitive process we are attempting to measure. An additional problem is that most contemporary measures of working memory also incorporate what is most likely short- and long-term memory functions.

Descriptions of Memory Components

Phonological Short-Term Memory is a passive short-term memory subcomponent that briefly stores speech-based information in phonological form. Phonological short-term memory continually receives information from auditory sensory stores and automatically activates related items held in long-term storage, such as phonologically similar items. In essence, phonological short-term memory is identical to Baddeley's phonological loop except that subvocal rehearsal is not always a function of phonological short-term memory. Specifically, conscious, directed rehearsal efforts are active processes that fall under executive working memory. However, processing occurring below the level of awareness, such as automated rehearsal, is under the purview of phonological short-term memory.

Visuospatial Short-Term Memory is another passive short-term memory subcomponent that briefly stores visual (object and color) and spatial (location and direction) information. Visuospatial information is refreshed automatically and continually as objects in the environment change and as the focus of attention changes.

Verbal Working Memory consists of complex working memory operations in which analysis, manipulation, and transformation of verbal material takes place. One of the primary functions of verbal working memory is to extract a meaningful representation that corresponds to the phonological information taken in by phonological short-term memory (Crain et al., 1990). Verbal working memory incorporates items from both short- and long-term working memory, including activated long-term memory items and structures. In essence, verbal working memory involves processing of verbal information that either is in current short-term storage or has been retrieved recently from long-term storage. In contrast to phonological short-term memory, verbal working memory is viewed as higher level, meaning-based processing, whereas phonological short-term memory is simple, passive processing, more phonologically based. For measurement purposes, verbal working memory sometimes includes phonological short-term memory (see Chapter 6 for details).

Visuospatial Working Memory, another aspect of working memory operations, combines visuospatial information held in both short- and long-term working memory. For example, visuospatial working memory is involved whenever images are being manipulated. The main distinction between the short-term memory and working memory aspects is that visuospatial short-term memory requires only passive retention of information, whereas with visuospatial working memory, a processing component is added, such as reversing the sequence of objects or transforming the information. When a secondary processing task introduces interference, executive working memory will become involved. Until recently, visuospatial working memory was seldom acknowledged as a separable working memory component, most likely because there were few efforts to measure and study it. For a review of empirical support for visuospatial working memory, see Alloway, Gathercole, and Pickering (2006).

Executive Working Memory is distinct from broad executive processes in that it is restricted to the management of memory systems. It is similar to Baddeley's central executive in that it involves coordinating interaction between memory subsystems and inhibiting irrelevant memory items. In particular, executive working memory is involved whenever tasks require the coordination of storage and processing. Executive working memory also enacts strategies that extend short-term memory span and guide retrieval of information stored in long-term memory. Executive working memory is not domain specific and does not itself have any storage capacity; working memory storage capacity is provided by the working memory operations component.

Long-Term Retrieval, as used in this text, refers to conscious, directed searches for specific information held in long-term memory. From this perspective, long-term retrieval is a working memory function (not a long-term memory function) that can be considered a component of working memory for assessment and intervention purposes. Excluded from this working memory component is automated long-term retrieval that occurs instantly and subconsciously. This type of retrieval is excluded because it does not require any involvement or resources from working memory. Effortful long-term retrieval occurs whenever specific information is demanded of the individual. It is also involved during learning activities in which information is repeatedly encoded and retrieved.

Working Memory Operations consists of all the working memory functions of a nonexecutive nature, including manipulating, encoding, transforming, recoding, and retrieving information. Working memory operations modify and transform items drawn from short- and long-term storage. For example, working memory operations modify long-term memory structures before they are returned to storage. Working memory operations also have limited storage capacity, which is typically used to hold information until the processing of that information is complete. For measurement purposes, working memory operations are divided into verbal working memory and visuospatial working memory.

Activated Long-Term Memory is a large pool of recently activated long-term memory items and structures to which working memory has quick access. Many of the units in the pool are automatically activated by short-term memory.

Capacity of Working Memory Operations

In the integrated model of working memory, capacity, while still limited, may be greater than indicated by span measures. For example, we routinely accomplish working memory feats that go beyond predictions based on memory spans of only a few items. Incorporating an activated pool of long-term memory items greatly expands the amount of information available to working memory at any one point in time. Despite the readily accessible pool of information from long-term memory, the working memory operations component has limited capacity. Consistent with Cowan's embedded process model, the integrated model of working memory adheres to the hypothesis that working memory operations are limited to the simultaneous processing of approximately four units of information. However, the size of the units or chunks may vary, depending on the content and the individual's level of expertise. Perhaps the whole question of quantifying span or capacity is a moot issue. At best, a measure such as backward digit span provides only a superficial assessment of working memory capacity. Furthermore, the number of discrete items that can be stored in short-term memory is less important than the processing capacity of working memory. Maybe what matters most is the ability to maintain relevant information in an active, quickly retrievable state.

Efficiency and Strategies

It is also proposed here that the ultimate capacity of an individual's working memory is partially determined by how effectively the individual utilizes his or her innate capacity. For example, the development of expertise in a particular knowledge or skill area will enhance working memory performance by increasing the size of the memory chunks that are manipulated. Practicing procedures until they are thoroughly mastered will allow them to be performed automatically without drawing on working memory resources, consequently improving working memory performance during tasks involving those procedures. Acquiring effective memory strategies (see Chapter 9) will also enhance working memory performance.

Measurement Implications

Any discussion of working memory capacity is marred by poor control over confounding variables. Nearly all research designs and assessment tools fail to discriminate among the contributions of short-term memory, long-term memory, general executive processes, and working memory; usually, they are all lumped together as *working memory*. For example, complex span procedures require retrieval of information from long-term memory, meaning the predictive power of complex working memory span procedures is directly influenced by activated and available information in long-term memory. Moreover, the application of the integrated model increases the complexity of assessment and interpretation of results from existing measures. For example, verbal working memory capacity is not determined by short-term memory span alone. Until measurement procedures are refined, selective testing and informed clinical judgment will be necessary.

Educational Intervention Implications

One of the implications of the integrated model is that interventions for working memory deficits should include methods that are usually considered long-term memory interventions. For example, providing learners with effective and appropriate retrieval cues should reduce working memory differences. Strengthening peripheral systems, such as broad executive processing, may also enhance working memory performance. Overall, the teaching and application of effective memory strategies and mnemonics will allow individuals to more fully utilize their working memory capacities (see Chapter 9).

Caveat

The various components of the integrated model proposed here are not original; all of them have been proposed and researched previously. Rather, this integrated model is an attempt to pull together the commonalities among existing models and to address all aspects of working memory functioning related to academic learning. It is also an attempt to provide a more complete model by addressing the full extent of working memory's involvement with both short- and long-term memory, with an emphasis on the interaction between long-term memory and working memory. Nonetheless, the model is somewhat speculative and is not intended as a guide for future research. The integrated model is proposed because of the perceived need for an applied model of working memory that allows educators and psychologists to better understand the functioning of working memory and its impact on learning and daily functioning. Hopefully, such a model will lend itself to practical clinical assessment and to the design and implementation of interventions that can facilitate learning when working memory deficiencies exist.

Key Points

Whenever possible, the remainder of this text will associate information and recommended practices with the integrated model. Consequently, the reader may find this review of the key points helpful:

1. Short-term memory, working memory, and long-term memory are all distinct and independent forms of memory.

2. Working memory is more interactive with long-term memory than with short-term memory. During complex cognitive processing, most of the contents of working memory consist of long-term memory representations that recently have been activated or retrieved.

3. Short-term memory structures and processes are limited to those that are passive, instantaneous, and fairly automatic. Conscious rehearsal aspects are the responsibility of working memory.

4. The working memory operations component has some temporary storage capacity of its own.

5. Much of the content in working memory and in the activated long-term pool is the result of automatic activation, initiated by short-term memory.

6. Working memory initiates and conducts effortful long-term memory searches that deliberately retrieve information for active restructuring and encoding.

7. Working memory is only one of the cognitive processes controlled by a broader and higher level executive processing system.

8. There is a distinction between broader, higher level executive processes and the specific memory-management responsibilities embedded within working memory.

9. Executive working memory and working memory operations can be differentiated. Working memory operations include active processing of information, such as the transformation, manipulation, and restructuring of information from short-term and long-term memory. Executive working memory includes direct manipulation of content in other memory systems, such as inhibiting irrelevant information or enacting a rehearsal strategy.

CHAPTER 4

Working Memory Development and Related Cognitive Processes

Rudimentary forms of short-term and working memory are probably in place early in infancy. In object-permanence studies, infants begin to search for hidden objects as early as 4 to 8 months of age (Brainerd, 1978). Later in infancy, children begin to imitate speech sounds, a behavior that necessarily requires phonological short-term memory. By age 4, normal children demonstrate functioning of diverse working memory components. At 16 years of age, adult levels of working memory performance are pretty much established. Working memory development means more than growth in span and capacity. As development proceeds, children become more accurate, can process information more quickly, can handle more information at a time, can deal with more complex information, can process information in a more automatized manner, and can increasingly use strategies. The major change that occurs during development is not so much an increase in capacity but rather increases in operating efficiency and speed, as well as increased use of strategies (Gathercole & Baddeley, 1993). Deploying strategies changes how goals are accomplished and how tasks are approached and managed. As individuals develop, strategy use becomes more frequent, consistent, and sophisticated.

When working memory fails to unfold normally, the consequences can be profound. Educators are coming to the realization that one of the primary causes of learning disabilities may be deficits in one or more aspects of working memory (see Chapter 5 for a discussion of learning disabilities). Furthermore, scientific inquiries have discovered working memory deficits in many developmental, cognitive, behavioral, and mental disorders. The pervasive influence of working memory on so many diverse cognitive functions can mean only one thing—working memory is the linchpin of cognitive processing. Working memory has a hierarchical relationship with some processes and more of a peer relationship with others. Sometimes, working memory is so interwoven with another cognitive function that it is difficult to discriminate between the two. Accordingly, the development of working memory proceeds in conjunction with other related cognitive processes, such as executive functioning, which is one reason why working memory span continues to grow into adolescence.

Development of Working Memory Capacity

Developmentally, verbal short-term and working memory spans increase two- to three-fold between the ages of 4 and 16, with more gradual improvement after age 8 (Gathercole, 1999). At age 4, the typical child can recall an average of three digits in order. By 12 years of age, the span has doubled to about six digits, and by 16, digit span has plateaued at 7 to 8 digits (Hulme & Mackenzie, 1992). Although the functioning of each dimension differs from that of adults, separable working memory components appear to be present in children as young as 4 years of age (Hitch, 1990). Using the Working Memory Test Battery for Children (see Chapter 8), Gathercole, Pickering, Ambridge, and Wearing (2004) have determined that Baddeley's tripartite working memory structure is basically in place by age 6. From 6 onward, there is no evidence of any significant change in structure; the working memory subsystems of childhood closely resemble those of adulthood.

Although the working memory functioning of children and adults is generally equivalent in terms of structure and processes, there are some notable differences. In general, young children seem to depend more heavily on phonological short-term memory than do adults. In particular, the phonological features of words are more influential in children's processing, whereas adults rely more on semantic associations, as indicated by the finding that phonological similarity and nonwords are less disruptive to adult functioning (Conlin & Gathercole, 2006). Over the course of development, the strength of the relationships among components varies, the functioning and interaction of the components evolve, and individuals learn to utilize components in different ways. In early childhood, the three Baddeley components are relatively independent, but as executive functions of working memory mature, there is a greater degree of interdependence between the functioning of the executive and the short-term components. For example, in the Gathercole et al. (2004) study, the correlation between the central executive and phonological short-term memory increased from .73 at age 6 to .90 or greater for 10- to 15-year-olds. The growing interdependence is probably a function of more executive coordination, as well as increased strategy use. Moreover, growth in related processes and the acquisition of skills alter the nature of working memory functioning. For instance, the requirements of the task at hand and one's expertise at performing the task also affect how diverse working memory functions are tapped.

In early childhood, working memory may consist of little more than short-term memory processes. From preschool on, developmental increases in short-term memory span and working memory capacity appear to be interrelated. For example, both simple span (which measures passive storage) and complex span (which measures storage while processing) expand throughout childhood. Moreover, the growth of short-term memory span seems to be at least partially dependent on increases in the overall capacity of working memory. As working memory processes become faster and more efficient, more resources are available for short-term storage (Case et al., 1982). When processing activities take longer to complete, the result is lower short-term spans, probably because items to be remembered cannot be refreshed before they decay (Barrouillet & Camos, 2001). On the other hand, limitations in short-term span can constrain the development of working memory (Bayliss, Jarrold, Baddeley, Gunn, & Leigh, 2005). The evolving relationship between short-term memory and working memory is apparent from the changing relations each has with overall cognitive ability. In childhood, phonological short-term memory plays a greater role in cognitive functioning than it will later in life. Although phonological short-term memory span is a significant predictor of general cognitive ability in childhood, it is not a reliable predictor in adolescence and adulthood (Hutton & Towse, 2001), when working memory has the stronger relation.

Whereas some theorists presume actual changes in working memory capacity (e.g., Riggs et al., 2006), many researchers contend that storage capacity remains constant throughout childhood (Case et al., 1982; Hulme & Mackenzie, 1992). The majority attribute the growth in memory span to the better utilization of available capacity that results from improved efficiency and greater use of strategies. Some theorists argue that the development of related cognitive processes, such as increases in processing speed, account for most of the improved efficiency (Henry & Millar, 1993), whereas others cling to the traditional position that the bulk of memory span expansion results from faster speech rate, which in turn allows faster subvocal rehearsal. Regardless of one's position on capacity, most psychologists agree that increased use of sophisticated control processes and strategies can only enhance the operating efficiency of working memory. See Chapter 2 for more on the conflicting theories of capacity.

Phonological Short-Term Memory Span

In most children, phonological short-term memory appears to be firmly established by 3 years of age (see Chapter 2 for more information on phonological short-term memory). At 4 years of age, the typical child can remember two or three words in sequence. However, the more consequential occurrence at age 4 is the emergence of subvocal rehearsal, an attribute of phonological short-term memory. Evidence for articulatory rehearsal comes from studies that discovered 4-year-old children are sensitive to phonemic similarity and word-length effects (Gathercole & Adams, 1993). The rudimentary subvocal rehearsal at this age is a precursor of the more deliberate and strategic rehearsal procedures that develop around 7 years of age (Gathercole & Pickering, 2000a). Although phonological short-term memory is basically passive storage, increased subvocal rehearsal is thought to at least partially account for growth in span (Conway et al., 2002).

Despite extensive research, the actual mechanisms involved in phonological short-term retention and retrieval are not entirely understood, especially those that account for the growth in memory span. The traditional explanation for growth in phonological short-term memory span is that age-related improvements in span depend primarily on increases in speech rate (Hulme & Mackenzie, 1992). Increases in articulation rates during childhood are assumed to enhance the effectiveness of subvocal rehearsal processes and hence reduce the decay of memory items in the phonological store prior to output (Swanson & Howell, 2001). While the retention interval of phonological short-term memory (as little as 2 seconds) is thought to remain constant during development and aging, the number of items retained increases as more words can be rehearsed in the same amount of time. Faster articulation during oral recall also reduces the total retention interval, meaning that more words can be recalled before they decay (Henry & Millar, 1993). Consistent with these explanations is the finding that speech disordered children have lower short-term memory spans (Raine et al., 1991).

However, some contemporary investigators (e.g., Leonard et al., 2007) propose that phonological short-term memory span is not solely determined by speech rate and word length. There are several indications that a faster speech rate and subsequent increases in subvocal rehearsal speed do not entirely account for memory span: (a) the number of words articulated within 2 seconds is usually less than the number that can be recalled sequentially—for example, at age 10, speech rate is about three words per second, whereas the average number of words recalled is about four; (b) there is still a word-length effect (shorter words are easier to remember) even when rehearsal is prevented; (c) the verbal short-term spans of preschool children grow even before they have acquired subvocal rehearsal; (d) older experimental subjects can retain sequential stimuli even when they are prevented from rehearsing; (e) most individuals can remember verbal information well beyond the alleged 2-second decay window; (f) an individual's memory span varies, depending on the material and the individual's level of expertise—for example, children with poorly developed arithmetic skills have more difficulty recalling digits; and (g) improved speed of information processing may underlie the relationship between speech rate and memory span. Processing speed also increases retrieval speed, which means words can be recalled quicker, thereby allowing more words to be spoken before they decay (Case et al., 1982).

Despite the challenges to the speech-rate hypothesis, other explanations for the growth in span have also been found wanting. Realistically, growth in span is probably the outcome of several combined factors: increased processing speed, increased speech rate, greater efficiency of working memory processes, attainment of expertise and automaticity, development of related cognitive processes, growth in knowledge and skills, and the conscious application of strategies after age 7. In general, faster processing speed (see the Processing Speed section later in this chapter) and increased support from long-term memory are probably the main determinants. As processing speed increases and the knowledge base in long-term memory expands, activation and retrieval speed, sometimes referred to as *item identification speed*, increases. Thus, as items enter short-term memory, long-term memory immediately identifies them. The item identification speed hypothesis was proposed by Henry and Millar (1993). Identification time is known to become more rapid with age, leaving more short-term and working memory capacity free for remembering items. Because younger children expend more effort simply identifying items in a span test, they have less residual capacity for retaining them. Familiarity with the items is one factor that affects identification time.

Nairne (2002) is another skeptical researcher who has proposed an alternative to the hypothesis that memory span grows as a result of increased speech rate and subvocal rehearsal. To account for inconsistencies in the traditional models, Nairne postulates that short-term retrieval is similar to long-term retrieval in that it is cue dependent. Evidence for cue-based short-term retrieval arises from studies in which subjects have longer spans for words than nonwords. The implication is that cues are immediately, automatically, and subconsciously attached when related long-term memory representations are activated. The frequently reported phonemic similarity effects do not disprove this hypothesis because the effectiveness of phonemically similar cues could be diminished through proactive interference. It seems that Nairne is proposing that growth in short-term span may be a consequence of learning. As long-term memory representations develop, they enhance short-term span by cuing recall of partially decayed items. Nairne suggests that the contents of short-term memory are not direct information but rather activated cues that can be used to reconstruct the information acquired only moments before. Accordingly, short-term forgetting occurs when attached cues are not well matched to the target items.

Verbal Working Memory Span

Similar to the reasons given for short-term memory-span growth, the predominant explanation for improved verbal working memory performance during development is that working memory operations become faster and more efficient, leaving more mental resources available for storage and reducing the time items are held in storage before they are processed and retrieved (Case et al., 1982). Verbal working memory span is shorter than phonological short-term span because the items must be retained while a secondary processing task is completed. Verbal working memory span, which is generally considered more complex than phonological short-term span, doubles in size from two items in 5- to 7-year-olds to four items in 11- to 12-year-olds, at which point it approximates adult levels (Cowan et al., 1999; Gathercole, 1999). The only exception to this developmental progression is listening span, which shows constant improvement up to 16 years of age. The longer developmental period of listening span is consistent with the later development of the frontal lobes, the brain region associated with complex working memory. Given working memory capacity of only a few items of sequenced verbal information, how do some individuals comprehend sentences of considerable length and complexity? Perhaps well-established long-term memory structures assist with retention and processing, compensating somewhat for the storage limitations of working memory.

Visuospatial Working Memory Span

Four-year-old children can typically remember a sequence of two to three pictures (Gathercole & Baddeley, 1993). Then the capacity of visuospatial working memory doubles between the ages of 5 to 11, when span reaches an adult level of approximately four items (Riggs et al., 2006). Unlike phonological and verbal span, much of the improvement seems to result from actual growth in capacity, rather than improved system efficiency or use of strategies. As individuals mature, visuospatial working memory becomes more closely associated with executive working memory. Similarly, in adults, measures of verbal working memory and visuospatial short-term memory share approximately 40% of their variance (Kane et al., 2004).

The most unique characteristic of visuospatial memory functions is that retention and rehearsal of visuospatial information depends heavily on verbal working memory. It seems that nearly all humans naturally gravitate toward recoding visuospatial information into verbal code. Visuospatial recoding emerges between the ages of 6 to 8 years, at about the same time children learn to read. Prior to recoding, children must remember nonverbal information in visuospatial form. By the age of 10, individuals consistently recode visuospatial material into verbal information. The recoding process capitalizes on the superior verbal storage systems most individuals possess, and recoding is actually a form of rehearsal. When called on to recall visuospatial information, the stored verbal code is used to reconstruct the images or spatial orientation. The ability to use verbal working memory to encode and retain visuospatial information contributes to the expansion in visuospatial working memory span. Notably, the ability to retain material in visuospatial form also increases during childhood. Moreover, tasks that involve retention of complex visuospatial information place heavy demands on the executive (Gathercole & Baddeley, 1993). Interestingly, the development of visuospatial recoding may mirror the development of executive working memory (Palmer, 2000), thereby providing a window on the progression of executive working memory capacity.

Executive Working Memory Development

Neuropsychological studies have documented that growth in executive working memory, and in general working memory capacity, is related to prefrontal cortex maturation (Kane & Engle, 2002). Hence, full development of the executive component occurs later than that of the phonological, visuospatial, and verbal components.

Inhibition of irrelevant information, one of the primary functions of executive working memory, has frequently been measured and provides a means of tracking executive development. Whereas 9-year-old children have considerable difficulty preventing unrelated information from entering working memory, 14-year-olds have much better developed inhibitory mechanisms (Swanson & Howell, 2001). Thus, younger children may need more executive resources to inhibit or resist potential interference from irrelevant items, leaving fewer executive resources for other tasks. Efficient allocation of executive resources also depends on engagement of effective executive strategies. Executive working memory develops until 16 to 17 years of age (Luciana et al., 2005). In old age, the decline of the central executive seems to precede that of the other three components (Baddeley, 1986). As executive working memory functions decline among older adults, susceptibility to interference increases and working memory performance suffers (Hedden & Yoon, 2006).

Recent research (reviewed in Cowan, 2005) has demonstrated that the efficacy of executive working memory processes is related to individual differences in working memory capacity. Similarly, superior working memory performance depends on proficient functioning of executive working memory processes. Executive processing efficiency impacts the functioning and capacity of nearly all working memory operations and makes more resources available for different types of storage. With increasing age, executive working memory becomes more strongly associated with verbal working memory and less connected with visuospatial functioning (Pickering & Gathercole, 2001b). Also, phonological short-term memory is the least associated with executive working memory, as phonological capacity will increase even without concomitant increases in executive working memory (Gathercole & Baddeley, 1993).

Working Memory Strategies

Increased use of strategies, such as subvocal verbal rehearsal, chunking, and organization, is also partially responsible for the apparent expansion in working memory (Minear & Shah, 2006). Broad executive processing and strategy use develop and increase with age, leading to more efficient functioning of cognitive resources in general. Strategy use and working memory span are positively correlated; higher span individuals are more likely to use strategies, such as chunking, imagery, and elaboration (St. Clair-Thompson, 2007). Nevertheless, the predictive power of working memory does not arise from strategy use. Nor does strategy use always speed up processing. Implementing strategies that increase span may actually increase the amount of time spent processing (St. Clair-Thompson).

Verbal Rehearsal Strategies

Rehearsal strategies can be applied in both short-term memory and working memory. The debate over when rehearsal strategies emerge and their relative influence in part results from a failure to distinguish between short-term memory rehearsal and working memory rehearsal strategies. From the perspective of this text, rehearsal in short-term memory consists of a process that is subconscious and automated, usually referred to as *subvocal rehearsal*. Subvocal rehearsal most likely develops from overt speech, becoming internalized and automatized during early childhood. Conversely, verbal rehearsal strategies in working memory need not be subvocal; rather, they tend to be conscious and effortful, often consisting of more than simple serial repetition. What working memory rehearsal shares with short-term memory rehearsal is the goal of preserving the same verbal items. Working memory may actually have more capacity and opportunity for rehearsal (Hutton & Towse, 2001), resulting in the ability to apply more sophisticated strategies. Regardless of where or how it takes place, verbal rehearsal is essentially a serial repetitive process that allows information to be maintained for a longer period of time (Gathercole, 1999), thus facilitating long-term encoding.

Although many children begin using a simple rehearsal strategy around 5 years of age, spontaneous rehearsal does not begin until age 7, and consistent use of verbal rehearsal strategies may not occur until the age of 10 (Gill et al., 2003). The development and increased use of verbal rehearsal strategies is thought to be at least partially responsible for the sizable growth in memory capacity, especially for the increase in span after 6 years of age (Gathercole et al., 2004; Minear & Shah, 2006). Children with disabilities often fail to independently develop or utilize verbal rehearsal strategies. Several studies have found explicit rehearsal training to significantly improve the working memory performance of children, with and without disabilities (Comblain, 1994; Conners, Rosenquist, & Taylor, 2001). Adults with low working memory spans have also shown improvement after training in simple rote rehearsal strategies (McNamara & Scott, 2001; Turley-Ames & Whitfield, 2003).

Despite their perceived importance, rehearsal strategies are not a panacea for working memory limitations. First, although there are strong indications that subvocal rehearsal extends phonological short-term memory span, it appears to have less impact on maintaining or increasing complex verbal working memory span (Engle et al., 1992). Perhaps this is because subvocal rehearsal consists of phonetically based encoding whereas higher level processing of information is semantically oriented. Second, differences in the use of rehearsal only partially account for individual differences in working memory performance, and rehearsal training does not eliminate age differences on working memory tasks (Hulme & Mackenzie, 1992). Third, some researchers (e.g., Henry & Millar, 1993) dispute the claim that increases in rehearsal are responsible for the increase in memory span with age.

Chunking

Although less is known about its developmental progression, the strategy of *chunking* has also been hypothesized to contribute to the growth in memory span. Chunking, the grouping or clustering of discrete items into larger units, appears to be a naturally occurring process, much like blending phonemes into a word. Miller (1956) was the first to demonstrate that apparent memory span could be increased by grouping items or units into *chunks*. Perhaps chunking explains why we can recall more information than is indicated by the results of simple span tests. Although adults can typically remember a sequence of only five or six unrelated words, chunking allows them to recall sentences of about 15 words. Chunking also accounts for the apparent extended working memory capacity of experts (Ericsson & Kintsch, 1995). Most of the evidence for the influence of chunking comes from intervention studies that find chunking to improve working memory performance (see Chapter 9). Chunking may also enhance working memory performance indirectly, through enriching the organizational structure of long-term memory (Richardson, 1996a).

Long-Term Memory

Because of the interwoven functioning of working memory and long-term memory, an overview of long-term memory structure and functions is necessary. Long-term memory is a complex storage system with several different types of storage distributed throughout the brain. Numerous classifications of long-term memory have been proposed, including memory for faces and music, but the focus of this section is on types of memory essential for academic learning. Although the same material can be stored in multiple ways with multiple retrieval cues (Berninger & Richards, 2002), information is generally stored as visual images, verbal units, or both. Consequently, long-term storage is generally partitioned into visual and auditory or verbal memory. The retention and reconstruction of visual images are the main characteristic of visual memory. Auditory and verbal memory are more complex, with several subtypes.

Since the early decades of memory research, one camp of cognitive psychologists has argued for a unitary theory of memory, maintaining that short-term and working memory functions could both be accounted for by long-term memory processes and storage. Other theorists have proposed that working memory is a subsystem of long-term memory. Although both groups have been discredited, it now appears that they were at least partially correct. Much of what appears to be working memory processing may actually be originating from long-term memory (Logie, 1996). Instead of information first passing into working memory and then long-term memory, the flow may actually be the other way around (Logie). That is, incoming information may automatically activate representations in long-term storage before working memory initiates any transformation of that information. Nevertheless, as discussed in Chapter 3, short-term and working memory are viewed as functionally distinct from long-term memory. An abundance of laboratory research and neuropsychological case studies support this conclusion. For instance, Baddeley (1986) cited evidence indicating that short-term storage depends mostly on phonological coding, whereas long-term storage relies heavily on semantic coding.

Semantic Memory

In classic information processing theory the major categories of long-term memory are semantic and episodic memory. Semantic memory, which is primarily a verbal form of memory, includes all the general knowledge we possess. Semantic memory is fundamental for academic learning, as it involves memory for facts, concepts, principles, and rules. Semantic memory is thought to be organized by categories, classifications, associations, and meaning—that is, items in the same category are more closely linked with one another than are unrelated items. The meaning-based, organizational structures are referred to as *networks* or *schemas*. For example, most people have a schema for insects that includes the characteristics of insects, and their insect schema will be closely connected with related schemas, such as the one for animals. Within each schema there are subcategories; within the insect schema there might be a grouping of insects that bite and insects that are beneficial. As learning occurs, schemas are modified and connections between related schemas are strengthened. Cognitive psychologists divide semantic memory into the two major classifications of learning—declarative (factual knowledge) and procedural. *Procedural memory* is a store of the steps required to complete various tasks; for example, a math algorithm may be stored as procedural memory. Successful academic learning and performance depend on a well-organized semantic memory for declarative and procedural knowledge.

Episodic Memory

In contrast, episodic memory is primarily visual, autobiographical, and contextual; it is focused on specific events or episodes. From an academic learning perspective, episodic memory contains information that is associated with the particular time and place information is learned (Leahey & Harris, 1989). For example, remembering the name of your state's capital is semantic memory; remembering that you first learned this on a class trip to the state capital is episodic memory. Semantic and episodic memory are usually interrelated during formation and retrieval. For instance, semantic memory may be acquired from a succession of episodes, and recalling episodic memories depends on semantic memory for the words themselves.

Explicit and Implicit Memory

Long-term memory is also divided between explicit and implicit. *Explicit memories* consist of knowledge the individual is aware of and can consciously manipulate. In contrast, individuals are not aware of the information stored in *implicit memory* or the learning that brought it about. For example, prior exposure to visual stimuli has been shown to facilitate rapid identification, and problem solving improves with repeated trials when individuals demonstrate little to no explicit learning (Reber & Kotovsky, 1997). Like explicit learning, implicit learning is thought to depend on working memory capacity.

Encoding and Retention

Encoding is the process of creating enduring codes or representations for long-term storage in the brain. All of the separate components of short-term and working memory systems encode information. Encoding seems to vary according to the type of sensory input and the long-term store in which it is placed. Short-term memory transforms sensory data into a representational code, such as a phonological code, that can be efficiently stored in long-term memory (Torgesen, 1996). Encoding handled by working memory tends to be meaning-based, and it usually occurs by modifying relevant long-term representations that are fully activated (Swanson, 1992). Encoding can be automatic or effortful, with automatic encoding thought to be more shallow and insufficient for the semantic coding required for academic learning. Elaborative rehearsal—associating meaning while rehearsing the information—is a type of meaning-based encoding conducted by working memory. Those with high working memory capacity spend more time encoding because they can keep more information simultaneously activated (Kyllonen & Christal, 1990). If information cannot be maintained temporarily, then it can not be registered in a longer-term store. For example, new vocabulary cannot be stored directly in long-term memory. Working memory must first create a representation of a new word that can interact with existing related vocabulary so that storage of the new word is consistent with current long-term organization, such as derivations of a root word being stored together. Meaning-based encoding may require more processing time and resources but the result is efficient storage that facilitates retrieval.

The retention of information in long-term storage depends on a variety of factors. First, total memory load determines how much will be retained; recall of information is a decreasing function of how much needs to be remembered (Estes, 1999). Second, it is assumed in all memory models that as duration of a retention interval increases, the amount of information recognized or recalled decreases (often referred to as *decay*). Third, loss of learning can result from changing the context between the learning and the test or recall event. Fourth, information is sometimes encoded in a manner that makes it difficult to store and retrieve, leading to apparent forgetting (Leahey & Harris, 1989).

Activation and Retrieval Processes

Although retrieval models often describe a linear or sequential process, retrieval is a complex process. The brain is capable of handling several retrieval procedures in parallel at any given time. Despite its complexity, most of long-term activation and retrieval is automatic and nearly instantaneous. When automated searching fails, conscious retrieval efforts, directed by executive working memory, are enacted. Whether directed or automated, the foundation of retrieval is subconscious activation. Given retrieval cues, we select information and bring it into working memory after relevant representations have been automatically activated. If the wrong representation is activated and recognized as incorrect, automatic activation continues to spread to related concepts until the search is complete (Leahey & Harris, 1989).

For the most part, long-term memory retrieval processes do not depend on limited-capacity working memory (Conway & Engle, 1994). Only when there is a retrieval failure, an error is detected, or the accuracy of the retrieved information questioned is a controlled, effortful retrieval necessary. In directed long-term retrieval, an individual consciously generates cues to guide the search and monitors the output for goal completion. A controlled, strategic long-term memory search seems to be a working memory function, as there is a significant relationship between working memory span and directed retrieval from long-term memory. Compared to those with low working memory spans, high-span individuals retrieve items more often and more quickly, retrieve more items and clusters, and retrieve larger-sized clusters (Rosen & Engle, 1997). Clearly, working memory capacity influences the effectiveness of conscious long-term memory retrieval (Cantor & Engle, 1993). According to Baddeley (1986), concurrent demands on working memory, such as maintaining rehearsal, take precedence over retrieval. Hence, working memory capacity limitations can have a detrimental impact on the long-term retrieval of existing associations and representations (Barrouillet & Lepine, 2005). Individuals with severe working memory limitations may not possess enough capacity to conduct active searches, and their searches may be more automatic and passive in nature, resulting in less output. When working memory is deficient or overloaded, retrieval is less frequent, slower, and less efficient, in part because there are fewer resources to devote to inhibiting irrelevant and incorrect information. During retrieval, multiple competing memory traces and structures are activated. Working memory considers these competing sources of information, selects the most appropriate ones for the current task, and reduces interference from irrelevant information by inhibiting it (Radvansky & Copeland, 2006).

Although working memory limitations constrain the efficiency and accuracy of conscious long-term retrieval efforts, some individuals have deficiencies in automated long-term retrieval itself. In extreme cases, their slow retrieval speed is observable. For instance, it is well established that individuals with a mathematics disability have difficulty automatically retrieving math facts from long-term storage. Exceptionally slow retrieval speed is also associated with general learning problems and reading disabilities. For example, difficulties with rapid automatic naming (RAN) are associated with a basic reading skills disability. Thus, assessment of long-term retrieval should be included in any comprehensive assessment of working memory.

Relationship with Short-Term Memory

There are several characteristics of long-term memory that distinguish it from short-term memory: (a) long-term representations change slowly and incrementally after repeated exposures to the same information, whereas short-term memory can instantaneously represent new information; (b) long-term memory is based on neuronal growth, whereas short-term memory consists of temporary electrical activation (Hebb, 1949); and (c) long-term memory maintains long-term, relatively stable, structured representations of the world, whereas short-term memories are less structured and less distinct (Brown & Hulme, 1996). These differences illustrate why long-term memory must certainly make a contribution to short-term memory performance. When information enters phonological short-term memory, related phonological and semantic information is immediately and automatically activated. When the individual is required to recall the information temporarily stored in short-term memory, long-term memory enhances recall by drawing on the activated phonological and semantic representations (Logie, 1996). This explains why memory span is greater for words than nonwords (Gathercole & Martin, 1996). Long-term memory also facilitates short-term recall in another way. According to Frick (1988), each verbal item recalled must be re-recognized from the stream of information in the phonological store. This re-recognition is aided by long-term memory representations. This process explains how partially decayed information can be recalled and why those with normal memory span have more difficulty recalling rhyming than nonrhyming words. In conclusion, the overlap between short-term and long-term recognition and recall processes makes it difficult to identify which store is actually being tapped by retrieval.

Relationship with Working Memory

Since long-term memory is basically a passive repository, most of the work of encoding and retrieving information falls on working memory operations (Shiffrin, 1999). The meaning-based encoding function of working memory is constantly required during the initial stages of learning. Once an individual has acquired schemas and other long-term representational structures, encoding of new conceptual information amounts to little more than rearranging and adding the new information to already existing schemas. Regarding retrieval, not only does stored knowledge automatically reconstruct partially decayed short-term traces, but long-term representations are consciously used by working memory to reconstruct larger units of information. This process of reassembling information to be recalled is referred to as *redintegration* (Turner, Henry, & Smith, 2000). By 6 years of age, it is apparent that children are consciously using long-term knowledge to reconstruct partially decayed information, a process thought to become more effective with further development (Gathercole, 1999).

In summary, working memory and long-term memory have reciprocal influences on each other that are difficult to separate. At the very least, working memory and long-term memory are very interactive. (More details on the interdependency of working memory and long-term memory can be found in Chapters 2 and 3.) The relationship is clearly bidirectional: Long-term knowledge is used to recall and enhance short-term and working memory representations; and working memory facilitates the building and retrieval of long-term structures.

Expertise and Automatization

Expertise is thought to increase working memory capacity, not just expertise in a particular domain, but also expertise at utilizing working memory resources. Expertise in a content area allows the formation of larger chunks; for example, compared to ordinary chess players, chess masters recall significantly larger chunks (Cowan, 2005). Most individuals naturally develop expertise at operating their own working memory systems by discovering and using effective strategies, such as subvocal rehearsal. Expertise with executive control processes, such as directing long-term memory searches, is even more important. Similar to expertise at a skill, the outcome of increased expertise at working memory processes is an increase in the size of the chunks that can be simultaneously manipulated and retained.

When a task is overlearned to the point where it can be conducted without conscious processing, it is referred to as being *automatized*. For example, when a reader becomes fluent at reading decoding, the process has become automatized. At this level, tasks are controlled by established procedures stored in long-term memory, thereby reducing the need for working memory involvement. Much of the apparent expansion of working memory capacity is a function of expertise and automaticity. Consequently, the improved efficiency of working memory depends on automatization of skills and strategies. When a task becomes automatized, its performance requires little assistance from working memory resources. (See Chapter 5 for a discussion of the impact of automaticity on learning.)

Deficit Models

The perspective that educators and practitioners take on the development of working memory capacity partly determines how they will view deficits. There are two main contrasting viewpoints. The traditional deficit model assumes a neuropsychological basis for poor performance. That is, there is a processing constraint that is viewed as stable and manifested across a variety of tasks. The processing constraint is not necessarily specific to working memory; it may originate with a function, such as processing speed, that underlies working memory performance. In contrast, the processing efficiency-deficit perspective assumes that the poorly performing individual is not effectively utilizing his or her normal working memory capabilities. If processing inefficiency underlies what are perceived as working memory impairments, then the implications for educational intervention are different. That is, the constraints should be modifiable (Swanson, 2000); for example, teaching the individual to use more effective strategies should lead to improved working memory performance.

Some researchers, most notably Swanson (2000), have attempted to resolve this dilemma, at least in regards to learning disabilities. Several investigations centered on this issue led Swanson (2000) to conclude that the working memory deficits of individuals with learning disabilities reflect deficits in capacity, not efficiency. However, the most pragmatic view is that it depends on the individual. Given low working memory performance and related learning problems, it could be either a processing deficit, a lack of efficiency, or both. The learner's response to intervention may provide further evidence as to causality. Those who respond well to intervention presumably do not have an innate, stable deficit, but rather need to learn more effective strategies for utilizing their existing capacity. Those who do not respond to interventions most likely have a capacity deficit that cannot be ameliorated. Swanson (2000) concluded that the working memory deficits of individuals with a reading disability are resistant to improvement because the deficits are due to actual capacity limitations in domain-general working memory. In cases where this is true, then interventions need to focus on compensatory approaches (see Chapter 9).

At this point, it may be helpful to define *deficit*, contrast it with *weakness*, and suggest a method of distinguishing between the two. In research, psychoeducational evaluations, and educational environments, the term *deficit* is often used loosely or inconsistently; many educators and practitioners equate *deficit* with any sort of *weakness* or difficulty. However, the term *deficit* should apply only to significantly lower than normal functioning that is also a relative weakness for the group or individual. When researchers say that working memory is a deficit for a particular population, they do not mean that it is simply a below average ability for that group. Rather, the implication is that when members of that group are matched with controls, working memory stands out as a significant group weakness. For example, when it is reported that working memory is a deficit among the learning disabled population, it does not mean simply that their working memory performance is well below average. Rather, it means that working memory is significantly lower than their other abilities or lower than the working memory of nondisabled individuals with the same IQ. The same principle (discussed further in Chapter 6) applies to determining deficits within individuals. To be classified as a deficit, performance should be both below average and a significant intraindividual weakness. Of course, the important implication is that a deficit is likely causing an impairment in functioning. In contrast, everyone has intraindividual weaknesses and many have weaknesses relative to population norms (referred to as *normative weaknesses*). However, the mere existence of either a normative or intraindividual weakness does not mean the individual or population has a deficit.

Relations with Other Cognitive Processes

Working memory plays a critical, integral role in most higher level cognitive activities, including reasoning, comprehension, and executive functioning (Dehn, 2006; McNamara & Scott, 2001). Thus, higher level cognitive functioning results from the interplay between working memory and several cognitive processes. Some of the relationships are hierarchical, some are reciprocal, and some are between parallel

Table 4.1 Correlations Between WJ III Cognitive Clusters, Ages 6–8

Cognitive Cluster	Working Memory	Short-Term Memory
General Intellectual Ability	.74	.74
Comprehension-Knowledge	.49	.47
Long-Term Retrieval	.51	.48
Visual-Spatial Thinking	.28	.25
Auditory Processing	.38	.37
Fluid Reasoning	.53	.49
Processing Speed	.49	.41
Short-Term Memory	.81	1.00
Broad Attention	.90	.78
Executive Processes	.51	.46
Delayed Recall	.39	.36
Phonemic Awareness 3	.54	.52

Note: The Numbers Reversed test is part of both the Short-Term and Working Memory clusters, producing greater similarity in the correlations each has with cognitive clusters.

Source: Woodcock-Johnson III Technical Manual (McGrew & Woodcock, 2001, p. 175).

processes. Sometimes there is such close interaction that it is difficult to distinguish between the two. The processes that are linked most closely with working memory include attention, phonological processing, executive functioning, fluid reasoning, and processing speed (McNamara & Scott). The correlations among the processes tested by the Woodcock-Johnson III (WJ III) Tests of Cognitive Abilities are similar to those reported in the scientific literature (see Table 4.1).

Deficient cognitive processes can reduce working memory's efficiency and performance, whereas strong cognitive processes can enhance working memory. For example, exceptionally fast processing speed may compensate somewhat for a working memory with subaverage capacity. For its part, working memory capacity sets limits on related higher level processes (Conners et al., 2001). An impaired working memory system may place serious limitations upon other cognitive functions that in themselves do not involve the retention of information. At times, even a working memory with normal capacity and efficient functioning can have deleterious effects on other processing. For example, when an individual is trying to maintain and rehearse unrelated information, a computational task will require more processing time, with increased risk of errors. The effect that working memory load has on another process reflects the level of dependence the related process has on working memory. The effect also could indicate that working memory and other cognitive functions draw from the same pool of processing resources. The interdependency of working memory and associated processes means that growth and development in other cognitive processes will contribute to the expansion of working memory capacity. For example, working memory capacity expands along with a child's growing attention span. Despite the difficulty in quantifying the reciprocal influences, undoubtedly, normal working memory processes are essential for higher level cognitive functioning, and, in turn, various cognitive processes support working memory operations.

Phonological Processing

Phonological processing is the manipulation and encoding of phonemes, which are the smallest distinguishable units of speech. Phonological processing involves recognizing, segmenting, and blending phonemes into whole words. Proficient phonological processing requires phonemic awareness—the conscious knowledge that words are composed of different sounds. The English language consists of about 41 phonemes (25 consonant and 16 vowel sounds) that are represented by hundreds of different graphemes—the written letters or combinations of letters that can be decoded into phonemes. Normal phonological processing and phonemic awareness are not only necessary for language development but are also critical for the acquisition of literacy skills. Developmentally, children first learn whole words without recognizing the units that comprise them. Later children can isolate syllables within words, and then finally phonemes within words. Phonemic awareness typically develops during the preschool years. An indication that a child has acquired phonemic awareness is the ability to segment, blend, omit, and rhyme phonemes. Research (National Reading Panel, 2000) has reported that a sizable number of children, perhaps as high as 30%, enter school with deficient phonemic awareness skills. The deficiency can have profound effects on literacy, as learning to read depends heavily on phonemic awareness (National Reading Panel).

The exact nature of the relationship between phonological short-term memory and phonological processing is not entirely known but certainly the two processes are integrally related (Hulme & Mackenzie, 1992). Adequate phonological short-term memory is necessary for proficient phonological processing; conversely, phonological processing affects short-term memory span. Studies (reviewed by Wagner, 1996) have found measures of phonological awareness and short-term memory span to be highly correlated with each other. To some extent, phonological processing and phonological short-term memory seem inseparable; they are certainly strongly associated throughout development. It is possible that phonological processing is the underlying process that determines the capacity and functioning of phonological short-term memory. The consensus among researchers is that the two processes have a reciprocal effect on each other. However, the extent of the bilateral influence is difficult to resolve (Cohen-Mimran & Sapir, 2007). (More discussion of their relationship can be found in the Reading section of Chapter 5.)

Auditory Processing

Auditory processing is the ability to perceive, analyze, synthesize, and discriminate all auditory stimuli, not just oral language. Although much is known about subsidiary phonological processing, unfortunately, very little memory research has been conducted on the temporary retention of nonspeech sounds. For example, there is certainly short-term retention, processing, and retrieval of musical tones; we just do not know as much about these functions and capabilities. Nonetheless, there are indications of a relationship between general auditory processing and working memory, as measures of verbal working memory have moderate correlations with auditory processing (Hitch, Towse, & Hutton, 2001).

Linguistic Processing

Researchers in the field of linguistics (for a review, see Leonard et al., 2007) generally concur that there is a strong relationship between language processing and working memory. There is sufficient evidence that linguistic processing is constrained by general working memory capacity and effective utilization of that capacity (Moser, Fridriksson, & Healy, 2007). Most psychologists and linguists (Just & Carpenter, 1992) believe that language processing is conducted by a general purpose, functionally separate working memory system. In contrast, a few (MacDonald & Christiansen, 2002) argue that verbal working memory and linguistic processing are not distinct entities. Instead, verbal working memory is a language subsystem specifically designed for mediating language comprehension (Waters & Caplan, 1996). (See Chapter 5 for an in-depth discussion of the relationship between working memory and language development.)

Visuospatial Processing

Visual processing is the ability to perceive, analyze, synthesize, manipulate, and transform visual patterns and images, including those generated internally. The spatial aspect of the processing has more to do with location of objects, such as the ability to scan a field and identify a configuration. Integration of visuospatial processing and subconscious visuospatial short-term memory processing seems necessary in order for individuals to remain oriented in space and retain the location of moving objects. It is hypothesized that visuospatial short-term memory is constantly refreshing the perceptual image of the visual field, even when the field is unchanging. When individuals must consciously recall or manipulate objects or mental images, then visuospatial working memory becomes involved. Not enough is known about visuospatial working memory and its separability from visual processing because more research has been conducted on visual perception and visual processing than on the functioning of visuospatial working memory. Nevertheless, we do know there is strong relationship between the two (Hitch et al., 2001). It is also well established that visual mnemonics are powerful methods of retaining and cuing information that needs to be learned (see Chapter 9).

Processing Speed

In general, processing speed refers to how quickly information moves through the information processing system and how efficiently simple cognitive tasks are executed over a sustained period of time. Processing speed is typically measured with tasks requiring an individual to perform overlearned procedures that require little reasoning or higher level processing. Because processing speed involves encoding, retrieval, and other working memory functions, it is difficult to separate from working memory. Processing speed has an exceptionally strong relationship with working memory. For example, Ackerman, Beier, and Boyle (2002a) reported a correlation of .477 between working memory tests and processing speed abilities. Moreover, age-related increases in processing speed may mediate most of the developmental increases in working memory capacity. Fry and Hale (1996) reported that 71% of the age-related changes in working memory capacity were related to developmental changes in processing speed. Undoubtedly, the processing and storage capacity of working memory is extremely dependent on the general speed of cognitive processing. Nonetheless, there is ample evidence for the functional separation of processing speed and working memory (Leonard et al., 2007).

Processing speed heavily influences working memory because memory processing and storage is time related (Swanson, Howard, & Saez, 2006). Faster processing speed allows more information to be processed in less time, thereby increasing the functional capacity of working memory. Faster speed also reduces the interval over which information must be maintained, resulting in less short-term forgetting. Other ways faster processing speed enables working memory processing and storage are: making it possible to shift more rapidly between competing tasks (Kail & Hall, 2001); increasing the speed at which perceptual information is encoded into a memory representation; increasing the speed at which long-term memories are activated and retrieved; increasing the speed of associative learning; and increasing response speed. Faster processing speed also allows more efficient access to representations maintained in working memory or the activated pool, and it reduces the pressure on executive working memory to resist interference. Conversely, slow processing speed impairs the efficient use of the working memory system. In general, individuals who process more rapidly have more time to encode, rehearse, and process the to-be-remembered material, resulting in improved short-term and long-term retention.

The influence of processing speed on phonological short-term memory retention has been explored in depth. As discussed in Chapter 2, increases in speech rate are highly related with the growth of short-term span. Processing speed mediates articulation rate and rehearsal rate, which in turn determines the number of items that can be rehearsed before decay. Thus, faster processing speed extends short-term memory span. In the case of curtailed phonological short-term capacity, processing speed can compensate somewhat by rapidly encoding information into long-term storage or rapidly moving information into working memory for higher level processing. Luckily, verbal working memory span is not solely determined by speed-related factors, such as rehearsal rate. Interestingly, processing speed seems to be more closely related with working memory development than with short-term memory development (Bayliss, Jarrold, Baddeley, Gunn, & Leigh, 2005).

Successive Processing

Successive processing, also referred to as *sequential processing*, is the maintenance of serial order, or the sequential arrangement and encoding of stimuli. Stimuli arranged sequentially form a chainlike progression in which each stimulus is related to the one it follows. Most successive processing is automatized, but demands to recall information sequentially will enlist working memory resources. Successive processing is required to understand speech and decode written material. By its nature, subvocal rehearsal is also a sequential process. Nevertheless, the relation between successive processing and phonological short-term memory measures is probably a function of the usual testing requirement that the items be recalled in the correct order. It is perhaps unfortunate that most testing paradigms are structured this way, as there is probably more to short-term capacity than is indicated by the ability to retain sequences.

Executive Processing

Executive processes modulate and coordinate the operation of many disparate cognitive processes, including multiple-component processes such as working memory. Although some psychologists argue that executive processing is a unitary function, the complex supervisory roles of executive functioning lead others to conclude that executive processing consists of several separate but related subcomponent processes, much like a board of directors (Berninger & Richards, 2002). One of the primary subcomponents of executive processing must have responsibility for managing working memory. The close interaction, supported by their joint location in the frontal lobes, makes it appear that executive processing and working memory are inextricably intertwined. And it has led some working memory theorists to conclude that working memory may be little more than the executive processes called into action whenever automated and passive short- and long-term memory processes are insufficient for the task at hand. Although this may be a valid interpretation of the relationship between these constructs, this author (as argued in Chapter 3) stresses the importance of maintaining a distinction between the two, and relegating within-memory management functions to executive working memory. Hence, general executive abilities should not be viewed as the equivalent of working memory. Certainly, working memory can vary independently of higher level executive functioning (Bayliss et al., 2003). Nor should it be assumed that the relationship is hierarchical; it is most likely reciprocal. Some theorists (e.g., Roberts & Pennington, 1996) even take the perspective that working memory actually underlies a wide range of executive function processes. In other words, executive processing depends on working memory's ability to hold and manipulate information "on-line" for a few seconds. For example, planning, which is considered an executive process, requires the use of working memory resources.

Fluid Reasoning

Fluid reasoning, which includes inductive and deductive reasoning, is the ability to reason and solve problems, especially when confronted with novel tasks. It is considered to be one of the primary intelligence factors (Carroll, 1993), if not the essence of what is considered general intelligence. Reading comprehension and mathematical reasoning are academic skills that draw heavily on fluid reasoning. Like executive processing, with which it is also intertwined, fluid reasoning is a cognitive process that does not reach full development until early adolescence.

Several studies have found extremely high correlations between fluid reasoning and working memory capacity. In research reviewed by Kane and Engle (2002), working memory span tasks correlate between .60 and .80 with fluid reasoning. Kyllonen and Christal (1990) even found correlations as high as .90. Furthermore, the strong relationship between fluid reasoning and working memory holds over a broad range of different tasks (Sub et al., 2002). The close relation between working memory and fluid reasoning is also supported by neuroimaging studies that have found the same regions of the prefrontal cortex to be involved during both types of tasks (Kane & Engle, 2002). The high correlations between the two variables may result from a third variable that they are both related to. What working memory and fluid reasoning may have in common is some aspect of controlled attention (Engle, Tuholski, et al., 1999). Or, perhaps, fluid reasoning and working memory capacity reflect the joint ability to keep a memory representation active. Another explanation for the strong link between working memory and fluid reasoning is offered by Conway et al. (2002), who contend that performance in both domains depends on successful application of strategies.

Some theorists (e.g., Kyllonen & Christal, 1990) even suggest that individual differences in fluid reasoning are due to differences in working memory capacity. For example, Kail (2007) reported longitudinal evidence demonstrating that an increase in working memory capacity is one of the factors driving developmental growth in inductive reasoning. Despite this evidence, a reciprocal relationship is implicated, with differences in fluid reasoning at least partially constrained by working memory capacity and differences in working memory partially reflecting one's ability to reason effectively. The working memory component that has the strongest relationship with fluid reasoning is executive working memory. In contrast, phonological short-term memory does not appear to have a strong connection with fluid reasoning (Engle, Tuholski, et al., 1999). As with other processes, strong fluid reasoning abilities may help to compensate for an impaired working memory; for example, fluid reasoning may produce a correct response when details have been partially forgotten. Although some (e.g., Buehner et al., 2006) argue that fluid reasoning and working memory are identical constructs, the consensus is that working memory and fluid reasoning are not identical factors, despite their extremely close relationship (Kyllonen & Christal).

General Intelligence

It is generally accepted that working memory is the central cognitive factor in human information processing. Recently it has been proposed that working memory capacity, broadly defined, may to a large extent account for individual differences in intellectual functioning (Cowan, 2005; Kyllonen, 1996; McGrew, 2005). It seems that working memory capacity correlates with the general intelligence factor, referred to as g, as much or more so than it does with specific processing domains. The correlations between working-memory capacity and g have typically been around .6 (see Conway, Kane, & Engle, 2003, for a review of related studies), with working memory accounting for a third to half of the variance in g. Kyllonen and Christal were the first to assert that "working memory is *the* general factor in cognition" (1990, p. 401). However, their initial research was criticized for using measures that were essentially measuring the same construct. Subsequent studies have replicated the original findings, using more carefully selected working memory tasks that were distinguishable from general reasoning tasks. For example, Sub et al. (2002) recently found general working memory capacity to be highly related with general intelligence. Recent factor-analytic results in support of this claim have also found working memory to have the highest correlation (.93) with g, supplanting fluid reasoning as the primary first-order factor (Colom et al., 2004). The relationship is so strong that g is almost perfectly predicted by working memory capacity, making working memory capacity the best predictor of g (intelligence). The relationship is bidirectional; g is also a good predictor of working memory. Findings of such strong relationships have led some to claim that working memory and intelligence are unitary constructs. However, the current consensus seems to be that working memory capacity and g are highly related factors but are not identical (Conway et al., 2003; Kyllonen & Christal). In contrast, other researchers have argued that working memory and g are quite different, having a common variance as little as 25% (Ackerman, Beier, & Boyle, 2002b).

Specifically, the strong relation most likely results from the necessity for working memory involvement whenever complex cognitive activity occurs. That is, a considerable amount of information must be actively maintained during most complex cognitive functioning. For both fluid reasoning and g, the working memory components that account for the relationship are the verbal and executive components, not passive short-term storage components. Short-term memory tasks that measure simple storage typically do not have significant relations with fluid reasoning or g. With tasks that demand processing in addition to storage, the basis of the relation is most likely an executive-attention control mechanism, which is mediated by portions of the prefrontal cortex—the brain location where fluid reasoning and g are also centered (Conway et al., 2003). For example, when additional processing is required, the executive control mechanism focuses attention, maintains activation of goal-relevant information, and combats interference. Actively maintaining a memory representation while inhibiting distracting interference may account for much of the variance working memory and *g* have in common (Kane & Engle, 2002).

Attention

Maintaining attention to the task at hand is another cognitive function that often seems indistinguishable from working memory. There is an exceptionally strong relationship between working memory and attention, with no clear distinctions between the many aspects of attention and the functioning of working memory, especially executive working memory (Cornish, Wilding, & Grant, 2006; Morris, 1996). Individuals who score high on tests of executive working memory capacity are better at suppressing, or inhibiting, distracting information than low-span individuals (Conway, Cowan, & Bunting, 2001). Conversely, children with poor attentional control are likely to have concomitant difficulties in some aspects of working memory. For example, Cornish et al. found that children rated by their teachers as having poor attention performed poorly on working memory measures.

Not surprisingly, some working memory theorists identify the maintenance of attention as the core working memory operation (see Chapter 2). Engle, Kane, and Tuholski (1999) propose that individual differences in working memory performance primarily reflect differences in controlled attention capability because controlled attention is necessary during almost every aspect of working memory functioning. Accordingly, working memory appears to be the seat of higher level attentional processes, including the ability to sustain attention, to divide attention, and to focus attention on a particular item or process. Working memory is also responsible for resisting interference and for shifting attention from one task to another, without losing relevant information. With controlled attention and other aspects of attention frequently identified as core mechanisms of working memory, there is a significant overlap between the constructs of attention and working memory, to the point where they might be considered one and the same. Undoubtedly, working memory and attention have much in common: Both selectively focus attention on desired information while inhibiting interference from irrelevant stimuli; in the visual domain, both involve selectively activating representations; they frequently focus on the same content at the same time; they share the same control processes; and they seem to share the same resources (Olivers, Meijer, & Theeuwes, 2006). Perhaps the common underlying process is inhibition—not only inhibition of irrelevant stimuli and internal representations, but also inhibition of inappropriate responses (Cornish et al., 2006). Another plausible explanation for the large overlap in functioning is that they both are controlled by the same subset of executive processes. If attention and working memory share the same cognitive resources, they have a combined capacity of around four items at a time. Therefore, when working memory is engaged at capacity, attention will suffer, and working memory will be impaired when maintaining attention is the priority, especially when attention and working memory are focused on different content (Awh & Jonides, 2001). For instance, who has not had the experience of having difficulty paying attention to environmental stimuli while engaged in unrelated mental processing? About the only difference between the two is that working memory has responsibility for retaining information.

If working memory and attention are separate processes, there is certainly a significant amount of interaction between them. Working memory may act in the service of selective and divided attention (Kane & Engle, 2002), determining which stimuli are selected for focused attention (Soto et al., 2005). Support for this hypothesis comes from neuroimaging studies that discovered working memory plays a critical role in controlling attention (Conway et al., 2001). On the other hand, stimuli that have captured attention frequently become working memory content. Furthermore, attention may play an integral function in working memory subprocesses; for example, rehearsal may be little more than an attention-based process (Smyth & Scholey, 1994). Despite the extremely close connection between working memory and attention, they are best regarded as separable processes and functions, with attention tasked with selecting relevant information and working memory responsible for processing and remembering information. For instance, Buehner et al. (2005) found evidence to support the claim that selective attention and working memory are distinct constructs. Additional support for the disassociation has been offered by Siegel and Ryan (1989), who reported that their subjects with ADHD did not have deficits in working memory tasks.

Disorders and Conditions with Working Memory Deficits

Given the interplay working memory has with so many cognitive processes, it is only logical to presume that impairments in any higher level cognitive process or skill are either impacting working memory functioning or can be partially attributed to working memory dysfunctions. Not all working memory impairments are innate: some are acquired through injury or illness, others appear after the onset of a disorder, and others result from life's natural ebb and flow. For instance, children born prematurely are at risk for working memory weaknesses (Espy et al., 2004). (For a discussion of learning disabilities, see Chapter 5.)

Attention-Deficit/Hyperactivity Disorder (ADHD)

Children with ADHD comprise a sizable group who typically perform poorly on measures of short-term and working memory (Klingberg, Forssberg, & Westerberg, 2002). Prevailing models of ADHD (Barkley, 1997a, 1997b) suggest that working memory impairments are central to ADHD because working memory deficits and ADHD both are associated with specific deficits in executive skills (Wu, Anderson, & Castiello, 2006). Barkley, a recognized expert in ADHD, has asserted that the core deficit of ADHD is the inability to use inhibitory processes when needed. Inhibition, an executive processing function, also performs a crucial function in working memory processing by suppressing and deactivating information that is not relevant to the task at hand (Cowan, 2005). When inhibition fails, irrelevant information interferes with the retention and processing of information that should be the focus of attention, negatively impacting working memory performance. In general, working memory deficits among ADHD children can be attributed to their poor control of attentional processes and limitations in attentional capacity, both important aspects of working memory functioning.

Numerous studies have found ADHD children and adolescents to have deficits in working memory. For example, Brown, Reichel, and Quinlan (2007) reported that over 74% of the ADHD youth in their sample displayed a significant impairment in working memory. In a meta-analysis of 26 studies on working memory impairments found in children with ADHD, Martinussen, Hayden, Hogg-Johnson, and Tannock (2005) concluded that children with ADHD exhibit deficits in multiple components of working memory. Relative to normal controls, the subjects exhibited large impairments in visuospatial working memory and moderate impairments in verbal working memory. Martinussen et al. suggest that poor academic progress in children with ADHD may be the result of working memory deficiencies rather than a direct consequence of inattention, a suggestion that has important implications for education.

An assessment of working memory components may even provide data for differentiating among different ADHD subtypes (Quinlan & Brown, 2003). Martinussen and Tannock (2006), along with other researchers, have found that children with the ADHD Combined subtype perform worse than normal students on all short-term and working memory components, whereas the Primarily Inattentive subtypes are deficient in visuospatial and executive working memory and the Primarily Hyperactive-Impulsive subtypes may not display any significant deficits. When those who are Primarily Hyperactive-Impulsive have a working memory impairment, it tends to be in the executive domain (Martinussen & Tannock). Thus, children with ADHD are not necessarily impaired in all aspects of working memory. For example, they generally do not possess verbal working memory deficits unless they have ADHD Combined subtype or have a comorbid learning disability. The consensus among researchers is that working memory is more strongly related to symptoms of inattention than to symptoms of hyperactivity-impulsivity. Some researchers (e.g., Denckla, 1996) have even asserted that verbal and executive working memory deficits may be a common neuropsychological weakness in children who have both Primarily Inattentive ADHD and a learning disability. Perhaps the most important educational implication from this research is that a working memory impairment may be the cognitive factor that actually underlies the academic learning problems experienced by children with ADHD. Finally, children with both ADHD and a reading disability tend to have more severe deficits in executive working memory (Martinussen & Tannock, 2006). However, unlike children with reading disabilities, children with ADHD generally do not exhibit a deficit in phonological short-term memory.

Autism

Because autism is thought to be an executive disorder arising from frontal lobe dysfunction, working memory has been hypothesized to be deficient in individuals with autism. However, investigations have yielded equivocal results. In particular, some studies have discovered intact verbal working memory in individuals with autism (see Williams et al., 2005, for a review). In a study involving high-functioning subjects with autism, Williams et al. found the subjects to be deficient in visuospatial but not verbal working memory. Steele, Minshew, Luna, and Sweeney (2007) also found that individuals with autism are deficient in visuospatial working memory and attributed this finding to the involvement of the prefrontal cortex in visuospatial working memory. A current prevailing hypothesis is that children with autism are impaired in working memory because they fail to develop and utilize working memory strategies (for a review, see Minear & Shah, 2006), probably because they have poor or nonexistent inner speech. If a strategy deficit exists, then their working memory deficits will not become apparent until they are older or until complex tasks are demanded of them.

Cognitive Disabilities

Research on the working memory development of children with cognitive or intellectual disabilities (reviewed by Henry & MacLean, 2002) has frequently found such children to have weaknesses in working memory relative to their other cognitive abilities. In this population, it seems that working memory performance does not keep pace with overall cognitive development. When children with cognitive disabilities are matched with subjects of the same mental age, they exhibit significantly lower digit and word spans (Hulme & Mackenzie, 1992), and the gap seems to grow over time. In addition to working memory being a relative weakness, recent findings indicate that children with intellectual disabilities have areas of relative strengths and weaknesses within working memory (Henry & MacLean). Their most consistent area of weakness is verbal working memory, which is most likely related to their delayed use of verbal rehearsal strategies.

Several studies have found that children with Down's syndrome typically have lower working memory than their overall cognitive ability, and, as their mental abilities grow, their memory span lags farther behind (Comblain, 1994; Conners et al., 2001; Hulme & Mackenzie, 1992). However, the working memory research with this population has been equivocal; little agreement exists on whether working memory performance keeps pace with overall cognitive development (Henry & MacLean, 2002). The inconsistent findings may be due to the fact that working memory performance in children with mental retardation depends on the task. Some aspects of working memory may be better than others; for example, children with Down's syndrome usually have weaker verbal working memory than visuospatial working memory. Furthermore, children with low cognitive abilities may not be using certain strategies.

Acquired Brain Injury

Acquired brain injury subjects have provided valuable information on the composition of memory systems, and the impact of working memory dysfunction on other cognitive functions. A closed-head traumatic brain injury (TBI) usually involves the vulnerable frontal lobes, where executive processes and core working memory operations are headquartered. It is well established that children who suffer head injuries are at risk for ongoing memory problems, especially working memory impairments. Levin et al. (2004) completed a valuable 2-year longitudinal study of 144 children with mild to severe brain trauma. The study found that the subjects' working memory improved during the first 3 months after injury, regardless of age or severity. However, in children who sustained severe TBI, working memory performance went on to deteriorate during the second year, whereas those less severely injured continued to demonstrate growth in working memory. Such an unexpected finding is consistent with developmental neuroscience research, which has identified other delayed effects of TBI on cognition (Levin et al.). Possible deterioration after initial improvement makes it imperative that neuropsychologists and related professionals monitor the working memory functioning of children with TBI for at least 2 years following the injury, as continued improvement or even maintenance of initial improvement cannot be assumed. Another educationally relevant finding of Levin et al. is that the academic performance of children with TBI is often poorer than would be predicted from academic achievement measures, a finding consistent with intact long-term storage but now damaged working memory.

Schizophrenia

Impairments in working memory capacity, as well as in executive functions, are reported widely in Schizophrenia research (Harvey et al., 2006; Stephane & Pellizzer, 2007). Processing and working memory demands that would be minimal for healthy individuals reveal significant limitations in patients with Schizophrenia. These deficits appear to be related to overall reductions in cognitive processing capacity, caused by dysfunction in the prefrontal cortex. Van Snellenberg, Torres, and Thornton (2006) found subjects with Schizophrenia who performed poorly on minimally challenging working memory tasks had greater dorsolateral prefrontal cortex activation than normal subjects. But as the working memory demands increased, the subjects' prefrontal activation declined, indicating that they were no longer engaging working memory or were using alternative ineffective strategies. All aspects of working memory—visuospatial, verbal, and executive—seem to be affected, both in children and adults with Schizophrenia (for a review see Minear & Shah, 2006). Even individuals with Schizotypal Personality Disorder demonstrate deficits in both verbal and executive working memory (Harvey et al., 2006). In fact, in children who are genetically at risk for Schizophrenia, the extent of their working memory deficit has been shown to be predictive of the likelihood of developing the disorder (Erlenmeyer-Kimling et al.,

2000). Goldman-Rakic (1992) hypothesizes that a schizophrenic's difficulty balancing immediate stimulation with internal and past information results from the breakdown of the working memory processes.

Stress

Stress is another factor that can be detrimental to working memory functioning (for a review, see Klein & Boals, 2001). Stress diminishes an individual's working memory capacity because working memory must dedicate attentional resources to inhibit irrelevant, unwanted, intrusive thoughts about stressful events. Consequently, the additional competition for working memory resources reduces performance on tasks that depend on working memory. Evidence on the effects of stress on working memory illustrates that working memory functioning depends on more than innate capacity, strategies, and the novelty of the task. Certain life events can have a significant, if only temporary, impact on working memory functioning.

Aging

It is widely known that there is an age-related decrement in working memory performance, although the cause of the decline is disputed. Declines in working memory with aging have generally been associated with the slowing in general speed of information processing, a decline in fluid intelligence, a slower retrieval speed, and a general reduction in the ability to inhibit irrelevant information (Baddeley, 1996b; Rypma & D'Esposito, 2000). Any of these possibilities would reduce the speed with which information is processed in working memory, thereby decreasing the efficiency of working memory overall. Some investigators have concluded that an age-related reduction in processing speed accounts for reduced memory span (reviewed by Engle, 1996). However, diminished working memory capacity in the elderly is more likely due to declines in the functioning of executive working memory (Baddeley, 1986), which leads to less efficient inhibition, an intrinsic working memory dimension that controls access to relevant information and removes irrelevant information (Hasher & Zacks, 1988; Pennington et al., 1996). Deficient inhibitory control over the contents of working memory results in difficulties retrieving and maintaining the information needed for the current task, resulting in curtailed working memory performance.

Conclusions and Implications

There are multiple, complex influences on the development of working memory. Growth in working memory seems to depend heavily on the concomitant development of several closely related cognitive processes, such as reasoning, executive control, and processing speed. In turn, several processes require working memory resources. Given the reciprocal interaction with so many processes and skills, attributing improved working memory performance to a single variable, such as increasing speech rate, seems to be an oversimplification. To complicate matters further, the influence of different factors varies by age, level of expertise, and the requirements of the task. The existence of working memory deficits in so many disorders further exemplifies the core relationships working memory has with most types of cognitive functioning. In addition to wide ranging relationships with various abilities, there are significant interactions among the components and processes of short-term, long-term, and working memory, interactions that change over the course of development. After all the developmental variation is examined, we still cannot answer an essential question: Is the expansion of memory span primarily due to increases in capacity or is it a function of increased efficiency?

The most important implication of the information reviewed in this chapter is that working memory assessment and intervention will be challenging because of the reciprocal influences it has with other processes and because of the evolving nature of working memory components. When working memory impairments are suspected, the assessment of working memory needs to include measures that allow some differentiation of the short-term and working memory components. To add to the challenge, hypotheses will even vary by age. Also, processes highly related with working memory will need to be assessed in order to investigate influences and underlying causes. Furthermore, evaluations for some cognitive and behavioral disorders, such as ADHD, should also include an assessment of working memory (see Chapter 6 for recommended assessment strategies). Overall, the deeper our understanding of working memory, the more obligations we have to seek answers that can guide interventions toward the actual areas of need.

CHAPTER 5

Working Memory and Academic Learning

"Working memory capacity is more highly related to . . . learning, both short-term and long-term, than is any other cognitive factor"

—P. Kyllonen

Educational and psychological research on working memory (e.g., Gathercole, Lamont, & Alloway, 2006; Swanson, Cochran, & Ewers, 1990) over the past 20 years has repeatedly affirmed the hypothesis that working memory processes underlie individual differences in learning ability. Working memory is required whenever anything must be learned because learning requires manipulation of information, interaction with long-term memory, and simultaneous storage and processing of information. Long-term memory, the vast storehouse of knowledge and experience, is also necessary for learning, but is able to acquire very little knowledge and skills without support from short-term and working memory. Clearly, working memory plays a critical role in learning; it is where knowledge is constructed and modified and where information is processed for semantic encoding. Nearly all of what must be learned and remembered must pass through working memory. Hence, the capacity and effective functioning of working memory determines the rate and extent of learning. In addition to learning, working memory capacity predicts performance on a wide range of real-world cognitive tasks (Engle, 2002).

Classroom performance and the development of verbal and academic skills, such as reading decoding, reading comprehension, mathematics, and written expression,

Table 5.1   Correlations Between WJ III Working Memory and Achievement, Ages 6–8

Achievement Cluster	Working Memory	Short-Term Memory
Broad Reading	.54	.48
Broad Math	.58	.50
Broad Written Language	.54	.48
Oral Expression	.38	.38
Listening Comprehension	.53	.49
Basic Reading Skills	.56	.50
Reading Comprehension	.53	.47
Math Calculation Skills	.51	.42
Math Reasoning	.59	.52
Basic Writing Skills	.51	.45
Written Expression	.52	.45

Note: The Numbers Reversed test is part of both the Short-Term and Working Memory clusters, producing greater similarity in the correlations each has with achievement clusters.

Source: Woodcock-Johnson III Technical Manual (McGrew & Woodcock, 2001).

depend heavily on the adequate functioning of working memory. The strong relations between specific areas of academic achievement and short-term and working memory components are well established (Berninger & Richards, 2002; Swanson, 2000; Swanson & Berninger, 1996). Overall, correlations between working memory measures and achievement range as high as .55 to .92 (Swanson, 1995). For example, the Working Memory cluster from the Woodcock-Johnson III (WJ III) Tests of Cognitive Ability has moderate correlations with the WJ III achievement clusters (see Table 5.1). In research reviewed by Engle (1996) and Engle, Tuholski, et al. (1999), working memory capacity has documented significant relationships with:

- Reading decoding
- Reading comprehension
- Language comprehension
- Spelling
- Following directions
- Vocabulary development
- Note taking
- Written expression
- Reasoning

- Complex learning
- Grade point average

In the typical classroom learning environment, continuous, heavy demands are placed on working memory. Common classroom activities that impose simultaneous demands on storage and processing include: listening to a speaker while trying to take notes, following complex instructions, decoding unfamiliar words, writing sentences from memory, and mental arithmetic. In each case, the learner must process new information and integrate it with previously stored knowledge or information that was just recently encountered. Learning is reduced, or at least slowed, when available working memory capacity is reduced through overloading of working memory or by requiring divided attention. Experimental research with dual-task paradigms has confirmed that a secondary working memory task impairs working memory performance on the primary task, as well as interfering with learning. For example, Reber and Kotovsky (1997) found that additional working memory load interfered with learning to solve a novel problem and that the impairment was proportional to the degree of working memory load. Even for those with normal working memory capacity and functioning, classroom instruction and learning activities can overwhelm working memory many times during the course of a day. For those with weak working memory functions or capacity, highly demanding working memory requirements can make learning extremely difficult. For example, children with poor working memory often lose track of their place in a complex task, require frequent repetitions of directions, skip procedural steps, and often abandon a task before completing it (Alloway et al., 2005).

The case of an actual student, referred to as "Joey," will illustrate how deficient working memory capacity can severely compromise a child's ability to make normal educational progress. When Joey was in fourth grade, his parents brought him to a private educational center so that he could receive tutoring in reading. At his school, Joey had been receiving special education services for a reading disability since first grade. Before tutoring began, a school psychologist at the center completed a psychoeducational evaluation of Joey using the WJ III cognitive and achievement batteries. On the cognitive scale, Joey obtained a General Intellectual Ability (similar to an IQ) standard score of 106, indicating that his overall cognitive potential was solidly average. In contrast, his reading and written expression standard scores were low average, ranging from 81 to 84. Using the discrepancy approach to identifying learning disabilities, Joey had significant discrepancies for these WJ III cluster scores: Broad Reading (-1.90), Basic Reading Skills (-1.63), Reading Comprehension (-2.09), Broad Written Language (-1.96), and Written Expression (-1.84). Clearly, Joey had learning disabilities in reading and written language.

When Joey's cognitive processes and different types of memory were tested with the WJ III, the difficulties underlying his disabilities became apparent. The first hypothesis was that Joey had a deficit in phonological processing, as measured by phonemic awareness on the WJ III. This hypothesis was supported by the parent and school report that Joey had always struggled with phonics and spelling. Nevertheless, Joey's Phonemic Awareness score was at the 97th percentile, indicating that his phonological processing was intact. However, his memory scores pointed to underlying processing problems: Short-Term Memory (25th percentile); Working Memory (18th percentile); Long-Term Retrieval (29th percentile); and, significantly, Numbers Reversed (7th percentile). These were not only weaknesses compared to his peers but they were also significant intraindividual weaknesses for Joey. Initial observations of Joey's oral reading were consistent with deficits in phonological short-term memory and verbal working memory: He had difficulty associating the correct phonemes with graphemes; he had difficulty blending phonemes into words; and he had difficulty remembering words that he had read or were provided to him only moments before. Apparently, short-term and working memory deficits were related to Joey's reading and writing problems. Interestingly, there was no record of these impairments ever being identified by school personnel or any indication that his individually designed instruction explicitly addressed these needs.

Working Memory and Learning Disabilities

In 2006, approximately 2.9 million children, or about 5.5% of the school-age population in the United States, received special education for a specific learning disability (U.S. Department of Education, 2006). Many educators and psychologists acknowledge that individuals with learning disabilities are likely to have a deficiency in one or more cognitive processes (Masoura, 2006), including phonological processing, auditory processing, long-term retrieval, attention, short-term memory, and working memory. In particular, research (Swanson & Berninger, 1996) has consistently found children with all types of learning disabilities and difficulties to display poor working memory performance, especially in verbal and executive working memory (see Table 5.2) When children with learning disabilities are matched with

Table 5.2 Working Memory Components *Most Highly Related* to Types of Academic Learning

Reading Decoding	Reading Comprehension	Written Language	Mathematics
Phonological STM	Executive WM	Executive WM	Visuospatial WM
Verbal WM	Verbal WM	Verbal WM	Executive WM
Executive WM		Phonological STM	

Note: STM = Short-Term Memory; WM = Working Memory.

controls who have the same IQ, the learning disabilities group displays within-child deficits in specific aspects of working memory (Swanson & Alexander, 1997). Another theme that emerges from the literature is that students with general or multiple specific learning disabilities (literacy and mathematics) perform poorly in all aspects of working memory. In contrast, children with only one specific learning disability demonstrate fairly distinctive working memory profiles, with deficits limited to one or two components. For example, children with a specific reading disability frequently have impairments in phonological short-term memory and verbal working memory (Pickering & Gathercole, 2004), whereas children with a specific mathematics disability tend to have deficits in visuospatial and executive working memory.

Research has consistently found students with specific learning difficulties to be the most deficient in the executive processing component of working memory (Swanson et al., 1990). Executive working memory serves a governing function, controlling and regulating memory subsystems. Executive-loaded working memory tasks provide the best discrimination between children with and without learning disabilities (Henry, 2001). For example, when compared with IQ-matched peers, students with learning disabilities have relatively more difficulty with a reverse digit span task (Gathercole & Pickering, 2001). Also, individuals with limited executive processing often fail to spontaneously use rehearsal, organization, and other executive-dependent strategies that allow effective and efficient use of working memory resources.

In addition to executive working memory deficits, the verbal working memory spans of children with learning disabilities are significantly lower than age- and ability-matched peers. In a sample of 11- to 12-year-old children, Henry (2001) determined that children with a moderate learning disability could retain verbal instructions that contained up to three units of information, whereas normal children could manage five units of information. When students must process other information while retaining verbal instructions (a typical classroom situation), those with learning disabilities can comfortably maintain only one item of information, whereas nondisabled students can handle an average of three units of information (Henry). A working memory deficit clearly puts those with learning disabilities at a significant disadvantage in the classroom.

The working memory deficits of those with learning difficulties seem to arise from neurobiological limitations in working memory and from inefficient use of working memory resources. Support for a neurological basis comes from evidence that working memory deficits are significantly resistant to change (Swanson, 2000). However, some researchers (e.g., Swanson, 2000) theorize that a working memory deficit is not entirely a capacity deficit. Rather, for some students with learning disabilities, a working memory problem is primarily a strategy deficit. That is, students with a learning disability often possess sufficient working memory resources and the ability to apply effective strategies but fail to use these strategies spontaneously or consistently. Thus, the working memory performance of students with learning disabilities often reflects the extent of effective strategy use (Ericsson & Kintsch, 1995).

The strong relationships between working memory deficits and a wide range of learning disabilities suggest that working memory should be assessed whenever a child is referred for a possible learning disability. The empirical evidence indicates that working memory performance is one source of data that can reliably differentiate between students with a learning disability and those who are slow learners (Swanson et al., 1990). Of course, working memory scores alone are insufficient for a diagnosis; other assessment data need to be taken into account. Furthermore, we must keep in mind that there are often multiple causes of a learning disability and that cognitive processing profiles will vary by individual. A working memory deficit is seldom the only deficiency found within individuals with learning disabilities. For example, those with a basic reading skills disability might have coexisting deficits in phonological processing or long-term storage. Individuals with lower general cognitive ability also are likely to be low in working memory. What sets those with learning disabilities apart is that working memory tends to be one of their intraindividual weaknesses.

Some investigators (e.g., Swanson & Siegel, 2001) believe that intrinsic working memory limitations are the primary *cause* of learning disabilities. However, because most of the research on working memory and learning disabilities is correlational, we cannot attribute causality. An alternative explanation is that a working memory deficit is the result of learning failure rather than its original cause (Torgesen, 2001). Also, some experts (e.g., Nation et al., 1999) claim that working memory problems are secondary to other cognitive processing deficits. Such arguments are consistent with MacDonald's and Christiansen's (2002) viewpoint that working memory is a subskill within various cognitive domains, such as language.

Working Memory and Oral Language

Strong relationships between verbal memory subsystems and both language development and oral language comprehension have been documented in a number of studies (e.g., Crain et al., 1990). Several aspects of language learning and comprehension depend on both phonological short-term memory and verbal working memory; for instance, Service (1992) found that verbal working memory accounted for 47% of the variance in the learning of a second language. Verbal working memory tasks have been found to discriminate between groups with different levels of language development. And developmental delays and disorders in language are often attributed to a curtailed capacity or dysfunction in verbal working memory. Although results have been inconsistent, correlations between language comprehension and short-term and working memory have ranged as high as .70 to .90. For instance, Montgomery (1996) reported a correlation of .62 between sentence comprehension and phonological short-term memory.

In oral language comprehension, working memory plays the critical role of constructing and integrating ideas from a stream of successive words (Just & Carpenter, 1992). To understand the meaning of a sentence, an individual must be able to remember previous words in order to relate them to later occurring words. During this complex process working memory must also store the partial results of comprehension, as well as encode some items for later retrieval. Difficulties in processing individual sentences have been related to deficient working memory capacity (Moser et al., 2007). Undoubtedly, one of the primary functions of verbal working memory is to extract a meaning representation that corresponds to the phonological input (Crain et al., 1990). An intact phonological store is also important for oral language comprehension because it stores word sequences long enough for the individual to decode these into their constituent meaning (Baddeley, 1990). Consequently, the capacity of the entire working memory system and the amount of temporary storage capacity have important implications for comprehensibility. Several studies (reviewed in Baddeley, 1986) have unequivocally found that placing demands, such as interference tasks, on working memory impairs language comprehension and slows down retrieval from long-term storage.

On the other hand, much of spoken-language processing occurs without assistance from working memory (Gathercole & Baddeley, 1993). For example, most comprehension of spoken sentences occurs immediately (Montgomery, 1996), as concepts and other representations in long-term memory are directly accessed. This activated long-term information automatically facilitates comprehension without the necessity of creating a working memory representation. However, if the syntactic structure or meaning of the sentence is confusing, then verbal and executive working memory will be brought into play. Therefore, it is likely that working memory only becomes involved after immediate comprehension fails or when the initial understanding turns out to be incorrect. Working memory processing of the discourse will then rely on phonological short-term memory for verbatim recall of the sentence. This places phonological short-term memory in a supportive backup role. That is, phonological memory is not initially involved in comprehension but may be called on later when further analysis is required for comprehension. Of course, if the information has been lost, the individual can usually ask the speaker to repeat what was said. Thus, oral comprehension does not depend exclusively on phonological short-term memory, which is why some individuals with severely impaired phonological short-term memory can comprehend discourse quite well (Wagner, 1996).

Nevertheless, the role of phonological short-term memory should not be discounted. It appears to play a prominent role in the language development and processing of young children. Poor language development seems to be directly connected with impaired functioning of phonological short-term memory (Baddeley, 1996). Individuals with delayed language development often have a deficit in the ability to retain unfamiliar pseudowords. This poor verbal memory span is thought to be one cause of delayed language development. In particular, vocabulary learning has been directly linked with phonological short-term memory capacity (Gathercole & Baddeley, 1990). If children are unable to retain the phonological sequence that makes up a new word, they will probably require repeated exposures to the word before they retain its phonetic and semantic representation (Leonard et al., 2007). Verbal working memory is also necessary for the acquisition of new vocabulary, as it links the correct pronunciation with a semantic representation. Not surprisingly, nonword repetition is also a good predictor of second-language learning. Superb functioning of the executive and verbal working-memory components can help to compensate for shortcomings in phonological short-term memory. However, despite assistance from other working memory subsystems, it is imperative that information in a curtailed phonological short-term store be rapidly encoded and transferred for higher level processing. In addition to quick processing and retrieval that rapidly moves information, fluid reasoning may enhance comprehension by attaching correct meaning to incomplete details.

Working memory impairments affect more than listening comprehension. Once thought to be a completely automatic process, oral language production places demands on working memory, especially during the conceptualizing and sentence formulation stages. Not only must the speaker retrieve words that convey the intended meaning, but he or she also must plan for correct syntax. For example, accurate production of subject-verb agreement depends on verbal working memory processes. Even in normal speakers, sentence planning is hindered when speakers have insufficient verbal working memory capacity (Hartsuiker & Barkuysen, 2006), such as when there is a secondary processing task.

There has been a debate among language researchers over the relationship between language processing and working memory. Some language theorists argue that verbal working memory is a language subsystem specifically designed for mediating language comprehension (Waters & Caplan, 1996). However, the consensus seems to be that language processing is conducted by a general purpose, domain-free working memory system that is not limited to linguistic processing. Thus, language development and linguistic processing are constrained by general working memory capacity and effective utilization of that capacity (Moser et al., 2007). For example, difficulties in comprehending spoken language may stem more from inefficiencies in verbal working memory than from failure to acquire critical language structures (Crain et al., 1990).

Oral Language Disabilities

An oral language disability refers to a condition in which a child experiences a delay in language development despite adequate progress in other cognitive areas. Research has established that individuals with language impairments perform poorly on verbal working memory tasks, especially those involving phonological processing (for a review, see Masoura, 2006). For example, children with a language impairment typically exhibit poor performance on digit span and nonword repetition tasks (Baddeley, 2003a). Gutierrez-Clellen, Calderon, and Weismer (2004) found children with a specific language impairment to possess word recall two standard deviations below the mean for their age. Gathercole and Baddeley (1990) reported that children with a language disability have poor phonological short-term memory compared to controls matched on nonverbal intelligence. Children with a language disability also exhibit specific difficulties on dual-processing tasks. Interestingly, children with disordered language development display phonological and verbal memory deficits that are of even greater magnitude than their deficient language skills (Gathercole & Baddeley, 1993), and limitations in working memory may persist even after language delays have been resolved (Bishop, North, & Donlan, 1996).

There are several related contributions and reciprocal influences connected with oral language impairments: (a) the weak phonological memory performance of individuals with a language impairment may originate from their slow recognition and discrimination of speech sounds, a function of phonemic awareness (Masoura, 2006); (b) articulation rate may be a cause of memory span deficits that in turn inhibit language processing; (c) slow processing speed may allow auditory traces to fade before meaning can be extracted; and (d) difficulties with word retrieval may also play a role. Overall, children with a language impairment have a limited capacity for processing and remembering verbal information (for a review, see Gill et al., 2003).

Working Memory and Reading

Over the past 3 decades, numerous studies (e.g., Smith-Spark & Fisk, 2007; Swanson & Jerman, 2007) have reported strong relationships between working memory performance and reading skills. Reading skills are typically divided into two main categories—reading decoding, also known as *basic reading skills*, and reading comprehension. Reading decoding is primarily dependent on phonological processing—the ability to detect and manipulate the sound units (phonemes) of oral language. Reading comprehension is more complex and involves several higher level cognitive processes (see Table 5.3). Each type of reading skill draws from short-term, long-term, and working memory somewhat differently. Reading decoding is primarily related to phonological short-term memory and verbal working memory, whereas reading comprehension is primarily related to verbal working memory, executive working memory, and long-term memory (Swanson et al., 2006). Verbal working memory span, also referred to as *complex span*, correlates highly with children's reading abilities, especially their reading comprehension (De Jong, 2006; Hulme & Mackenzie, 1992). Even short-term memory span, referred to as *simple span*, is highly related with reading, especially with basic reading skills. For instance, Hutton and Towse (2001) reported a correlation of .45 between digit span and tests of reading. The

Table 5.3 Cognitive Processes *Most Highly Related* to Types of Academic Learning

Reading Decoding	Reading Comprehension	Written Language	Mathematics
Phonological Processing	Working Memory	Working Memory	Working Memory
Short-Term Memory	Long-Term Memory	Executive Processing	Fluid Reasoning
Visual Processing	Executive Processing	Processing Speed	Visual Processing
Sequential Processing	Fluid Reasoning	Planning	Processing Speed
Working Memory			Planning
Long-Term Memory			

extent of involvement of visuospatial memory components during reading is less clear, as very little reading research has examined its role. Those who challenge the implication that working memory capacity underlies reading development sometimes claim that the relationship is merely an artifact of language development or verbal IQ. Yet, when verbal IQ, reasoning, processing speed, and other cognitive abilities are factored out, a significant correlation between working memory and reading remains (Swanson & Jerman, 2007).

Reading Decoding

In addition to short-term memory and most aspects of working memory, several other cognitive processes are involved in reading decoding (Evans et al., 2002; see Tables 5.2 and 5.3). Of the other cognitive functions, phonological processing, a subtype of auditory processing, and long-term retrieval, especially rapid automatic naming, are the most important. In fact, phonological processing, which includes phonemic awareness, is thought to be the foundation of reading decoding (Kamhi & Pollock, 2005). *Phonemic awareness* is the recognition that words are composed of different sounds. *Phonological processing*, essentially the manipulation of phonemes, involves recognizing, segmenting, and blending phonemes. Many sources of evidence support the conclusion that reading decoding problems stem primarily from deficiencies in phonemic awareness and phonological processing (for a review, see National Reading Panel, 2000). During reading, phonological processing depends on phonological short-term memory. For example, beginning readers sequentially convert printed letters into sounds that need to be held in the correct sequence until the last letter is converted and the full sequence of sounds is blended into a complete word (Palmer, 2000). Thus, phonological processing requires temporary storage of phonemes in phonological short-term memory. Fortunately, most readers have a phonological short-term memory span capable of handling the usual demands of phonological processing and reading decoding.

To convert written words into phonemes, phonological processing also depends on visual processing. The decoding process involves accessing learned phonetic codes for visually presented letters and words (graphemes). Readers must phonologically recode visual stimuli by matching the graphemes with the phonemes they represent. The matching process requires high-quality grapheme–phoneme conversion information from long-term memory. Although visual processing is involved in reading decoding, it is primarily phonological processing ability that determines the development of reading proficiency.

Phonological processing ability and phonological short-term memory, along with verbal working memory, are interdependent (De Jong, 2006), making it difficult to determine the root cause of limited phonological short-term memory span. In some cases, a deficit in phonological processing accounts for poor performance on phonological short-term memory tasks, whereas in other cases, phonological processing is normal and the limitation originates in short-term memory capacity. The possibility that phonological processing alone accounts for the relationship between working memory and reading has been considered by several studies (reviewed by De Jong, 2006). The majority have found that the phonological short-term memory and verbal working memory components make a contribution to reading skills beyond phonological processing. However, the consensus seems to be that phonological short-term memory and verbal working memory share a common underlying ability with phonological processing and that this common underlying ability accounts for the close association that short-term and working memory have with reading decoding (De Jong, 2006). From this perspective, short-term and working memory are relegated to subordinate, but nonetheless essential, roles in the acquisition of basic reading skills. When phonological processing skills are intact, poor readers are either not using phonological short-term memory effectively or have a reduced capacity in that memory subcomponent. Another possibility is that poor readers have an impairment in phonological short-term memory that makes it difficult for them to retain the sequence of sounds (Baddeley, 1986).

Other factors that may account for poor short-term and working memory performance are articulation speed and the use of verbal rehearsal strategies. Since efficient utilization of phonological short-term memory depends on articulation speed, it is not surprising that studies (reviewed by Baddeley, 1986) have found that articulation rate can distinguish between weak and strong readers. Although speech rate seems to have little relationship with individual differences among normal readers, it does seem to explain part of the short-term memory impairment in children with a reading disability. Also, poor readers may not be spontaneously using verbal rehearsal strategies to the same extent as normal readers (Torgesen & Goldman, 1977). For example, O'Shaughnessy and Swanson (1998) concluded that children with a reading disability inefficiently use phonological rehearsal processes.

Reading decoding involves more than simple storage of phonological sequences in short-term memory. Blending of the phonemes into a word requires processing of sequential information, thereby requiring a contribution from working memory, particularly verbal and executive working memory. For example, children with a reading disability have been found to perform poorly on measures of executive working memory (Siegel & Ryan, 1989). Of the executive functions, there is strong evidence that the updating of verbal information is essential for reading decoding (De Jong, 2006). A deficit in updating seems to be independent of the length of simple verbal memory span. Some studies have also discovered a role for inhibitory functions during reading. For instance, Palmer (2000) found that good readers were able to better inhibit visual representations (orthographic representations) and focus on the phonological representation. This finding indicates that poor readers may continue to focus on visual encoding when it would be more productive to recode phonologically. Palmer postulates that a delay in inhibiting the disruptive visual representations contributes to dyslexia. (Note that this text uses the terms *reading disorder, reading disability*, and *dyslexia* interchangeably.) Another role of executive and verbal working memory during reading decoding is to coordinate phonological processing with word-level analysis and semantic processing (Palmer).

In summary, most aspects of short-term and working memory are involved in reading decoding, with the initial burden falling mostly on phonological short-term memory. Verbal working memory and executive working memory are also directly linked with the ongoing development of basic reading skills. Despite extensive research, it remains unclear whether short-term phonological storage or executive and verbal working memory play the greater role in reading progress (Swanson & Jerman, 2007). What is clear is that once a reader becomes fluent and basic reading decoding becomes automated, short-term and working memory play a less critical role in reading decoding, and long-term memory becomes more prominent.

Reading Comprehension

To comprehend text, a reader must store recently decoded text while complex processes construct meaning (De Beni, Borella, & Carretti, 2007). As the reading of text progresses, working memory stores the gist of the information from one or more sentences until a meaning-based representation of the text's content, called a *mental model*, is formed. Text comprehension includes several skills and abilities that involve working memory: decoding individual words and accessing their meanings; assembling word meanings into larger meaning units; constructing representations of sentences; linking information across sentences; detecting inconsistencies between parts of the text; focusing attention on the main ideas; creating visual images; forming new knowledge representations; drawing plausible inferences on the basis of prior knowledge; monitoring the understanding of text as reading progresses; integrating information from different parts of a text; and integrating information with related long-term memory representations. Most of these comprehension components make exceptionally heavy demands on both the storage and processing functions of working memory. Overall, reading comprehension depends on the capacity of working memory to retain text information that facilitates the comprehension of subsequent sentences. Studies (e.g., Just & Carpenter, 1992) have found that individuals with greater capacities are more successful at integrating information across longer readings. Even carrying information from one sentence to the next requires proficient use of normal working memory capacity. The integration of information derived from text is the essence of comprehension. This integration cannot be accomplished without an adequately functioning working memory (Cain, 2006).

After reading decoding skills and vocabulary level, working memory capacity is the next highest predictor of reading comprehension in children, adults, and students with a reading disability (Seigneuric et al., 2000). Numerous studies have uncovered a moderate to strong relationship between working memory capacity and reading comprehension, with correlations typically around .50 (e.g., Daneman & Carpenter 1980; Seigneuric et al., 2000). In a meta-analysis of 77 studies by Daneman and Merikle (1996), the average correlation between reading comprehension and verbal working memory tasks was .41. The strength of the relationship between working memory capacity and reading comprehension grows from the early to the later grades (Seigneuric & Ehrlich, 2005). Differences in working memory capacity can greatly affect the success of reading comprehension, especially when the text is difficult or complex (Linderholm & Van Den Broek, 2002; Swanson, 1999b), and reading comprehension problems are highly associated with working memory deficits (Goff, Pratt, & Ong, 2005). For those who have a reading comprehension deficit but have normal phonological processing and word decoding skills, the specific reading comprehension deficit can frequently be attributed to a working memory impairment (Cain, Oakhill, & Bryant, 2004).

Phonological short-term memory, although necessary for reading decoding, appears to play only a minimal role in reading comprehension. Clearly, there is a much stronger relationship between verbal working memory and reading comprehension than between phonological short-term memory and reading comprehension (Engle, Carullo, & Collins, 1991). For instance, Leather and Henry (1994) found that phonological short-term memory accounted for only 5% of the variance in 7-year-olds' reading comprehension level, but that verbal working memory explained an additional 33% of the variance. In their pioneering work, Daneman and Carpenter (1980) argued that simple span tasks (i.e., phonological short-term memory tasks) do not tap higher level working memory processes necessary for reading comprehension. Since then, other researchers (e.g., Cain et al., 2004) have concurred; the passive, short-term storage of information does not correlate significantly with reading comprehension.

Daneman and Carpenter are credited with devising a verbal working memory test called *reading span* in which subjects have to recall, in order, the last word of each of three to seven sentences read aloud. Reading span, the number of final words recalled, is thought to represent the residual storage capacity of working memory when a person is actively engaged in reading (Dixon, LeFevre, & Twilley, 1988). Among college students, reading spans typically vary from 2 to 5.5 final words recalled, with an average span of 3 to 3.5 words. Daneman and Carpenter and subsequent researchers (Just & Carpenter, 1992; Turner & Engle, 1989) found reading span to have high correlations with reading comprehension, in contrast to simple-span measures that essentially tap phonological short-term memory. Critics of the reading span approach point out that performance on a reading span measure is partly dependent on general reading ability (Seigneuric et al., 2000). Thus, in part, reading skills account for the high correlation and make it difficult to differentiate between contributions from working memory processes and reading skills. An alternative that avoids this confound is to use a listening span task that has the same requirements.

Certainly, verbal working memory is a necessary prerequisite for successful reading comprehension. Results from Seigneuric et al. (2000) suggest that verbal working memory capacity constrains reading comprehension in young readers. Verbal working memory includes short-term memory for words and sentences, tasks that certainly include phonological short-term memory. At the basic level, verbal working memory facilitates reading comprehension by holding words and sentences in consciousness until there is enough information to complete an idea. The number of sentences that can be held in verbal working memory has been found to relate to reading comprehension (Daneman & Carpenter, 1980). The holding process appears to be subvocalization, an important form of inner speech in reading. Despite the strong relationship, it seems that the demands of reading comprehension typically exceed the limited storage capacity of verbal working memory. Consequently, readers must form some long-term representation of the text or combine the information in working memory with existing long-term representations. This is where a readily accessible pool of activated long-term memory items would play an important supportive role and account for the apparent discrepancy between working memory capacity and the elevated demands of reading comprehension.

Given the high-level processing demands of reading comprehension, there is little doubt that executive working memory is another primary determinant of successful comprehension. Research has repeatedly confirmed this relationship; for example, Swanson, Howard, and Saez (2006) concluded that the functioning of executive working memory, not phonological short-term memory, discriminates between skilled comprehenders and those with comprehension deficits. Executive working memory must coordinate many diverse processes, especially those that culminate in the integration of new information with an existing mental model. Of the specific executive functions, inhibition is one that has been directly linked with reading comprehension (Savage et al., 2006; Savage, Lavers, & Pillay, 2007). Discarding information that is no longer relevant and preventing the entry of unnecessary or irrelevant information affect the ability to engage in processes that are crucial for good comprehension (De Beni & Palladino, 2000). In general, inefficient inhibitory control during reading overloads the working memory system, causing comprehension problems. Adults and children with deficient inhibitory processes are more likely to remember irrelevant words and information, resulting in weak reading comprehension (De Beni & Palladino). Furthermore, individuals with an apparent lower working memory capacity and concurrent comprehension difficulties may be less efficient at regulating the activation level of long-term representations in the activated pool (Cain, 2006). Similarly, executive working memory may direct the retrieval of semantic information while the verbal component retains the words, phrases, or sentences long enough for text to be understood and integrated with long-term schemas.

There is also a general consensus that visuospatial working memory has little or no relationship with reading comprehension (Seigneuric et al., 2000; Swanson & Berninger, 1995). Daneman and Tardif (1987) reported no correlation between visuospatial working memory measures and reading comprehension. Later, Swanson and Berninger (1995) found that, although visuospatial working memory is correlated with reading comprehension, visuospatial performance does not differentiate between good and poor comprehenders. More recently, Seigneuric et al. (2000) also reported that visuospatial working memory was not significantly correlated with working memory. If visuospatial working memory has any involvement, it is likely to be during the early stages of reading development. Despite these consistent findings, recent research by Goff et al. (2005) reveals that the role of visuospatial working memory may have been prematurely discounted. Goff et al. found an exceptionally strong relationship between visuospatial working memory tasks and reading comprehension, a finding consistent with the belief that good comprehenders create a visual image of text as they read. Perhaps the equivocal findings are due to differences in how visuospatial working memory was measured.

Working memory is not alone in supporting reading comprehension; several other cognitive processes, as well as additional memory systems, are involved. Other cognitive processes that specifically facilitate reading comprehension include fluid reasoning, executive processing, and processing speed (see Table 5.3). Of course, reading comprehension also depends on verbal abilities, prior knowledge (Was & Woltz, 2006), vocabulary development, and adequate reading decoding skills. To fully comprehend text, working memory must interact with both short- and long-term memory. In doing so, working memory simultaneously manipulates recently read information (from short-term storage) and recently retrieved information (from long-term storage), with the integration of the two stores of information producing comprehension. Finally, the application of effective memory and reading comprehension strategies enhances reading comprehension, mostly because these strategies support the effective operation of working memory processes, such as semantic encoding. Interestingly, less skilled readers and those with a disability try to compensate for low working memory capacity by rereading text (Linderholm & Van Den Broek, 2002), instead of selecting a higher level memory or reading comprehension strategy.

In summary, there is myriad evidence to support the claim that reading comprehension performance depends heavily on working memory. The only controversy is over which working memory processes, components, and resources actually have the most significant effects on reading comprehension. The best working memory predictors of reading comprehension are tasks that require the coordination of storage and processing, namely those involving executive working memory and verbal working memory. The memory subprocesses that play a minimal role are those that can be classified as short-term memory functions. Because of the complexities involved, successful reading comprehension is almost always a challenge. Consequently, the working memory processes that support comprehension are far from automatic, even among good comprehenders. Individuals with a larger working memory capacity not only have an advantage in reading comprehension, but their extra resources allow them to better induce the meanings of unknown words and thereby acquire more vocabulary (Just & Carpenter, 1992). The strong relationship indicates that the development of reading comprehension skills is highly influenced by working memory capacity and efficiency (Seigneuric & Ehrlich, 2005).

Reading Fluency and Reading Comprehension

A discussion of reading comprehension would be incomplete without acknowledging the influence of reading fluency on reading comprehension. The level of reading fluency, which can be equated with reading decoding skills, is the foremost predictor of reading comprehension. Once decoding proceeds smoothly, quickly, and effortlessly, reading is considered to be fluent. Reading fluency is usually assessed with a test that measures the number of correct words read per minute. A high level of fluency is an indication that reading decoding has become automated. Once reading decoding, both sight-word recognition and phonetic decoding, becomes automated, more working memory capacity becomes available for reading comprehension. The development of automaticity facilitates reading comprehension by reducing the working memory resources necessary for decoding words—a demanding process that includes segmenting, blending, and holding phonemes. Automaticity in reading also results in automatic activation of semantic representations in long-term memory, which accounts for the pool of activated long-term memory items accessible to working memory. Poor readers who continue to struggle with reading decoding have fewer residual working memory resources for comprehension. That is, their inefficient word reading impairs comprehension. Even with normal phonological processing, short-term memory, and working memory, inadequate reading speed may hinder comprehension because information will be lost before it is fully processed and integrated with a current mental model. Readers with high working memory capacity have an advantage. Even before they achieve fluency, they have greater residual resources to devote to comprehension than low working-memory-capacity readers.

On the other hand, reading comprehension level is not entirely constrained by reading decoding skills; some readers with poor decoding skills are able to attain normal levels of reading comprehension. That is, reading comprehension skills are somewhat independent of phonological decoding abilities (Swanson & Berninger, 1995), and of phonological short-term memory span, in particular (Swanson & Howell, 2001). The difference can be accounted for by a strong overall working memory capacity, the application of other cognitive processes such as fluid reasoning, and well-developed reading comprehension and working memory strategies. Prior knowledge or expertise on a topic will also facilitate comprehension. Clearly, an adequate level of reading fluency is a prerequisite for advances in reading comprehension skills, but fluency alone is insufficient for higher level comprehension. Even after an adequate level of reading fluency is obtained, working memory makes a direct contribution to comprehension (Seigneuric & Ehrlich, 2005), a contribution that increases as readers mature. As readers progress through school, increased demands on working memory partially result from the increasing length and complexity of texts. In first grade, reading decoding skills explain most of the variance in reading comprehension. By the end of third grade, working memory capacity emerges as a specific and significant contributor (Cain et al., 2004).

Not all reading comprehension problems are the result of poorly developed reading fluency or insufficient working memory capacity. There is also a subset of students with poor reading comprehension skills who have average decoding skills, normal phonological short-term memory, and adequate working memory capacity. Approximately 10% of middle school students fall into this group (Nation et al., 1999). These readers tend to have poorer vocabulary knowledge, use context clues less efficiently, and have difficulty making inferences. In many cases, their comprehension difficulties are probably due to delayed language development, weak fluid reasoning, or insufficient reading comprehension strategies.

Long-Term Memory Involvement

To accomplish comprehension and learn from it, the mental models formed while reading must be integrated with existing long-term schemas. Thus, activating and maintaining relevant long-term memory representations is necessary for reading comprehension (Conway & Engle, 1996; Pascual-Leone, 2001). Much of the activation is automatic and prompted by the contents of short-term memory; the rest results from effortful searches conducted by working memory. Working memory then integrates new information with preexisting schemas. The level of semantic knowledge mediates comprehension and allows working memory to function more effectively, much like automated skills do. Therefore, readers with advanced prior knowledge or expertise on a topic achieve higher levels of comprehension. Evidence for this hypothesis is that we find it easier to remember words than we do nonwords (Cain, 2006), and that poor comprehenders have a shorter memory span for abstract words (Nation et al., 1999). Thus, all other factors being equal, reading comprehension and working memory performance will suffer when semantic knowledge in long-term memory is lacking. Reading comprehension and working memory may also be impaired when readers have difficulty efficiently retrieving information from long-term storage; however, most individuals with a reading disability have average ability to retrieve information from long-term memory (Savage et al., 2007). Undoubtedly, long-term memory plays a crucial role in working memory functioning during reading comprehension. Accordingly, the interaction between working memory and long-term memory may be a better predictor of reading comprehension than working memory tasks that have only a short-term memory component (Goff et al., 2005).

Conclusion

Regardless of the functioning levels of related processes and skills, high working-memory-capacity individuals have better reading comprehension because they have more working memory capacity to draw on. That is, total working memory capacity constrains reading comprehension. Comprehension differences between good and poor readers may be primarily attributed to differences in the processing capacity of working memory.

Reading Disabilities

An abundance of evidence in reading research implicates a deficit in phonological processing as the primary cause of reading disabilities (National Reading Panel, 2000). However, some readers with disabilities have no impairment in phonological processing, while nevertheless demonstrating very limited phonological short-term and verbal working memory spans. In such instances, weak short-term and working memory make it difficult to perform phonological processes, such as blending, that are necessary for word identification. Clearly, phonological processing ability is intertwined with phonological short-term memory. Consequently, difficulties with basic reading decoding skills are often associated with poor performance on short-term retention of phonological information, such as digits and nonwords (Jeffries & Everatt, 2004). Since the early 1960s, a large number of studies (cited in Torgesen, 1996) have reported that poor performance on short-term memory tests is one of the most common characteristics of children with reading disabilities. For example, Speece (1987) found that 15 to 20% of these children displayed serious difficulties on digit span tasks. This means that children with reading disabilities are not able to efficiently use phonological short-term memory, sometimes because they are deficient in articulatory speed. Their reduced ability to temporarily maintain phonological memory codes reduces recall and impairs reading decoding. Regardless of the qualitative differences among children with reading disabilities, impairment in phonological short-term memory seems to be a constant research finding (for a review, see Masoura, 2006).

Despite the predominant roles of phonological processing and phonological short-term memory in early reading development, there is evidence that the relationship between reading decoding and working memory reflects more than phonological processing ability and phonological short-term memory capacity (Gathercole, Alloway, Willis, & Adams, 2006; Kail & Hall, 2001). For example, Swanson (1992) found that, when simple phonological short-term memory tasks are factored separately from more complex working memory tasks, short-term memory is not significantly related to word decoding skills, whereas working memory performance is. Such a finding indicates that deficits in verbal working memory and executive working memory also may be responsible for reading decoding problems. In particular, there is considerable evidence that individuals with reading disabilities have impaired verbal working memory (e.g., De Jong, 1998). Children with a reading disability also have significant difficulty with the simultaneous storage and processing of information, the hallmark of executive working memory (Van Der Sluis et al., 2005). Simultaneous storage and processing of phonological information cannot be accomplished by the phonological store alone. Participation from executive working memory is required, especially when phonological processing during reading has not yet become automated. Swanson (1987) offered another explanation for reading decoding difficulties when he proposed that students with reading disabilities have failed to establish effective visual-verbal connections, a process mediated by executive working memory. Essentially, individuals with a reading disorder have overly independent visual and verbal coding systems, and show a preference for visual encoding of words (Johnston & Anderson, 1998). Their preference is not surprising, given their frequent weakness in phonological processing and their typically normal visual processing capability. Unfortunately, overreliance on visual encoding will restrain progress in reading development.

Further support for the role of working memory in reading disabilities comes from several studies that have found a deficiency in working memory capacity to be one of the variables that differentiates between normal and dyslexic readers (e.g., Swanson et al., 1990). For example, a standardization study of the Wechsler Intelligence Scale for Children–Fourth Edition (WISC-IV; Wechsler, 2003) found that a group of children with reading disabilities obtained their lowest index score (a mean of 87) on working memory, and that, compared to a matched control group, the Working Memory Index had the largest effect size. (See Chapter 7 for details on the WISC-IV working memory subtests.) The general consensus is that readers with a disability frequently have insufficient capacity in general working memory resources, not just a phonological processing deficit, a phonological short-term memory deficit, a language processing deficit, or a deficit in processing speed and efficiency (De Jong, 1998; Savage et al., 2007). Nevertheless, high correlations alone do not allow us to say that deficits in short-term and working memory are the cause of reading disabilities, or at least the primary cause (De Jong, 1998).

In response to those who might challenge the empirical evidence, poor phonological short-term memory and verbal working memory do not seem to be a consequence of reading problems. When poor readers are matched with younger control children of the same reading level, the poor readers have more difficulty repeating nonwords. Longitudinal studies have also provided convincing evidence that deficient reading skills can be attributed to phonological short-term memory and verbal working memory impairments. For example, early childhood phonological short-term memory scores have been found to be valid predictors of later performance on reading tasks (Gathercole & Baddeley, 1989). Thus, it appears that less skilled readers have a smaller short-term and working memory capacity and that this capacity is independent of their reading skills (Turner & Engle, 1989). Nevertheless, the influence of other memory stores and cognitive processes cannot be ruled out; for example, inadequate representations of phonological units in long-term memory or difficulty retrieving phonological units may also be detrimental to reading decoding (Torgesen, 1996).

Conclusion

Many reading and working memory researchers believe that diminished short-term and working memory capacities, particularly in the phonological and verbal subcomponents, are related to impaired development of reading decoding skills and reading comprehension. Frequently, the differences between skilled readers and those with a reading disability can be attributed to deficiencies in working memory (Swanson, 1992, 1993, 2000). Although working memory deficits have not yet been identified as one cause of reading disabilities, it is clear that working memory contributes a unique and significant variance to reading (McCallum et al., 2006). Because phonological processing, phonological short-term memory, and verbal working memory are highly interrelated (Torgesen, 1996), it is difficult to determine causality or the exact nature of their relations with reading. One possibility is that weak phonological storage is merely a reflection of deeper phonological processing problems (Baddeley, 2003a). For instance, poor readers do not display phonemic similarity effects like normal readers do. This is most likely because they are weak in phonological processing and consequently not relying on phonemic coding in short-term memory as much as normal readers. Another possibility is that early differences in phonological short-term span play an important role in the growth of phonological awareness skills (Torgesen, 1996). While it is true that phonological processing has a significant relationship with phonological short-term memory span, phonological processing can vary independently of phonological short-term memory functioning. For example, adults with acquired phonological storage deficits can possess perfectly normal phonological and linguistic skills (Baddeley, 2003a). All things considered, the current consensus among reading researchers is that phonological processing and phonemic awareness skills account for individual differences in reading more than phonological short-term and verbal working memory (Torgesen, 1996). Regardless of the direction of the relationship and relative importance of short-term and working memory, screenings and evaluations for reading disabilities should include tests of short-term and working memory, in addition to assessing phonological processing and phonemic awareness skills.

Working Memory and Mathematics

Educational and psychological research has documented strong relationships between mathematics performance and measures of working memory. Examples of the findings include: Hutton and Towse (2001) reported a correlation of .45 between digit span and performance on mathematical tests; Swanson and Beebe-Frankenberger (2004) reported a correlation of .54 between working memory and mathematics problem solving; and LeBlanc and Weber-Russell (1996) found that working memory variables accounted for up to 57% of the variance in children's word-problem solutions.

Mathematics skills are usually divided into two types—basic arithmetic calculation and mathematics problem solving. To varying degrees, both types of mathematics skills involve all short-term and working memory components and processes. Even the simplest mathematics calculations clearly require three working memory processes: temporary storage to hold problem information, retrieval that accesses relevant procedures, and processing operations that convert the information into numerical output (Brainerd, 1983). Complex problems, such as those involving carrying and borrowing, require multiple working memory operations. Any time multiple steps are required, additional digits from intermediary results must be held in working memory until they are retrieved at a later step. When this information is lost, errors occur. Working memory resources are needed most during the initial phases of mathematics skills acquisition, and fewer working memory resources are needed as knowledge and skills grow (Imbo & Vandierendonck, 2007). Assuming basic mathematics facts have been mastered, solutions to simple forms of mental arithmetic can be retrieved from long-term memory, thereby freeing up working memory resources.

Most studies attempt to isolate the working memory components and processes that are responsible for various aspects of mathematics skills (e.g., Fuchs et al., 2006). However, it is difficult to isolate all of the variables involved. Also, the utilization of specific storage and processing components varies as a function of age. Young students (first grade and under) depend more on visuospatial storage while older children primarily draw on phonological short-term memory as their mathematical functioning becomes more verbal and abstract. Older students may utilize visuospatial working memory again when they encounter geometry tasks. Even the manner of numerical presentation may determine which domain-specific short-term component stores the information. Trbovich and LeFevre (2003) found that the vertical presentation of two-digit arithmetic problems promotes visuospatial storage whereas horizontal (number sentence) presentation promotes phonological coding. In conclusion, the type and extent of working memory involvement is a function of working memory development, the type of mathematics problem, and mastery level of mathematics skills.

Mathematics Calculation

Except for simple arithmetic (single-digit addition and subtraction), most mathematical computation involves a succession of stages where each part is carried out and stored until the next step in the calculation is completed. Of course, some operands need to be stored until the entire operation is finished. The current consensus is that complex arithmetic calculation involves all short-term and working memory components to varying degrees (Tronsky, 2005). Most likely, all of the components are involved even during simple arithmetic, given that the majority of the research (reviewed by Tronsky) has found that even simple mental arithmetic requires executive working memory resources. According to Swanson (2006a), the working memory component that best predicts mathematics calculation is visuospatial. Others (e.g., Gathercole & Pickering, 2000a) have found the combination of visuospatial and executive to have the strongest association with mathematics calculation performance.

Mathematics Word Problems

Compared to basic mathematics calculation, strategy-based problem solving places a greater load on working memory. When solving mathematics word problems, individuals must mentally construct an adequate problem representation—a process that depends heavily on working memory. The initial stage of mathematics story problem solving requires verbal comprehension and temporary storage of the words, phrases, and sentences. Completing a mathematical word, or story, problem requires: (a) keeping track of incoming information; (b) integrating information; (c) retrieving mathematics facts and procedures from long-term storage; (d) matching the correct algorithm to the problem at hand; (e) updating the contents of working memory; (f) making on-line mathematical calculations; (g) monitoring the computational process; and evaluating the solution (Swanson & Beebe-Frankenberger, 2004). The dependence of problem solving on working memory is especially evident when the problem is novel. Once the individual has learned to solve a particular type of problem, less working memory capacity is necessary (Reber & Kotovsky, 1997). According to Swanson (2006a), the working memory component that best predicts mathematics problem solving is the executive.

Role of Visuospatial Working Memory

The role of visuospatial working memory in mathematics learning and performance seems to change significantly during childhood development. It plays a prominent role during the preschool years when the child's arithmetic mental model is primarily visuospatial, instead of verbal and abstract. Until young children acquire symbolic and verbal representations of arithmetic, they utilize a visual mental model (Holmes & Adams, 2006). Accordingly, Hitch, Halliday, Schaafstal, and Schraagen (1988) found that preschool children rely on visuospatial working memory more than older children do, and Rasmussen and Bisanz (2005) found visuospatial working memory to be the best and only unique predictor of preschool performance on standard nonverbal arithmetic problems. Hence, young children must be manipulating internal visual representations that are analogous to external objects. Concordant with this assumption is the finding that preschool children perform better on nonverbal than verbal problems (Rasmussen & Bisanz). Young children's reliance on visuospatial short-term memory was also supported by Brainerd (1983), who found that short-term storage failures, not higher level working memory processes, were responsible for most arithmetic errors. Brainerd (1983) reported that the average percentage of arithmetic errors due to short-term storage failure was 74% for 4- and 5-year-olds and 65% for first graders.

The prominence of visuospatial working memory in arithmetic computation is short-lived. By the end of first grade, verbal working memory has become the best predictor of arithmetic performance. Even when older children are presented with a visual arithmetic problem, they tend to recode the visual information into a verbal code that passes through phonological short-term memory (Rasmussen & Bisanz, 2005). Recoding allows children to manage greater quantities, as the number of items that can be manipulated in a visual mental model is relatively small. By the time children reach mid-elementary years, there is no evidence that visuospatial working memory plays any significant role in arithmetic (for a review, see Imbo, Vandierendonck, & Vergauwe, 2007). Nevertheless, visuospatial working memory is sometimes involved in arithmetic functioning, at least minimally; for example, it seems to be particularly necessary in multidigit problems where visual and spatial knowledge of column positioning is required (McLean & Hitch, 1999).

Role of Phonological Short-Term Memory

Individual differences in mathematical problem solving have been partially attributed to phonological short-term memory (for a review, see Swanson & Sachse-Lee, 2001). Because numbers are words and story problems are text, phonological storage and processing are involved in both basic arithmetic calculation and the solution of story problems. At least in the initial stage, the solution of a mathematical word problem relies heavily on phonological processing. Consequently, if phonological short-term memory is deficient in capacity or inefficient in processing, it creates a bottleneck that constricts the flow of information to the higher levels of processing, including verbal working memory, that are necessary for mathematical problem solving (Swanson & Beebe-Frankenberger, 2004). Not surprisingly, children with specific mathematics disabilities have been found to suffer deficits in short-term retention of verbal information (Swanson & Beebe-Frankenberger). Of course, inefficient utilization of the phonological rehearsal process may be as much to blame as any shortcomings in phonological span.

When considering the involvement of phonological short-term memory, the age of the child must be taken into account. During mathematics performance, older children utilize phonological short-term memory more so than younger children (Holmes & Adams, 2006). Older children also tend to use subvocal rehearsal to retain mathematics problem information. Phonological short-term usage may also depend on the specific mathematics function; for example, phonological short-term memory directly supports counting processes but has less involvement during calculations that rely on direct retrieval from long-term memory. It appears that phonological short-term memory is most related to arithmetic during the learning of basic mathematics facts and concepts. Although preschool children rely heavily on visuospatial working memory for mathematical operations, phonological short-term memory is thought to be very important for the acquisition of number facts in early childhood (Holmes & Adams). When phonological memory span is inadequate, some of the integers are lost before they can be associated and encoded together in long-term storage. Although there is some controversy about the extent of phonological short-term memory involvement in mathematics activities, Swanson and Sachse-Lee (2001) concluded that, although phonological short-term memory may not be more important than other memory processes, it does contribute unique variance to mathematics solution accuracy.

Role of Verbal Working Memory

Although it plays a role, phonological short-term memory alone is insufficient for successful mental arithmetic. Undoubtedly, verbal working memory is involved in mathematical computation, especially during complex mental arithmetic calculations. It seems that verbal working memory storage is most in demand when digits must be temporarily stored during multistep procedures. For example, Imbo et al. (2007) reported that verbal working memory is involved in complex subtraction where borrowing is required. In contrast, simple multiplication places fewer demands on working memory because multiplication relies predominantly on long-term retrieval. Wilson and Swanson (2001) concluded that verbal working memory is a better predictor of mathematical computation than visuospatial working memory.

Role of Executive Working Memory

Of the specific short-term and working memory domains, executive working memory plays an indispensable role during all types of mathematical computation and reasoning tasks (Andersson & Lyxell, 2007; Imbo & Vandierendonck, 2007). This finding is not surprising, given that mathematics requires the simultaneous processing and storage of numerical and visual information. Executive working memory appears to be responsible for coordinating, monitoring, and sequencing all of the processing steps involved in mathematical procedures. Specifically, executive working memory is necessary for estimating, counting, maintaining order of information, keeping track of information in multistep procedures, and selecting and executing problem-solving strategies (Imbo et al., 2007). Fundamentally, limited executive working memory capacity or high demands on working memory resources results in slower calculation and more errors, even after mathematics facts have been mastered.

All aspects of executive working memory (for a review, see Swanson & Siegel, 2001) seem to make an important contribution to mathematics problem-solving performance: (a) resource monitoring and coordination of multiple tasks is required, including keeping track of subproducts and other information; (b) switching is required, for example, in a problem that requires both addition and multiplication; (c) selective attention is necessary when attention must be paid to specific parts of the problem while suppressing irrelevant information; and (d) activation and manipulation of relevant facts and algorithms from long-term storage is also involved (McLean & Hitch, 1999). Above all, an executive working-memory-inhibition deficit that allows irrelevant information to enter or remain in working memory during the processing of targeted information may largely account for poor mathematics performance (Passolunghi & Siegel, 2001). Good problem solvers are better able to inhibit irrelevant information; for example, children with ADHD make more errors when problems contain irrelevant numeric or verbal information (Bull & Espy, 2006). Flexible switching of operations and strategies, controlled by executive processing, is another aspect of complex arithmetic and mathematical problem solving.

Although executive working memory seems to be the primary mediator, mathematics performance also depends on other memory systems and working memory components. However, the proficiency of other memory components is insufficient when there are fundamental processing problems in executive working memory or in higher level executive processes (Swanson & Beebe-Frankenberger, 2004). The growth in mathematics problem-solving ability seems to depend significantly on the capacity and development of executive working memory (Swanson, 2006a). For example, Passolunghi and Siegel (2004) found that children who were poor at mathematics problem solving had significant difficulty with tests of executive working memory. Clearly, executive working memory plays a critical role in mathematical problem solving.

Factors that Reduce Working Memory Load During Mathematical Processing

Processing Speed

Working memory is not the sole cognitive processing contributor to mathematics performance. Processing speed is another indispensable cognitive process that also underlies the working memory performance observed during mathematics activities. In fact, Bull and Johnston (1997) found that processing speed was the best predictor of arithmetic competence among 7-year-olds, and Fuchs et al. (2006) found processing speed to be a stronger predictor of mathematics competencies than working memory. For a broader discussion of the role of processing speed, see Chapter 4.

Long-Term Memory

Long-term memory is another significant mediator of the influence of working memory on mathematics performance because knowledge of mathematical facts and algorithms reduces the demands on working memory (Swanson & Siegel, 2001). During arithmetic procedures, long-term memory needs to be accessed frequently and repeatedly, as different facts and algorithms are retrieved and checked for accuracy (Imbo & Vandierendonck, 2007). Working memory operations then select the correct information and answers from long-term storage, while inhibiting incorrect information. For proficient mathematics calculation and problem solving, mathematics facts and algorithms need to be firmly established in long-term memory. Once computation procedures have been acquired, calculation is accomplished primarily through direct retrieval from long-term memory. Until then, mathematics computation places a heavy load on working memory. The more automated, direct, and frequent the retrieval, the fewer demands are made of working memory. Therefore, a readily accessible pool of activated relevant information allows working memory to conduct mathematical operations efficiently.

Automaticity

Once arithmetic facts, procedures, and strategies are thoroughly committed to memory, arithmetic functioning becomes more automated. Automatization increases the speed and efficiency of mathematical processing, with a consequent reduction in working memory involvement (Bedard et al., 2004). Quick and direct retrieval from long-term memory is one way that automatization reduces the need for working memory during arithmetic calculation. Thus, for those with limited working memory resources, the development of automaticity is essential.

Strategy Use

Given an adequate working memory span, the application of working memory strategies also affects mathematical performance. Even the stability of strategy choices is important, most likely because consistent utilization of a particular strategy leads to strategy expertise and automaticity. For example, individuals who repeatedly select the same rehearsal strategy during a verbal task have higher verbal working memory spans and higher mathematics performance (Keeler & Swanson, 2001). Many children also discover the use of external memory aides to reduce the load on working memory during mathematical computation. For example, young children will use their fingers to keep track of amounts.

Developmental Variables

Age-related changes in mathematics functioning seem to be correlated with age-related changes in working memory (Swanson, 2006a). Preschool and early elementary children, for whom arithmetic is primarily a visuospatial task, rely primarily on visuospatial short-term memory. As mathematics operations become more verbal and abstract, children depend more on verbal and executive working memory. By the age of 8, children seem to rely on both visuospatial and verbal working memory during mathematical calculation. By 9 to 10 years of age, children depend primarily on phonological short-term memory and verbal working memory for the solution of mathematical problems (Holmes & Adams, 2006). At any age, word problems necessitate executive management to integrate the information and processes involved. In adolescence and adulthood, when mathematics algorithms are firmly represented in long-term storage, executive processes play the primary role. Even though executive working memory is preeminent in adolescence and adulthood, in general, working memory resources are less in demand during mathematical computation and problem-solving, as manifested by several studies (reviewed by Wilson & Swanson, 2001) that found the relationship between working memory and mathematics performance to be stronger in children than in adults. Therefore, working memory capacity places greater limits on the mathematics performance of children than on that of adults.

Conclusion

Clearly, there is not a unidimensional relation between working memory and mathematical skill. To varying degrees, each short-term and working memory component and process is involved in each type of mathematics operation. The nature of the relationships is dependent not only on specific features of the task but also on the developmental levels of both working memory and mathematical skills.

Mathematics Disabilities

Approximately 3 to 6% of school-age children have mathematics disabilities and many more children struggle with mathematics. Empirical investigations have consistently implicated working memory as a central deficit in children with mathematical disabilities (for a review, see Passolunghi & Siegel, 2004). Compared to their same-age peers, children with a specific mathematics disability have been found to be deficient in verbal working memory, visuospatial working memory, executive working memory, and working memory in general (Swanson & Sachse-Lee, 2001). Also, children with a mathematics disability frequently display an intraindividual deficiency in the short-term storage of phonological information, especially when they possess co-morbid reading and written language disabilities (Siegel & Ryan, 1989). Some studies (e.g., Siegel & Ryan) have found children with mathematics disabilities to demonstrate poorer performance on visuospatial working memory than verbal working memory, whereas others report that both verbal and visuospatial working memory influence mathematical performance. Nevertheless, executive working memory is more frequently implicated than either verbal working memory or visuospatial working memory (Andersson & Lyxell, 2007; Holmes & Adams, 2006). Individuals with executive deficits are unable to activate a sufficient amount of information from long-term memory and have difficulty integrating activated units with information in the verbal and visuospatial components. Moreover, those with an executive working memory deficit have difficulty inhibiting irrelevant information (Passolunghi & Siegel) and switching between operations (e.g., from addition to subtraction). To date, the distinctive contributions from different working memory components have not been disentangled, but all researchers agree that a deficit in some aspect of working memory exists in nearly all mathematics disabilities (Masoura, 2006).

Alternatively, for some individuals with a mathematical disability, the source of the problem may be difficulty retrieving basic mathematics facts from long-term memory, thus creating an unnecessary load on working memory (Geary et al., 2004). Children with mathematical difficulties have difficulty using direct memory retrieval to solve arithmetic problems, even after they have acquired basic mathematics knowledge (Barrouillet & Lepine, 2005). Of course, retrieval is ineffective for some because they have weak, incomplete networks of number facts in long-term memory (Holmes & Adams, 2006). Low working memory capacity itself may be the reason those with a disability are less likely to use long-term retrieval. That is, low working memory capacity may result in slower and less efficient retrieval processes, as well as difficulty resisting the interference to which mathematics retrieval is particularly prone.

Although children with mathematics disabilities may demonstrate normal overall storage capacity in phonological short-term memory, they typically have shorter digit spans and shorter spans on complex tasks that involve counting (Siegel & Ryan, 1989). Their storage deficit for numerical information may be a result of delayed growth in mathematical knowledge. There is evidence that mastery of mathematics facts may have a reciprocal relationship with short-term numerical memory span (Andersson & Lyxell, 2007). Students with mathematics disabilities have problems acquiring long-term representations of basic mathematics facts, a difficulty that has been attributed to short-term memory deficits (Geary et al., 2004; McLean & Hitch, 1999). Initially, the learning of mathematics facts may be restrained by a low phonological short-term memory capacity that results in the first number decaying before the child can encode the mathematics fact into long-term storage. When numerical knowledge acquisition is delayed, age-appropriate short-term retention of numerical information, such as digits, may be affected, as long-term representations are unable to make sufficient contributions during recall. Nonetheless, most children with mathematical disabilities have a persistent deficit in working memory that goes beyond a deficit in the processing and storage of numerical information (Passolunghi & Siegel, 2004). Moreover, failure to master mathematics facts prevents automatization of mathematics computation, creating even more demands on an easily overloaded working memory. Overloading can be compounded further in cases where the learner also has slow processing speed or long-term retrieval difficulties.

Compared to those with a mathematical disability only, students with comorbid mathematical and reading disabilities seem to have short-term and working memory deficits that also involve storage of nonnumerical verbal information, and their executive working memory is even more affected (Andersson & Lyxell, 2007). Children with comorbid learning disabilities perform worse in mathematics that is mediated by language, such as story problems (Andersson & Lyxell). Students with comorbid learning disorders also may have difficulty recoding visuospatial information into verbal information, continuing to use less effective visuospatial storage and processing when their normal peers have moved on. Similarly, those with comorbidity may struggle even more in mathematics because they cannot effectively use alternative verbal strategies to solve mathematics problems.

Working Memory and Written Language

Written expression is a complex cognitive activity that requires the integration of several cognitive processes and memory components. Writing begins with a planning phase during which the writer generates ideas and constructs a preverbal message that corresponds to the ideas she or he wants to communicate. Next, the composer must translate the ideas into words and construct grammatically correct sentences that involve retrieval of the semantic, syntactic, and morphological properties of words. After motor programs have transformed the linguistic message into text, the writer must evaluate by comparing the text with the intended meaning. Of course, written language production is not a lock-step sequence; writing is a parallel and iterative process requiring constant shifting among the procedures. In addition to reliance on the executive, the planning phase draws on the visuospatial component, as many writers visualize images, and the translating phase imposes demands on the verbal component (Kellogg, 1996; Olive, 2004). All of these steps place very heavy demands on working memory, especially on the executive and verbal components. In addition to substantial reliance on executive and verbal working memory, phonological short-term memory contributes to writing by briefly storing phonological representations of the words or sentence under construction. Also, visual working memory is involved (Kellogg, Olive, & Piolat, 2007) in the planning phase of written language production and during recalling definitions of concrete nouns (but not abstract nouns). Overall, written expression places so many demands on working memory that several aspects of written language production are probably competing for the same working memory resources (Kellogg, Olive, & Piolat).

Similar to the relationship between reading decoding proficiency and the working memory resources available for reading comprehension, it appears that mastery of elementary writing processes, such as punctuation, spelling, and transcribing, allows greater working memory capacity for the higher level writing processes of generating, organizing, and revising (Swanson & Berninger, 1996). Furthermore, even with well-developed written language skills, written expression will always place extensive demands on working memory because processes such as constructing ideas can never become fully automatized. Moreover, written expression also involves retrieval and temporary storage of information from long-term memory while the writer juggles multiple writing tasks.

Compared to reading and mathematics, there have been fewer scientific inquiries into the relationship between working memory and written language. Findings from the few existing investigations are consistent with the usual hypotheses;

for example, individuals with longer verbal spans write more complex sentences than those with shorter spans. Also, the correlation between verbal working memory span and written language increases as written language skills increase (Swanson & Siegel, 2001). Despite the limited research, there can be little doubt that written language production depends heavily on working memory and all aspects of verbal and executive working memory are fully involved, even in proficient writers.

Implications for Assessment, Instruction, and Intervention

Assessment of Learning Disabilities

Knowing the relationships between specific academic skills and specific working memory functions is valuable information that can guide assessment, interpretation of results, and diagnosis of learning disorders. Children with different specific learning disabilities tend to demonstrate unique types of working memory deficits (Siegel & Ryan, 1989; Swanson et al., 2006). Thus, an individual's working memory profile, at least to some extent, can help to differentiate among specific learning disabilities. For example, children with a reading disability usually perform significantly below normal on verbal short-term and working memory tasks, whereas children with a mathematics disability primarily have difficulties in the visuospatial and executive domains but also struggle with some verbal working memory tasks, especially those that involve counting (Van Der Sluis et al., 2005). Children with comorbid reading and mathematics disabilities have lower scores on both verbal and visuospatial tasks, as well as deficiencies in executive working memory (Siegel & Ryan). Consequently, assessment procedures that allow discrimination of working memory components can help to differentiate among academic learning dysfunctions and disabilities.

Given the well-established relationship between poor working memory capacity and academic failure, a working memory measure would be an appropriate addition to early school screenings. Working memory assessments hold the potential to identify children at risk of future low achievement (Gathercole & Pickering, 2001). With the emphasis on early intervention, most school systems now conduct universal screening of reading and arithmetic skills. Processing assessment, namely phonological processing, is already embedded in most reading assessments. Including a brief measure of phonological short-term span and verbal working memory span may improve early identification of children at risk for academic failure and learning disabilities. For example, longitudinal research in England discovered that a backward digit-recall task administered at school entry is a good predictor of who will need special education 3 years later (Pickering and Gathercole, 2004). Because of its high predictive validity, Gathercole, Brown, and

Pickering (2003) modified the backward digit-recall task to make it appropriate for use with children as young as 4 years of age.

Importance of Automaticity

When teaching and assessing students with learning difficulties, be aware that a lack of skill fluency, or automaticity, may give the appearance of a working memory deficiency. Automaticity is attained when a skill or procedure is mastered so well that it no longer requires conscious, effortful cognitive processing. The burden on working memory is greatest in the early stages of skill development (Kyllonen & Christal, 1999). As students master skills and develop expertise, the skills and procedures become automated and require less processing by working memory. Automated processing requires only minimal working memory resources, and it does not interfere with effortful concurrent processing (Richardson, 1996a). Another important characteristic of an automated task is that it is less subject to interference from a competing task (Just & Carpenter, 1992). Students who do not obtain automaticity at the same time as their peers have relatively fewer residual working memory resources for other tasks. For example, a fifth grader still struggling with reading decoding has fewer resources to devote to comprehension. When observing such students, it often appears that they are lacking in working memory capacity. Actually, they may have a working memory impairment, and their slow progress may be due to the impairment, but it is important to know the difference. Regardless of a student's working memory capacity, it is crucial that basic skills be taught to a high level of mastery so that automaticity is assured and working memory can focus on higher level processing. Consequently, practice is essential; only repeated pairings of stimulus and response lead to skill automaticity.

The principle of automaticity also applies directly to working memory functions themselves. More resources are freed up as working-memory routines and strategies, such as subvocal rehearsal and chunking, become automated. In fact, chunking may be the primary process that underlies automaticity. Available capacity also is a function of how efficient the individual is at specific working memory operations (Richardson, 1996a). Consequently, extensive opportunities to deliberately practice a strategy may improve working memory performance without expanding preexisting working memory capacity (MacDonald & Christiansen, 2002).

When it comes to individual differences in working memory capacity, the development of automaticity may be the great equalizer. For learners with working memory impairments, acquiring expertise and automaticity is more important than it is for those who have ample working memory resources. As basic skills develop to the point of full automaticity, working memory capacity becomes less of a factor in skill performance (Conway and Engle, 1994), thereby allowing students with working memory deficiencies to progress academically. The only problem is that some higher level cognitive processes, such as those involved in written expression, can never be fully automatized, and working memory must always strive to maintain the focus of attention, even during automatized tasks. Nevertheless, automaticity essentially creates higher processing efficiency, leading to stronger working memory performance, as well as better products and outcomes for the processing or learning task at hand. For students with working memory deficits, reaching automaticity is crucial.

Educational Interventions and Classroom Instruction

There are many educational implications that arise from the empirical evidence regarding the relationships between working memory components and academic learning. An in-depth discussion, with more detailed recommendations for intervention and instruction, can be found in Chapter 9. For now, a few high points are worthy of review:

1. There is a strong relationship between working memory span and overall learning rate; greater memory span is related to faster learning (Radvansky & Copeland, 2006). Even basic short-term memory functions have significant relationships with learning. For example, scores on word and nonword repetition tasks are closely linked with vocabulary learning (Gathercole & Adams, 1993). Therefore, knowing the working memory span of each student can provide a basis for adapting instruction.

2. With the exception of mathematics, academic learning and performance depend more heavily on phonological short-term memory and verbal working memory than on visuospatial memory components. Fortunately, most learners have a substantially longer memory span for verbal information than for visually presented information (Baddeley, 1986). Verbal information also seems to be more durable and resistant to interference than is visually encoded material. The typical individual capitalizes on this verbal strength by converting most visually presented material into a phonological code (Logie, 1996). As one might expect, visual processing has a very low correlation with academic learning (Mather & Wendling, 2005).

3. Working memory functioning is most important during the initial stages of learning. It declines in importance as facts and procedures become firmly established in long-term memory and tasks are performed automatically and effortlessly (Geary et al., 2004). The initial learning of procedural knowledge, such as mathematics problem-solving procedures, is particularly demanding of working memory. For example, during the early stages of procedural learning, working memory must hold instructions and other knowledge of the task while performing the steps involved. Consequently, teachers should strive to keep working memory demands to a minimum during initial learning phases.

4. Some of the relationships between academic learning and working memory are reciprocal. Not only does working memory capacity restrain learning, but skill development influences working memory development and capacity, at least

available capacity for a specific task (Henry & Millar, 1993; Van Der Sluis et al., 2005).

5. Although it has been frequently assumed that the probability of long-term encoding is a function of the amount of time an item is maintained in short-term or working memory, the probability of long-term storage is also a function of how many times an item enters working memory (Anderson, 1983). Thus, repeated practice and review is an effective instructional method for all students. Regarding reading comprehension, individuals with weak working memory capacity need ample time to reread sections and need continued access to the text while answering questions.

6. The relative importance of each working memory component changes during development and skill acquisition. For example, the relationship between visuospatial working memory and learning is stronger in preschool and early grades (Swanson & Siegel, 2001). The phonological system is more highly related with reading decoding and reading comprehension in children younger than 9, after which the executive system plays an equally important role (Swanson & Siegel).

7. Elementary teachers need to be aware of the evolving role of working memory in mathematics performance. Through first grade, children rely more on the visuospatial components of short-term and working memory during mathematics learning and performance. After first grade, verbal and executive working memory take precedence. These developmental changes should inform curriculum and instruction, as well as remediation. For example, visuospatial presentation of mathematics problems is very important until the end of first grade.

8. In general, the most influential working memory component when it comes to academic learning is the executive. The development, capacity, and effective use of executive working memory has important consequences for academic learning and performance. Children with executive working memory shortcomings have greater difficulty monitoring resources, utilizing effective strategies, inhibiting irrelevant information, and maintaining task-relevant information (Swanson & Siegel, 2001). These deficiencies lead to difficulties acquiring knowledge and developing new complex abilities, especially in language, literacy, and mathematics (Gathercole & Pickering, 2001).

9. The direct teaching of rehearsal strategies, mnemonics, and other working memory strategies can improve the efficiency of working memory (Torgesen & Goldman, 1977), thereby augmenting academic learning and performance. For older children, effective executive management strategies should be taught, such as how to monitor procedures and assess accuracy. For those with executive working memory weaknesses, external supports, such as cards listing step-by-step procedures, should also be helpful.

10. When mathematics performance is being measured, unrelated demands on working memory should be eliminated or reduced. For example, when reading skills are adequate, written presentation of word problems will reduce the load on short-term and working memory. For those with working memory impairments, external aides, such as calculators, should be allowed at an early age.

11. Similarly, for children deficient in working memory, irrelevant information should be eliminated from mathematics word problems, or, at the very least, students should explicitly be taught how to distinguish between relevant and irrelevant information. For example, they might be taught how to underline relevant information or cross out the irrelevant information.

12. If students with working memory deficits are to attain normal achievement, they must experience frequent learning situations that place only minimal demands on working memory, thereby allowing them to attain skills and knowledge comparable to peers who possess average working memory capabilities. In particular, the methods and materials used with students who have a learning disability should keep working memory processing demands to a minimum.

13. Finally, teachers should encourage the development and application of related cognitive processing strengths that allow learners to compensate for their working memory weaknesses.

CHAPTER 6

Working Memory Assessment Strategies

S everal years ago, after the release of the Wechsler Intelligence Scale for Children Fourth Edition (WISC-IV; Wechsler, 2003), the Wisconsin Department of Public Instruction began receiving phone calls from concerned school psychologists who had been using the new scale. The WISC-IV was different from its predecessor, the WISC-III, in that it had a Working Memory Index and more working memory and processing speed subtests were included in the computation of the Full Scale IQ (FSIQ). Some school psychologists were reporting that the additional working memory and processing speed subtests were "pulling down" the FSIQ of students referred for learning disabilities, preventing the students from qualifying for learning disability services. At the time, a discrepancy model was being used to determine eligibility; thus, higher FSIQ scores were needed to produce a significant discrepancy between FSIQ and achievement scores. Some of the callers asked if they could omit the working memory and processing speed scores from computation of the FSIQ. Later, the publisher of the WISC-IV (Wechsler, 2003) would offer that option by providing norms for a 6-subtest FSIQ called the General Ability Index (GAI).

It is ironic that one of the strongest indicators of a learning disability, a low working memory score, was thought to be preventing the identification of learning disabilities. Since then, the discrepancy model has been abandoned, providing an opportunity for appropriate diagnostic use of low working memory scores. Even before the discrepancy model met its demise, some psychologists (e.g., Naglieri, 1999) were suggesting that we should look for consistency between processing scores and achievement, instead of discrepancy. That is, if a processing weakness is accounting for an academic skill deficit, then both scores should be low, instead of related cognitive processing scores being significantly higher than the academic skill score. For example, when working memory and basic reading skills scores are both low, there is evidence of a learning disability in basic reading skills.

Proponents of the Response-to-Intervention (RTI) model now being applied in most states argue that working memory and other processing scores are just as irrelevant as FSIQ because they provide no information about the existence of a disability or about interventions. This author agrees that the FSIQ and the discrepancy approach were ineffective diagnostic methods and that the FSIQ provided little direction about course or outcomes of intervention. However, given the extensive evidence documenting the relationships between working memory and specific learning disabilities (see Chapter 5), working memory and other related processing scores can provide valuable information in the determination of learning disabilities. This author also believes that treatment for working memory impairments is an appropriate component of a disabled student's educational plan (see Chapter 9). Advocates for RTI might respond to these arguments by saying that the cause of the learning disability is irrelevant and that educational interventions should focus on proven academic methods. They also believe that RTI can be used to identify students with learning disabilities. In RTI programs, students who do not obtain academic benchmarks receive increasingly intensive educational interventions. Students who do not respond to these evidence-based interventions are determined to have a learning disability. Unfortunately, for students with learning disabilities, RTI programs may be delaying the specialized interventions and individualized education that they need. In many instances, low working memory scores could have predicted academic failure and the need for special education (Gathercole, Brown, & Pickering, 2003). From this author's experience, it is frequently a deficit in working memory, or some other related process, that prevents students with learning disabilities from responding well to interventions. As such, their failure to respond to regular education interventions could have been predicted.

If working memory tests measure a capacity that is crucial for cognitive functioning and fundamental for academic learning, then working memory measures should be a central part of every assessment of cognitive abilities, especially when learning difficulties are a referral concern. An abundance of empirical evidence confirms that deficiencies in working memory skills are implicated whenever learners have difficulty acquiring any academic skill (e.g., Gathercole et al., 2005). Given the strong relationships working memory has with all areas of academic learning, working memory scores can provide valuable diagnostic information. Even if working memory scores are not used for diagnostic purposes, they can provide a better understanding of the learner's cognitive strengths and weaknesses. Once a learner's processing strengths and weaknesses have been identified, this knowledge can be used in designing individualized interventions and appropriate educational programming. Educational interventions are likely to be more effective when they take into account the specific processing weaknesses associated with the learning problem. For example, there are many potential processing problems that can account for a delay in basic reading skills. An intervention for a student with a phonemic awareness deficit should be distinct from an intervention designed for a student whose phonemic awareness is normal but whose working memory is deficient. Thus, assessment of working memory and related cognitive processes should be conducted with treatment in mind.

Although a comprehensive assessment of working memory and related cognitive processes is recommended when students are referred for learning problems, the informal methods and standardized tests should vary somewhat, depending on the specific referral concerns, the age of the student, and the measurement tools available. As such, there is not a standard battery for testing working memory; assessment procedures should be individualized for each case. The selection of informal procedures and tests should be determined by the hypotheses generated to account for the specific learning problems. Systematic planning before conducting an assessment is likely to increase the efficiency of the process and the usefulness of the results. Similarly, there is no standardized interpretative procedure that applies to all working memory test results. Also, the meaning of any given test score varies, depending on the examinee's other abilities and characteristics. Furthermore, the level of functioning indicated by test scores needs to be corroborated by other assessment data. In essence, the interpretation of test results should be based on both statistical analysis and clinical judgment.

In addition to recommendations for planning and organizing selective, cross-battery testing, this chapter describes informal assessment methods and materials that include interviews, observations, and records review. General guidelines for selecting and using working memory subtests, tests, factors, and batteries are offered (see also Chapters 7 and 8). To provide the reader with a knowledge base for subtest selection, a variety of working memory assessment paradigms are explained in detail, along with their intended use. The information will allow readers to determine which memory systems and which working memory components are tapped by various types of memory subtests. Furthermore, there are recommendations for assessing cognitive processes that are closely associated with working memory. Most importantly, this chapter contains detailed procedures for analyzing and interpreting working memory test results. The analytical and interpretative procedures apply to any and all working memory test batteries, especially those constructed in a cross-battery fashion. (Test-specific interpretative suggestions are provided in Chapters 7 and 8.) In addition, this chapter will confront the challenges associated with working memory assessment.

Working Memory Assessment Challenges

Psychologists and related practitioners must resolve several challenges when conducting a formal assessment of working memory. To begin with, there are no recently normed test batteries that are designed specifically for an in-depth assessment of working memory. (At least not any that are normed in the United States.) Several cognitive and memory scales include measures of short-term and working memory. Unfortunately, the majority of these scales only tap certain aspects of working memory; for example, some only tap the phonological and verbal dimensions of working memory while ignoring visuospatial components. These half-measures force the practitioner to administer additional instruments in a cross-battery fashion (discussed later in this chapter) whenever a comprehensive assessment is desired. Other batteries classify all types of temporary storage and processing either as short-term memory or as working memory, leaving the practitioner the responsibility of trying to separate the two. Cognitive batteries and memory scales seldom differentiate well between short-term memory and working memory, even when subtest and composite names indicate such. For example, digit span, the most widely used measure of temporal memory, has traditionally been used to produce a scaled score that combines digits forward and digits backward. Unfortunately, this procedure confounds assessment of two distinct memory components: phonological short-term memory (measured by digits forward) and executive working memory (measured by digits backward). Not surprisingly, digit span is sometimes categorized as a short-term memory subtest and sometimes classified as a working memory subtest.

For practitioners who wish to differentiate among a client's processes and components within short-term and working memory, selective testing and clinical interpretation is necessary. In nearly all batteries, working memory subtests do not discriminate well between subprocesses within working memory. One reason is that span measures taken during concurrent processing tasks are used to measure the capacity of executive working memory instead of attempting to directly measure an executive function, such as inhibition. Consequently many working memory subtests are appraising multiple aspects of working memory and short-term memory. Moreover, no standardized tools are available that explicitly attempt to assess Baddeley's episodic buffer or the ability to maintain long-term representations in an active, quickly retrievable state, an essential aspect of most contemporary theories. Also, there are no measures that allow direct assessment of specific working memory operations, such as the ability to recode visuospatial input into verbal code.

Another concern with existing cognitive and memory instruments is that, despite the perceived importance of strategies, there is only one scale that attempts to assess their influence: The Swanson Cognitive Processing Test (S-CPT; Swanson, 1995; reviewed in Chapter 8) attempts to broadly assess the use and impact of memory strategies on working memory performance. Span procedures, the most common form of measurement, provide little indication of strategy selection, use, or efficiency. In fact, digit span does not even correlate with strategy selection and efficiency (Imbo & Vandierendonck, 2007). Of course, examinees are often utilizing strategies, such as subvocal rehearsal. Following the paradigms of laboratory researchers, some test authors have designed tasks that prevent strategy use by introducing irrelevant interference. Sometimes, the intent of interference is to measure *pure* short-term memory span. *Pure* short-term span is thought to indicate the capacity of short-term memory when it receives no assistance from working memory. To obtain a pure span, distracting interference is introduced that prevents rehearsal and further processing of the stimuli. It is not surprising that such restricted measures are poor predictors of academic performance. In the real world, short-term and working memory operations typically function in conjunction with concurrent processing and strategic applications.

From the perspective of contemporary theories of working memory and the applied model proposed in this text, another major concern with existing measures is their complete failure to assess the interaction between long-term and working memory, as well as long-term memory's contributions to short-term and working memory (Masoura, 2006). For example, almost no existing measures provide a means of determining how much recall can be attributed to short-term storage and how much to long-term storage, a problem that might be solved by the opportunity to contrast retention of words with that of nonwords. Moreover, omitting any attempt to factor in the influence of long-term memory or long-term retrieval results in an incomplete picture of total working memory capacity. The amount of information currently active in working memory may be greater than indicated by the length of a short-term memory span; that is, memory span may not provide an accurate appraisal of total working memory capacity (Richardson, 1996b). Similarly, some tasks identified as long-term memory subtests may actually be measuring working memory components.

To complicate matters further, existing assessment tools, as well as texts on the subject, provide little guidance on when to assess and how to interpret related processes. For example, discovery of a phonological short-term memory impairment in a preschooler should mandate testing of phonological processing. Furthermore, there are multiple interpretation challenges when trying to make sense of data gathered during a multidimensional assessment of working memory. For instance, how does a six-digit span impact learning differently than a five-digit span? From a broader perspective, it is difficult to determine the ramifications short-term and working memory scores have for academic learning and interventions.

Finally, one has to wonder how often we are actually measuring working memory capacity. The typical working memory subtest is a dual-task paradigm that requires examinees to concurrently perform a secondary task that prevents strategy use and adds to the working memory load. The outcome of adding to the working memory load is typically a reduction in short-term memory span, such as the decline in span from digits forward to digits backward. In one sense, it is paradoxical because we believe that working memory capacity is greater than that of short-term memory capacity alone. On the other hand, the effect of the secondary task is to mostly prevent working memory from assisting short-term memory through rehearsal. So, the resulting span may be nothing more than an indication of pure short-term memory span. What does pure short-term memory span tell us about overall working memory performance and capacity? Would it not make more sense to measure working memory capacity by presenting examinees with a complex task and allowing them to freely use all of their resources and strategies to preserve information? Wouldn't that be a more accurate appraisal of real-world working memory functioning? Fortunately, the additional processing required during many complex test activities does not totally disrupt efforts to maintain information. Nonetheless, preventing working memory from full normal functioning when trying to evaluate it seems counterintuitive. Experimental assessment paradigms originally designed to determine the extent of resource sharing between memory systems seem to have questionable validity when the purpose is to measure the overall level of an individual's working memory capacity.

Perhaps working memory measures should not be so harshly criticized; all types of psychological testing present challenges. And all types of test performance are subject to various influences. For example, at first glance, a digits forward subtest appears to be a narrow measure of temporary phonological storage. Nevertheless, it cannot be assumed that only passive storage is being tapped, as some examinees may be using sophisticated executive strategies to extend the span. Clearly, there is a need for additional assessment tools that are designed to specifically measure and differentiate among critical aspects of working memory. Until such products become available, this chapter and the following two chapters are intended to provide practitioners with appropriate guidance, particularly in test selection and the interpretation of results.

Distinguishing Between Short-Term and Working Memory Measures

Most of the standardized working memory subtests found in contemporary test batteries have their origins in experimental research paradigms. The theoretical basis for the majority of these research paradigms and associated subtests is Baddeley's (1986) tripartite model. Because Baddeley views the short-term stores as subsidiary components of working memory, many standardized measures take the same perspective, resulting in "working memory" subtests and factors that do not discriminate between short-term memory and working memory. Despite the lack of differentiation, most test authors adhere to the traditional definition of working memory as processing while trying to retain information in the short-term. Given this definition, a subtest is considered a measure of working memory whenever mental processing is required while trying to maintain information, and a subtest is considered a measure of short-term memory whenever storage but no additional processing is required. The assessment challenge is not that some measures of working memory contain elements of short-term storage, but that test batteries often do not provide measures that isolate short-term memory. The ability to measure short-term memory and working memory separately is important because the functions are different.

Even when test batteries have separately labeled subtests and factors, the titles may not accurately reflect what is being measured. For example, many subtests identified as short-term memory tasks may be primarily measuring working memory. To determine whether a subtest is primarily measuring short-term memory or working memory, consider the task and ask:

1. Is passive, serial recall of the information the only requirement? If so, the task can be classified as short-term memory.

2. Is any manipulation or transformation of the information required? If so, the task is essentially measuring working-memory functions.

3. Is any concurrent or intervening processing required, such as the insertion of an interference task? If so, the task clearly involves working memory.

4. Are both storage and processing required? If so, the task is primarily measuring working memory.

5. Does the task involve the concurrent retention of both visuospatial and verbal information or the recoding of one modality into the other? If so, it is primarily measuring working memory.

Short-Term and Working Memory Testing Paradigms

Nearly all measures of short-term and working memory developed to date involve the measurement of span. In general, memory span is defined as the maximum amount of sequential information an individual can remember accurately (Gathercole, 1999). In measurement, span is the number of items the examinee can recall after a short interval; usually, the items must be recalled in serial order. A span procedure typically begins with only one or two items to remember. When the individual responds correctly to enough trials at a given level, the amount of material to be remembered is increased, usually by one item at a time. Short-term memory span is the number of items retained when no concurrent processing is required, whereas working memory span is the number of items recalled after processing the same or other information. Span activities can be classified as either *simple span* or *complex span*. Simple span is presumed to measure short-term memory, whereas complex span is considered a measure of working memory. Measures of simple span require only the passive retention of information. Examples of simple-span tasks include the serial recall of letters, digits, words, or nonwords.

Complex span activities require effortful processing of information while trying to retain a list of items for a short interval (Bayliss, Jarrold, Baddeley, & Gunn, 2005). Complex spans are considered measures of working memory because they require the involvement of executive working memory. The classic example of a complex-span task is the reading span task (Daneman & Carpenter, 1980) in which the examinee reads aloud a sentence, responds to a simple question about it, and then later must sequentially recall the final word of each sentence. Other complex span activities include listening span, operation span, and counting span. Whereas simple-span tasks are used to measure phonological short-term memory, complex-span activities measure verbal and executive working memory. Complex-span tasks require the coordination of storage and processing—coordination is one of the primary functions of executive working memory. Although verbal working memory plays a role, individual differences in complex-span tasks seem to be primarily due to differences in the executive component of working memory (Conway et al., 2002).

Complex-span tasks are usually constructed in a manner that is intended to replicate real-world memory functioning, such as that which occurs while reading for comprehension. This may be why complex spans generally have higher correlations with academic learning and higher cognitive functions than simple spans do. There is no denying that complex-span activities put executive working memory to the test. It is the responsibility of executive working memory to cope with the challenge of retaining information while minimizing the impact of the interference that has been introduced. If the interference cannot be inhibited, rapid switching between processing the interference and rehearsing the information may preserve some of the span. Therefore, the span resulting from complex-span activities does allow us to make inferences about the effectiveness of executive working memory. A sub-average complex span is one indication of a deficiency in executive working memory.

In the following sections, several common measurement paradigms are categorized and described (see Table 6.1). All of these have been used in experimental research and the majority have been incorporated into one or more standardized test batteries. Additional working memory assessment paradigms may be found in Strauss, Sherman, and Spreen (2006).

Phonological Short-Term Memory
Forward Digit Span

Nearly everyone in education and psychology is familiar with the most frequently used measure of short-term and working memory. Joseph Jacobs, a London schoolmaster who wanted to measure the mental capacities of his pupils, developed the first digit span test in the 1880s. It was later incorporated into Binet and Simon's 1905 intelligence scale and has been a mainstay of cognitive assessment ever since. Forward digit span measures phonological short-term memory, whereas backward digit span is categorized under executive working memory. Compared with forward span, backward span usually yields a reduction in span of at least one digit, with more of a reduction with older subjects. In most standardized procedures the examiner says the digits at the rate of one per second, although some tests double the presentation rate to reduce the opportunity for rehearsal. Some applications also explicitly prevent examinees from chunking the numbers when responding.

Table 6.1 Common Measurement Paradigms for Memory Components

Short-Term Phonological	Short-Term Visual	Working Verbal	Working Visuospatial	Working Executive	Long-Term Retrieval
Forward digit span; Letter span; Word span; Nonword span	Forward block-tapping span; Visual digit span	Memory for sentences; Memory for stories; Listening span; Reading span; Operation span	Backward block-tapping span; Counting span	Backward word span; Backward digit span; Computation span; Trail-making; Stroop; Trail-making; N-Back; Random Generation	Retrieval fluency; Rapid automatic naming

Letter Span

Almost identical to digit span in structure and administration, letter span, which also has a backwards option, is ideal for use with examinees who are deficient in mathematics skills. Delayed mathematics development can influence the recall of digits, producing a score that underestimates overall phonological short-term storage capability. Letter span also keeps the processing close to the phonological level because letters activate fewer meaning-based long-term representations than words.

Word Span

As the name implies, word span is a series of words the examinee must recall in order. Like digits, they are typically presented at the rate of one per second. The words should be unrelated and categorical groupings should be avoided so that verbal working memory and long-term representations have less impact on performance. Also, the words should be relatively short, typically one or two syllables in length. Because of the influence of total articulation time on retention, spans with a greater number of syllables are more difficult to maintain than spans with fewer syllables.

Nonword Span

Nonwords, also know as pseudowords or nonsense words, are particularly ideal material for narrowing the assessment to simple phonological short-term memory span. With nonwords, the examinee cannot rely substantially on long-term semantic memory to supplement recall, as such items have no long-term representations other than basic phonetic properties. Consequently, when articulation time is equivalent, nonword span is typically shorter than word span. The best nonwords are those that bear almost no resemblance to recognizable syllables or words, and the number of syllables in each nonword should be limited to two. Also, sequences of nonwords should not include any items that rhyme. Individuals with phonological processing problems often have even more difficulty with nonwords than actual words. Interestingly, nonword span is a better predictor of vocabulary development than is word span (Gathercole, 1999).

Verbal Working Memory

Phonological short-term memory handles verbal information when only a few verbal items are involved and no transformation of the information is required. In contrast, verbal working memory is required when the information is long and complex, is more meaningful, needs to be manipulated, or when long-term semantic memory plays a significant role during recall. The purest measures of verbal working memory are those that do not introduce interference, a dual-processing task, or a secondary processing task. Thus, the complex spans classified here as verbal working memory tasks also tap executive working memory. Verbal working memory span tasks also depend on knowledge and processes beyond working memory; for example, many tasks involve verbal ability and some tasks require quantitative ability (Conway et al., 2003).

Memory for Sentences

Memory for sentences may be the purest form of verbal working memory, as it does not involve any dual processing that would enlist executive working memory processes. It also has the benefit of being distinct from phonological storage because meaning-based encoding will occur with sentences, resulting in spans that are significantly longer than spans for series of unrelated words.

Memory for Stories

Another short-term retention activity that is a relatively pure form of verbal working memory involves the retelling of brief stories. Immediately after hearing a story, the examinee is directed to retell as much of the story as he or she can remember. Complete and sequential recall is not required; points are awarded for each key element recalled and paraphrasing is usually allowed. Even more so than memory for sentences, success at this meaning-based task will depend heavily on support from activated long-term semantic memory structures.

Reading Span

Reading span, the complex-span task originally developed by Daneman and Carpenter (1980), has been a prototype for many verbal and executive working memory measures. Reading span typically requires the examinee to read a series of sentences and then sequentially recall the final word of each sentence. The task has been used in a variety of forms; for example, one version limits rehearsal by requiring a simple response to each sentence (Duff & Logie, 2001). Sentences that are more complex are thought to lead to a greater demand on working memory resources and a consequent reduction in span.

Listening Span

With listening span, the examiner reads a series of sentences to the examinee, and then the examinee recalls the final word of each sentence. The task can be made more challenging by inserting a question, typically a verification question, the examinee must answer before the next sentence is read. For example, the sentence might be "Cats bark at dogs," followed by the question "Is that true?" A cloze procedure can also be used with listening span (Siegel & Ryan, 1989). In this version, the examiner reads aloud sets of short sentences in which the final word is missing—for example, "Apples are red and bananas are ————." Examinees are instructed to complete the sentences. When all the sentences in the set have been completed, the examinee must repeat, in order, the words he or she used in completing the sentences. The word used to complete each sentence should be obvious, but selection of the correct word is not required.

Operation Span

The operation span task is another complex-span task similar to reading span. Subjects read aloud a mathematical equation and then state whether or not the equation is correct before reading a word aloud. Another variation is to have examinees solve a simple math problem before being exposed to the stimulus word. After completing a set of such items, subjects must recall the words in the correct sequence (Engle, 2002).

Visuospatial Short-Term Memory

Visual Digit Span

Rather than hearing orally presented digits, the examinee views printed digits. Although some tasks display the entire set of digits simultaneously, it is best to uncover one digit at a time at the rate of one per second. Sequential presentation seems reasonable when ordered recall is required, and it reduces the opportunities for chunking. Moreover, a direct comparison with auditory digit span is more valid when the method of presentation is similar.

Block-Tapping Span

The classic Corsi block-tapping task, or variations thereof, is often used to assess visuospatial short-term and working memory. The Corsi block task, which consists of an array of nine randomly placed blocks, is the visuospatial equivalent of digit span. Thus, the forward span is a measure of visuospatial short-term memory, whereas the backward span measures visuospatial working memory and executive working memory. To administer the task, the examiner taps or touches a set of two to nine blocks in a preselected random sequence at the rate of one per second. Examinees must then recreate the tapping sequence. In models that distinguish visual and spatial memory, the Corsi task is thought to primarily measure spatial span (Baddeley, 1996). In normal individuals, Corsi block span is typically about two items less than aural digit span.

Visuospatial Working Memory

Counting span involves counting a series of visual arrays and subsequently recalling the totals in order. An informal version can be constructed with index cards. The examinee counts the dots on the card (usually an amount not exceeding 10), turns the card over, and reports the number of dots. Then a second card is added and, after counting the dots on it, the examinee reports the number of dots that were on the first card followed by the number on the second card. More cards are added to increase the difficulty level. A variation that prevents grouping of dots for quick counting is to intersperse red dots with black dots and have the examinee count only the red dots.

Executive Working Memory

The dual-task technique is the classic method for assessing executive working memory. Dual-task activities require the subject to simultaneously perform two tasks—the primary and the secondary. The primary task is the short-term maintenance of stimuli. The secondary task is designed as interference with the purpose of disrupting any strategies that would facilitate maintenance of the information in the primary task. The introduction of interference assures the involvement of executive working memory. The notion behind the dual-task paradigm is that there is a limited pool of working memory resources that the primary and secondary tasks must share. Without the full amount of resources usually available, performance on the primary task (retaining the information) is presumed to decrease. Dual-task measures apply well to working memory functioning in the real world. For example, in the classroom, students must continually deal with distracting interference, some of it internally generated. In order to introduce the most interference, the secondary tasks should be in the same modality. For example, the maintenance of visuospatial information is disrupted by concurrent visuospatial tasks but not by secondary verbal tasks (Olive, 2004). Because of the additional complexity, memory spans measured with executive processing components are often shorter than their uninterrupted, straightforward memory counterparts (phonological short-term memory or verbal working memory). For individuals with an executive working memory deficiency, their difficulty will become more pronounced as the complexity of dual-processing increases. Individuals who do not display a decrement in span usually take longer to complete the secondary task, probably because they are shifting back and forth between the two tasks. In addition to the following tasks, all of the complex span tasks listed under verbal working memory involve executive working memory to some degree.

Computation Span

Computation span is another variation of complex span (De Jong, 1998) in which the examinee must retain digits while making simple computations. The examinee orally reads simple addition and subtraction problems and gives the answers aloud. After each computation, the examiner orally presents a digit. To prevent rehearsal, the examinee is required to begin the next problem immediately after presentation of the digit. After the series of computations is complete, the examinee must recall the digits in order.

Star Counting

Star counting is a task that especially requires inhibition. In the first part, the examinee is directed to count stars in rows of differing amounts, with the number at the beginning of the row showing the total number of stars in that row. However, a plus or minus sign is inserted at varying locations between the stars. These signs indicate the direction, forward or backward, in which subsequent stars have to be counted. The final count is the answer to the item. In the second part, more inhibition is required, as the meaning of the signs is reversed, with a plus meaning backward counting.

Stroop Task

In experimental research, the classic Stroop task has been repeatedly used to measure working memory, specifically the executive ability to focus attention and to inhibit overlearned responses or irrelevant information. The most challenging Stroop task is to read a list of color words that are printed in ink colors incongruent with the printed word (e.g., the word *red* in green ink).

Trail-Making

Cognitive psychologists have used trail-making tests to assess the ability to switch between operations or retrieval strategies. This paper-and-pencil task usually consists of numbers or letters on a page that must quickly be connected in numerical or alphabetical order. Difficulty may be increased by combining numbers and letters and requiring the examinee to connect them in an alternating fashion (e.g., 1-A-2-B).

N-Back

The *n-back* task is another popular cognitive neuroscience paradigm that has been widely used. The general procedure requires the examinee to respond to a stimulus, for example a number, when it matches a previously presented item that is a predetermined number of items back. The presentation of stimuli and reporting by the examinee is continuous (Cicerone, 2002). For example, using a deck of cards in a

2-back task, the participant is required to name the card that was exposed two cards prior to the one currently exposed. So if the exposure sequence is "10," "2," "6," "8," the subject says "10" when the "6" is exposed and "2" when the "8" is exposed, and so on. The *n*-back task is often used to measure executive functioning. Recently, the validity of the *n*-back task was challenged by Kane, Conway, Miura, and Colfiesh (2007), who argue that the *n*-back task may not be a valid measure of working memory as it does not correlate significantly with other measures of working memory span.

Random Generation

Random generation is another task that is typically employed with a concurrent storage task. In this approach, the subject must randomly generate numbers, letters, or words from a semantic category while avoiding repetitions. With letters, subjects sometimes are required to generate triads while avoiding acronyms, natural letter sequences, or words.

Verbal-Spatial Association

A new working memory measurement paradigm was recently proposed by Cowan et al. (2006). They developed an experimental task that requires verbal-spatial associations. The task involves remembering the location of names presented on a computer screen. Such a task is thought to measure working memory for abstract information. The task is also unique in that it creates a challenging working memory measure without introducing an unrelated processing task that disrupts normal working memory functioning or prevents retention strategies. The new paradigm may also be the first to tap Baddeley's episodic component of working memory. Thus, the task is similar to real-world functioning in that cross-modal associations are required.

Long-Term Retrieval

Retrieval Fluency

Tasks of this nature are sometimes referred to as *associational fluency* or *verbal fluency* tasks. These activities are intended to measure the examinee's speed of long-term memory retrieval. During these effortful searches, semantic categories, such as food, are commonly used, but initial phoneme sounds are also used sometimes. Working memory plays a role during directed searches; for example, working memory determines whether retrieved items meet search criteria.

Rapid Automatic Naming

Rapid Automatic Naming is a timed long-term retrieval task found in several types of scales, including achievement batteries. Typically, the examinee is required to say the names of symbols or pictured objects. Proficiency at the task is influenced by several factors, including processing speed and the strength of the associations stored in long-term memory. Rapid Automatic Naming probably requires fewer working memory resources than retrieval by category.

Paired Associate Learning

As learning is inextricably linked to memory, most memory batteries include learning subtests that involve repeated trials of the same information. These tasks require the examinee to learn pairings of unrelated words or pairings of words with symbols. The activities are distinct from short-term and working memory paradigms in that there are repeated trials during which corrective feedback is provided. Such subtests are intended to measure how efficiently the examinee can learn novel material. Although long-term retention is necessary, working memory is thought to play an essential role because new information must be encoded meaningfully—a function of working memory. The benefit of including such tasks in working memory testing is that they allow clinicians to assess how the individual's working memory is influencing learning. Nonetheless, for the sake of consistency, paired associate and related learning tasks should be interpreted as measures of learning, not working memory per se or even as the long-term retrieval function associated with working memory (see working memory component definitions in Chapter 3). Also, delayed-recall subtests should be interpreted as measures of long-term storage, a capacity that is distinct from short-term and working memory capacities.

Hypothesis-Driven Assessment of Working Memory

Psychologists and related professionals who conduct psychological and educational evaluations often come across individuals who have been suffering from a disability but have never been diagnosed. Sometimes these individuals have been evaluated previously but the disability was missed or another disorder was diagnosed instead. For example, young children with learning and behavior problems are sometimes diagnosed with ADHD when they actually have a learning disability. Even when children are correctly diagnosed with a specific learning disability, the underlying cause of their learning problems usually remains unknown or is misunderstood. The occurrence of misdiagnoses and the limited understanding of *why* an individual has learning problems can often be attributed to assessment procedures that missed the mark or were too superficial. Such assessment procedures usually consist of "standard battery" procedures (i.e., the same procedures and the same set of tests are used in every case, regardless of the specific referral concerns). An alternative that can reduce misdiagnoses and increase in-depth understanding of the individual is to adopt a hypothesis-driven approach to psychoeducational assessment that results in an individualized assessment plan for every referral.

Prior to selecting informal procedures and standardized tests, evaluators should generate and select hypotheses that account for the specific referral concerns. *Referral hypotheses* are statements that explain or account for the presenting problem. These hypotheses get at the underlying cause of the problem or at *why* the problem is occurring. In a sense, referral hypotheses point toward the suspected deficit. Whether we express them or not, we all generate hypotheses about other people's problems; for example, when we suspect someone is performing poorly because he or she lacks motivation, we have, in effect, hypothesized that the individual lacks motivation. This text promotes hypotheses for working memory and related processing problems but evaluators should not restrict hypotheses to these domains; behavioral instead of cognitive hypotheses can also be chosen.

The generation and selection of appropriate memory and processing hypotheses begins with a careful examination of the presenting problems. Especially when it comes to assessing memory, the referral reasons need to be examined and clarified so that all relevant concerns are investigated. This preassessment step may require a preliminary interview with the client or person making the referral to determine the precise nature of the concerns. Simply relying on the initially stated presenting problems is often ineffective because the individual seeking an assessment or intervention often fails to report important behaviors or performance. The client or the person making the referral may posit some hypotheses of their own. If these hypotheses are appropriate, they should be considered and included in the assessment plan. For example, a parent will sometimes hypothesize that poor instruction is the cause of the child's reading problems. Such a hypothesis should be considered but will not be included in a psychoeducational assessment. The generation and selection of referral hypotheses can be completed once all of the referral concerns have been examined and clarified. One structured approach to accomplishing this task is to use the *Working Memory Assessment Plan* form provided in Appendix B. When learning disabilities are a possibility, hypothesis-driven assessment planning keeps the focus on working memory components that have the strongest relationships with the areas of academic deficiency. For example, whenever basic reading decoding skills are a concern, the first memory-based hypothesis should be that the examinee has a significant weakness in phonological short-term memory. After logical or empirically based hypotheses worthy of investigation have been selected, the examiner selects assessment methods (e.g., observations, interviews, and standardized tests) that will allow the testing of each hypothesis. The case of Joey (introduced in Chapter 5) will be used to illustrate hypothesis-driven assessment planning (see Table 6.2). In Joey's case, extreme difficulty in basic reading decoding is one of the primary concerns. Hypotheses with a high likelihood of explaining this difficulty are: (a) Joey has difficulty decoding because of weak phonological processing; (b) Joey has difficulty decoding because of weak phonological short-term memory; and (c) Joey has difficulty decoding because of weak long-term storage and retrieval. For some reminders of plausible memory and processing hypotheses see Tables 5.2 and 5.3 in Chapter 5.

After the memory and processing hypotheses have been selected, the next step is to determine the best assessment procedure for testing each hypothesis. In many cases,

Table 6.2 Working Memory Assessment Plan

Examinee's Name: Case Study of "Joey" DOB: —— Age: 9 Grade: 4 Testing Dates: —— Completed By: ——

Referral Concerns	Memory or Processing Hypotheses	Memory Factors or Subtests	Observations	Interviews	Other Method
1. Difficulty decoding words when reading	1.a. Phonological processing weakness 1.b. Phonological STM weakness 1.c Long-term storage and retrieval weakness 1.d Visuospatial STM or WM weakness	1.a. WJ III Phonemic Awareness cluster 1.b. WJ III Memory for Words 1.c. WJ III Rapid Picture Naming and Retrieval Fluency 1.d WISC-IV Integrated Spatial Span Forward and Backward	1.a. Observe while reading in the classroom	1.a. Question parent about rhyming 1. b.c.d. Question teacher about signs of weaknesses	1.a.b.c. Review special education records
2. Difficulty with reading comprehension	2.a. Fluid reasoning weakness 2.b. Executive WM weakness 2.c. Long-term storage and retrieval weakness	2.a. WJ III Fluid reasoning cluster 2.b. WJ III Numbers Reversed and Auditory Working Memory 2.c. See 1.c.	2.c. Observe retention of material in classroom	2.c. Question teacher about long-term retention	2.c. Check early childhood history for long-term retention problems
3. Difficulty with written expression	3.a. Executive WM weakness 3.b. Processing speed weakness 3.c. Language development delay	3.a. See 2.b. 3.b. WISC-IV Processing Speed 3.c. Refer to speech/ language therapist	3.b. Observe for processing speed in classroom and during testing	3.c. Question parent about language development	3.c. Check early childhood history for language delay

Directions: Under Memory Factors or Subtests, specify the name of the battery, factor, and/or subtest that will be used. Under Observations, specify when and where. Under Interviews, specify with whom.

an informal procedure, such as an observation, will provide enough data to test one or more hypotheses. For other hypotheses, standardized testing will be necessary. In most situations, one instrument, such as a comprehensive memory scale, can be used to test several hypotheses. For many hypotheses, a single subtest will provide an adequate test of one hypothesis; however, the use of two subtests provides a more reliable sampling of the component or process being investigated. Selection of a specific subtest should be based on the extent to which the subtest measures the specific underlying process thought to account for the problem. To determine subtest classifications based on the Integrated Model of Working Memory, see Chapters 7 and 8 and consult Appendices A and E. The hypothesis-driven method meshes well with a cross-battery, selective testing approach (discussed later in this chapter) because selective testing limits standardized testing to the subtests that address the hypotheses, avoiding administration of entire batteries just because they contain the subtests of interest. For example, in Joey's case (see Table 6.2), only one subtest from the Woodcock-Johnson III (WJ III) was selected to test the phonological short-term memory weakness hypothesis, and two WJ III subtests were selected to test his long-term storage and retrieval. Effective use of the hypothesis-testing approach depends on delaying the selection of standardized measures until after the hypotheses have been identified. In conclusion, memory and processing assessment should be hypothesis driven, not battery driven. Selecting the instrument(s) in advance of choosing hypotheses, or using the same instruments with every assessment, is not only inefficient but poor practice as well.

After hypotheses that account for the problems have been selected, it may be necessary to expand the assessment further. One drawback to limiting testing to the areas of concern is that potential strengths are ignored. Assessing strengths creates a balanced view of the individual and allows the identification of assets that can be utilized during interventions. There are also instances when not enough is known about the individual's difficulties, as in the case of a young child, or the individual is experiencing a broad range of difficulties related to working memory. In such cases, a more comprehensive assessment that goes beyond the derived hypotheses is warranted. Nonetheless, "standard" assessment batteries and redundant testing should still be avoided. In instances where the information is so limited that it is difficult to select any plausible hypotheses, it may be best to begin with screening. In such cases, a broad-based but short measure with high predictive validity will serve the purpose. For instance, a digit-span task is ideal, as digits forward measures phonological short-term memory and digits backward measures executive working memory. If performance on either is subaverage, then these memory components and verbal working memory should be tested in depth.

From a scientific perspective, the main purpose of generating hypotheses before collecting and analyzing data is to increase the objectivity of the investigation and the interpretation of results. When using a hypothesis-testing approach to assessment, it is critical that evaluators keep an open mind and avoid hypothesis confirmation bias

(Hale & Fiorello, 2004). Confirmation bias leads to ignoring data that do not support a hypothesis while focusing on pieces of data that do support it. The data for and against a hypothesis should be carefully weighed before reaching a conclusion. The best way to counteract confirmation bias is to assume that the hypothesis is false unless there is considerable convergent evidence supporting it.

When hypotheses are selected prior to assessment, they are known as *a priori hypotheses*. As data are collected and analyzed, new insights often arise and more hypotheses are added. Also, when the results are inconsistent or are not what was predicted from the hypotheses, it is often necessary to generate new hypotheses that account for the unexpected findings. These new hypotheses are referred to as *a posteriori hypotheses*. When additional hypotheses are considered, the examiner should cycle back to an earlier step in the planning and assessment process. Follow-up testing may be necessary. In some instances, a posteriori hypotheses can be evaluated by reexamining already existing assessment data.

Basing memory evaluations on hypothesis testing serves several functions and has several advantages. First, explicitly generating and selecting hypotheses forces the examiner or multidisciplinary evaluation team to carefully think about and consider the referral concerns and how best to assess them. Each hypothesis should be one possible explanation for *why* the individual is experiencing a specific problem. Second, the hypothesis approach can increase the understanding of the learner even before assessment begins. Third, following a hypothesis-testing approach truly individualizes the assessment, forcing the evaluator to abandon a standard battery approach and adapt to the unique concerns of each case. Fourth, following the hypothesis-testing method, coupled with selective testing, results in an efficient, time-saving assessment that avoids redundancies while measuring all of the processes that need to be assessed. In conclusion, using hypotheses as the basis for assessment planning results in an individualized, comprehensive, and efficient assessment. Hypothesis-driven assessment should result in an in-depth understanding of the examinee. It also provides direction for subsequent interventions.

As this point, the reader may be wondering why we should bother with generating hypotheses—why not complete a comprehensive assessment of working memory in all cases? The main reason is that it is not necessary in every case. Some specific reasons include:

1. Not all memory components have a strong relationship with every problem. For example, if the only referral concern is mathematics reasoning (and mathematics calculation skills are above average), it is highly unlikely that phonological short-term memory has much to do with the problem.

2. Some hypotheses are determined by the age of the examinee. For example, if a 4-year-old is having speech and language development problems, a hypothesis involving executive working memory would be premature because executive working memory has hardly begun to develop.

3. The functioning level in some memory components may have already been evaluated during previous testing and found to be quite normal.

4. The functioning level in a memory component may already be a clear strength. For example, a child with superb spelling, vocabulary, and phonetic decoding skills is highly unlikely to possess a weakness in phonological short-term memory.

Multimethod Assessment of Working Memory

A test score alone should never be used to define an individual. Psychological tests and the scores they produce are fraught with inherent weaknesses, among them measurement error and limited construct validity. When cognitive abilities, such as working memory processes, are assessed, it is crucial that data collected through other methods are considered along with the test scores. Informal assessment methods include observations, interviews, rating scales, and records review. These informal procedures also have serious drawbacks, such as inconsistent application and being easily influenced by biases. Moreover, it is difficult to analyze, interpret, and draw suitable inferences from informally gathered data. Clearly, standardized testing is necessary during a memory assessment, despite the shortcomings of standardized batteries. Standardized measures are particularly necessary when a learning disability diagnosis is being considered or when the goal is to determine whether the examinee has strengths, weaknesses, or deficits in working memory. Furthermore, contemporary measures of working memory capacity do reliably predict real-world performance in academic learning and daily functioning (see Chapter 5). Thus, standardized testing is recommended whenever working memory weaknesses are hypothesized; however, informal procedures should always be conducted along with testing. Generally, the validity of assessment results improves as the number of data-collection methods increases. When different sources of data provide convergent evidence, evaluators can be more confident of test results. Diagnostic and programming decisions should never be based on one source of data alone. Best practices in assessment of working memory and related cognitive processes require multidimensional assessment.

Reviewing Records for History

Unless there has been an acquired brain injury, subnormal capacity in short-term and working memory has usually been present since birth. That is why gathering the individual's history is an important aspect of working memory assessment. Although much of the history can be obtained through interviews, reviewing available psychological and educational records can provide documentation of previous performance and ongoing problems. When reviewing educational records, one must often play detective in looking for clues indicative of ongoing problems because records seldom contain explicit comments about memory, especially working memory. When the records are anecdotal, the reviewer should look for reports of behaviors that are associated with working memory difficulties (see Table 6.6 for a listing of working memory related behaviors). For instance, a teacher's comment that a fourth-grade student is still using his or her fingers during arithmetic calculation is a sign of working memory deficiencies. When searching for evidence of ongoing memory and processing weaknesses, the reviewer should pay particular attention to the first report of the suspected weakness and how frequently and consistently it has been reported. Isolated reports should not be accepted as adequate documentation but rather as red flags that need to be investigated further. Some reported difficulties may be situation-specific behaviors that serve a function in a particular environment but are not actual memory or processing deficiencies. Moreover, deficits in basic processes, such as short-term and working memory, should be evident as soon as a child enters school. However, deficits in the higher level processes such as fluid reasoning and executive working memory may not become apparent until the later childhood years when the frontal lobes become fully developed.

In addition to educational records, a review of medical, neurological, and psychological reports is pertinent whenever there are concerns about memory and cognitive processing. When test records are available, it is important for the informed reviewer to reexamine, reanalyze, and reinterpret the test scores instead of relying on the analysis and interpretation found in the existing report(s). The primary reason for this is that previous examiners may have been uninterested or unaware of working memory measures embedded in the scales that were used. For example, a child may have obtained an extremely low Digit Span subtest score, but it was interpreted as a measure of distractibility, instead of short-term and working memory. To reanalyze previous test scores from a contemporary working memory perspective, practitioners should classify subtests according to the tables in Appendices A and E, use the *Working-Memory Clinical Analysis Worksheet* found in Appendix C, and follow the interpretative guidelines discussed later in this chapter and subsequent chapters.

Interviews

Teacher, parent, and student interviews are an essential component of any comprehensive psychoeducational assessment. Information garnered during preliminary interviews can be used to generate hypotheses that will guide remaining assessment and testing procedures. Subsequent interviewing allows more in-depth investigation of variables thought to underlie the referral concerns and the test results. Unfortunately, structured and semistructured interview formats seldom include items specifically related to working memory. Therefore, the interviewer must make a special effort to develop questions that allow assessment of possible working memory impairments. Information obtained from interviewing should never be used alone to confirm hypotheses or reach diagnostic decisions. Rather, interview data need to be corroborated by other assessment data before their accuracy is accepted.

Teacher Interviews

With teachers, the most efficient and focused strategy is to first clarify the academic learning concerns. Then, proceed with specific short-term and working memory items that are known to be highly related with the academic area of concern (see Table 6.3). For instance, when a third-grader is struggling significantly with mathematics learning and performance, ask about behaviors, such as finger counting, that are known to be associated with working memory weaknesses. Also, ask questions intended to identify which working memory components may be implicated. For example, when older elementary students are referred for math problems, a likely working memory hypothesis is that there is a deficit in executive working memory. After questioning the teacher about the student's ability to stay focused on relevant information, the interviewer might proceed with asking about a related cognitive process, such as fluid reasoning. In general, an effective interviewing technique is to begin with open-ended questions and progress to closed questions. When the

Table 6.3 Suggested Teacher Interview Items for Working Memory

1. What types of learning activities are most difficult for the student?
2. How well does the student remember information?
3. Does the student have difficulties memorizing information?
4. How well does the student retain information during multistep operations, such as when completing a complex arithmetic problem without paper and pencil?
5. How much repetition does the student require before learning new information?
6. How often does the student ask you to repeat directions?
7. Does the student have any difficulties with listening comprehension?
8. How well does the student stay focused on the task at hand?
9. How well can the student do two things simultaneously, such as listen and take notes?
10. Is the student slow to recall information that he or she knows?
11. Does the student have difficulty expressing ideas orally or in writing?
12. Does the student seem to be stronger in either visual or auditory learning?
13. What memory strategies, if any, have you observed the student using?
14. To what do you attribute the student's learning problems?
15. What signs have you observed that indicate the student might have problems with short-term memory?

interviewee seems unfamiliar with the behavior in question, the interviewer should provide examples.

Near the end of the initial interview, it is important to elicit the teacher's hypotheses regarding the student's learning problems. The expression of these hypotheses may illuminate other cognitive difficulties that could account for the concerns. For example, it may be the teacher's hypothesis that the student is struggling because of long-term retrieval problems. One way to encourage the expression of processing hypotheses is to ask the teacher *why* she or he thinks the student is experiencing each specific learning problem. When teachers seem uncertain about possible memory and processing hypotheses, the interviewer may need to provide more structure by asking questions, such as "Do you think the student is having difficulty with math because he can't memorize the facts?"

Parent Interviews

Whether the evaluation is conducted in a school or a clinic, parents can be a valuable source of information regarding a student's working memory functioning. Because many parents of struggling students attempt to support their child's learning, parents are often more aware of the child's learning and memory processes than might be expected. Consequently, many of the interview items suggested for teachers in Table 6.3 can easily be adapted for parent interviews. To make the interview more relevant, the interviewer should also create items that are specific to the child's functioning in the home environment. In particular, the interviewer should ask how often the child forgets to complete daily activities. Also, the interviewer might ask how well the child remembers to complete all the steps in a multistep task. Similar to teacher interviews, parents should also be asked questions about strategy use and their hypotheses regarding the child's learning difficulties. A unique feature of parent interviews are questions about early development; in particular, interview items about early speech and language development are especially relevant to working memory. This author remembers a case where a parent volunteered that she knew her child had a memory problem when the child could not remember nursery rhymes after repeated readings. Finally, interviewers should be prepared to offer some consultation, even during the initial interview. After questioning parents about their child's memory functioning, it is often appropriate to explain to them how working memory functions relate to academic learning.

Student Interviews

Although students vary widely in their ability to self-appraise, student interviews can also be a valuable source of assessment data. Certainly, students who are middle school age or older should be directly questioned about behaviors related to working memory, and age-appropriate interview items also should be attempted with elementary students. Given the lack of structured interviews that include any items related to memory, it will be necessary for the interviewer to construct items. Of course, the

Table 6.4 Suggested Student Interview Items for Working Memory

1. Do you ever forget to do something? Can you give me an example? How often does this happen?
2. Do you sometimes forget what the teacher just talked about?
3. Do you sometimes ask the teacher to repeat directions?
4. Do you sometimes raise your hand in class and then forget what you were going to say?
5. When you study something, do you have difficulty remembering it the next day?
6. Do you plan things but then forget to do them?
7. When you are writing, do you leave out letters or words without knowing that you did?
8. Is it hard for you to listen and take notes at the same time?
9. Do you have difficulty memorizing facts?
10. Do you sometimes lose your place when reading?
11. Is it hard for you to do arithmetic in your head?
12. What do you do when you want to remember information that is difficult to remember?

main challenge with student interviews is using age-appropriate terminology and limiting the items to behaviors of which the student is aware. Questions that ask the student to make inferences about his or her memory are usually inappropriate. It is important to include items related to strategy use, especially when working memory interventions are under consideration. See Table 6.4 for some suggested student interview items.

Observations

Observation of behavior is a fundamental assessment method that should be included in every comprehensive assessment of working memory. To increase the validity of observations regarding working memory, the observer needs to become familiar with the intricacies of working memory and the behaviors that are indicative of limitations or dysfunctions. Knowledge of the relationships between academic functioning and working-memory processes (see Chapter 5) will also be particularly beneficial when conducting observations. In addition to an in-depth understanding of working memory functioning and associated behaviors, the observer should analyze the processing demands of the task the examinee is engaged in (Hale & Fiorello, 2004). Even an observer with expertise in working memory needs to be cautious about making inferences from observed behaviors, mainly due to the lack of one-to-one correspondence between behaviors and processes. That is, any one of several cognitive processes may underlie a specific observable behavior; for example, observers should not assume that failure to follow directions can be attributed to a working-memory shortcoming. Nevertheless, observations serve an indispensable purpose; they provide data that can be used to corroborate the results of testing.

Observation During Testing

Unstructured observations during the administration of standardized tests can provide valuable clinical information about the examinee's working memory strengths and weaknesses. Insights into an examinee's working memory functioning can be gained from observations during any type of testing, not just during working memory subtests. Familiarity with observable indicators of working memory processes will increase the examiner's awareness of behaviors that are noteworthy. Many of the behaviors suggested for classroom observation (see Table 6.6) should also be observable during testing. Because much of cognitive and achievement testing requires complex processing, there should be ample opportunities to observe how the examinee behaves when heavy demands are made of working memory. See Table 6.5 for testing behaviors that are indicative of an overloaded working memory.

When observing during testing, it is important to note when the behaviors occurred; do not just make general observations after all of the testing is finished. A convenient method of tracking behaviors is to record the observation alongside the item or subtest associated with it. After completing the administration, review the recorded observations and consider the demands of the task at the time each one occurred. Task analysis can provide insights into which working memory components, processes, or strategies may be deficient. Keep in mind that observations gathered during testing are informal data that should be considered, along with other data, when weighing the evidence regarding possible working memory weaknesses.

Table 6.5 Testing Behaviors Related to Working Memory

—Asking for directions to be repeated.
—Requesting supplemental materials, such as paper when the task is mental arithmetic.
—Inability to work quickly.
—Increasing frustration as the complexity of the task increases.
—Difficulty elaborating upon a response when requested to do so.
—Difficulty retrieving simple information on demand.
—Difficulty staying focused on the task at hand.
Also, observe for these indications of strategy use:
—Whispering or lip movements (subvocal rehearsal).
—Grouping or clustering information (chunking).
—Thinking aloud.

Classroom Observations

Much can be learned about a referred student's working memory characteristics through careful observation of the student in the classroom. At the very least, observations can lead to hypotheses that can be tested through later formal assessment. It is most productive to observe the referred pupil when she or he is engaged in academic areas that are challenging, because the student is less likely to display working memory related behaviors during simple, routine activities. Until the observer becomes versed in grade-appropriate working memory expectations, it is helpful to compare the subject's behavior with that of one or more random peers. For example, when a second-grader uses finger counting to complete arithmetic calculation, observe peers for the same behavior and compare frequency of occurrence. Similar to observing for other learning and behavior concerns, not much weight should be awarded to isolated behaviors. Behaviors that are indicative of underlying working memory problems should be reoccurring and similar behaviors should also be evident. For example, finger counting alone may be insufficient evidence. A stronger case for a working memory problem can be made if the learner is also having difficulties with learning math facts, retrieving known math facts, remembering partial solutions, and confusing known math facts.

The behaviors suggested in Table 6.6 are derived from observations reported in the research literature on working memory deficits and learning disabilities. The reader is encouraged to use the items in Table 6.6 with the caveat that these items have not been piloted or used in research. Therefore, these items should be used cautiously and it should be assumed that the items lack reliability and validity. For instance, many of the behaviors are also characteristic of other cognitive deficits. The suggested observations are intended for informal, clinical use only. They should mainly be used to generate hypotheses for further investigation. The information gathered during observations using these items can be used as collateral evidence for diagnostic and intervention decisions; however, the items should be given no more weight than any other informal data.

Cross-Battery and Selective Testing

Hypothesis-driven assessment frequently leads to cross-battery and selective testing. Even when a practitioner has access to a comprehensive memory scale, there are times when additional subtests should be drawn from other scales. For instance, when the primary scale measures phonological short-term memory with digits only, the practitioner may decide to replace the digits subtest with one that uses words. However, the more likely scenario for cross-battery testing is when the examiner is required to or decides to first administer a comprehensive cognitive battery. Within that cognitive battery are subtests that measure some but not all aspects of short-term and working

Table 6.6   Suggested Items for Classroom Observation of Working Memory

General Working Memory
—Classroom performance is poorer than would be predicted from standardized achievement test scores.
—Has difficulty staying focused during cognitively demanding activities but attends well when cognitive demands are minimal.
—Prefers to simplify tasks whenever possible.
—Fails to complete complex activities.
—Has difficulty keeping track of place during challenging activities.
—Has difficulty retrieving information when engaged in another processing task.
—Has difficulty associating current situation with past experience.
—Has difficulty integrating new information with prior knowledge.
—Rarely contributes to class discussions.
—Make comments such as, "I forget everything."
—Has difficulty organizing information during written expression.
—Has difficulty retaining partial solutions during mental arithmetic.
—Has difficulty memorizing and retaining facts.
—Is very slow at arithmetic computation.
—Is slow to retrieve known facts.
—Confuses known facts.

Phonological Short-Term Memory
—Has difficulty remembering multistep oral directions.
—Has difficulty restating instructions.
—Has more difficulty remembering digits than words (indicative of mathematics disability).
—Makes many counting errors.
—Has difficulty blending phonemes into words when reading.
—Has difficulty with phonetic decoding of text.
—Has difficulty with phonetic recoding (spelling).
—Has difficulty learning new vocabulary.
—Has difficulty producing multiword utterances.

Visuospatial Working Memory
—Does not notice the signs (e.g., "+") during arithmetic calculation.
—Has episodic memory lapses for the relatively recent past.
—Loses place when reading.

Verbal Working Memory
—Requires frequent reminders.
—When called on, forgets what was planning to say.
—Forgets the content of instruction.
—Has difficulty paraphrasing spoken information.
—Has difficulty comprehending syntactically complex sentences.

(Continued)

Table 6.6 (Continued)

—Has difficulty taking meaningful notes.

—In third grade and above, continues to finger count during arithmetic calculation.

—Rereads text when there has not been a decoding problem.

—Has difficulty remembering the first part of the sentence or paragraph when reading.

—Has difficulty detecting targets in spoken or written language, such as identifying the rhyming words in a paragraph.

—Produces only short sentences during written expression.

—Has frequent subject-verb agreement errors in written expression.

—Omits some of the content when writing a sentence.

—Repeats words when writing a sentence.

Executive Working Memory

—Answers to oral comprehension questions are off-topic or irrelevant (has difficulty inhibiting irrelevant information).

—Has difficulty switching between operations (e.g., from addition to subtraction problems).

—Has difficulty taking notes and listening at the same time.

—Inaccurately estimates memory performance before, during, or after a task.

—Does not use learning strategies or does not use them on a consistent basis.

—Prefers to use simple instead of complex learning strategies.

—Does not use the most basic strategies, such as subvocal rehearsal.

—Selects inefficient strategies during problem solving.

memory. To complete the assessment of working memory, the evaluator need only select subtests that tap the working memory components that remain untested. Informal cross-battery assessment is not new; many practitioners have mixed tests and batteries when conducting psychoeducational or neuropsychological evaluations. However, a systematic method of cross-battery cognitive assessment has only recently been advocated by Flanagan and Ortiz (2001, 2007). The approach to analyzing working memory test scores recommended in this text (see Appendix C) is an adaptation of the cross-battery model proposed by Flanagan and Ortiz (2001, 2007).

The cross-battery method involves administering a compilation of subtests from different batteries in order to systematically measure all of the areas selected for assessment. It can actually be time saving and efficient even though more than one scale is utilized. From the cross-battery perspective, evaluators should not administer an entire battery just because it contains some desired subtests. Rather, they should administer only those subtests that measure the memory components and cognitive processes selected during assessment planning. Redundant testing should be avoided; there is no need to test the same process twice. For example, if the entire WISC-IV has been administered and then is supplemented with another scale, there is no need to measure executive working memory again as it has already been adequately sampled (see Appendix A). Administering only selected factors and subtests is acceptable, unless a test's authors specifically state that the entire scale or a certain subset must be administered for the results to be valid. A battery's subtests each have their own scaled score that can be used independently to determine an individual's functioning in the primary process measured by that subtest. Nevertheless, cross-battery testing does not give practitioners permission to abandon testing standards. Also, the number of batteries involved should be restricted to three at the most. Restricting the amount of battery crossing serves to maintain the reliability and validity of the resulting scores, as well as keeping the interpretation manageable. Furthermore, there should be a psychometric or empirical basis to the selection of subtests. Appendices A and E are intended to provide guidance for subtest selection.

Cross-Battery Assessment Concerns

Although the cross-battery method is well suited for assessment of memory components and processes, a cautious interpretation of cross-battery results is necessary because of the inherent weaknesses of the method. The lack of cross-battery norms is the main concern. There are no norms for any of the numerous cross-battery "scales" that can be created. The composite, factor, and subtest scores obtained from different batteries are based on standardization samples, distributions, and norms unique to each test. Caution is particularly urged when a specific memory subprocess, such as phonological short-term memory, is assessed with subtests from more than one scale. This source of error can be reduced somewhat by using tests that were normed about the same time. When conducting an intraindividual, or *ipsative*, analysis, subtest and "clinical" factor scores representing memory components are usually compared to a cross-battery mean computed by averaging the scores of the subtests involved. This cross-battery mean has no norms and there are no statistical tables for determining significant discrepancies between it and individual factor or subtest scores. Flanagan and Ortiz (2001) recommend using a one standard deviation discrepancy as the criterion for significance, but the number of points necessary for a statistically significant difference will vary. Despite these concerns, a structured, systematic procedure to cross-battery assessment and interpretation is preferable to a completely clinical approach. For a further discussion of strengths and weaknesses of cross-battery assessment and interpretation see Flanagan and Ortiz (2001, 2007).

Selective Testing

Selective testing is associated with cross-battery assessment, as well as with the hypothesis-testing approach to assessment. The principle behind selective testing is that evaluators should select and administer only those subtests that measure what needs to be assessed. When the primary battery does not supply all of the necessary measures, portions of other batteries should be included in the assessment. Informed judgment is necessary when selecting subtests that measure specific memory components and processes. The names assigned to memory factors and subtests can be misleading. Before making a decision, examiners should examine the task and consider how it compares to the usual working memory paradigms described at the beginning of this chapter. If the task changes during the subtest, it is likely that more than one working memory component is being measured. Further guidance in subtest selection is provided in Appendices A and E.

Testing Related Processes

Cross-battery selective testing for short-term and working memory concerns should also include assessment of related cognitive processes. Some examinees who appear to be struggling because of working memory deficiencies may actually have impairments in related processes, instead of working memory itself. Processes that influence performance on working memory tasks include attention, phonological processing, processing speed, long-term retrieval, long-term storage, general executive processing, fluid reasoning, visual processing, and auditory processing (see Chapter 4 for details). The selection of cognitive processes for testing should be based on the generation and selection of hypotheses. Testing of related cognitive processes can also be conducted on a selective and cross-battery basis. For a breakdown of processing subtests by cognitive scale, see Appendix G and see Dehn (2006) for additional details.

Assessment Recommendations for Specific Disabilities

Reading Disabilities

When referral concerns include the possibility of a reading disability, the primary memory components to assess are phonological short-term memory, verbal working memory, and rapid automatic naming. In children older than 6 years of age, executive working memory should also be examined. When executive working memory is included it is advisable to use subtests that allow the discrimination of verbal working memory from executive working memory. For example, memory for sentences could be contrasted with a last word task (see Appendix A). Using reading span tests to assess verbal working memory can confound results, even in older children; listening span is preferable. The testing of related cognitive processes should include phonological processing. For children who are able to decode words, a test of reading fluency is essential, as it reveals the level of automaticity and has implications for reading comprehension.

Mathematics Disabilities

When testing for the possibility of a mathematics disability, practitioners should include the administration of short-term and working memory subtests that do not include numbers. As research has documented (Andersson & Lyxell, 2007), students with mathematics learning difficulties often have a storage-specific deficit for numerical information. Although children with mathematics disabilities may possess normal overall storage capacity in phonological short-term memory and verbal working memory, they typically have shorter spans for numbers. Their phonological and verbal spans that do not involve numbers may be normal. Also, those with mathematics disorders are known to have difficulty quickly retrieving arithmetic facts. To determine if their long-term retrieval difficulty is specific to numerical information, examiners might administer a rapid automatic naming task that does not involve numbers. Finally, the visuospatial short-term and visuospatial working memory components should be assessed, especially in younger children, when mathematics performance and visuospatial abilities are closely related.

Written Language Disabilities

First and foremost, executive working memory should be scrutinized with two or more subtests. Phonological short-term memory and verbal working memory should also be assessed, regardless of age. When there are written expression problems, several related cognitive processes should be tested, including: general executive functions, planning, and processing speed. Furthermore, an assessment of oral language development should be considered if not previously conducted.

ADHD

For children with ADHD or suspected ADHD, executive working memory should be examined in depth. Subtests that introduce interference or require dual processing are particularly relevant but they should be contrasted with executive working memory subtests that involve simple transformation (e.g. digits backward). Contrasting executive working memory with verbal working memory subtests that do not introduce interference is also helpful. The idea is to factor out the influence of attentional control in an effort to determine if poor working memory performance is a result of attentional problems or if there is also a deficiency in working memory itself.

General Guidelines for Interpreting Test Scores

Interpretation of working memory test results presents some unique challenges. These challenges arise whenever there is cross-battery testing, computation of clinical factor scores, realignment of subtests, and intrasubtest analysis. Realignment of subtests occurs when subtests are used to measure a different memory component than the test's author(s) intended. These unique procedures require more reliance on clinical judgment than is usually encouraged by experts in psychometrics. Concerns about clinical judgment are justified. Open-ended clinical interpretation is analogous to implementing interventions that are not research based. On the other hand, actuarial-based, statistical analysis also has its limitations. Ultimately, the meaning of test scores, discrepancies, and other statistical findings must be determined by the clinician (examiner). Thus, clinical judgment needs to be balanced with the actuarial-based, statistical procedures recommended by experts in psychometrics. In addition to informal analysis of test scores, clinical interpretation includes an examination of all the data, including: history, observations of the examinee, information gathered through interviews, and data collected through other informal methods.

There are several factors that enhance the quality and meaningfulness of interpretation. First and foremost, interpretation should be theory based. Regarding working memory, the practitioner has several theories to choose from, including: a general information processing theory, Baddeley's theory, Cowan's theory, or the integrated theory suggested in this text. A practitioner might even develop his or her own theory that combines elements of various research-supported theories. The benefits of theory-based interpretation are consistency across cases, a structure for integrating information, research-based support, and terminology other professionals understand. Interpretation is also facilitated when data result from planned and organized testing that addresses all of the referral concerns. The hypothesis approach to planning an assessment discussed earlier in this chapter provides a structure for interpretation. After testing is complete, the data regarding each hypothesis are considered and conclusions are drawn.

Meaningful and beneficial interpretation is focused on the individual, not the test scores. Because the goal of assessment is to better understand the individual and why that individual is experiencing problems, simply reporting scores, reviewing data, and documenting symptoms is insufficient. The meaning of assessment data will vary, depending on the individual being evaluated. Identical test scores do not have the same meaning and implications across individuals. Test scores take on meaning that is dependent on the characteristics of the examinee. For example, an average working memory score of 91 might be an individual strength for one person but an individual weakness for another. The implications of a specific memory component score depend on how that score relates to the rest of the individual's memory and cognitive profiles.

Profile Analysis

The traditional interpretative approach of analyzing subtest scores and identifying patterns of strengths and weaknesses within the individual is known as *profile analysis*. Profile analysis is conducted by computing the mean of the subtest scores involved, and then using the mean to determine which subtest scores are significantly discrepant. Generally, the .05 or .01 level of significance is used. When statistical tables are unavailable for making this determination, a one standard deviation discrepancy is usually considered significant. Subtests with significantly lower scores are interpreted as intraindividual weaknesses, whereas significantly higher subtests are individual strengths. Thus, profile analysis is an intraindividual analysis.

There is a longstanding controversy surrounding subtest profile analysis. Critics (Glutting, McDermott, & Konold, 1997) contend that profile analysis is unreliable and that the resulting profiles have no diagnostic validity. Their criticism stems mainly from the low reliability of subtests and the fact that each subtest measures more than one ability. Nevertheless, valuable information about the examinee's memory strengths and weaknesses and how these relate to overall cognitive processing will be lost if a profile analysis is not conducted. Short-term and working memory components and processes are mostly measured by subtests; there are very few factor or composite scores that are truly representative of these memory constituents. Therefore, complete analysis of separate memory elements depends on profile analysis. With profile analysis, clinicians can better understand the interactive functioning of the examinee's memory systems.

Despite the criticism of subtest profile analysis, the practice is defensible. First, the reliability and specificity of many subtests have increased as batteries have been revised. More importantly, empirical investigations and factor-analytic studies have identified the specific subprocesses measured by subtests. Similarly, brain research has documented the separate memory components that the subtests purport to measure. Moreover, profile analysis can be justified when the interpretation is grounded in theory and when the test results are corroborated by other data. When theory and research support the conclusions drawn from profile analysis, those interpretations have increased validity. Finally, profile analysis is more credible when it is conducted hand-in-hand with a normative analysis that compares the individual's performance to the distribution of test scores for his or her age group.

Weakness versus Deficit

Depending on how *weakness* is defined, nearly everyone can lay claim to at least one weakness in a cognitive process or memory component. In psychological test interpretation, it is important to adhere to the usual ground rules so that the term is not used loosely. When examining an individual's test scores there are two types of weakness: normative and ipsative. Any test score that falls below the average range (below a standard score of 90 when the mean of the distribution is 100 and the standard deviation is 15) represents a *normative weakness*. An *ipsative weakness* occurs when a subtest or factor score is significantly lower than the individual's mean for the broad domain, with a discrepancy of approximately one standard deviation an acceptable criterion for statistical significance. For example, when an individual's verbal working memory score is an 84 and the FSIQ is 99, the discrepancy is considered a significant ipsative, or intraindividual, weakness. In this text, the term *deficit* refers to a score that is both a normative *and* an ipsative weakness. Defined as such, a deficit is rare and it is indicative of an impairment because it represents poor performance relative to peers, as well as in comparison to the individual's overall abilities. When an examinee has a deficit in one or more short-term or working memory components, the deficit is most likely causing significant problems in learning or daily functioning. Although a deficit is clearly cause for concern, an ipsative or normative weakness alone may also severely interfere with the acquisition of academic skills or some aspects of daily life. Thus, all ipsative and normative weaknesses should be examined closely, with pertinent informal assessment data taken into account. Although a normative weakness may account for the difficulty an individual is experiencing, practitioners tend to ignore a specific normative weakness when all other cognitive scores are also subnormal. In such instances, it makes sense not to single out one score as worthy of attention; on the other hand, practitioners should not deny that performance associated with that ability is going to be difficult. The same guidelines can be applied to strengths. When a strength is both normative and ipsative, it is referred to as an *asset*.

Unitary versus Nonunitary Factors

When two or more subtests are aggregated and represented by one score, that score is referred to as a *factor* score. Depending on the extent of testing or the battery used, functioning of some memory components will be represented by factor scores. In such instances, it is important to examine whether the performance on the subtests comprising that factor is consistent. Inconsistent performance will produce divergent scores. When the difference between the highest and lowest subtest scores within a factor is extreme, the factor is said to be *nonunitary*. The criterion for this determination is an approximate discrepancy of 1.5 standard deviations. Accordingly, when the standard score (from a distribution with a mean of 100 and a standard deviation of 15) difference between two subtests is more than 22 points, the factor should be considered nonunitary. When a factor is nonunitary, the factor score may not represent a unitary ability. Nonunitary factors most likely occur because the underlying subprocesses measured by the subtests are not equivalent for that individual. When a factor is nonunitary, it is not appropriate to interpret the factor score as truly representing the component or process it is suppose to represent.

Nonunitary factors and the subtests they comprise should still be included in the computation of a mean cognitive processing or mean memory score. However, they should not be used in pairwise comparisons. Nonunitary factors should be interpreted, especially when they represent a weakness or a deficit, but the interpretation should be cautious. When a nonunitary factor occurs, the clinician should examine the subtests involved and generate hypotheses that account for the discrepancy, taking testing behaviors and other evaluation data into account. For instance, an examinee may perform poorly on one short-term memory subtest but not the other. Examining the content of the two subtests and the narrow abilities that they measure may reveal an explanation. For example, the low-score subtest might have involved the repetition of numbers while the other involved the repetition of words. One hypothesis might be that the examinee lacks number facility. Such hypotheses should be investigated through further testing and assessment. Another approach to dealing with nonunitary factors is to administer an additional subtest that taps another narrow ability within the broad factor. This approach will provide a broader sampling of the memory factor.

Base Rates

Base rate is another standardized test statistic usually considered when conducting profile analysis and interpreting test scores. Test manuals that provide critical values for significance testing also provide base rate tables that report the frequency of intraindividual differences in the standardization sample. The idea of using base rate information is to determine just how infrequent or rare a given discrepancy is. For example, a difference of 12 points between working memory and the mean processing score might be statistically significant but yet occur in approximately 25% of the population. Given that this discrepancy is not that uncommon, the practical significance of the finding is questionable. Many test authors and experts in psychometrics recommend interpreting significant ipsative strengths and weaknesses only when the base rate is lower than 15%. However, strictly following such an actuarial rule and not using clinical judgment may result in not identifying a weakness that is actually causing impairment. Just because a given ipsative weakness occurs in 15% or more of the population does not mean that it is not causing a serious memory problem for the individual. A relatively common significant weakness may still be an impairment for some individuals. Especially in cases where an actual *deficit* has been identified, base rates should be ignored. This is because *all* deficits can be considered unusual and infrequent (Naglieri, 1999). When cross-battery analysis is conducted, base rates for ipsative discrepancies are generally unavailable. Under such circumstances, clinicians should carefully consider all potential weaknesses that meet the criterion of one standard deviation below the mean or composite score used to represent the mean. When other assessment data support the existence of a weakness that is impairing functioning, the weakness should be regarded as being important and having practical significance. In general, each profile should be carefully examined and all assessment data taken into account. Rules regarding base rates should not take precedence.

Hypothesis Testing

After profile analysis is complete, the evaluator should weigh all of the evidence for and against each of the a priori hypotheses pertaining to memory components and related processes. The evidence consists of test scores and relevant data collected through other methods. The *Working-Memory Interpretative Summary* found in Appendix D is offered as a structure for summarizing the data and reaching a conclusion about each hypothesis. Even when the data clearly support a hypothesis, oral and written conclusions and generalizations should be stated cautiously. In many cases, the data will be inconclusive and the evaluator will not be able to reach a decision about the hypothesis. In instances where results are inconclusive or unexpected and answers are still sought, the evaluator should generate a posteriori hypotheses and investigate these through further assessment. As discussed earlier in this chapter, the clinician should be on guard against hypothesis confirmation bias.

Processing Strengths

If only suspected areas of weakness are tested, a profile analysis is unlikely to reveal any strengths or weaknesses because the individual's mean score is based mainly on weaknesses. Because assessments originate with referral concerns, areas of potential strengths and assets are often not tested, especially when the assessment is based on hypotheses that account for the referral concerns. Fortunately, not all hypothesized weaknesses turn out to be such; many memory components hypothesized to be deficient are discovered to be individual strengths in the normal range of functioning. Such findings restore some balance to the profile analysis mean. Another option of comparing memory component scores to a more valid estimate of overall cognitive ability is to use a FSIQ or similar composite score (see the next section). When interpreting test results, clinicians should emphasize strengths and assets as much as weaknesses and deficits because incorporating strengths into interventions may increase the probability of success.

Analysis of Working Memory Test Scores

The goal of conducting a profile analysis of an individual's working memory test scores is to gain a better understanding of the individual's memory strengths and weaknesses. Determination of strengths and weaknesses should take statistical guidelines into account but should not be bound by those guidelines. Scores and discrepancies between scores only provide indications of levels of functioning and the relative degree of strengths or weaknesses. Deciding that an individual has a deficit that is impairing functioning must ultimately be based on clinical judgment. To rule out the possibility of a deficit because the discrepancy pointing toward a deficit is barely significant or has a relatively high base rate in the population is poor clinical judgment. All relevant assessment data and information should be taken into account before such decisions are made because the same set of scores and the same degrees of discrepancy mean different things for different individuals. Consequently, the profile analysis procedure suggested in this section combines an actuarial and a clinical approach, with clinical judgment taking precedence.

The *Working Memory Analysis Worksheet* found in Appendix C provides consistent structure and guidelines for analyzing nearly every set of test scores. When a cross-battery assessment has been completed, the worksheet is ideal for combining scores into one comprehensive analysis, as opposed to a test-by-test analysis that leaves the evaluator and the clients wondering what it all means. The versatile analysis worksheet is also ideal for analyzing scores resulting from only one battery. Because the memory subtests and factors of many batteries do not align well with theoretical models, there is often a need to restructure the subtests and compute clinical factor scores. The primary purpose of the worksheet is to identify and compare the six main memory components of the Integrated Model of Working Memory, but additional related processes, such as processing speed, can also be incorporated. The procedures for completing the *Working Memory Analysis Worksheet* are described in the following, using Joey's completed worksheet in Table 6.7 as an example (an abbreviated set of instructions is also found on the blank worksheet in Appendix C).

1. *In the lower cells of the first column, include any related cognitive processes that were tested.* The six components of the Integrated Model of Working Memory are preprinted in the first column but the worksheet can still be used if one or more of the memory components is not tested. In the case of Joey, a priori hypotheses led to the inclusion of phonemic awareness, fluid reasoning, and processing speed (see Table 6.7).

2. *Write the name of the test battery in the second column.* This is the name of the scale or battery from which the subtests measuring that component are drawn. In instances where subtests from different batteries are used to measure the same component, put both batteries and related information in the same row. For an example of this, see the analysis of scores in Table 8.2.

3. *In the third column write the name(s) of the subtest(s) used to measure that memory component or process.* Classification of the subtests is found in Appendices A and E and in subsequent chapters. In instances where a factor score can be used as is, enter the battery's name for the factor.

4. *For each subtest or factor, calculate standard scores and enter these in the fourth column.* Scaled and standard scores found in the test's manual should be used. However, all subtest scores with a mean of 10 and standard deviation of 3 will first need to be transformed to scores that have a mean of 100 and a standard deviation of 15. Use the table in Appendix F to transform the subtest scores.

5. *Compute the mean of the subtest scores for each memory component and cognitive process and enter it in the fifth column.* For components that are assessed with only one subtest, simply carry over that subtest score from the fourth column. When two or more subtests are used, compute the mean, rounding to the nearest whole number. The mean of the subtests can be considered a *clinical factor* score that represents the broad functioning of that component or process. The computation of clinical factors is necessary whenever subtests from two different batteries are used to measure the same memory component or when subtests from the same scales are aligned differently than that test's structure. For example, the WJ III COG has a Long-Term Retrieval cluster but a clinical long-term retrieval cluster has been computed for Joey because Rapid Picture Naming is not one of the subtests that comprise the WJ III's Long-Term Retrieval factor. In Joey's case, the two subtests used to

Table 6.7 Working Memory Analysis Worksheet–Completed Example

Examinee's Name: Case Study of "Joey" DOB: ——   Age: 9 Grade: 4 Dates of Testing: ——

Memory Component	Battery Name	Subtest/ Factor Name	Subtest Score	Component Mean	Composite or Mean	Difference	Normative S or W	Ipsative S or W	Deficit or Asset
Phonological STM	WJ III COG	Memory for Words	106	106	WJ III GIA–106	0	Avg.	—	—
Visuospatial STM	WISC-IV Integrated	Spatial Span Forward	85	85	106	−21	W	W	Deficit
Verbal WM	WJ III COG	Auditory Working Memory	101	101	106	−5	Avg.	—	—
Visuospatial WM	WISC-IV Integrated	Spatial Span Backward	95	95	106	−11	Avg.	—	—
Executive WM	WJ III COG	Numbers Reversed Auditory Working Memory	77 101	89	106	−17	W	W	Deficit
Long-Term Retrieval	WJ III COG	Rapid Picture Naming Retrieval Fluency	95 87	91	106	−15	Avg.	W	—
Phonemic Awareness	WJ III COG	Phonemic Awareness	128	128	106	+22	S	S	Asset
Fluid Reasoning	WJ III COG	Fluid Reasoning	95	95	106	−11	Avg.	—	—
Processing Speed	WJ III COG	Processing Speed	107	107	106	+1	Avg.	—	—

(Continued)

Table 6.7 Working Memory Analysis Worksheet–Completed Example (Continued)

Subtest or Clinical Factor Score	Subtest or Clinical Factor Score	Discrepancy	Significant: Y/N
Phonological STM (106)	Phonemic Awareness (128)	22	Y
Phonological STM (106)	Visuospatial STM (85)	21	Y
Verbal WM (104)	Executive WM (89)	15	Y
Executive WM (89)	Long-Term Retrieval (91)	2	N
Long-Term Retrieval (91)	Processing Speed (107)	16	Y

Directions: (1) Convert all subtest scores to standard scores with a mean of 100 and an SD of 15. (2) For each component, compute the mean of the subtest scores and round to the nearest whole number. (3) Enter a cognitive composite, such as a FSIQ, or compute the mean of all available memory components. (4) Subtract the composite or mean from each component mean and enter amount in Difference column. (5) Indicate whether the component mean is a normative weakness or strength (90–109 is average). (6) Using a criterion of 12 points, determine intraindividual strengths and weaknesses. (7) Determine deficits and assets. A deficit is both a normative and intraindividual weakness; an asset is both a normative and intraindividual strength. (8) Determine which factors are nonunitary. Factors are nonunitary when the two subtests involved are significantly different or when the range between the highest and lowest subtest scores exceeds 1.5 standard deviations. Nonunitary factors should be interpreted cautiously and should not be used in pairwise comparisons. (9) Compare logical pairs of components, using a 15-point difference as an indication of a significant discrepancy.

evaluate long-term retrieval average out at 91. Not just any subtests should be paired to produce clinical factors. It should be apparent that the tasks involved are measuring that memory component to a significant degree. The classification of subtests in this text is based on which research paradigms have consistently been used to measure specific memory components, and it is based on the functions of the components in the Integrated Model (see Chapter 31). Classifications of subtests from numerous batteries are found in Chapters 7 and 8, as well as in Appendices A and E. Clinical factor scores need to be interpreted more cautiously than the regular factor scores provided by batteries.

6. *Enter a cognitive composite or mean in the sixth column.* In general, this score should represent overall cognitive processing ability, overall memory functioning, or a combination of memory functioning and related cognitive processes. The first option is to use an IQ score or similar composite from an intellectual or cognitive scale. In Joey's case, the General Intellectual Ability (GIA) score is used. An IQ or cognitive composite is appropriate for memory profile analysis because of the high correlations between IQ and working memory. In the absence of an IQ or cognitive composite score, the next option is to compute an overall processing mean from the set of memory and other cognitive processes that are being analyzed on the Worksheet. To arrive at this mean, average the scores found in the "Component Mean" column, rounding to the nearest whole number. When assessment has been restricted to suspected areas of weakness or when all of the memory scores are low, the mean of the scores will also be low, resulting in fewer discrepancies. In such instances, it is better to use an IQ or other global cognitive score, even if that score was obtained during a previous evaluation. Another option is to use a global memory score obtained from a memory battery or compute a memory mean based only on memory component scores. Each cell in the sixth column will have the same value. When reporting results later on, the practitioner should always identify the source of the value entered in this column so that colleagues and clients know what the memory components were compared with.

7. *Calculate and enter difference scores in the "Difference" column.* Subtract the composite or mean from each component score and enter the difference with a + or −. For example, Joey's composite of 106 was subtracted from his visuospatial short-term memory score of 85, resulting in a difference score of −21.

8. *Determine normative strengths and weaknesses.* In the "Normative S or W" column, enter an *S* (strength) for component means that are above 109. Enter a *W* (weakness) for component means that are below 90. For scores in the average range (90 to 109), simply put an *A* for average. For the sake of consistency, classify all scores on this basis, even scores from tests that describe the average range as 85–115.

9. *Determine intraindividual strengths and weaknesses and enter an S or W in the appropriate cells of the "Ipsative S or W" column.* Enter a *W* for weakness when the memory component mean is 12 or more points lower than the individual's cognitive composite or mean, and enter an *S* for strength when the memory component mean is 12 or more points higher than the individual's cognitive composite or mean. For example, Joey has an ipsative weakness in executive working memory because he has a negative discrepancy of 17 points. Whenever clinical factors have been computed or only part of a test has been administered, tables for determining significance and base rates are unavailable. In these instances, a discrepancy of 12 points or more (see the "Difference" column) is indicative of a significant difference. In a cross-battery analysis with clinical factor scores and a cognitive composite drawn from another scale, it is highly unlikely that a 12-point discrepancy is actually statistically significant at the .05 level. A 15-point discrepancy, roughly a difference of one standard deviation or more, is more likely to achieve a satisfactory level of significance. However, very few relative strengths or weaknesses will be identified if a criterion of 15 points is applied. Working memory weaknesses and deficits that are actually causing impairments in the individual may be missed if a 15-point discrepancy is required. When 12 points is used as the cutoff, it is very important that other assessment data corroborate the existence of the specific intraindividual weakness.

10. *Determine processing deficits and assets and enter in the last column.* Enter "Deficit" for components that have both a normative and ipsative weakness. Enter "Asset" for components that have both a normative and ipsative strength.

11. *Determine whether each component is unitary.* Using standard scores that have a mean of 100 and a standard deviation of 15, compare the lowest and highest subtest scores within each component or cognitive process. When the difference is greater than 22 points (greater than 1.5 standard deviations), consider the factor to be nonunitary. Nonunitary factors should be included in the profile analysis, but they should be interpreted cautiously. Practitioners should generate hypotheses to account for the disparity within the nonunitary memory component. Additional testing will often clarify the reasons for the discrepancy. Nonunitary factors should not be included in pairwise comparisons.

12. *Conduct pairwise comparisons in the lower portion of the worksheet.* Compare the scores of logically related components and processes, such as phonological short-term memory versus visuospatial short-term memory or phonological short-term memory versus phonological processing (see Tables 6.8 and 6.9). For example, Joey has a significant 16-point discrepancy between his Long-Term Retrieval score of 91 and his Processing Speed score of 107. When both components are represented by single subtest scores from the same

Table 6.8   Pairwise Comparisons of Short-Term and Working-Memory Components

—Phonological short-term memory versus visuospatial short-term memory
—Phonological short-term memory versus verbal working memory
—Phonological short-term memory versus visuospatial working memory
—Phonological short-term memory versus executive working memory
—Phonological short-term memory versus long-term retrieval
—Visuospatial short-term memory versus verbal working memory
—Visuospatial short-term memory versus visuospatial working memory
—Visuospatial short-term memory versus executive working memory
—Visuospatial short-term memory versus long-term retrieval
—Verbal working memory versus visuospatial working memory
—Verbal working memory versus executive working memory
—Verbal working memory versus long-term retrieval
—Visuospatial working memory versus executive working memory
—Visuospatial working memory versus long-term retrieval
—Executive working memory versus long-term retrieval

Table 6.9   Suggested Pairwise Comparisons of Memory Components and Related Processing Scores

—Executive working memory versus attention
—Executive working memory versus executive processing
—Executive working memory versus fluid reasoning
—Executive working memory versus general intelligence
—Executive working memory versus processing speed
—Executive working memory versus rapid automatic naming
—Executive working memory versus retrieval fluency
—Verbal working memory versus verbal ability
—Visuospatial working memory versus visual processing
—Phonological short-term memory versus auditory processing
—Phonological short-term memory versus phonological processing
—Phonological short-term memory versus processing speed
—Phonological short-term memory versus successive processing
—Long-term retrieval versus verbal ability

battery, check the battery's manual for statistical tables for determining pairwise discrepancies. When such tables are unavailable or when clinical factors have been calculated, use a 15-point discrepancy as indicative of significance and infrequency. (With pairs, a higher critical value is necessary than when comparing scores to a mean.) Discrepancies of 20 points or greater are very likely to be significant. Discrepancies in the 15- to 19-point range need more support from other evaluation data before they are interpreted.

Interpretation of Working Memory Assessment Results

The meaning of test scores and other data is more easily discerned when the practitioner has expertise in the domains assessed. Most professionals who are assessing working memory have extensive experience and strong background knowledge in cognitive development, learning disabilities, standardized testing, and related domains. Nonetheless, they are encouraged to pursue more reading on current research in working memory. Expertise is also acquired through experience. Once practitioners begin to test working memory on a regular basis, they will begin to recognize common cognitive profiles associated with working memory difficulties and associated learning challenges. The remainder of this chapter offers suggestions intended to facilitate interpretation of working memory weaknesses and deficits. (See Chapter 10 for advice on how to present results orally and how to explain them in evaluation reports.)

The general strategy for interpreting working memory functioning is to pull it apart and examine the components and subprocesses. Current testing technology, as well as theory and research, gives us the ability and rationale for doing so. Restricting interpretation to global working memory leaves many questions unanswered and can result in a misunderstanding of what is actually happening. Most individuals are likely to possess strengths and weaknesses within working memory. Identifying these will increase the evaluator's understanding of the individual (and hopefully the individual's self-awareness as well), resulting in the ability to select interventions, accommodations, and strategies most likely to improve the individual's working memory performance. For example, a blanket interpretative statement, such as "Joey has a deficit in working memory" (see Table 6.7), may mask the fact that Joey's phonological short-term and verbal working memory are just fine. His problems lie mainly with executive working memory. In other situations, impairments erroneously attributed to working memory may actually be due to phonological short-term memory. Furthermore, each aspect of working memory has unique relationships with other processes and functions. Of course, the risk of pulling cognitive processes apart and examining the subprocess is that an understanding of the system is lost. Thus, evaluators need to ultimately put the pieces back together, integrating the information and explaining how the components and processes relate to one another. The evaluator may very well conclude with the global statement that "the examinee has a working memory deficit"; but by the end of the interpretation, all listeners or readers should understand which memory components are involved.

Other general strategies for interpreting working-memory assessment results include: (a) checking for similarities by domain (e.g., if visuospatial working memory is high, visual processing is also likely to be high); (b) determining areas of expertise (e.g., a student with exceptionally high mathematics skills may perform exceptionally well on any task involving numbers); (c) contrasting performance with related cognitive functions, such as processing speed (see Table 6.9); (d) taking into account related influences (see Table 6.10); (e) checking for consistency between memory components and closely related academics (see Table 5.2); (f) considering the extent of strategy knowledge and usage—in particular, the automaticity of strategies; and (g) contrasting performance with overall cognitive ability, such as an IQ score.

Pairwise Comparisons

The most direct and primary method of examining memory components and disentangling influences is to contrast test scores that differentiate between different components and processes. For comprehensive lists of suggested pairings, see Tables 6.8 and 6.9. Some prominent pairings and the explanations and implications of discrepancies are discussed in the following. (There should be at least a one standard deviation discrepancy between paired components before the difference is considered significant.)

Table 6.10   Memory Components and Related Cognitive Processes and Influences

Phonological short-term memory: speech development, speech rate, phonological processing, phonemic awareness, sequential processing, processing speed, rote learning, auditory processing, and auditory discrimination. For tasks involving numbers—arithmetic skills and number facility.

Verbal working memory: verbal abilities, language development, reading fluency, long-term semantic memory, long-term retrieval speed, and fluid reasoning.

Visuospatial short-term memory and visuospatial working memory: visual processing, spatial ability, simultaneous processing, attention, verbal recoding, and executive processing.

Executive working memory: general executive processes, attention, metacognition, metamemory, planning, and fluid reasoning.

Short-Term Memory Components versus Working Memory Components

When short-term memory scores are higher, the examinee tends to do well with simple, rote tasks but struggles with more complex cognitive and learning activities. Short-term memory can function adequately without normal working memory but the converse is less likely because impairments in short-term memory place more demands on working memory as it tries to compensate for impaired short-term functions. Also, when the load on working memory increases, short-term span tends to decline as much as 30% (Duff & Logie, 2001). Thus, it is normal for the digits backward span to be lower than the digits forward span. When individuals do perform significantly better on more complex working memory tasks than they do on simple-span tasks, it may be that they find the tasks more engaging and thus focus their attention better than they do on the simple-span activities.

Short-Term Memory or Working Memory versus Long-Term Memory

When long-term storage is weaker than short-term and/or working-memory components, the initial and common hypothesis is that there is a problem with long-term retention of information. However, the problem may be at the encoding level. Just because short-term retention is stronger does not mean that working memory successfully encoded the information into long-term memory. Support for such a hypothesis is indicated when verbal and/or executive working memory is weaker than short-term memory. For example, effective semantic encoding requires associating new information with existing long-term schemas. When the converse—impaired short-term or working memory but normal long-term memory—occurs, it seems paradoxical at first. The unexpected profile might be attributable to many opportunities to learn under "low load" conditions (see Chapter 9), or the deficit might be limited to one or two specific short-term or working memory processes that have less of an impact on long-term encoding.

Phonological Short-Term Memory versus Visuospatial Short-Term Memory

Discrepancies between these two components, and similarly between verbal working memory and visuospatial working memory, primarily reflect relative differences in the development and strength of the two modalities: visuospatial and auditory/verbal. The difference between these two components may change with age. In particular, visuospatial performance may improve as verbal recoding develops and as executive working memory is able to provide more coordination between visuospatial and verbal processes.

Phonological Short-Term Memory versus Verbal Working Memory

This comparison is crucial whenever an examinee is experiencing academic learning problems. When phonological short-term memory is lower, it is frequently because delayed phonological processing or slow speech rate is influencing auditory short-term retention, and there is little that strategies can do to improve performance. Conversely, verbal working memory is more amenable to strategies, is enhanced by well-developed fluid reasoning, and is directly supported by long-term memory retrieval. It could be that the individual has diminished short-term memory capacity, but in such cases it is unlikely that verbal working memory would be much higher, as short-term and working memory resources are interdependent. Conversely, when phonological short-term memory is higher than verbal working memory, it implicates shortcomings in the higher level processes associated with verbal working memory, whereas the processes associated with short-term memory are intact. Such individuals may do well in simple activities, such as spelling, but struggle with complex tasks like written expression.

Verbal Working Memory versus Executive Working Memory

A discrepancy in favor of verbal working memory implicates poor executive management of working memory resources relative to well-developed verbal abilities. Other hypotheses that might account for this difference include: (a) there is high capacity for storing and encoding verbal information but not when it needs to be transformed; (b) strong long-term memory structures provide more support for verbal working memory than executive working memory; and (c) the individual has difficulty dealing with interference but otherwise has good ability to manipulate and store verbal information. This profile is likely to be observed in an intelligent child who has ADHD. The reverse discrepancy indicates well-developed executive coordination of memory tasks and a strong ability to inhibit irrelevant information in contrast to weak verbal abilities, poor verbal encoding, and/or weak long-term semantic memory structures.

Educational Implications and Assessment Recommendations for Specific Deficits

Because of the complex interrelationships various working memory components and processes have with other cognitive processes and academic learning, it is imperative to consider how specific short-term and working memory processes may be interacting with other cognitive processes and how they may be impacting aspects of academic learning (see Table 5.2). It is not enough to thoroughly explain working memory performance; the evaluator must also accept responsibility for discussing the implications for learning and daily functioning. When short-term and working memory weaknesses and deficits have been identified, the evaluator needs to closely examine performance in related domains (see Table 6.10). In some instances, further assessment may be necessary. Regarding the assessment recommendations listed in the following, it is assumed that all other short-term and working memory components have already been tested. Identification of the deficits discussed in this section results from a profile analysis procedure (see Appendix C), not from pairwise comparisons. See Chapter 9 for intervention recommendations for each area of deficiency.

Deficit in Phonological Short-Term Memory

First, do not base this determination on a digits-only subtest; a word or nonwords subtest should be included. The primary related areas to examine are phonological processing and basic reading decoding skills. When digits are low, counting and arithmetic skills should also be scrutinized. In addition to the acquisition of basic reading and arithmetic skills, deficient phonological short-term memory capacity is also likely to impact: rote learning, spelling, vocabulary development, and speech development. It is essential that additional testing include: phonological processing or phonemic awareness; sequential processing; processing speed; auditory processing; and verbal abilities. It is also important to informally evaluate the examinee's development and use of rehearsal and other basic strategies.

Deficit in Visuospatial Short-Term Memory

Visuospatial memory has its strongest relationship with visual processing; thus, poor performance in this domain necessitates assessment and examination of visual processing ability. In general, visual processing has low correlations with all types of academic learning, and deficits in visuospatial memory do not have the consistent relationships with learning domains that phonological and verbal deficits have. Nonetheless, in young elementary school children, arithmetic skills should be assessed. Also, it would be helpful to determine whether the child has developed the strategy of recoding visuospatial stimuli into verbal information.

Deficit in Verbal Working Memory

A specific deficit in verbal working memory is indicated by poor performance recalling sentences or stories. The size of this sentence-based working memory is related to reading comprehension (Daneman & Carpenter, 1980), as the retention of sentences that have already been read is a critical feature of reading comprehension. Other activities that are likely to be difficult are: taking notes while listening; remembering multistep directions; relating new information to prior knowledge; verbal fluid reasoning; written expression; oral language comprehension; and oral expression, especially paraphrasing and summarizing. Areas that should be assessed include: reading comprehension; reading fluency; long-term retention of information; long-term retrieval; fluid reasoning; and language development.

Deficit in Visuospatial Working Memory

Similar to a visuospatial short-term deficit, general visual processing ability is the primary consideration. As visuospatial working memory depends on the manipulation of mental images, a weakness or deficit indicates that visual mnemonics may not be beneficial and that verbal recoding of visuospatial information will be important. Also, visuospatial working memory depends heavily on executive working memory; thus, an executive deficiency may impact visuospatial performance.

Deficit in Executive Working Memory

In general, these individuals will have more difficulty with complex activities that require the coordination of memory systems, such as a task that requires both visual and auditory processing. The more severe the deficit, the broader the range of difficulties the individual will experience; for example, more than one area of academics may be impacted. Upon discovering such a deficit, it is incumbent on the examiner to use all available means (unfortunately, there are no standardized tests for this purpose) to assess the extent of strategy use, as executive working memory efficiency is partly a function of strategy development and usage. Inefficient executive working memory processing will have a detrimental impact on other working memory functions but not necessarily on short-term components. When executive working memory performance is poor, additional testing should be conducted in: attention, fluid reasoning, broad executive processes, reading comprehension, written expression, and mathematics reasoning.

The Use of Nonstandardized Working Memory Measures

In applied settings, there are times when informally constructed working memory tests are appropriate or even necessary. Such instances include group or individual screenings, progress monitoring during interventions, or times when standardized working memory tests are unavailable. In such instances, informally constructed tests can provide useful data for decision-making purposes. To prepare an informal measure, first review the frequently used paradigms described near the beginning of this chapter and select one or more appropriate methods. Once the content and procedure have been selected, construction of progressively more difficult items is relatively easy. In constructing span tasks, simply add one more item to be remembered at each level, and allow about three trials at that level of difficulty. When testing, stop after the examinee fails all three trials at one level and record the longest span of items the examinee responded to correctly. Keep in mind that a task will not measure the full extent of working memory capacity unless it presents enough of a challenge. Overly easy tasks or activities for which the individual has attained automated processing are not challenging measures of working memory. For example, to assess executive working memory, construct a dual-task procedure in which the examinee is required to remember items sequentially while a brief processing task is interspersed between items. Complex tasks that require additional processing will result in shorter spans than simple-span tasks. After completing a set of test items, pilot the informal measure by sampling a few students. Piloting will provide feedback on clarity of directions and ease of administration, as well as assess the difficulty level of the test. If broad use of the test is intended, collected data can even be used to establish local norms.

Preschool Screening

Preschool screening is one situation in particular in which informally constructed tests, adapted standardized tests, or local norms may be beneficial. According to the work of Gathercole and Pickering (2000b) in the United Kingdom, screening the working memory of all children entering school can provide valuable information about who is at risk for learning problems. Gathercole and Pickering modified a backwards digit recall task to make it age-appropriate for 4 year olds. Similar procedures that can be efficiently administered and scored might also be created from the paradigms described in this chapter.

Progress Monitoring

Informally constructed measures of working memory may also be appropriate for measuring progress during interventions involving working memory. Similar to measuring academic skills progress with formal tests, standardized scores from working memory tests are often poor indicators of change. Furthermore, the repeated administration of standardized tests will create practice effects that will invalidate the results. Informally constructed working memory measures are similar to curriculum-based measurement procedures in that the content should relate to the goals for the intervention. In such applications, only raw data are necessary and it is left to the practitioner to assess the clinical or practical value of the improvement, based on his or her knowledge of working memory capacity and development. Also, standardized scores are unnecessary for intervention purposes, as progress is usually determined by comparing the individual's baseline data to subsequent data. For example, when trying to improve the complex working memory span of an 8-year-old, the trainer might use an originally created counting span as the dependent measure. During baseline testing, it is determined that the 8-year-old has a counting span of three. As the intervention proceeds, the learner's counting span might increase to four. The relevant question at that point is the extent to which the data represent an improvement that will translate into better academic performance or improved academic skills. Perhaps, in the future, helpful *benchmarks* for working memory will be created to assist educators and related professionals in making judgments about the development of children's working memory abilities.

Key Points

1. Processing deficits, particularly deficits in working memory, are one of the main reasons students with disabilities are unable to respond successfully to regular education interventions.

2. When short-term and working memory components are being assessed, closely related cognitive processes should also be tested.

3. Short-term and working memory subtests evolved out of experimental research paradigms, not all of which are valid measures of real-world working memory functioning.

4. The memory subtests found in most cognitive and memory scales are often incorrectly classified. For example, a subtest purported to measure phonological short-term memory may be primarily measuring executive working memory.

5. Simple-span activities measure short-term memory and complex-span tasks measure working memory. Simple-span tasks require little more than passive retention of sequential items. Complex-span tasks introduce a secondary processing task that interferes with short-term retention.

6. Working memory assessment should begin with the generation and selection of hypotheses that account for the referral concerns. Hypotheses point toward memory components and cognitive processes that are likely to be deficient. Subtests that allow the testing of these hypotheses are then selected.

7. The cross-battery approach can be an efficient method of organizing and conducting working memory assessment. However, because cross-battery analysis is lacking the usual psychometric statistics, interpretation of results should be cautious.

8. Although clinical judgment is necessary, it needs to be balanced with acceptable actuarial-based, statistical procedures.

9. Profile analysis is a justifiable method of determining an individual's memory strengths and weaknesses.

10. A normative weakness is indicated when a score is below a standard score of 90, and an ipsative weakness is indicated when there is at least a 12-point discrepancy between the score and a relevant broad domain or IQ score. A deficit exists when both a normative and an ipsative weakness are present. Deficits are rare and are indicative of an impairment. Whenever scores meet the criteria for a deficit, the usual rules regarding base rates and nonunitary factors can be suspended.

11. The *Working Memory Analysis Worksheet* (Appendix C) can be used to analyze scores from one battery or scores obtained during a cross-battery assessment.

12. When interpreting working memory results, clinicians should first analyze the separate memory components and processes. Then, integrate the information so that the functioning of the overall working memory system can be understood.

CHAPTER 7

Using Cognitive Scales to Assess Working Memory

N early all tests of intelligence, cognitive abilities, and cognitive processes include measures of short-term and working memory. With the round of revisions that began in the mid-1990s, many popular scales added working memory subtests and created working memory composites. Short-term and working memory subtests factor into FSIQs and other composites more than they ever have before. The recent addition of working memory subtests seems to have been influenced by the growing awareness of the central role working memory plays in cognitive functioning and learning. Despite the expanded offerings, some of the intellectual and cognitive instruments tap only some aspects of short-term and working memory. Consequently, a selection of memory subtests from two or more batteries may be necessary in order to complete a comprehensive assessment of working memory. Whether the practitioner elects to use one scale or multiple scales, she or he will have a better understanding of how each scale measures working memory and how to interpret results after reading this chapter. The intent of this chapter is to provide detailed information about the memory measures contained in several popular contemporary cognitive scales. The emphasis will be on identifying the specific working memory components measured by each subtest, with specific recommendations for how to interpret the memory scores produced by each scale.

Cattell-Horn-Carroll (CHC) Theory and Working Memory

The short-term and working memory subtests incorporated into intellectual and cognitive scales are derived from well-established measurement paradigms that were developed during decades of research in cognitive psychology. Thus, using an

Table 7.1 CHC Theory Broad Abilities

Fluid Intelligence
Quantitative Intelligence
Crystallized Intelligence
Reading and Writing
Short-Term Memory
Visual Processing
Auditory Processing
Long-Term Storage and Retrieval
Processing Speed
Decision/Reaction Time/Speed

intellectual scale to assess working memory should be considered no less valid than using a recognized memory battery. Although intellectual and cognitive scales utilize traditional memory measures, their theoretical foundations are intellectual and cognitive theories, not memory theories. As such, the structure of short-term and working memory factors within intellectual and cognitive scales may vary from the prominent research models, such as Baddeley's.

Currently, CHC theory (McGrew, 2005) is the most recognized intelligence theory that includes memory factors. The majority of intellectual and cognitive scales are now aligned with CHC theory or are influenced by it. CHC advocates (e.g., Flanagan & Ortiz, 2001; McGrew) have developed a taxonomy based on factor-analytic studies that allows the classification of all factors and subtests found in contemporary intellectual and cognitive scales. The origins of CHC lie with Cattell-Horn theory (Horn & Blankson, 2005) and John Carroll's (1993) colossal meta-analysis of intellectual factors. CHC theory posits a trilevel hierarchical model, with *g*, or general intelligence, at the top; 10 broad abilities (see Table 7.1) at the middle level, or stratum; and approximately 70 narrow abilities at the lowest level (McGrew & Woodcock, 2001).

In CHC theory working memory is classified as a subtype of short-term memory. This hierarchy may be incorrect and outmoded for two reasons: (a) only pre-1990 tests that seldom contained working memory measures were included in Carroll's (1993) analysis; and (b) research since Carroll's analysis has consistently found working memory to be a primary intellectual factor (see Chapter 3). Nonetheless, most interpretive guidelines found in the manuals of CHC-based batteries assume that Carroll's classification is correct. Consequently, clinicians should be aware of CHC's hierarchical arrangement of short-term and working memory. Despite the subsidiary placement of working memory, the CHC definitions of short-term memory and working memory are consistent with Baddeley's theory (McGrew, 2005). For instance, *short-term memory* is defined as "the ability to apprehend and maintain awareness of elements of information in the immediate situation" (McGrew, p. 153). *Working memory* is defined as the "ability to temporarily store and perform a set of cognitive operations on information that requires divided attention and the management of the limited capacity resources of short-term memory" (McGrew, p. 154).

General Guidelines for Selecting Working Memory Subtests

Chapter 6 provided guidelines for selecting subtests based on referral hypotheses and cross-battery procedures. When searching for subtests that measure the memory components chosen for assessment, practitioners should review reliability and validity information before making the final selections.

Subtest Reliability

Global and factor scores produced by intellectual and cognitive scales are almost always at an acceptable level of reliability. However, the reliability of individual subtests is another matter because it is more difficult to attain high subtest reliability, especially when the subtest contains only a few items. The higher the reliability coefficient, the less measurement error is associated with the subtest score. When reliability coefficients are .90 or above, reliability is considered adequate and practitioners can be confident using these scores to make diagnostic decisions. However, very few short-term and working memory subtests, if any, meet this high standard. For subtests with reliability coefficients between .80 and .90, clinicians should use the scores to test referral hypotheses and analyze strengths and weaknesses but should be cautious about basing diagnostic decisions on these scores. Subtests that have reliability coefficients of less than .80 should be combined with other subtests that measure the same component, if possible. For instance, a clinical factor score is likely to have higher reliability than a single subtest score. Furthermore, when subtest reliability is weak, much more weight should be given to other sources of data. When the memory subtests being considered have a reliability coefficient below .70, the practitioner should seek out alternatives with higher reliability. For most of the subtests reviewed in this chapter and in Chapter 8, reliability coefficients are not provided, mainly because the coefficients vary by age and by the type of reliability study. When planning a working memory assessment, the reader is advised to consult the technical manual of the battery containing the subtests of interest.

Validity

When conducting evaluations involving learning problems, validity studies conducted with clinical populations are the most relevant. Given the overwhelming evidence documenting the significant relationships between working memory components and all areas of academic learning, clinical studies should report findings that would be predicted from these established relationships. In general, it can be predicted that a clinical sample, such as a group of children with reading disabilities, will perform poorly on short-term and working memory subtests relative to matched control subjects. Concurrent validity studies with achievement tests can also provide pertinent evidence. For these, expect to find high correlations between academic skills and working memory. When results confirming predictions are reported, clinicians can be relatively confident that the subtests under consideration are valid measures of short-term and working memory. Each test review contained in this chapter and the next provides a synopsis of validity evidence pertaining to memory.

General Guidelines for Administering Working Memory Subtests

Certainly, evaluators need to strictly adhere to the manual's administration and scoring rules when conducting standardized testing. Due to the somewhat unique characteristics of short-term and working memory subtests, additional caveats and recommendations are offered here. Keeping these in mind will help to ensure the integrity of testing procedures and the validity of the results.

1. With memory subtests in particular, standardized rules need to be strictly followed. No discretion is allowed when every second counts, as it does in most measures of simple span. Accordingly, examiners may need to practice unfamiliar memory subtest procedures more so than other unfamiliar cognitive subtests.

2. Because these are memory tests, no item or part of any item should be repeated, unless the contrary is clearly specified. The only exception applies to learning subtests (often grouped with memory subtests) in which corrective feedback and multiple trials are allowed.

3. Keen observation is necessary. Because repetition of items is not allowed, it is critical that the examiner check for nonverbal behavior that indicates the examinee is ready and paying attention before presenting each item. Observation during memory testing is also important because it may reveal strategy usage and other relevant behaviors (see Table 6.5 for specific behaviors).

4. Close observation will also prevent examinee strategies and tactics that may invalidate the results. Most of these are obvious, such as responding before the examiner has finished presenting the list. Whether a strategy such as chunking of numbers is allowed will vary with each test battery.

5. During testing, examiners should avoid making any comments that might suggest strategy use or nonuse. After all testing is completed, examiners should question examinees about their use of strategies during the short-term and

Table 7.2 Stanford-Binet Intelligence Scales–Fifth Edition (SB5)

Author: Gale Roid
Publisher: Riverside Publishing
Publication Date: 2003
Age Range: 2:0–85+

Memory Composites
 Working Memory

Memory Tasks and Associated Memory Components
 Delayed Response—Visuospatial STM
 Block Span—Visuospatial WM
 Memory for Sentences—Verbal WM
 Last Word—Executive WM

working memory subtests. Such questioning should not be done between sub-tests, as it may prompt the examinee to apply certain strategies.

6. Additional clinical information may be obtained by testing the limits. This method involves returning to a subtest and conducting some informal testing. For example, the clinician might suggest that the examinee try subvocal rehearsal during a span subtest. Then administer additional items to determine if the strategy makes a difference.

7. For individuals lacking English proficiency, there is no harm in translating directions so that the examinee understands the task. However, translation of verbal items is completely inappropriate, given the direct relationship between articulatory length and phonological memory span. When batteries in the examinee's primary language are unavailable, only visuospatial measures should be administered.

Stanford-Binet Intelligence Scales–Fifth Edition (SB5)

From its inception, the Stanford-Binet has included measures of short-term memory. In the most recent revision of the Stanford-Binet (Roid, 2003; see Table 7.2), the name of the memory factor was changed from "Short-Term Memory" to "Working Memory" and two new working memory subtests were added. Despite structural changes, the SB5 remains true to its origins. It is still very much a test of *g*, with processing factors that load low on *g* omitted from the battery. From a CHC perspective, the SB5 measures five factors: fluid reasoning, crystallized intelligence, quantitative reasoning, visual-spatial processing, and short-term memory. The SB5 attempts to measure the verbal and nonverbal dimension of each factor, resulting in a Verbal and Nonverbal IQ, in addition to the global IQ score. (For more details on the SB5, see Roid and Barram, 2004.)

Unique Features

With six levels of difficulty, SB5 administration begins with two routing subtests—one verbal and one nonverbal—to determine remaining subtest entry levels. The two routing subtests, which increase the efficiency of testing, can also be used to compute an Abbreviated Battery IQ for screening purposes. The most unique characteristic of SB5 administration is that the subtests are divided into groups of six items or less, referred to as *testlets*. After completing a testlet, the examiner goes on to three other subtests in the same verbal or nonverbal domain before returning to the subtest and continuing with the next testlet. This unique administration procedure can be challenging for examiners to master, but it is actually more efficient and perhaps less stressful for the examinee, as a range of abilities are tested at a comparable level before going on to a more difficult level within a subtest. In order to better track cognitive development over time, the SB5 offers the option of *change-sensitive* scores. These special standardized scores, which have a mean of 500 for age 10:0, change with cognitive growth even if the examinee's rank in the distribution remains the same.

Validity Evidence Regarding Working Memory

The SB5 manual (Roid, 2003) reports factor means for a study of students with specific learning disabilities. The results are what would be predicted from research on the relations working memory scores have with specific areas of achievement. The group of students with a mathematics disability obtained its lowest mean on the Quantitative and Working Memory factors. Students with a reading disability had the lowest factor means in Knowledge and Working Memory. And, for those with a written language disability, Working Memory was the lowest mean. Unfortunately, the data are not broken down by verbal and visual domains.

Memory Subtests and Tasks

The SB5 has one verbal working memory subtest and one nonverbal working memory subtest. Because the tasks change as difficulty level changes, this discussion will focus on the tasks instead of the subtests.

Delayed Response

Young children and those with low level functioning are administered a testlet of working memory items referred to as *Delayed Response*. In this variation of the classic "shell game" a small toy is hidden under a plastic cup that either remains in position, is switched with another cup, or is hidden behind a screen. After a brief delay, the child must identify the location. Because of the movement of the objects and the likelihood the child is using a strategy to track and retain the location, this task is probably tapping visuospatial working memory in addition to visuospatial short-term memory.

Block Span

Beginning with Level 2, the Nonverbal Working Memory subtest consists of a block span task, a nonverbal analog to the classic digits forward and backward tasks. In this variation of Corsi block span, eight blocks are placed on a card that has two rows, one yellow and the other red. Using another block, the examiner taps a sequence of blocks at the rate of one per second with an exaggerated up and down motion of the hand. At level three, the task becomes more challenging as the examinee must mentally sort the taps occurring on the blocks placed on the yellow strip from those placed on the red strip and then tap the yellow series before the red. Clearly, this task is measuring visuospatial working memory. When the task requires sorting, executive working memory also becomes involved.

Memory for Sentences

This activity requires examinees to repeat brief phrases or sentences. At the lowest level (Level 2) there are brief phrases; at Level 3, the stimuli are complete sentences. Two points are awarded for perfect recall; one point if the examinee makes a single mistake. As there is no transformation of the information or any secondary processing task, this activity seems to be a fairly pure measure of verbal working memory.

Last Word

The Last Word task, which is introduced at Level 4, is clearly more challenging and involves verbal working memory in addition to executive working memory. Executive working memory is called into action because the task introduces interference by asking two unrelated questions after each sentence. The Last Word task is the classic listening span (Daneman & Carpenter, 1980) in which the examinee must retain the last word in a series of sentences while dealing with interference. Similar to Memory for Sentences, the examinee earns two points for all words in the correct sequence and one point if the sequence is incorrect or if one word is omitted or incorrect.

Interpretation of Memory Scores

Begin by computing the Working Memory factor score (a combination of the Nonverbal and Verbal Working Memory subtests) and comparing this to a global cognitive score in order to determine whether overall working memory functioning might be an intraindividual strength or weakness. Proceed with comparing the Working Memory score with relevant cognitive processes, including any other SB5 factors that were administered. Then, contrast the Verbal and Nonverbal Working Memory scores, keeping in mind that the verbal subtest measures verbal and executive working memory, whereas the nonverbal is measuring visuospatial short-term memory and visuospatial working memory. If the SB5 Visual-Spatial Processing factor has been completed, it is worthwhile to compare it with the Nonverbal Working Memory score (converting the subtest score to the factor metric will be necessary). Should Nonverbal Working Memory be significantly lower that the Visual-Spatial Processing factor, the implication is that the problem lies within working memory, not within broad visual-spatial processing. Unfortunately, it is difficult to interpret a subtest analysis of the SB5's memory subtests because the two tasks (for which there are no scaled scores) within each subtest are tapping different memory components. An alternative is to rely on clinical judgment and examine within subtest performance divided by tasks. One difference between the Delayed Response and Block Span tasks is that Delayed Response does not require sequencing or any advanced strategies. Within the verbal domain, Memory for Sentences is mainly verbal working memory, whereas Last Word primarily involves executive working memory. Both of these verbal tasks are influenced by long-term semantic memory. In cases where working memory is retested with the SB5, change sensitive scores can be compared to determine the extent of growth.

Strengths and Weaknesses As a Working Memory Measure

Despite the distinct tasks within each subtest, there are some advantages to using the SB5 in a working memory assessment: (a) none of the stimuli are digits, eliminating a potential confound caused by poorly developed arithmetic skills; (b) it covers a wide age range and the tasks are age appropriate; and (c) the gain scores are useful for measuring progress. Disadvantages to SB5 use include: (a) there is no phonological short-term measure; and (b) it does not have a broad short-term memory factor. When a comprehensive working memory assessment is desired, practitioners will need to supplement the SB5 with subtests from other scales.

Differential Ability Scales–Second Edition (DAS-II)

The DAS-II (Elliott, 2006; see Table 7.3) is a cognitive abilities battery designed to measure reliable profiles of specific cognitive strengths and weaknesses. An American version of the British Intelligence Test, the DAS-II was originally based on Gustafsson's model of intelligence (Elliott) but is now aligned with CHC theory. In addition to its primary composites—Verbal Ability, Nonverbal Reasoning Ability, and Spatial Ability—the scale provides three optional diagnostic clusters: Working Memory, Processing Speed, and School Readiness. The Working Memory cluster is comprised of two subtests: Recall of Digits Backward and Recall of Sequential Order. However,

Table 7.3   Differential Ability Scales–Second Edition (DAS-II)

Author: Collin Elliot
Publisher: PsychCorp
Publication Date: 2006
Age Range: 2:6–17:11
Memory Composites
  Working Memory
Memory Subtests and Associated Memory Components
  Recall of Digits Forward—Phonological STM
  Recall of Digits Backward—Executive WM
  Recall of Sequential Order—Executive WM
  Recall of Designs—Visuospatial STM
  Recognition of Pictures—Visuospatial STM
  Recall of Objects Immediate—Learning
  Rapid Naming—Long-Term Retrieval

the DAS-II also includes several other subtests that tap various short-term and working memory components (see Table 7.3).

Unique Features

The DAS-II has a variety of appealing, child-friendly tasks with age-appropriate manipulatives that make it an ideal scale for preschoolers and young elementary-aged children. A unique property of the DAS-II is its emphasis on high subtest specificity and reliability. Subtest specificity refers to the degree to which a subtest measures a specific ability, as opposed to multiple abilities. With its high subtest specificity, examiners can more confidently interpret profiles of subtest strengths and weaknesses, a desirable quality when assessing working memory components. Also, the DAS-II is particularly useful when evaluating children with exceptional abilities, as it allows out-of-age-level testing. Finally, the DAS-II minimizes the sense of failure by using an item-set approach instead of traditional basals and ceilings.

Validity Evidence Regarding Working Memory

Similar to validity studies conducted with other intellectual scales, students with learning disabilities performed as predicted on the DAS-II's short-term and working memory subtests. In a standardization study, a group of children with a reading disability performed significantly lower than matched normal children on several memory subtests: Recall of Digits Forward, Rapid Naming, Recall of Sequential Order, and Recall of Objects (Elliott, 2006).

Memory Subtests and Tasks
Recall of Digits Forward and Recall of Digits Backward

Although these two subtests are administered separately, the administration and scoring procedures are identical. For both subtests, the examiner utters the digits at the rate of two per second, a speed twice as fast as traditional digit span tasks. The quicker delivery of the items is intended to virtually prevent rehearsal; however, it appears that the forward and backward spans obtained on the DAS-II are very similar to those from digit span subtests that present digits at the traditional rate of one per second. Perhaps the shorter retention interval counterbalances the reduced opportunity to rehearse between digits. The separation of the forward and backward tasks (see Appendix A) facilitates profile analysis and interpretation of short-term and working memory scores, and results in a working memory cluster that is distinct from short-term memory.

Recall of Sequential Order

In Recall of Sequential Order, the child hears a list of body parts and must order them from highest to lowest. For the easiest items, a picture of a child remains exposed as the examinee orders and recalls the body parts. At the next level, the examinee recalls body parts without a picture; and at the highest level, the examinee must sequentially recall body parts when other object names are mixed in with the list. Because this task requires the integration of verbal and visual information, it mainly involves executive working memory.

Recall of Designs

According to the DAS-II factor structure, this subtest is primarily aligned with visual-spatial processing. However, in this text it is classified as a measure of visuospatial short-term memory because the task involves the short-term recall of visual and spatial relationships. After viewing an abstract line drawing for 5 seconds, the child is required to reproduce it with pencil and paper. Because of the abstract nature of the stimuli and short exposure time, verbal recoding of the stimuli is unlikely, making it an appropriate measure of visuospatial short-term memory.

Recognition of Pictures

During this subtest, the examinee is shown a picture of one or more familiar objects for 5 seconds, and then must select the previously viewed object(s) from a response page that includes distracters. Although examinees can apply verbal recoding during this activity, it seems to be primarily measuring visuospatial short-term memory.

Recall of Objects-Immediate

The examiner displays a card and says the names of 20 pictured objects. When the card is removed, the examinee is directed to recall as many objects as possible. There is a second and third trial with the same items; thus, this subtest is classified as a learning task. An optional delayed version can be administered 10 to 30 minutes later but the examinee should not be informed that this will occur.

Rapid Naming

Although the DAS-II structure places Rapid Naming under the Processing Speed cluster, this subtest might also be considered a measure of long-term retrieval. Similar to other rapid automatic naming (RAN) subtests, the task includes the naming of colors and pictures and has a time limit of 2 minutes.

Interpretation of Memory Scores

The DAS-II Record Form and computer-scoring software apply the usual discrepancy analysis procedures, comparing the Working Memory cluster with the GCA and Processing Speed, the other clinical cluster. Included in the statistical procedures is a time-saving subtest profile analysis that compares each diagnostic subtest with the mean score of the core subtests. This analysis of intraindividual strengths and weaknesses is particularly useful, given that all of the diagnostic subtests involve short-term or working memory, or are very closely associated with working memory. To more clearly identify the individual's short-term and working memory strengths and weaknesses, the *Working Memory Analysis Worksheet* (see Appendix C) should be used to analyze the DAS-II subtest scores (see Table 6.7 for an example of how to complete the worksheet). When doing so, refer to Appendix A to determine the classification of the subtests; for example, Recall of Digits Forward should be used to represent phonological short-term memory. Because the DAS-II subtest standard scores are *T*-scores with a mean of 50 and a standard deviation of 10, a 10-point discrepancy between subtest scores should be considered significant. When DAS-II subtests are part of a cross-battery analysis, the *T*-scores will first have to be transformed (to a metric with a mean of 100 and a standard deviation of 15) by multiplying the *T*-Score by 1.5 and then adding 25. Notable pairwise comparisons with the DAS-II are: (a) comparing Recall of Digits Forward with Recall of Designs because both are relatively pure short-term measures of their respective modality; (b) contrasting the DAS-II's Working Memory cluster with each short-term memory component; and (c) contrasting the Working Memory cluster with a clinical short-term memory factor derived from averaging the three short-term memory subtests (see Appendix A).

Strengths and Weaknesses As a Working Memory Measure

The DAS-II is ideal for conducting a profile analysis of individual strengths and weaknesses because of the exceptionally high specificity of its subtests. In regards to working memory assessment, the DAS-II also has several other advantages: (a) it includes assessment of cognitive processes (phonological processing, visual processing, and processing speed) that are closely associated with working memory; (b) because the diagnostic subtests are designed to stand alone, they are suitable for cross-battery assessment; (c) the Working Memory cluster measures working memory components only, instead of a combination of short-term and working memory; and (d) Recall of Digits Forward is a relatively pure measure of phonological short-term memory span because it reduces the opportunity for rehearsal. Some of the drawbacks of DAS-II usage include: (a) the need to transform *T*-scores whenever a cross-battery analysis is completed; and (b) the lack of verbal measures that do not include digits.

Kaufman Assessment Battery for Children–Second Edition (KABC-II)

The KABC-II (Kaufman & Kaufman, 2004a; see Table 7.4) is a five-factor cognitive assessment instrument with a bitheoretical structure. Like the original KABC, the recent revision operationalizes Luria's neuropsychological theory (Luria, 1970) by measuring planning, learning, sequential processing, and simultaneous processing. By adding a fifth factor—knowledge—the KABC-II offers the option of assessment and interpretation from the CHC perspective. The authors recommend selection of the Lurian model whenever inclusion of crystallized ability (the knowledge factor) would compromise the validity of the full-scale composite, such as when the examinee is bilingual. When evaluating children referred for a learning disability, the Kaufmans recommend the CHC model. Examiners should select the model that best applies to each case before administering the battery. With the exception of the Knowledge subtests, the same subtests are administered under both approaches; however, the meaning ascribed to the results will vary, depending on the model chosen.

Table 7.4 Kaufman Assessment Battery for Children–Second Edition (KABC-II)

Authors: Alan and Nadeen Kaufman
Publisher: Pearson AGS
Publication Date: 2004
Age Range: 3:0–18:11

Memory Composites
  Sequential Processing/Short-Term Memory
  Learning Ability/Long-Term Retrieval

Memory Subtests and Associated Memory Components
  Number Recall—Phonological STM
  Word Order—Executive WM
  Hand Movements—Visuospatial STM
  Face Recognition—Visuospatial STM
  Atlantis—Learning
  Rebus—Learning

For example, the CHC Short-Term Memory factor is interpreted as sequential processing under the Lurian model, and the CHC Long-Term Retrieval factor is interpreted as learning under the Lurian model. (For more information on the KABC-II, see Kaufman et al., 2005.)

Unique Features

In addition to its bitheoretical foundation, the KABC-II is unique in that it allows teaching of the task when the child fails teaching items, typically the first and second items of each subtest. On some subtests, it is even permissible to readminister easy items when a child subsequently passes harder items. Other options that make the KABC-II ideal for students of varying abilities and characteristics include: (a) norms are available for out-of-level testing for children aged 3 through 7; (b) for Spanish-speaking examinees, Spanish directions to all subtests, sample items, and teaching items are printed in the easels; and (c) for bilingual children, a Nonverbal Index comprised of five subtests is an option. The KABC-II also has a reputation for reducing differences between racial and ethnic groups. For each of the African American, Hispanic, and Native American groups, FSIQ is only a few points lower than the mean FSIQ of whites. According to the *KABC-II Manual* (Kaufman & Kaufman, 2004a), ethnicity accounts for no more than 2% of test score variance among preschoolers and no more than 5% among older children. These reduced ethnic differences may be related to the fact that the KABC-II primarily measures processing, which tends to be less culturally loaded than knowledge-based scales. Also, the test seems to be very "child friendly," thereby affording children who are less "test wise" the opportunity to perform well.

Validity Evidence Regarding Working Memory

Validity studies of students with learning disabilities produced profiles consistent with learning disabilities research, if not with working memory per se. For students with a reading disability, the Long-Term Retrieval and Knowledge scores were the lowest, and the Short-Term Memory score was lower than the Visual Processing score. The group of students with a mathematics disability obtained its lowest means on the Knowledge and Fluid Reasoning factors.

Memory Subtests and Tasks

The set of memory subtests administered varies with age. Visuospatial short-term memory measures are not included in the 4- to 18-year-old factors, but they are part of the Nonverbal Index and battery for 3-year-olds. The Long-Term Retrieval/Learning subtests, which involve the presentation of stimuli in both a visual and auditory format, require the examinee to learn and retain new information with efficiency. These subtests are unique in that corrective feedback is given every time the examinee makes an error. The auditory Short-Term Memory/Sequential subtests are traditional measures that require the sequential repetition of numbers or words. Also, there are optional delayed recall subtests for both of the Long-Term Retrieval/Learning scale subtests—Atlantis and Rebus.

Number Recall

The Number Recall subtest, which does not include a backward condition, measures phonological short-term memory. After listening to a series of numbers ranging from two to nine numbers in length, the examinee is required to repeat the numbers in order. Although the digits are presented at the typical rate of one per second, examiners should not drop their voice at the end of sequence, a practice that is typical with other batteries. Interestingly, the number *seven* is omitted from the subtest because it has two syllables.

Word Order

Word Order is classified as an executive working memory task because it requires both visuospatial and verbal processing, and because the higher level items include interference. For the lower level items, the examinee is shown a card with five pictures (silhouettes of common objects), the pictures are covered, the examiner says the names of some pictures, the pictures are uncovered, and then the examinee points to the pictures in the exact sequence. When the higher level items are reached, the number of pictures is increased to seven and interference is introduced. The interference consists of naming the colors of two rows of colored squares before pointing to the correct pictures.

Hand Movements

This measure of visuospatial short-term memory is intended to replace the two verbal short-term memory subtests when a nonverbal ability estimate is desired. The items consist of hand movements (there are three positions) presented at the rate of one per second. The examinee must repeat the movements in the correct sequence.

Face Recognition

The KABC-II places the Face Recognition subtest under the Visual Processing factor; however, it is also a measure of visuospatial short-term memory. Neurologically, memory for faces is probably distinguishable from memory for other visual-spatial content. Nonetheless, it seems appropriate to place it under the visuospatial short-term memory component. The task consists of showing the examinee one or two faces for 5 seconds and then having the examinee pick out the faces from a group of faces on the response page. Interestingly, the stimulus photos are tightly cropped so as to display only the face, whereas most of the body is shown on the response page.

Atlantis

This task requires the examinee to use working and long-term memory to associate new names with drawings of a fish, shell, or plant. After the stimuli are presented, the examinee must point to the correct drawings on a response page containing several items. Immediate corrective feedback is provided every time the child makes an error. This learning task goes beyond short-term retention because the examinee must recall random items introduced previously, along with items introduced moments ago. In addition to routine working memory operations, the task surely enlists executive working memory to initiate strategies for remembering the information and to coordinate visual and auditory input. Examinees receive one point instead of two any time an incorrect response is in the correct category—for example, the correct response is a fish but the examinee points to the wrong fish.

Rebus

This task also requires the examinee to use working and long-term memory to learn and retain new associations. Rebus is a cumulative learning task similar to Atlantis, with the main difference being that no corrective feedback is given when the child makes an error. However, when going on to the next item, there is a review of previous symbols before new ones are introduced. The sequence involves teaching a rebus (abstract symbol for a word) and then having the child read rebus sentences. Along with Atlantis, Rebus taps several processes besides working memory and long-term retrieval, including attention, encoding, executive processing, and visual and auditory processing.

Interpretation of Memory Scores

Because of the need to realign the KABC-II memory subtests with specific components, clinicians should use the *Working Memory Analysis Worksheet* (Appendix C) when conducting a profile analysis. To determine individual strengths and weaknesses, memory component scores can be compared to the KABC-II composite or a processing mean that includes the memory subtests. The Learning/Long-Term Retrieval subtests may be included in the profile analysis, but should be classified as *learning* because they include corrective feedback and repetition of stimuli. When conducting pairwise comparisons, the KABC-II Learning/Long-Term Retrieval score should be contrasted with Number Recall (representing phonological short-term memory) and with Word Order (representing executive working memory). For intra-subtest analysis, clinicians should consider performance on Word Order items before and after the introduction of the interference task. Finally, Kaufman et al. (2005) recommend that examiners observe the examinee's strategies during memory subtests and take these qualitative indicators into account when interpreting results.

Strengths and Weaknesses As a Working Memory Measure

The KABC-II makes several contributions to a comprehensive assessment of working memory, including: (a) the subtests are carefully constructed to control for potentially confounding variables—for example, with the number *seven* omitted, all of the Number Recall digits are one syllable only; (b) partial credit is given for categorically correct responses in Atlantis, acknowledging the contributions of semantic memory and an activated pool of long-term representations; (c) age-appropriate visuospatial memory measures are included; and (d) the learning/long-term retrieval factor allows for a within-battery comparison with verbal short-term and working memory components. The main drawback to the KABC-II is that the sampling of short-term and working memory components is limited.

Supplementing the KABC-II with the Kaufman Test of Educational Achievement–Second Edition (KTEA-II)

If an assessment of the long-term retrieval component is desired, especially the specific aspect of rapid automatic naming (RAN), the evaluator should consider using select subtests from the KTEA-II (Kaufman & Kaufman, 2004b). The KTEA-II is a comprehensive and diagnostic individual achievement test that was conormed with the KABC-II. It offers an optional Naming Facility (RAN) subtest along with an optional Associational Fluency subtest. The Naming Facility subtest has three separated timed rounds that include naming pictures of common objects, naming colors, and naming letters. Associational Fluency has four separated timed tasks that require rapid retrieval of common objects and words that start with specific sounds. In instances where a child performed poorly on the KABC-II's Learning/Long-Term Retrieval factor, administration of these KTEA-II subtests allows the clinician to differentiate the child's long-term retrieval from his or her learning ability. Learning is distinct from long-term retrieval in that learning is a combination of several memory processes, including encoding and short-term retention. The KTEA-II can also be used in situations where phonological processing abilities are a concern, as it includes a phonological awareness measure.

Cognitive Assessment System (CAS)

The CAS (Naglieri & Das, 1997; see Table 7.5) is another cognitive abilities test based on Luria's theory of cognitive processing. Although the authors of the scale do not claim that their test measures any memory dimensions, examination of the battery's Successive Processing scale reveals that it is comprised of three classic verbal short-term and working memory assessment paradigms. Also, the Simultaneous Processing scale contains a task that taps visuospatial short-term memory. Because these subtests can be interpreted as short-term and working memory measures, the CAS is included among cognitive batteries that measure working memory. The four cognitive processes purportedly measured by the CAS are Planning, Attention, and Simultaneous and Successive processing (referred to as PASS; Naglieri, 1999). Adherents of working memory theories that view working memory as an executive attention control system would also consider some of the subtests comprising the Attention and Planning scales to be working memory measures, as the Attention scale

Table 7.5 Cognitive Assessment System for Children (CAS)

Authors: Jack A. Naglieri and J. P. Das
Publication Date: 1997
Publisher: Riverside
Age Range: 5:0–17:11

Memory Composites
   (Successive Processing)
   (Simultaneous Processing)

Memory Subtests and Associated Memory Components
   Word Series—Phonological STM
   Sentence Repetition—Verbal WM
   Sentence Questions—Executive WM, Verbal WM
   Figure Memory—Visuospatial STM

includes a Stroop task called *Expressive Attention* and the Planning scale includes a trail-making task called *Planned Connections*. Nevertheless, the discussion herein is restricted to subtests from the Successive and Simultaneous scales. (For more details on the CAS, see Naglieri, 1999.)

Unique Features

Among cognitive ability scales, the CAS is unique in that it strictly adheres to a processing theory of cognitive abilities. Because of its theoretical basis, it does not contain any measures of verbal ability or crystallized intelligence. A unique administration feature of the CAS Planning subtests is the structured observation of strategies and questioning about strategies after each subtest. After recording the observed strategies, the examiner asks the child to report how he or she did the items. Unfortunately, the observation and questioning of strategies is not required on the subtests that are primarily measuring memory. Another feature of the CAS is that it measures speech rate in children aged 5 to 7, providing the examiner with a unique opportunity to compare speech rate with other indicators of short-term memory capacity.

Validity Evidence Regarding Working Memory

There has been controversy surrounding the CAS factor structure; that is, the main factors underlying CAS performance may not be the four PASS factors. Although the CAS manual (Naglieri & Das, 1997) reports both exploratory and confirmatory factor-analytic support for the four-factor PASS structure, Keith, Kranzler, and Flanagan (2001) argue that the CAS is primarily measuring processing speed and short-term memory. The case for attributing performance on the Successive scale to short-term memory is consistent with Kaufman and Kaufman's (2004a) acknowledgment that sequential processing is essentially the same as short-term memory. Furthermore, a standardization study of children with reading disabilities (Naglieri & Das) reported that the group performed poorest on the Successive Scale (a mean of 87.8), a finding concordant with research on the strong relationship short-term memory has with reading. Finally, the CAS is known for having extremely high correlations with measures of achievement. These strong relations are not surprising, given that a substantial portion of the CAS is tapping short-term and working memory.

Memory Subtests and Tasks

According to the manual (Naglieri & Das, 1997), the Successive Processing scale measures the integration of stimuli into a specific serial order that forms a chain-like progression in which each element is only related to those that precede it. Just like other short-term memory measures, the CAS Successive processing subtests require the examinee to repeat the items in serial order.

Word Series

This is a classic phonological short-term memory measurement paradigm. Words are presented at the rate of one per second and the child must repeat them in the same order. Although there is a different sequence and selection each time, the words for each item are selected from the names of nine common objects. At first glance, this appears to make the task easier; however, this is unlikely, as proactive interference probably builds throughout the test.

Sentence Repetition

These sentences are nonsensical, as all the nouns, verbs, and modifiers are colors. For example, a sentence might be something like "A blue greened a brown purple." Although the examinee can depend somewhat on knowledge of sentence structure, semantic knowledge and visual imagery will be of little use during recall. Thus, the subtest is probably measuring phonological short-term memory as much as verbal working memory.

Sentence Questions

After reading the same type of nonsense sentences (with nearly every word a color), the examiner asks the examinee a question about the sentence, such as "Who greened a brown purple?" With the questions complicating the task, the subtest is surely tapping both executive working memory and verbal working memory, as the child struggles to make sense out of nonsense. Given the challenge, it seems appropriate that this subtest is not administered to those under 8 years of age.

Figure Memory

Classified as a Simultaneous processing task by the CAS authors, Figure Memory seems to be measuring visuospatial short-term memory as much as broad visual processing. After a 5-second exposure to a geometric figure, the examinee must draw the same figure within a more complex design. The test is unique in that a verbal response to a visual stimulus is not required.

Speech Rate

Given the established connection between speech rate and phonological short-term memory, this subtest should be administered whenever the CAS is given to a child from 5 to 7 years of age. The task requires a child to repeat a series of words as fast as possible 10 times. All of the series are three words long, and all of the words were used previously in the Word Series or Sentence Repetition subtests.

Interpretation of Memory Scores

Psychologists and related professionals tend to restrict their test interpretation to the factors suggested by the test's purported structure. Thus, practitioners who use the CAS to assess short-term and working memory will need to preface their oral and written interpretations with an explanation as to why these CAS subtests are actually measuring memory and why it is appropriate to interpret them accordingly. Otherwise, the recommendations for analysis and interpretation are the same as for most other cognitive scales. Clinicians should use the *Working Memory Analysis Worksheet* in Appendix C, entering scores in the cells suggested in Appendix A. They should then proceed with comparing each memory component with the CAS composite, another global cognitive score, or the mean of the processes and memory components that have been assessed. Finally, logical pairs should be compared, such as contrasting phonological short-term memory with visuospatial short-term memory. When interpreting CAS subtests, keep in mind that the Successive processing subtests are relatively uninfluenced by semantic long-term memory. Finally, there is a unique opportunity to compare the speech rate of 5- to 7-year-olds with their phonological short-term memory span.

Strengths and Weaknesses As a Measure of Working Memory

Despite the fact that the CAS does not claim to measure short-term and working memory, the test has much to recommend it, including: (a) it presents an opportunity to obtain a standardized measure of speech rate and compare this with the child's short-term memory span; (b) it factors out the influence of long-term semantic memory, thereby creating a purer measure of short-term and working memory; (c) none of the subtests introduce interference, again allowing for a cleaner measure of specific memory components; and (d) it does not mix visual and verbal modes. Unfortunately, most practitioners are unlikely to utilize the memory subtests or interpret them as such because the short-term and working memory factors on the CAS are labeled as *Successive Processing*.

Table 7.6   Woodcock Johnson III Tests of Cognitive Abilities (WJ III COG)

Authors: Richard Woodcock, Kevin McGrew, and Nancy Mather
Publisher: Riverside Publishing
Publication Date: 2001
Age Range: 2:0–90+

Memory Composites
  Working Memory
  Short-Term Memory
  Long-Term Retrieval

Memory Subtests and Associated Memory Components
  Numbers Reversed—Executive WM
  Auditory Working Memory—Verbal WM, Executive WM
  Memory for Words—Phonological STM
  Picture Recognition—Visuospatial STM
  Visual-Auditory Learning—Learning
  Retrieval Fluency—Long-Term Retrieval
  Rapid Picture Naming—Long-Term Retrieval

Woodcock-Johnson III Tests of Cognitive Abilities (WJ III COG)

The WJ III COG (Woodcock, McGrew, & Mather, 2001b; see Table 7.6) battery is an appropriate choice whenever a broad-based assessment of cognitive processes is planned. In addition to sampling seven CHC broad cognitive abilities that are interrelated with working memory, the scale measures several related clinical factors: phonemic awareness, attention, cognitive fluency, executive processes, and delayed recall. Furthermore, the WJ III COG is conormed with the Woodcock Johnson III Tests of Achievement (WJ III ACH), which itself has some subtests that tap working memory and related processes. Even though the WJ III COG was not designed solely for memory assessment, practitioners frequently utilize it for this purpose because the design of the battery facilitates selective and cross-battery testing. See Schrank (2006) for more information on the specific cognitive processes involved in WJ III COG performance.

Unique Features

The WJ III COG was designed with selective testing in mind. The authors encourage examiners to select subtests as needed instead of administering the entire battery. The WJ III COG comes with Compuscore, a sophisticated computerized scoring, analysis, and report writing program that analyzes the data from several perspectives.

Another unique feature of the WJ III COG that makes it particularly applicable for assessing individuals with a suspected learning disability is that it includes controlled learning subtests in which immediate corrective feedback is given each time the examinee commits an error. Two of the controlled learning subtests are measures of fluid reasoning.

Validity Evidence Regarding Working Memory

In a standardization study of children with learning disabilities and ADHD, the subjects obtained their lowest score (88.2) on the Auditory Working Memory subtest, the most demanding working memory subtest on the WJ III COG. The group also obtained a below average mean (89.0) on Rapid Picture Naming.

Memory Subtests and Tasks
Numbers Reversed

Numbers Reversed is the classic backward digit span paradigm, with the examinee required to repeat a series of numbers in reverse sequential order. Although a backward digit span task is usually considered a measure of executive working memory, the WJ III authors (Woodcock et al., 2001b) have Numbers Reversed contributing to the battery's Short-Term Memory cluster, as well as its Working Memory factor. The WJ III COG does not include a forward digit span task.

Auditory Working Memory

Because the examinee must transform verbal information, Auditory Working Memory involves both verbal and executive working memory. The task requires the examinee to listen to a series of intermixed words and digits, then to recall the words in sequential order first, followed by the digits in the order they were presented. Partial credit can be earned if one of the series is correct, but only if the words are attempted first.

Memory for Words

Memory for Words is a classic test of phonological short-term memory span in which the examinee is directed to repeat lists of unrelated words in the correct sequence.

Picture Recognition

Consistent with the CHC model, Picture Recognition is placed under the Visual-Spatial Thinking cluster because short-term visual-spatial memory is considered a narrow ability of visual-spatial processing. Nonetheless, Picture Recognition is ostensibly a measure of visuospatial short-term memory and should be interpreted as such when assessment of working memory is being conducted. One or more pictures of common objects are presented for 5 seconds and then the examinee selects the previously presented items from a page that includes distracters. Picture Recognition makes verbal recoding of the stimuli difficult, as each item contains varieties of the same category.

Visual-Auditory Learning

Success on this rebus learning task depends on the effective coordination of working memory and long-term retrieval. As the associations between the visual stimuli and the words are completely novel, this activity relies on working memory to effectively attach new representations with known words. Because the task extends for several minutes, the fresh associations must be maintained in a readily accessible pool within long-term memory while working memory accesses the relevant associations and inhibits irrelevant information. Because immediate corrective feedback is provided whenever the examinee responds incorrectly, examinees with short-term and working memory weaknesses may eventually learn most of the material. The amount of long-term storage resulting from this learning exercise can be assessed with the Visual-Auditory Learning Delayed subtest, which can be administered after a minimum of 30 minutes. Although the WJ III authors (Woodcock et al., 2001b) classify this subtest as long-term retrieval, such tasks are also considered measures of learning.

Retrieval Fluency

During Retrieval Fluency, working memory must direct an efficient search of related items in long-term storage. The examinee is given 1 minute to name as many examples as possible from a specified category. The task consists of three different well-known categories, with a 1-minute time limit for each.

Rapid Picture Naming

Rapid Picture Naming is a RAN activity that measures long-term retrieval speed. The examinee is given 2 minutes to recall the names of pictured common objects as quickly as possible. Rapid Picture Naming is part of the WJ III COG's Cognitive Fluency cluster but is classified herein as a measure of long-term retrieval.

Interpretation of Memory Scores

Unfortunately, the analysis provided by Compuscore is of little use when interpreting the short-term and working memory scores. Because the Short-Term Memory cluster contains a subtest (Numbers Reversed) that is typically not considered a short-term memory measure, the subtests that comprise the Short-Term Memory cluster need to be realigned. However, the Working Memory cluster score can be used as is to represent executive working memory. Also, Compuscore's Intra-Cognitive Discrepancy table can be used to assess how executive working memory relates to the individual's overall cognitive ability. When the Working Memory score is more than one standard deviation of discrepancy below the predicted score, it can

Table 7.7   Universal Nonverbal Intelligence Test (UNIT)

Authors: Bruce A. Bracken and R. Steve McCallum
Publisher: Riverside Publishing
Publication Date: 1998
Age Range: 5–17

Memory Composites
   Memory Quotient

Memory Tasks and Associated Memory Components
   Symbolic Memory—Visuospatial STM
   Spatial Memory—Visuospatial STM
   Object Memory—Visuospatial STM

be considered a statistically significant weakness. The remainder of the analysis should be conducted with the *Working Memory Analysis Worksheet* in Appendix C, with subtests classified according to their placement in Appendix A.

Strengths and Weaknesses As a Working Memory Measure

The main advantage of using the WJ III COG to test short-term and working memory is the wide range of related cognitive processes found in the same battery, as well as in-depth sampling of learning and long-term retrieval. The drawbacks of using the WJ III COG for memory assessment are minor. Although it does not contain a digits forward task, Memory for Words provides an adequate sample of phonological short-term memory. Overall, the WJ III COG would be more useful if it sampled the short-term and working memory components in more depth.

Supplementing the WJ III COG with the Woodcock Johnson III Tests of Achievement (WJ III ACH)

Story Recall, a subtest on the WJ III ACH (Woodcock, McGrew, & Mather, 2001a), is a typical story-retelling activity that can be considered a measure of verbal working memory. The WJ III ACH uses the task to measure oral language expression but it is clearly tapping verbal working memory, with assistance from long-term semantic memory. The examinee listens to a story and then retells as much as can be remembered. Points are awarded for elements that are recalled; some elements must be stated verbatim, whereas others can be paraphrased. Because the two WJ III batteries were conormed, there are no concerns about including the Story Recall score in a profile analysis with WJ III COG scores.

Universal Nonverbal Intelligence Test (UNIT)

The UNIT (Bracken & McCallum, 1998; see Table 7.7) is designed to provide an accurate assessment of nonverbal intellectual functioning in children and adolescents for whom traditional language-loaded measures may not be appropriate due to: speech, language, or hearing impairments; differences in cultural or linguistic background; or certain childhood disorders, such as autism. The UNIT's six subtests produce four composite scores: memory, reasoning, symbolic processing, and nonsymbolic processing, with fluid reasoning and short-term memory being the primary factors.

Unique Features

The most unique characteristic of the UNIT is that the administration and response formats are entirely nonverbal. Even the directions are nonverbal; eight easily understood hand and body gestures are used to communicate. To ensure that the examinee understands the task, each subtest begins with a nonverbal demonstration, coupled with the standardized gestures, that is followed by sample items and teaching items.

Validity Evidence Regarding Working Memory

The UNIT's FSIQ, 50% of which is based on short-term and working memory performance, was found to be highly predictive of academic achievement (Bracken & McCallum, 1998). Validity studies conducted with students who have learning disabilities found that these individuals can be differentiated most easily on the basis of symbolic processing (two of the memory subtests load on the symbolic processing factor).

Memory Subtests and Tasks

The three memory subtests are very similar in what they measure: the visual and spatial aspects of short-term and working memory. The subtests require short-term recall of content (shape and color), location, and sequence. An individual with normal visuospatial short-term memory can probably perform well without any verbal mediation. However, an examinee who has developed verbal recoding of visuospatial information can easily apply such a strategy, as all of the stimuli and their locations can be named. The more recoding that is involved, the more likely the task will also involve visuospatial working memory, as well as some strategy coordination from executive working memory. All of the subtests have a similar administration format in that each stimulus page is displayed for only 5 seconds and the examinee responds by moving objects or placing chips on the response page.

Symbolic Memory

The examinee is shown a sequence of universal symbols for baby, girl, boy, woman, and man, depicted in green or black. After viewing the sequence for 5 seconds, the examinee re-creates the sequence using response cards. Of the three subtests, this is the only one with a sequencing requirement.

Spatial Memory

The examinee is shown a random pattern of green and black dots on a 3 × 3 or 4 × 4 grid. After viewing the stimulus for 5 seconds, the examinee re-creates the pattern by placing green and black chips on a response grid. The authors view Spatial Memory as less amenable to verbal mediation (i.e., verbal recoding). However, colors and locations can be verbally coded; thus, this task appears very similar to the other two.

Object Memory

The examinee is shown a page with a random array of pictures of common objects. After viewing the stimulus page for 5 seconds, the examinee is presented with a second pictorial array that includes all of the original stimulus figures plus foils. The examinee must select the original stimulus figures by placing chips on them. This subtest probably enlists executive working memory more than the other two, as the examinee must inhibit the incorrect stimuli.

Interpretation of Memory Scores

When administered alone, interpretation of the UNIT's memory scores is relatively straight forward. The interpretative worksheet in the UNIT Record Form provides tables for completing a thorough actuarial analysis. Standardized data are available for: comparing each memory subtest to the overall memory score; some pairwise comparisons of memory subtests; and comparing the memory composite with the reasoning composite. In cases where the UNIT is part of a cross-battery assessment, the practitioner should follow the procedures on the *Working Memory Analysis Worksheet* found in Appendix C.

Strengths and Weaknesses As a Working Memory Measure

In accord with its main purpose, the UNIT provides an opportunity to assess the short-term memory capacity of individuals for whom a verbal assessment is inappropriate. Furthermore, it allows an in-depth evaluation of short-term retention of visuospatial information. The UNIT's subtests are more challenging than most alternatives because examinees must recall more than one visuospatial characteristic for most of the items. In cross-battery assessment cases, the UNIT may serve as an appropriate supplement to a scale that lacks visuospatial memory subtests. The obvious weakness of the UNIT is its limited sampling of working memory processes; however, this constraint is expected, given its nonverbal format.

Table 7.8   Wechsler Adult Intelligence Scale–Third Edition (WAIS-III)

Author: David Wechsler
Publisher: The Psychological Corporation
Publication Date: 1997
Age Range: 16:0–89:11

Memory Composites
 Working Memory Index

Memory Subtests
 Digit Span Forward—Phonological STM
 Digit Span Backward—Executive WM
 Letter-Number Sequencing—Verbal WM, Executive WM
 Arithmetic—Executive WM

The Wechsler Scales

The Wechsler Adult Intelligence Scale–Third Edition (WAIS-III; Wechsler, 1997a; see Table 7.8) and the Wechsler Intelligence Scale for Children–Fourth Edition (WISC-IV; Wechsler, 2003; see Table 7.9) share the same short-term and working memory subtests: Digit Span, Letter-Number Sequencing, and Arithmetic. Of course, the WAIS-III has a more difficult set of items because it goes into adulthood. On the WAIS-III, all three subtests are needed to compute the Working Memory Index, whereas only Digit Span and Letter-Number Sequencing are needed on the

Table 7.9   Wechsler Intelligence Scale for Children–Fourth Edition (WISC-IV)

Author: David Wechsler
Publisher: The Psychological Corporation
Publication Date: 2003
Age Range: 6:0–16:11

Memory Composites
 Working Memory Index

Memory Subtests
 Digit Span Forward—Phonological STM
 Digit Span Backward—Executive WM
 Letter-Number Sequencing—Verbal WM, Executive WM
 Arithmetic—Executive WM

WISC-IV, with Arithmetic as a supplemental subtest that can be substituted for one of the other two. In previous editions of both scales, Digit Span and Arithmetic comprised a factor named "Freedom from Distractibility." The preschool version—the Wechsler Preschool and Primary Scale of Intelligence–Third Edition (WPPSI-III; Wechsler, 2002)—does not contain any short-term or working memory subtests.

Validity Evidence Regarding Working Memory

As predicted, samples of children and adults with learning disabilities perform worse on the working memory subtests than on other Wechsler factors. On the WAIS-III, both reading and mathematics disabled samples obtained their lowest mean index on Working Memory, a mean that was significantly lower than the Verbal Comprehension and Perceptual Organization index means. Furthermore, the WAIS-III Verbal Comprehension Index score was 15 points higher than the Working Memory Index score for 41.7% of those with a reading disability compared to only 13% of the WAIS-III standardization sample (Wechsler, 1997a). Evidence that the WISC-IV is measuring critical working memory functions was found in a standardization study of children with reading disorders. The children with reading disorders obtained significantly lower mean scores for all composites, with the largest effect size for the Working Memory Index mean of 87.

Memory Subtests and Tasks

Digit Span

This is the classic digit span task, with digits forward and digits backward combined into one subtest. As always, digits forward is classified as measuring phonological short-term memory and digits backward is categorized under executive working memory. However, for some individuals, digits backward can be managed by their verbal working memory alone.

Letter-Number Sequencing

After listening to a randomly ordered series of letters and numbers spoken by the examiner, the examinee must first repeat the numbers in ascending order, then the letters in alphabetical order. On the WISC-IV, credit is also given when the examinee says the letters before the numbers, as long as both groups are arranged correctly. The rationale for allowing this exception is that the load on working memory arises from arranging each series, not from remembering which group goes first. Because of the need to separate and reorder the two codes, the subtest seems to be measuring both verbal working memory and executive working memory.

Arithmetic

For the Arithmetic subtest, the child listens to orally presented arithmetic problems and tries to mentally solve them without pencil or paper within a specified time.

Although mental arithmetic certainly involves working memory, it may not be the primary process being tapped. Moreover, the Wechsler Arithmetic subtest is not based on any established working memory measurement paradigm. Not surprisingly, there is controversy over what it actually measures. Keith, Fine, Taub, Reynolds, and Kranzler (2006) believe that the WISC-IV Arithmetic subtest is primarily a measure of fluid reasoning. On the WAIS-III, Arithmetic loads on two other factors besides working memory. Despite the controversy, the Arithmetic subtest can be considered a measure of executive working memory, with significant influences from fluid reasoning, quantitative reasoning, visuospatial processing, and processing speed.

Interpretation of Memory Scores

Similar to analyzing and interpreting results from other intellectual scales, clinicians should consider the classifications of the subtests found in Appendix A and then follow the procedures for completing the *Working Memory Analysis Worksheet* found in Appendix C. Related processes, such as processing speed, should be included in the analysis, as well as other memory subtest scores gathered through cross-battery testing. The Digit Span subtest score should not be used because it confounds short-term and working memory. To make the most of the Digit Span subtest, performance on Digits Forward should be contrasted with Digits Backward. Essentially, this is comparing simple span to complex span, or phonological short-term memory with verbal working memory and executive working memory. On the WAIS-III, only the length of each span can be contrasted and only base rates are provided for the amount of the difference. However, the WISC-IV allows transformation of the forward and backward raw scores into separate scaled scores and provides critical values for the discrepancy between the two.

Strengths and Weaknesses As a Working Memory Measure

The main advantage of using the Wechsler scales to measure short-term and working memory is convenience. While administering the most frequently used intelligence scale, clinicians can also obtain a broad sample of working memory functions. Nevertheless, the sampling is not very deep or comprehensive. The visuospatial domain is not included and even the sampling of phonological short-term memory is limited. Therefore, a Wechsler scale will frequently need to be supplemented with subtests from other batteries whenever a comprehensive working memory assessment is needed.

WISC-IV Integrated

Although not designed solely for memory assessment, the Wechsler Intelligence Scale for Children–Fourth Edition, Integrated (WISC-IV Integrated; Wechsler et al., 2004a) offers an in-depth and efficient assessment of short-term and working memory (see Table 7.10). The WISC-IV Integrated is the combination of the standard

Table 7.10   WISC-IV Integrated

Authors: David Wechsler, Edith Kaplan, Deborah Fein, Joel Kramer, Robin Morris, Dean Delis, and Arthur Maerlander
Publisher: The Psychological Corporation
Publication Date: 2004
Age Range: 6:0–16:11

Memory Composites
  None

Memory Tasks and Associated Memory Components
  Visual Digit Span—Visuospatial STM
  Spatial Span Forward—Visuospatial STM
  Spatial Span Backward—Visuospatial WM
  Letter Span Nonrhyming—Phonological STM
  Letter Span Rhyming—Phonological STM
  Letter-Number Sequencing PA*—Verbal WM, Executive WM
  Arithmetic PA Part A—Executive WM
  Arithmetic PA Part B—Executive WM

Note: PA = Processing Approach.

WISC-IV battery (Wechsler, 2003) and 16 supplemental process subtests. The 16 process subtests are grouped under four domains—Verbal, Perceptual, Working Memory, and Processing Speed. The general purpose of the WISC-IV Integrated is to provide an opportunity for an in-depth assessment of suspected cognitive processing weaknesses. The development of the process portion of the WISC-IV Integrated has its roots in neuropsychological assessment and the belief that the WISC-IV is a valuable clinical instrument. Many of the process subtests are derivations of the standard WISC-IV subtests; only the scoring procedures or the presentation formats have changed. However, the WISC-IV Integrated subtests are not necessarily designed to measure the same ability as the WISC-IV subtests from which they are derived. In regards to working memory, the WISC-IV Integrated consists of some derived subtests and some new subtests. As a result, the WISC-IV Integrated provides a more in-depth assessment of working memory than the standard WISC-IV, as well as providing the opportunity to distinguish among different aspects of working memory. The most significant contribution of the WISC-IV Integrated is the inclusion of visuospatial memory, something not measured by the standard WISC-IV. This addition is particularly important when evaluating students for a learning disability, as they often have deficient phonological short-term memory and verbal working memory but adequate visuospatial memory. When administered in conjunction with the standard WISC-IV memory subtests, the WISC-IV Integrated's memory subtests provide the unique opportunity for within-battery comparisons of: (a) broad short-term memory with broad working memory; (b) visuospatial short-term memory with visuospatial working memory; and (c) phonological short-term memory with verbal working memory.

Intended for use after the usual WISC-IV administration, the expressed purpose of the WISC-IV Integrated process subtests is to provide additional information about the cognitive processes that underlie performance on the standard WISC-IV subtests. Because each WISC-IV core and supplemental subtest taps more than one cognitive process, following up with WISC-IV Integrated subtests allows the examiner to parse and distinguish among the cognitive processes involved, potentially leading to identification of a process or subprocess that accounts for the examinee's poor performance on a particular WISC-IV subtest. For instance, an examiner may hypothesize that a child's poor performance on Digit Span is due to poor number facility. In such a case, the Letter Span subtest of the WISC-IV Integrated could be administered to test the hypothesis. Some processing hypotheses may originate from observations of the child's behaviors. In such instances, the WISC-IV Integrated subtests afford the opportunity to quantify and corroborate these observations. Even in the absence of specific working memory hypotheses or prior administration of the WISC-IV, practitioners may elect to utilize the WISC-IV Integrated's memory subtests whenever a comprehensive assessment of working memory is needed.

Validity Evidence Regarding Working Memory

WISC-IV Integrated standardization studies conducted with learning disabled populations support the usefulness and validity of the scale as a working memory measure. Regardless of the type of specific learning disability, all of the groups demonstrated difficulties with tasks involving short-term and working memory. For example, compared to a matched control group, a sample of 45 children with a reading disorder had significantly lower scores on most of the working memory subtests. Consistent with predictions, those with a reading disorder did not differ from controls on Spatial Span Backward. On the working memory subtests, a group with ADHD obtained the largest effect size on the Arithmetic Process Approach subtest. Finally, the construct validity of the WISC-IV Integrated is supported through convergent and discriminant validity studies that reveal a pattern of correlations dividing working memory into visuospatial and auditory-verbal processes.

Memory Subtests and Tasks

The WISC-IV Integrated's authors (Wechsler et al., 2004b) divide the working memory process subtests into "Registration" and "Mental Manipulation" tasks, with all of the forward span subtests classified as registration subtests and the remaining subtests classified as mental manipulation subtests. The authors define *registration* as the temporary retention of information for the purpose of repeating it without modification and *mental manipulation* as the transformation of the information. The registration definition and tasks are consistent with the construct of short-term memory, whereas the manipulation tasks are consistent with the construct of working memory. WISC-IV Integrated administration may also include the standard WISC-IV working memory subtests, such as Digit Span. For details on these subtests, see the section on the Wechsler Scales earlier in this chapter.

Visual Digit Span

In Visual Digit Span, the examinee must repeat a sequence of digits that are visually presented for 1 to 5 seconds. Unlike the standard aural Digit Span, the entire string of digits is presented simultaneously, and there is no backward repetition condition. Although Visual Digit Span is classified primarily as a visuospatial short-term memory task, most examinees will also employ verbal and executive working memory. Verbal working memory becomes involved as examinees verbally recode the numbers. Also, exposure to the entire number string may facilitate chunking strategies, which depend on executive working memory coordination. Accordingly, helpful clinical information can be obtained by asking the examinee about his or her use of a chunking strategy. However, questioning about strategy use should be delayed until battery administration is complete.

Spatial Span

Spatial Span is a Corsi block task with both a forward and a backward condition. The child repeats a sequence of tapped blocks in the same order or reverse order that the blocks were touched by the examiner. Unlike the standard aural Digit Span, there is no overall Spatial Span score; rather, there are separate Spatial Span Forward and Spatial Span Backward scores. Spatial Span Forward is simpler and thus classified as primarily measuring visuospatial short-term memory, whereas Spatial Span Backward mainly measures visuospatial working memory. In contrast to Visual Digit Span, Spatial Span depends more on spatial memory (memory for location) as opposed to visual memory. Although useful, verbal recoding is unnecessary, as only a nonverbal response is required. Also, performance may be mediated by motor planning and execution.

Letter Span

The Letter Span subtest also consists of two item types and two separate scores: Letter Span Rhyming and Letter Span Nonrhyming, both of which measure phonological short-term memory. With Letter Span, the rhyming and nonrhyming items are interspersed, not divided into separate tasks like forward and backward spans. Each item consists of four trials, two with nonrhyming letters and two with rhyming letters. The examinee is not informed that some of the trials consist entirely of rhyming letters. Consistent with research, most children obtain lower Letter Span Rhyming than

Letter Span Nonrhyming scores because indistinct phonological traces are more difficult to recall.

Letter-Number Sequencing Process Approach

For this subtest, the examinee is read a series of letters and numbers that must then be ordered alphabetically and numerically. The process version of this subtest is the same as the standard WISC-IV Letter-Number Sequencing subtest except that two of three trials in each item have embedded words, and only the trials with embedded words are scored. The task seems to be measuring a combination of verbal and executive working memory, as well as tapping long-term memory more than typical working memory paradigms. The embedded word may provide a retrieval cue that utilizes a long-term representation and reduces the demand on working memory. Curiously, the examinee is never informed of the possibility of embedded words. Nor is there any standardized opportunity to inquire as to whether the examinee was even aware of the embedded words. Nonetheless, an appropriate clinical procedure would be to question the child after completion of the entire battery in an effort to determine whether the child was aware of the cues and attempted to utilize them. Without verifying the examinee's awareness of the cues, it is difficult to determine their influence on the individual's working memory performance.

Arithmetic Process Approach

Adapted from the standard WISC-IV Arithmetic subtest, Part A of this task requires the examinee to mentally solve problems that are presented in the stimulus book and read aloud by the examiner. In Part B, the items scored 0 in Part A are readministered, and this time the child is allowed to use pencil and paper to solve them. While mostly involving executive working memory, the Arithmetic Process Approach tasks progressively reduce the demands on working memory, from the high demands of the completely oral and mental aspects of the standard subtest to the lesser requirements of the Written Arithmetic subtest (Part C). The WISC-IV Integrated places its Written Arithmetic subtest under the working memory domain. However, for the purposes of this text, Written Arithmetic is not considered a measure of working memory.

Interpretation of Memory Scores

Analysis and interpretation of results should begin with the Process Analysis worksheet found in the WISC-IV Integrated Record Form. Because no domain or index scores are available for the processing portion of the test, analysis of working memory in the Record Form consists of 19 pairwise comparisons at the subtest and intrasubtest level. Some of the process-level discrepancy comparisons are between the scaled score of a standard WISC-IV subtest and the scaled score of a related process subtest.

Other scaled-score discrepancy comparisons are between two scores from the same subtest, such as Letter Span Rhyming versus Letter Span Nonrhyming. And some comparisons are between the longest spans for different content or procedures. The longest span scores are the highest number of correct items the examinee recalls. For example, if a child recalls 7 digits during one of the 7-digit trials but misses both 8-digit trials, his or her span score is 7. Except for the span discrepancies, which provide only base rates, the significance of the discrepancies can be determined using critical values of .15 or .05. For more details on recommended interpretative procedures using the Record Form, as well as hypotheses and implications of various pairwise discrepancies, see the *WISC-IV Integrated Technical and Interpretative Manual* (Wechsler et al., 2004b).

The subtest and span comparisons offered in the WISC-IV Integrated's Record Form help to differentiate among the examinee's short-term and working memory strengths and weaknesses. When evaluating these discrepancies, the critical values found in the WISC-IV Integrated's manual (Wechsler et al., 2004a) should be used to determine statistical significance. Here are some important pairings, along with the rationale and some a posteriori hypotheses to account for discrepancies:

1. *Letter Span Nonrhyming versus Digit Span Forward.* Poorly developed number and arithmetic skills can influence performance on memory tasks involving digits. Thus, Letter-Span Nonrhyming should be used to gauge the capacity of phonological short-term memory whenever it is significantly higher than Digit Span Forward. Comparing Digit Span Forward with Letter Span Nonrhyming is probably more helpful than comparing it with Letter Span Rhyming, as a series of rhyming letters often lowers performance.

2. *Visual Digit Span versus Spatial Span Forward.* Research and neuroimaging has revealed that visual and spatial memory can be differentiated. Although Visual Digit Span involves symbols instead of objects, comparing performance on these two subtests may provide some indication as to the relative strength of short-term spatial memory (measured by Spatial Span Forward) compared to visual short-term memory. In instances where there is a significant difference, additional testing with a subtest that uses objects or pictures of objects is recommended.

3. *Arithmetic versus Arithmetic Process Approach (Parts A and B).* Arithmetic performance is highly related with working memory. In cases where the student has subaverage classroom performance in arithmetic, these comparisons will help to determine the extent to which working memory limitations are influencing arithmetic performance. For example, if the student's score on Arithmetic is significantly lower than his or her score on Arithmetic Process Approach (Part A), a logical hypothesis is that the student has adequate arithmetic knowledge and skills, but has difficulty demonstrating these due to working memory limitations.

Clinical Interpretation

The next step in analyzing WISC-IV Integrated working memory subtest results is to compare short-term and working memory processes with overall cognitive ability. This task can be accomplished by using the worksheet found in Appendix C and following the classification of the subtests in Appendix A. For an example of a completed worksheet, see Table 7.11. In addition to the pairings in the WISC-IV Integrated's Record Form, clinical interpretation should include several other pairings. When single subtests are being compared there is no need to transform the standard scores that have a mean of 10 and a standard deviation of 3. In such instances, a three-point discrepancy can be assumed to be statistically significant. Some of the additional pairings should involve clinical factor scores, which are calculated by averaging two subtest scores. Computing clinical factor scores is particularly applicable to the WISC-IV Integrated because of the numerous and diverse memory measures it incorporates. When subtests scores are combined to produce clinical factor scores, the scaled scores should first be transformed to a metric with a mean of 100 and standard deviation of 15 (see Appendix E) before computing the average, which is used as the clinical factor score. The suggested pairings of subtests are indicated in the cells found in Appendix A. For these clinical pairings, a discrepancy of one standard deviation should be taken as an indication of a significant difference.

1. *Phonological short-term memory versus visuospatial short-term memory.* Use Digit Span Forward and Letter Span Nonrhyming (avoid using Letter Span Rhyming because of the phonemic similarity confound) to calculate a clinical phonological short-term memory factor, and use Visual Digit Span and Spatial Span Forward to represent visuospatial short-term memory. This comparison allows investigation of modality specific strengths and weaknesses within short-term memory. In the event of a probable difference, proceed with a comparison of the visuospatial and verbal components within working memory.

2. *Verbal working memory versus visuospatial working memory.* Contrasting the Letter-Number Sequencing Process Approach and Spatial Span Backward subtests will reveal whether a modality difference exists at the working memory level.

3. *Phonological short-term memory versus verbal working memory.* Using the phonological short-term memory score computed in number 1, compare it with the Letter-Number Sequencing PA score. The purpose of this comparison is to evaluate how short-term and working memory are related within the verbal mode. If verbal working memory is significantly weaker, the implication is that the

Table 7.11 Working Memory Clinical Analysis Worksheet

Examinee's Name: WISC-IV Integrated Case Study DOB: _____ Age: 8 Grade: 3 Dates of Testing: _____

Memory Component	Battery Name	Subtest Name	Subtest Score	Component Mean	Composite or Mean	Difference	Normative S or W	Ipsative S or W	Deficit or Asset
Phonological STM	WISC-IV Integrated	Digit Span Forward; Letter Span Nonrhyming	(8) 90 (8) 90	90	(WISC-IV FSIQ) 105	−15	—	W	—
Visuospatial STM	WISC-IV Integrated	Visual Digit Span; Spatial Span Forward	(11) 105 (12) 110	108	105	+3	—	—	—
Verbal WM	WISC-IV Integrated	Letter-Number Sequencing PA	(6) 80	80	105	−25	W	W	D
Visuospatial WM	WISC-IV Integrated	Spatial Span Backward	(7) 85	85	105	−20	W	W	D
Executive WM	WISC-IV Integrated	Digit Span Backward; Spatial Span Backward; Letter Number Sequencing PA	(5) 75 (7) 85 (6) 80	80	105	−25	W	W	D

Subtest or Clinical Factor Score
Phonological STM—90
Verbal WM—80
Phonological STM—90
Visuospatial STM—108
Phonological STM—90
Visuospatial STM—108

Subtest or Clinical Factor Score	Discrepancy	Significant Difference: Y/N
Visuospatial STM—108	18	Y
Visuospatial WM—85	5	N
Verbal WM—80	10	N
Visuospatial WM—85	23	Y
Executive WM—80	10	N
Executive WM—80	28	Y

Directions: (1) Convert all subtest scores to standard scores with a mean of 100 and an SD of 15. (2) For each component, compute the mean of the subtest scores and round to the nearest whole number. (3) Enter a cognitive composite, such as a FSIQ, or compute the mean of all available memory components. (4) Subtract the composite or mean from each component mean and enter amount in Difference column. (5) Indicate whether the component mean is a normative weakness or strength (90–109 is average). (6) Using a criterion of 12 points, determine intraindividual strengths and weaknesses. (7) Determine deficits and assets. A deficit is both a normative and intraindividual weakness; an asset is both a normative and intraindividual strength. (8) Determine which factors are nonunitary. Factors are nonunitary when the two subtests involved are significantly different or when the range between the highest and lowest subtest scores exceeds 1.5 standard deviations. Nonunitary factors should be interpreted cautiously and should not be used in pairwise comparisons. (9) Compare logical pairs of components, using a 15-point difference as an indication of a significant discrepancy.

examinee's performance will drop significantly whenever the complexity and processing demands of a verbal task increase.

4. *Visuospatial short-term memory versus visuospatial working memory.* Using the visuospatial short-term memory score calculated in number 1, compare it with the Spatial Span Backward score. The rationale and hypotheses for this comparison are the same as in number 3; only the modality has changed.

5. *Phonological short-term memory versus executive working memory.* All three subtests found in the executive working memory cell in Appendix A should be used to derive an executive working memory clinical factor. Essentially, this factor represents broad working memory, as it is comprised of working memory subtests involving both visuospatial and verbal components.

6. *Visuospatial short-term memory versus executive working memory.* This is the same rationale and procedure as in number 5 but this time executive working memory is compared to visuospatial short-term memory.

Case Study Interpretation

The case study analyzed in Table 7.11 illustrates some of the benefits of using the WISC-IV Integrated when a comprehensive assessment of working memory and short-term memory is desired. The Working Memory Index derived from the standard WISC-IV administration can mask differences between basic short-term memory and the more complex functioning of working memory. Moreover, the Working Memory Index only measures phonological and verbal memory components. The analysis in Table 7.11 reveals that this individual's visuospatial short-term memory is a relative strength compared with all other aspects of short-term and working memory. The other dimensions of short-term and working memory are also weaknesses relative to the individual's overall cognitive ability (as measured by the WISC-IV FSIQ). The weaknesses in working memory are not modality specific, whereas they are modality specific within short-term memory. Overall, the profile is a strong indication that this individual's working memory is significantly weaker than his or her short-term memory. Given the same content, performance declines every time the task increases in complexity; for example, Spatial Span Backward is significantly lower than Spatial Span Forward. A student with this memory profile would certainly be at risk for learning problems.

Strengths and Weaknesses As a Working Memory Measure

The WISC-IV Integrated is one of most comprehensive short-term and working memory assessment instruments commercially available and is ideal whenever the examinee has been referred for a possible learning disability. Among the WISC-IV Integrated's strengths: (a) it has two or more subtests for some short-term and working memory components; (b) it is conormed with the WISC-IV, allowing for more reliable comparisons with general cognitive ability and other cognitive processes;

(c) it samples both visuospatial and phonological/verbal dimensions of short-term and working memory; (d) it has norm-referenced data on longest spans; (e) it divides subtests, such as Digit Span, that have historically aggregated short-term and working memory skills; and (f) it lends itself well to clinical interpretation. Depending on how a practitioner wants to use the WISC-IV Integrated, some challenges may arise: (a) there are no composite or factor scores available, such as a short-term memory or working memory composite; (b) standardized administration procedures do not allow the examiner to determine the impact of cues and strategies, such as whether the examinee is chunking numbers in Visual Digit Span; and (c) there are no standardized critical values for comparing working memory scores with other cognitive processing domains.

The NEPSY II: A Developmental Neuropsychological Assessment

The NEPSY II (Korkman, Kirk, & Kemp, 2007; see Table 7.12) is a neuropsychological instrument designed specifically for children ages 3 to 16:11. It consists of 34 subtests that are used to assess six domains: executive functioning, language, sensorimotor functioning, visuospatial processing, social perception, and memory and learning. Although the NEPSY (Korkman, Kirk, & Kemp, 1998) and NEPSY II

Table 7.12 NEPSY-II

Authors: Marit Korkman, Ursula Kirk, and Sally L. Kemp
Publisher: The Psychological Corporation
Publication Date: 2007
Age Range: 3–16:11

Memory Components
   None

Memory Subtests and Associated Memory Components
   Memory for Faces—Visuospatial STM
   Memory for Names—Learning
   Narrative Memory—Verbal WM
   Sentence Repetition—Verbal WM
   List Learning—Learning
   Word List Interference—Verbal WM, Executive WM
   Memory for Designs—Visuospatial STM
   Speeded Naming—Long-Term Retrieval
   Repetition of Nonsense Words—Phonological STM
   Verbal Fluency—Long-Term Retrieval

have their origins in neuropsychological traditions and Lurian theory, their use is not restricted to neuropsychologists, as long as those untrained in neuropsychology restrict their interpretation to the cognitive processing level (Kemp, Kirk, & Korkman, 2001). When the NEPSY was revised the most significant changes were the removal of domain scores, the addition of new subtests, and an upward extension of the test to 16 years, 11 months.

Unique Features

The NEPSY-II offers opportunities to explore several cognitive processing domains in depth. Three of its domains—Executive, Language, and Visuospatial Processing— are closely related to working memory. A full NEPSY-II administration can be lengthy, taking up to 3 hours. Consequently, the authors recommend beginning an evaluation with a brief core assessment that samples all five domains. If the core assessment reveals any potential deficits, the examiner should select additional subtests in the affected domains. In addition to selective testing, the NEPSY-II encourages close observation of behaviors by providing base rates on some testing behaviors. See Kemp et al. (2001) for behaviors to observe during each subtest.

Memory Subtests and Tasks

Memory for Faces

The examinee views photos for 5 seconds each, stating the gender of each face during its exposure. After the faces have been presented, the child identifies the faces from arrays of three faces. This activity taps visuospatial short-term memory.

Memory for Names

During this activity the examinee learns the names of six to eight line drawings of children. Because of the corrective feedback and multiple trials, this is essentially a test of learning, with a delayed-recall option administered 30 minutes later.

Narrative Memory

Narrative Memory is a story-retelling task that measures verbal working memory and long-term retrieval. In this variation of the commonly used paradigm, the examinee is questioned for additional details (cued recall) after retelling the story (free recall). If the child produces significantly more information during cued recall, the implication is that the material was encoded by verbal working memory but there is a problem with accessing it.

Sentence Repetition

This is another classic measure of verbal working memory. As no interference or secondary processing is introduced, Sentence Repetition does not appear to draw on executive working memory.

List Learning

This is a traditional multiple-trial learning task and there is the option of measuring delayed recall. After the child has five opportunities to learn the list, an interference trial is administered and then the child must recall the original list.

Repetition of Nonsense Words

The NEPSY-II authors have placed this classic measure of phonological short-term memory under the language domain.

Word List Interference

This task requires examinees to recall a list of words following interference. It is most likely tapping a combination of verbal working memory and executive working memory.

Speeded Naming

Although the battery's authors classify this subtest as a language measure, it is essentially a rapid automatic naming task in which the child must name colors, shapes, letters, numbers, or sizes. For the sake of consistency, it is herein categorized as a measure of long-term retrieval. In addition to a retrieval or naming deficit, poor performance might be due to: impulsivity (the child is fast but inaccurate); slow processing speed in general; and poor knowledge of the names.

Memory for Designs

As implied by the subtest's name, this task assesses visuospatial short-term memory.

Verbal Fluency

This task requires the child to rapidly generate words within specific semantic and phonemic categories, constituting a directed search—a function of working memory. Consequently, it is classified under the long-term retrieval component of working memory.

Interpretation of Memory Scores

Neuropsychological assessment and interpretation focus on identification of subprocesses that underlie impairment in a domain. This approach is consistent with the interpretative approach advocated in this text; that is, clinicians should evaluate the components and processes of working memory in an effort to better understand the cause of poor working memory performance. Because there are no composite scores, interpretation of NEPSY-II results meshes well with the profile analysis method. To analyze short-term and working memory performance, practitioners should use Table 7.12 to determine which memory components subtests are measuring, and then they should complete the *Working Memory Analysis Worksheet* found in Appendix C. Pairs of interest should also be contrasted, using Tables 6.8 and 6.9 for reference.

Strengths and Weaknesses As a Working Memory Measure

One of the major advantages of using the NEPSY-II for working memory assessment is that it allows in-depth assessment of language and executive functions within the same battery. For instance, poor executive functioning in inhibition (measured by an executive subtest) can influence working memory performance. Some of the drawbacks of the NEPSY-II include the lack of factor scores and complex administration, recording, and scoring procedures for some of the subtests.

Key Points

1. Most intellectual and cognitive scales include subtests that measure various components of short-term and working memory. These subtests are derived from established research paradigms developed by cognitive psychologists.

2. Regardless of which scale or scales are used, the subtests that measure memory will need to be realigned with the specific memory components they measure (see Appendix A). After realignment, a clinically oriented profile analysis can be conducted (see Appendix C) and a theory-based interpretation can be completed. For suggested pairwise comparisons, see Tables 6.8 and 6.9.

3. Most intellectual and cognitive scales offer only limited sampling of short-term and working memory components, often entirely omitting some components. Thus, memory subtests from additional scales will be necessary to complete a comprehensive assessment.

4. For additional scales, see Table 7.13.

Table 7.13 Other Cognitive and Neuropsychological Scales that Measure Working Memory

Kaplan Baycrest Neurocognitive Assessment
Authors: Larry Leach, Edith Kaplan, Dmytro Rewilak, Brian Richards, and Guy B. Proulx
Publisher: The Psychological Corporation
Publication Date: 2000
Age Range: 20–89

Memory Composites
  Immediate Memory Recall
  Delayed Memory Recognition
  Delayed Memory Recall

Working Memory Subtests
  Word-Lists 1—Recall
  Complex Figure 1 —Recall
  Repetition
  Numbers

(*Continued*)

Table 7.13   (Continued)

Leiter International Performance Scale–Revised
Authors: Gale H. Roid and Lucy J. Miller
Publisher: Stoelting
Publication Date: 1998
Age Range: 2:0–20:11

Memory Composites
  Attention and Memory
  Memory Screen
  Associative Memory
  Memory Span
  Memory Process
  Recognition Memory

Working Memory Subtests
  Associated Pairs
  Immediate Recognition
  Forward Memory
  Reverse Memory
  Spatial Memory

Reynolds Intellectual Assessment Scales
Authors: Cecil R. Reynolds and Randy W. Kamphaus
Publisher: Psychological Assessment Resources
Publication Date: 2003
Age Range: 3–94

Memory Composites
  Composite Memory Index

Working Memory Subtests
  Verbal Memory
  Nonverbal Memory

Repeatable Battery for the Assessment of Neuropsychological Status
Authors: Randolph Christopher
Publisher: The Psychological Corporation
Publication Date: 1998
Age Range: 20–89

Memory Composites
  Immediate Memory
  Delayed Memory

Working Memory Subtests
  List Learning
  Digit Span

Ross Information Processing Assessment–Second Edition
Author: Deborah Ross-Swain
Publisher: PRO-ED
Publication Date: 1996
Age Range: 15–90

Memory Composites
  None

Working Memory Subtests
  Immediate Memory
  Recent Memory

CHAPTER 8

Assessing Working Memory with Memory Scales

This chapter contains reviews of two types of memory scales: (a) those designed for a broad assessment of memory and learning, and (b) those designed specifically for working memory assessment. In general, broad memory scales emphasize learning, the product of memory. Although broad scales include "immediate" memory subtests, many of these short-term measures involve learning procedures. The learning tasks typically involve corrective feedback, multiple trials with the same content, and sometimes an interference trial. Improved retention across trials is used to calculate a learning curve. Each of the learning subtests has a delayed-recall counterpart that is typically administered about 30 minutes later. With the introduction of learning procedures, immediate memory subtests become measures of learning, even when traditional short-term memory paradigms are used.

The structure of broad memory scales is not surprising, given their "generic" theoretical orientation. For the most part, broad memory scales are based on long-accepted classifications of memory systems: (a) auditory/verbal versus visual/nonverbal, and (b) immediate versus long-term. Traditional broad memory scales seem to pay little heed to contemporary theories of working memory; most of them do not include a working memory composite. Working memory measures that are included are often placed under an "Attention/Concentration" factor. Thus, broad memory scales are more concerned with learning and long-term retention than with short-term and working memory. Consequently, it might be more valid, if not efficient, to assess working memory with cognitive batteries rather than with broad memory batteries.

In contrast, there are recently developed assessment instruments that focus entirely on short-term and working memory. Unfortunately, there are only a few of these and one of them does not have working memory in its title. Two of these contemporary scales (Alloway, 2007; Pickering & Gathercole, 2001a) have been developed in the United Kingdom and are based on Baddeley's theory. The single American counterpart (Swanson, 1995) is consistent with the theory of Daneman and Carpenter (1980). The working memory batteries also have their drawbacks, but they at least recognize and attempt to measure separate memory components, such as executive working memory. In the sections that follow, several prominent and contemporary memory scales are reviewed (additional options are listed in Table 8.10).

Wechsler Memory Scale–Third Edition (WMS-III)

The WMS-III (Wechsler, 1997b; Table 8.1) is a comprehensive, in-depth memory assessment battery designed for adults and older adolescents. With the WMS-III, an examiner can assess both the visuospatial and verbal aspects of the three core memory systems: immediate (short-term), working, and long-term. Although the WMS-III assigns only two subtests to a working memory composite, many of its other subtests tap various aspects of working memory. Moreover, the WMS-III measures learning as much as memory; for example, many of the immediate auditory memory subtests measure the ability to learn new material. Of the eight available factor scores, the most global are Immediate Memory and General Memory. Immediate Memory is composed of the Auditory Immediate and Visual Immediate Indexes. General Memory consists of the Auditory Delayed, Visual Delayed, and Auditory Recognition Delayed Indexes. Within the Auditory Delayed Index, recognition and recall can be evaluated separately. The General Memory Index is a global measure of *delayed* memory only; it should not be construed as representing working memory or general memory functioning. The Working Memory Index is comprised of a visually presented subtest and an auditorily presented subtest. There are also four supplemental Auditory Process Composites that are scored only on a percentile metric. For more details on the WMS-III see Lichtenberger, Kaufman, and Lai (2002).

Validity Evidence Regarding Working Memory

Standardization studies of the WMS-III were conducted with several clinical groups. A reading disabled group exhibited average performance on all of the WMS-III memory indexes, but did obtain its lowest mean on the Working Memory Index. When matched with a normal control group, participants with reading disabilities had a significantly higher forgetting rate for auditorily presented material.

Memory Subtests and Tasks

Six of the subtests have both an immediate recall condition and a delayed-recall condition that is administered 25 to 35 minutes later. During the immediate subtests, examinees are told to remember the information because they will be asked to recall

Table 8.1

Wechsler Memory Scale–Third Edition (WMS-III)

Author: David Wechsler
Publisher: The Psychological Corporation
Publication Date: 1997
Age Range: 16–89

Memory Composites
  Immediate Memory
  Auditory Immediate
  Visual Immediate
  General Memory
  Auditory Delayed
  Visual Delayed
  Auditory Recognition Delayed
  Working Memory

Memory Subtests and Associated Memory Components
  Logical Memory I—Verbal WM, Learning
  Faces I—Visuospatial STM
  Verbal Paired Associates I—Learning
  Family Pictures I—Visuospatial STM
  Word Lists I—Learning
  Visual Reproduction I—Visuospatial STM
  Letter-Number Sequencing—Verbal WM, Executive WM
  Spatial Span—Visuospatial STM, Visuospatial WM
  Mental Control—Long-Term Retrieval, Executive WM
  Digit Span—Phonological STM, Executive WM

it later. Examiners completing only a partial battery must be careful to maintain the interval between the immediate and delayed versions of the subtests selected. When an abbreviated battery is given, the examiner also should avoid administering several verbal or visual subtests in a row. Only three of the subtests have discontinue rules; the majority are administered in their entirety. Lichtenberger et al. (2002) suggest several specific behaviors to observe during each subtest. As with other batteries reviewed in this text, the WMS-III subtests are classified according to the Integrated Model of Working Memory (see Chapter 3), not necessarily according to the structure identified in the WMS-III manual (Wechsler, 1997b).

Logical Memory I

Logical Memory I consists of two paragraphs that are read aloud. After hearing each brief, but detail-loaded story, the examinee is instructed to start at the beginning and retell as much as can be remembered. Points are award for each element of the story the examinee recalls. This task is primarily a measure of verbal working memory, as no interference or additional processing is introduced. This subtest also provides a snapshot of how effectively verbal working memory is sustaining learning. When a second trial of Story B is administered immediately following the first trial, the amount of improved recall provides insight into the rate of learning.

Faces I

This subtest displays a set of 24 photos of unique faces, with one closely cropped face per page, each exposed for only 2 seconds. The presentation of the stimuli is immediately followed by a recognition paradigm, with 48 faces, each displayed on a separate page. The examinee views each page and indicates whether or not the face is one that was previously presented. Memory for faces is a type of visuospatial short-term memory.

Verbal Paired Associates I

For this activity, the examinee is given four opportunities to learn a list of eight semantically unrelated word pairs. After the pairs have been presented, the first word is provided and the examinee is to recall its associate. The response is provided if there is an error or no response after 5 seconds. Although the WMS-III manual classifies it as an auditory immediate task, this subtest seems to be primarily a learning task, with encoding contributions required from short-term and working memory, and retrieval from long-term memory playing a significant role. Although the paired words are unrelated, success on repeated trials depends heavily on long-term retrieval. The delayed version has both a recognition and recall component.

Family Pictures I

During this subtest, four scenes with characters (drawn from a character pool of seven) are displayed for 10 seconds each. Examinees are then asked who was in each scene, in which quadrant of the page the named character was located, and what the named character was doing. The task seems to measure primarily visuospatial short-term memory.

Word Lists I

Because there are five trials and preservation of sequence is not required, this is not the classic word span task. Like most of the other WMS-III auditory immediate subtests, it is really a measure of learning rate. Although short-term memory has initial responsibility, overall success on the task depends on executive working memory and long-term retrieval. Four times, the examiner presents the same list of 12 words at the rate of 1.5 seconds per word. Each time, the examinee recalls as many words as possible. Then, a new list designed to create interference is introduced, followed by a final recall of the original list.

Visual Reproduction I

After an exposure of 10 seconds, the examinee is directed to draw figural designs from memory. Four of the seven designs are in pairs. This subtest is a fairly direct measure of visuospatial short-term memory.

Letter-Number Sequencing

In this measure of verbal and executive working memory, the examiner reads strings of letters and numbers ranging in length from two to eight items. The examinee must then say the numbers first, in ascending order, and then the letters in alphabetical order. Letter-Number Sequencing is one of the two subtests the WMS-III classifies as working memory. There is no need to readminister this subtest if the WAIS-III Letter-Number Sequencing subtest has already been completed.

Spatial Span

This is the traditional Corsi block span task, with a forward and backward condition. The forward procedure measures visuospatial short-term memory, whereas the backward procedure measures visuospatial working memory. The combined Spatial Span score also contributes to the WMS-III's Working Memory composite score.

Mental Control

This optional subtest is primarily a measure of executive working memory, with rapid automatic retrieval predominating during the initial timed recitation of over-learned sequences, such as days of the week. The executive working memory trials involve backward recitation of numbers, days of the week, and months.

Digit Span

This is the traditional digit span paradigm, with a forward and backward condition. As usual, the forward span represents phonological short-term memory, whereas backward span is more indicative of executive working memory. There is no need to include this subtest if the WAIS-III Digit Span subtest has already been administered.

Interpretation

If the entire WMS-III battery, or the core battery, has been administered, the initial round of interpretation should adhere to the structure and procedures suggested in the WMS-III manual and Record Form, without regard for how the subtests align with specific working memory subprocesses (see Appendix E). This level of interpretation may prove particularly fruitful when there are questions about how the individual's broad visual memory compares with his or her broad auditory/verbal memory and when there are questions about how short-term memory functions compare with long-term storage and retrieval. When following the standard interpretative route, the discrepancy analysis procedures in the Record Form should be used, along with the statistical tables in the WMS-III manual. If the WAIS-III has been administered, complete the Ability-Memory Differences table in the Record Form. The use of the WAIS-III FSIQ is appropriate, given that the two scales were conormed and that there is a high correlation between memory and IQ. Significant differences between IQ and any of the eight WMS-III primary indexes are indicative of ipsative weaknesses that can impair learning. Emphasis should be given to the General Memory Index, as it subsumes three delayed indexes and is thought to provide the best estimate of overall memory functioning. Continuing to use the Record Form, proceed with pairwise discrepancy analysis of the primary indexes. The pairings allow contrasting of visual and auditory within the immediate and delayed domains, as well as comparing the Working Memory and General Memory scores.

Clinical Analysis

After gleaning available information from the Record Form, evaluators should conduct a clinical analysis of working memory subprocesses by completing the worksheet in Appendix C, using Table 8.1 or Appendix E to reassign WMS-III subtests to short-term memory and working memory processes. The clinical approach allows a subprocess analysis of working memory that may shed light on individual strengths and weaknesses unidentified by the procedures in the WMS-III Record Form. In the clinical analysis, the WAIS-III FSIQ can still be used, or another cognitive ability composite can be used if the WAIS-III was not administered (see Table 8.2 for a completed example). If some WMS-III subtests were used to supplement another test in a cross-battery fashion, all available scores should be used, including relevant cognitive processes and any working memory subtest scores from cognitive batteries. Finally, "learning" subtests from the WMS-III can be combined to form a clinical factor that should be included in the analysis.

An alternative to examining working memory strengths and weaknesses within the context of overall cognitive processing ability is to conduct a within broad memory analysis. This approach particularly applies to instances in which there has been a comprehensive assessment of memory systems, such as when the entire WMS-III battery has been completed. In such instances, memory component means can be compared to the broad memory composite provided by the scale. Otherwise, the mean of all memory components should be computed, and each working memory component should be compared with that mean (see Table 8.3 for a completed example). However, profile analysis should not be restricted to memory scores; analysis with an IQ or cognitive composite (discussed in the previous paragraph) is also

Table 8.2 Working Memory Analysis Worksheet

Examinee's Name: <u>WMS-III Case Study with WAIS-III</u> DOB: _____ Age: <u>10</u> Grade: <u>5</u> Dates of Testing: _____

Memory Component	Battery Name	Subtest/Factor Name	Subtest Score	Component Mean	Composite or Mean	Difference	Normative S or W	Ipsative S or W	Deficit or Asset
Phonological STM	WAIS-III	Digit Span Forward	(9) 95	95	WAIS-III FSIQ - 97	−2	—	—	—
Visuospatial STM	WMS-III	Faces I; Visual Reproduction I	(13) 115 (11) 105	110	97	+13	S	S	A
Verbal WM	WMS-III	Logical Memory I	(10) 100	100	97	+3	—	—	—
Visuospatial WM	—			—					
Executive WM	WMS-III WAIS-III	Mental Control; Digit Span Backward	(7) 85 (6) 80	83	97	−14	W	W	D
Processing Speed	WAIS-III	Processing Speed	NA	90	97	−7	—	—	—
Learning	WMS-III	Paired Associates I; Word Lists I	(7) 85 (8) 90	88	97	−9	W	—	—
Long-Term Storage	WMS-III	General Memory	NA	82	97	−15	W	W	D

Subtest or Clinical Factor Score
WMS-III General Memory (82)
Phonological STM (95)
Verbal WM (100)

Subtest or Clinical Factor Score
Executive WM (83)
Visuospatial STM (110)
Executive WM (83)

	Discrepancy	Difference: Y/N
	1	N
	15	Y
	17	Y

Directions: See Appendix C.

Table 8.3 Working Memory Analysis Worksheet

Examinee's Name: <u>WMS-III Case Study with Memory Mean</u> DOB: _____ Age: <u>10</u> Grade: <u>5</u> Dates of Testing: _____

Memory Component	Battery Name	Subtest/Factor Name	Subtest Score	Component Mean	Composite or Mean	Difference	Normative S or W	Ipsative S or W	Deficit or Asset
Phonological STM	WAIS-III	Digit Span Forward	(9) 95	95	Memory Mean—93	+2	—	—	—
Visuospatial STM	WMS-III	Faces I; Visual Reproduction I	(13) 115 (11) 105	110	93	+17	S	S	A
Verbal WM	WMS-III	Logical Memory I	(10) 100	100	93	+7	—	—	—
Visuospatial WM	—			—					
Executive WM	WMS-III WAIS-III	Mental Control; Digit Span Backward	(7) 85 (6) 80	83	93	−10	W	—	—
Learning	WMS-III	Paired Associates I; Word Lists I	(7) 85 (8) 90	88	93	−5	W	—	—
Long-Term Storage	WMS-III	General Memory	NA	82	93	−11	W	—	—

Subtest or Clinical Factor Score	Subtest or Clinical Factor Score	Discrepancy	Difference: Y/N
WMS-III General Memory (82)	Executive WM (83)	1	N
WMS-III Auditory Delayed (84)	WMS-III Auditory Recognition Delayed (85)	1	N
Phonological STM (95)	Visuospatial STM (110)	15	Y
Verbal WM (100)	Executive WM (83)	17	Y

Directions: See Appendix C.

important. For example, if all memory scores are low, intraindividual weaknesses will not be identified when only a low memory mean is used for profile analysis.

Pairwise analysis is the final step in the clinical procedure, regardless of which composite or mean is used in the profile analysis (see Tables 6.8 and 6.9 for applicable pairings). With the WMS-III, there is an opportunity for some unique pairings among memory systems and processes. Begin by comparing all short-term and working memory components with the General Memory Index (it represents long-term memory). Also, contrast the Auditory Recognition Delayed score with the Auditory Delayed Index (this comparison is in the Record Form). Contrasting delayed recognition with delayed recall allows the evaluator to differentiate between a long-term storage problem and long-term retrieval problem. If an individual can recognize learned information but has difficulty recalling it on demand, the implication is that the information has been encoded and stored but there is problem with retrieval. Additional interpretative advice can be found in Dehn (2006) and Lichtenberger et al. (2002).

Finally, when interpreting the WMS-III's immediate auditory subtests, examine the subtest procedures. Several of these subtests do not require sequential recall, and they provide several trials with the same content. Consequently, these subtests are not measuring simple short-term memory span, as the titles of the subtests imply. Rather, they are primarily measuring learning efficiency. Because one of the primary functions of working memory is to support learning, these subtests may provide valuable information about working memory. Nevertheless, because of the additional processes and influences involved, the examinee's scores on these particular immediate memory subtests may diverge significantly from simple span measures like digit span.

Illustrative Case Study

Tables 8.2 and 8.3 illustrate options for completing a clinical analysis when the WMS-III has been used to evaluate memory. Table 8.2 compares memory processes to the WAIS-III FSIQ, an estimate of overall cognitive ability, whereas Table 8.3 compares memory processes to the mean of the memory components involved. These test scores represent the case of a student who has always done poorly on classroom examinations, despite extensive preparation. On previous psychological evaluations, the student has consistently performed in the mid-average range on tests of short-term memory and has often performed in the average range on tests of working memory. The results of the WMS-III evaluation reveal important information about the student's memory strengths and weaknesses. First, even though her phonological short-term memory is average, visuospatial short-term memory is significantly stronger in comparison, and visuospatial short-term memory is an asset whether compared to overall cognitive ability or overall memory. Second, she has deficits in executive working memory and long-term storage. Third, the within memory analysis (see Table 8.3) does not reveal any intraindividual weaknesses or any deficits, whereas deficits emerge when the memory components are compared to FSIQ (see Table 8.2). Fourth, the Auditory Delayed score and the Auditory Delayed Recognition score are commensurate (see Table 8.3), indicating that long-term retrieval and recognition are equivalent. Several hypotheses can be derived from these results. First, the student's problems with long-term memory are probably related to her deficit in executive working memory; not enough information is being adequately encoded when she studies. Second, her problems are not due to a long-term retrieval weakness per se; she appears to be retrieving the stored knowledge she has in her possession. Third, the student may benefit from mnemonic strategies that allow her to capitalize on her visuospatial short-term memory strength.

Strengths and Weaknesses As a Working Memory Measure

Although the WMS-III purports to be a broad memory measure, it may actually sample learning and long-term storage more directly than it samples short-term memory and working memory functioning. Nonetheless, the WMS-III taps a variety of working memory functions and allows meaningful comparisons between long-term memory and short-term and working memory, as well as providing valuable information about the examinee's ability to utilize working memory resources during learning. Other advantages the WMS-III has to offer include: (a) the availability of critical values for discrepancies when administered in conjunction with the WAIS-III; (b) the ability to compare visual versus auditory memory across different retention intervals; and (c) the opportunity to compare long-term encoding and storage with retrieval. Some disadvantages to WMS-III usage include: (a) a limited opportunity to assess how the examinee encodes, stores, and retrieves semantic information (the test emphasizes episodic learning and memory); and (b) the lack of a global memory score that can be used for intraindividual analysis.

Children's Memory Scale (CMS)

The CMS (Cohen, 1997; Table 8.4) is a broad memory scale designed for children aged 8 to 16. Although the CMS taps various aspects of short-term and working memory, it does not have any factors labeled as "Working Memory." The main processes explicitly measured by the CMS are attention, learning, immediate memory, and delayed recall. Different combinations of subtests yield eight index scores (see Table 8.4). The General Memory Index adequately represents global memory processing, as it includes immediate and delayed subtests in both the visual and auditory domains. Most of the immediate memory subtests have a delayed version. However, the Delayed Recognition Index includes only auditory/verbal subtests.

Validity Evidence Regarding Working Memory

In a CMS standardization study, a sample of children with learning disabilities obtained their lowest index mean (83.6) on Attention/Concentration, the index that

Table 8.4

Children's Memory Scale (CMS)

Author: Morris J. Cohen
Publisher: The Psychological Corporation
Publication Date: 1997
Age Range: 5–16

Memory Composites
   General Memory
   Verbal Immediate
   Visual Immediate
   Verbal Delayed
   Visual Delayed
   Attention/Concentration
   Learning
   Delayed Recognition

Memory Subtests and Associated Memory Components
   Dot Locations—Learning
   Stories—Verbal WM
   Faces—Visuospatial STM
   Word Pairs—Learning
   Family Pictures—Visuospatial STM
   Word Lists—Learning
   Numbers—Phonological STM, Executive WM
   Sequences—Long-Term Retrieval, Executive WM
   Picture Locations—Visuospatial STM

consists entirely of short-term memory and working memory measures. A sample of children with Combined ADHD also obtained their lowest mean (88.6) on Attention/Concentration, as did a group with specific language impairments (a mean of 85.6). As predicted, the learning disabled group also performed poorly on the Verbal Immediate Index (a mean of 86.6) in contrast to its average mean of 97.8 on the Visual Immediate Index.

Memory Subtests and Tasks

Most of the immediate memory subtests described in this section have a delayed-recall version that is administered approximately 30 minutes later. During the immediate subtests, the examinee is always instructed to remember the items for later testing.

Dot Locations

This subtest depends on visuospatial short-term memory but is primarily measuring learning. The examinee is required to remember the spatial locations of dots on a grid. After three learning trials and one interference trial, there is a final recall of the first dot array.

Stories

This verbal working memory subtest involves recall of meaningful and semantically related verbal material. Two stories are read by the examiner, and the examinee is asked to retell the stories. Credit is given for story units recalled verbatim and also for correctly recalled thematic units.

Faces

As the name implies, this subtest assesses the ability to remember and recognize faces. The examinee is shown a series of faces one at a time. After all the stimuli have been presented, another series of faces is presented and the examinee must state whether each face was one of the faces in the initial series. Immediate memory for faces is a type of visuospatial short-term memory.

Word Pairs

This subtest is a traditional paired associate learning task with four learning trials followed by a distractor word list.

Family Pictures

Scenes of family members engaged in various activities are presented for 10 seconds each. Then, another card with the characters missing is displayed and the examinee is asked to recall which characters were in each scene, where the characters were positioned, and what they were doing. This task is primarily a measure of visuospatial short-term memory.

Word Lists

This subtest is a multiple-trial learning activity involving word lists. The task is cumulative, in that new words are added with each trial. After the first trial, the examiner reads any forgotten words, plus a list of new words. The examinee is then directed to recall as many words as possible, including words from previous lists.

Numbers

The Numbers subtest is the traditional digit span task, with a forward and backward component. Although the CMS has Numbers placed under its Attention/Concentration factor, the forward procedure is herein classified as a phonological short-term memory measure, whereas the backward procedure measures executive working memory. Unfortunately, the CMS does not provide separate scaled scores for the different procedures.

Sequences

This subtest assesses the ability to mentally manipulate and sequence auditory/verbal information. All of the items involve common well-known sequences, such as the alphabet, days of the week, and months of the year. After doing a forward version of a common sequence, a backward version is requested after a couple other items have been interspersed. The task is thought to primarily measure both long-term retrieval and executive working memory, even though it is under Attention/Concentration in the CMS structure.

Picture Locations

In this subtest, the examinee is shown a stimulus page with pictures placed in various locations within a rectangle. The stimulus page is then removed from view and the examinee is asked to place response chips on a grid in the same locations as the pictures appeared. As the task is completely nonverbal, it is clearly a measure of visuospatial short-term memory.

Interpretation

Interpretation of the CMS should proceed in a fashion similar to that of the WMS-III (explained earlier in this chapter). First, the ability–memory discrepancy analysis found in the CMS record form can be completed but only in the unlikely event that the child was also administered the WISC-III or WPPSI-R (tests the CMS is linked to). Next, tables in the CMS manual can be used to evaluate the discrepancies between various pairs of CMS Index scores. The more relevant index pairings are: (a) Visual Immediate versus Visual Delayed; (b) Verbal Immediate versus Verbal Delayed; (c) Visual Immediate versus Verbal Immediate; and (d) Visual Delayed versus Verbal Delayed. When the Attention/Concentration factor is interpreted, it can be considered somewhat representative of executive working memory.

Clinicians should then proceed with two more profile analyses that follow the worksheet and directions found in Appendix A, realigning the subtests according to their classifications in Appendix E. The first clinical profile analysis should compare memory components to a cognitive composite or cognitive mean, and include relevant cognitive processes as well as any CMS memory indexes, such as Learning and Delayed Recognition, that do not correspond to any short-term or working memory components found on the worksheet (see Table 8.2 for an example of how this type of analysis was conducted with the WMS-III). The second profile analysis should be comprised only of memory and learning scores, using the CMS General Memory Index or a mean derived from the component scores (see Table 8.3 for an example of memory-only analysis with the WMS-III). Because the Numbers subtest score confounds short-term and working memory, it should not be used in either clinical profile analysis. Analysis should conclude with examining pairs of components for significant discrepancies.

Strengths and Weaknesses As a Working Memory Measure

For a broad memory scale, the CMS offers rather limited testing of short-term and working memory; only visuospatial short-term memory is sampled in depth. None of its index scores should be used to represent working memory, and even its immediate (short-term indexes) are confounded by learning procedures. When a comprehensive assessment of working memory is in order, the CMS will need to be supplemented with other scales. The CMS may be most helpful when the evaluator wishes to collect data on the referred child's rate of learning and long-term storage. Also, the General Memory Index is a particularly useful indicator of overall memory capacity, as it is comprised of both immediate and delayed subtests in both the visual and verbal modes.

Test of Memory and Learning–Second Edition (TOMAL-2)

The TOMAL-2 (Reynolds & Voress, 2007; see Table 8.5) is a revision of the TOMAL (Reynolds & Bigler, 1994), which was one of the first comprehensive memory batteries designed for children and adolescents. Like its predecessor, the TOMAL-2 emphasizes the distinction between verbal and nonverbal memory. It also focuses on measuring learning with tasks that present the same stimuli over multiple trials. The TOMAL-2 is comprised of eight core subtests whose scores contribute to a Composite Memory Index, Verbal Index, and a Nonverbal Index. It also offers five supplementary indexes and several optional subtests (see Table 8.5). Although several of the optional subtests are traditional short-term and working memory measurement paradigms, the TOMAL-2 has neither a working memory nor a short-term memory composite.

Unique Features

Among memory and learning batteries, the TOMAL-2 is unique in that it does not emphasize the distinction between immediate and long-term memory. The authors (Reynolds & Voress, 2007) simply classify the core subtests as "Verbal" or "Nonverbal," and only two subtests, both verbal, have delayed-recall versions. Furthermore, Reynolds and Voress barely acknowledge the working memory construct, preferring instead to classify traditional working memory subtests as measures of either sequential recall or attention/concentration.

Validity Evidence Regarding Working Memory

Some of the validity evidence cited by the authors (Reynolds & Voress, 2007) goes back to the original TOMAL, with the justification being that the two versions have

Table 8.5

Test of Memory and Learning–Second Edition (TOMAL-2)

Authors: Cecil R. Reynolds and Judith K. Voress
Publisher: PRO-ED
Publication Date: 2007
Age Range: 5–59:11

Memory Composites
    Composite Memory
    Verbal Memory
    Nonverbal Memory
    Verbal Delayed Recall
    Learning
    Attention/Concentration
    Sequential Recall
    Free Recall
    Associate Recall

Memory Subtests and Associated Memory Components
    Memory for Stories—Verbal WM
    Word Selective Reminding—Learning
    Object Recall—Learning
    Paired Recall—Learning
    Facial Memory—Visuospatial STM
    Abstract Visual Memory—Visuospatial STM
    Visual Sequential Memory—Learning
    Memory for Location—Visuospatial STM
    Digits Forward—Phonological STM
    Letters Forward—Phonological STM
    Manual Imitation—Visuospatial STM
    Digits Backward—Executive WM
    Letters Backward—Executive WM
    Visual Selective Reminding—Learning

nearly identical content. The TOMAL-2 manual reports a study in which children with reading disabilities were evaluated with the TOMAL. When matched with control children on IQ, the reading disabled group had particularly low Attention/Concentration and Sequential Recall Indexes. Given that both of these indexes are comprised primarily of short-term and working memory measurement paradigms, the lower scores are consistent with predictions based on the evidence-based relations between working memory and academic learning.

Memory Subtests and Tasks
Memory for Stories

As the name of the subtest implies, examinees must recall stories read by the examiner. Credit is given for each element of the story repeated correctly; elements need not be verbatim or in order. Although associations with long-term semantic memory may cue recall, the task seems to primarily tap verbal working memory. After 30 minutes has elapsed, there is the option of a delayed-recall version of the subtest.

Word Selective Reminding

This task measures a combination of short-term recall and learning. When the examinee attempts to repeat a word list, he or she is reminded of words left out and given another opportunity to repeat the entire list. Trials continue until mastery or until six trials have been completed. Although phonological short-term memory is involved, the score seems more representative of learning than short-term memory span.

Object Recall

In Object Recall, the examiner presents a series of pictures, names them, and then has the examinee recall them. The examinee has up to five trials to correctly recall all of the pictured items. Although there is initial pairing of verbal and visual stimuli, the response is entirely verbal. The TOMAL-2 classifies this subtest as a measure of Learning and Verbal Memory. Although long-term retrieval, verbal working memory, and executive working memory are all involved to some extent, the subtest seems to be primarily a measure of learning.

Paired Recall

This is a classic paired-associate learning task that measures learning of verbal information. Some of the pairs are easy because of their semantic connections but most of the paired words have no logical connection. Although the task is primarily measuring learning, long-term retrieval is also involved as long-term semantic associations facilitate memorization of the pairs.

Facial Memory

As the TOMAL-2 authors (Reynolds & Voress, 2007) point out, memory for faces is quite different from recalling inanimate objects and abstract stimuli. Nonetheless, Facial Memory is considered a type of visuospatial short-term memory, especially since the response is entirely nonverbal and no learning procedures are involved.

Abstract Visual Memory

This is another visuospatial short-term memory task, as no verbal recoding or manipulation of the stimuli is required. Also, the stimuli are meaningless abstract figures whose recall is unlikely to be assisted by long-term memory.

Visual Sequential Memory

This subtest is more challenging than the previous two subtests because it requires the examinee to retain the sequence of meaningless geometric designs. Because corrective feedback is involved, this activity becomes more of a learning task than a specific measure of visuospatial short-term memory.

Memory for Location

Memory for location is a visuospatial short-term memory task with an emphasis on the spatial component. Examinees are required to recall the distribution of dots on a page.

Digits Forward and Letters Forward

Both of these subtests are considered measures of phonological short-term memory. The Letters Forward subtest affords the opportunity to measure phonological short-term span without digits. Under the TOMAL-2 structure, these subtests and similar subtests are placed under the Attention/Concentration Composite and/or the Sequential Recall Composite.

Manual Imitation

There are four different hand movements that are used to present a sequence of gestures that the examinee must repeat. Although attention, sequencing, and psychomotor abilities all come into play, this subtest is classified as visuospatial short-term memory.

Digits Backward and Letters Backward

Digits Backward is administered in the traditional manner, and Letters Backward is the language-related analogue. Although the TOMAL-2 places these subtests under its Attention/Concentration factor, from a working memory perspective they are both executive working memory.

Visual Selective Reminding

This activity is similar to a Corsi block tapping task, the main difference being that a series of dots is used instead of three dimensional blocks. Because of the corrective feedback and multiple trials, this subtest is primarily a learning task.

Interpretation

If the evaluator wishes to interpret TOMAL-2 test results from a working memory perspective, much of the TOMAL-2 structure and suggested analysis will need to be ignored. As recommended previously in this chapter and in Chapter 6, subtests scores should be realigned based on the short-term memory and working memory components they are thought to measure (see Appendix E), and then the procedures for completing the worksheet in Appendix C should be followed. When conducting a clinical profile analysis, use of the TOMAL-2 Core Composite should be avoided unless the learning subtests are included in the analysis. An IQ score or mean derived from the subtests included in the analysis is preferable. After a profile analysis of short-term memory and working memory components, each component can be paired with the TOMAL-2's Learning Index. If the Learning Index is significantly higher than phonological short-term memory or verbal working memory components, one implication is that the child or adolescent has acquired learning strategies that compensate for a limited opportunity to encode verbal information into long-term memory. Conversely, if phonological short-term span exceeds learning, then the possibility of poor encoding strategies or poor retrieval should be considered.

Strengths and Weaknesses As a Working Memory Measure

Despite the fact that TOMAL-2's structure does not explicitly identify working memory, the battery actually provides some in-depth sampling of both modalities within short-term memory and adequate sampling of working memory components. Although the TOMAL-2 lives up to its claim of differentiating verbal from nonverbal memory through in-depth sampling of both the visual and verbal domains, it is unfortunate that it does not discriminate immediate from long-term retention within each of these modalities. Nonetheless, given its recent norming, strong technical properties, and ease of administration and scoring, the TOMAL-2 has much to recommend it as a memory assessment instrument, especially when there is a desire to contrast learning with short-term memory and working memory capacities.

Wide Range Assessment of Memory And Learning–Second Edition (WRAML-2)

The WRAML-2 (Adams & Sheslow, 2003; see Table 8.6) is an updated and expanded version of the WRAML. When the WRAML was revised, several new subtests were added, including two new working memory subtests that allow the computation of a Working Memory Index. The core WRAML-2 battery consists of six subtests, two for each of the three main factors: Verbal Memory, Visual Memory, and Attention/Concentration. In addition to the core subtests, the WRAML-2 has 11 optional subtests, 7 of which are delayed-recall and recognition subtests that are not reviewed here. Although the battery has three delayed-recall subtests, it does not have a delayed-recall index. Also, a memory screening option consisting of four subtests can be administered. Like most broad memory batteries, the WRAML-2 is not associated with any contemporary theory of working memory.

Unique Features

Compared to similar scales, the WRAML-2 has fewer learning subtests and more straightforward immediate memory subtests. When measuring long-term retention

Table 8.6

Wide Range Assessment Of Memory And Learning–Second Edition (WRAML-2)

Authors: Wayne Adams and David Sheslow
Publisher: Wide Range
Publication Date: 2003
Age Range: 5–90

Memory Composites
    General Memory
    Verbal Memory
    Visual Memory
    Attention/Concentration
    Working Memory
    Verbal Recognition
    Visual Recognition
    General Recognition

Memory Subtests and Associated Memory Components
    Story Memory—Verbal WM
    Verbal Learning—Learning
    Design Memory—Visuospatial STM
    Picture Memory—Visuospatial WM
    Finger Windows—Visuospatial STM
    Number/Letter—Phonological STM
    Sentence Memory—Verbal WM
    Sound Symbol—Learning
    Verbal Working Memory—Executive WM
    Symbolic Working Memory—Executive WM

of information, the battery emphasizes recognition over recall. Another unique feature of the WRAML-2 is that the authors encourage qualitative analysis at the intra-subtest level and provide several structured means for doing so.

Validity Evidence Regarding Working Memory

Of the WRAML-2 indexes, the Attention/Concentration Index, which can be equated with short-term memory, has the highest correlations with reading, mathematics, and written language scores from the WJ III Achievement battery. These high correlations occurred both in a normal sample and one that was made up of children with ADHD and LD (Adams & Sheslow, 2007). In another standardization study, a sample of 29 children with learning disabilities obtained significantly lower scores on all of the WRAML-2 indexes, when compared to a matched control sample. The largest mean difference between the two groups was on the Number/Letter subtest, a distinctive measure of phonological short-term memory.

Memory Subtests and Tasks

Story Memory

This traditional memory measure is classified as a verbal working memory subtest. Neither verbatim nor sequential recall is required of either of the two stories. However, the examiner has the option of contrasting verbatim versus "gist" scaled scores. For example, someone who remembers relevant themes but forgets details will obtain a higher gist than verbatim score. Story Memory has a delayed version that can be administered after an interval of about 15 minutes.

Verbal Learning

Verbal Learning is a list-learning task that allows four trials for the examinee to learn a list of either 13 or 16 words. Although phonological short-term memory is clearly involved, the score is more representative of learning. In addition to quantifying the rate of learning with a learning slope, the number of intrusion errors (words not on the list) can be tallied and analyzed with norm-referenced data. An unusually high number of intrusion errors may indicate that executive working memory is not effectively inhibiting incorrect responses.

Design Memory

This procedure consists of exposing geometric designs for 5 seconds and than having the examinee draw them from memory. This task is clearly a measure of visuospatial short-term memory.

Picture Memory

The examinee is shown four common but visually complex scenes for 10 seconds, then shown an alternate scene, and next asked to identify the elements that have moved, changed, or been added by marking each part of the picture that is different (no verbal response is required). Because of the transformations involved, this task is more challenging than basic visuospatial activities. Thus, it seems appropriate to classify Picture Memory as a visuospatial working memory measure.

Finger Windows

For this subtest, the examiner sequentially touches holes in a card at the rate one per second and the examinee repeats the sequence. The WRAML-2 classifies Finger Windows as a measure of attention/concentration. However, because the activity is analogous to the Corsi block task it seems more appropriate to classify it as a measure of visuospatial short-term memory.

Number/Letter

This variation of the traditional measure of simple short-term memory span combines digits and letters. Number/Letter is another task purportedly measuring attention/concentration, but the more appropriate classification is phonological short-term memory.

Sentence Memory

As the name implies, this subtest requires the examinee to repeat sentences dictated by the examiner. As no interference or multiple trials are involved, it seems to be a relatively clean measure of verbal working memory.

Sound Symbol

This is a multiple-trial, paired-associate learning task in which the examinee must recall sounds associated with various abstract symbols. It is different from the typical rebus learning tasks in that semantic memory is less helpful. Although it involves long-term retrieval, for the sake of consistency it is herein classified as a measure of learning.

Verbal Working Memory

Despite the subtest's name, it is measuring executive working memory more than verbal working memory. Not only must the examinee separate animal words from non-animal words, but he or she must cope with challenging secondary processing tasks before repeating the words in order. Two transformations of the stimuli are required: separating the words into two categories and arranging the animals and non-animals by size.

Symbolic Working Memory

At the higher level of this subtest, the examinee hears a list of numbers and letters, followed by the presentation of a card with numbers and letters on it. The examinee must first point to all the stimulus numbers in the correct sequence, followed by pointing to the letters in the correct sequence. Coordination, transformation, and inhibition are all required, making this another executive working memory measure.

Interpretation

Similar to the interpretation of other memory batteries, the WRAML-2 subtests should be realigned according to the classifications in Appendix E, clinical factor scores should be computed for the tested memory components, and the profile analysis completed, following the instructions in Appendix C. The General Memory Index is a poor choice for determining discrepancies, as it does not include the working memory subtest scores. An IQ score, cognitive processing composite, or mean of the subtests comprising the analysis is a better choice. Because the WRAML-2 does not have any learning or delayed-recall indexes, the options for assessing the influence of short-term memory and working memory components on learning are limited. Instead, pairwise comparisons should focus on the immediate and delayed versions of subtests (see the test's manual for critical values). At the intrasubtest level of interpretation, the WRAML-2 offers some unique diagnostic scores. For example, norm-referenced data are available for the number of intrusion errors on the Verbal Learning test. See the WRAML-2 manual (Adams & Sheslow, 2003) for a discussion of clinical and qualitative analyses at the intrasubtest level.

Strengths and Weaknesses As a Working Memory Measure

The authors of the WRAML-2 should be commended for a carefully constructed measurement tool. For example, only indexes supported through factor analysis are included in the WRAML-2's structure. Moreover, the WRAML-2 is supported by extensive validity evidence, including studies with several clinical populations and correlations with current cognitive and achievement batteries. Also, the manual (Adams & Sheslow, 2003) provides extensive advice on profile analysis and interpretation, including an in-depth discussion of qualitative analysis. The drawbacks of the WRAML-2 are not unique. For instance, it classifies traditional short-term memory measurement paradigms under attention/concentration, and like other batteries does not attempt to separately measure working memory components.

Working Memory Test Battery for Children (WMTB-C)

Based on 25 years of working memory research, the WMTB-C (Pickering & Gathercole, 2001a, 2001b; see Table 8.7) is the only norm-referenced battery specifically designed to measure Baddeley's triarchic theory of working memory. The WMTB-C measures the central executive, visuospatial sketchpad, and phonological loop, but excludes the episodic component. The WMTB-C subtests are based mainly on established experimental paradigms known to yield relatively pure assessments of particular aspects of working memory. The scale is comprised of nine recall subtests (see Table 8.7), each of which involves the child repeating a sequence of items to the examiner. Although the battery does not offer an overall working memory score, it does produce three composites: Phonological Loop, Central Executive, and Visuo-Spatial Sketchpad.

Test Development, Reliability, and Validity

This theory-based battery was standardized on a sample of 750 children drawn from seven schools in England. Although special needs learners were included in the sample, no demographic details about the special needs sample are provided. Intertester and test-retest reliability were assessed, with the reliability study involving 99 children who were retested after an interval of 2 weeks (see Table 8.7). For most of the

Table 8.7

Working Memory Test Battery For Children (WMTB-C)

Authors: Sue Pickering and Sue Gathercole
Publisher: The Psychological Corporation Limited (London)
Publication Date: 2001
Age Range: 4:7–15:9

Memory Composites
   Phonological Loop
   Visuo-Spatial Sketchpad
   Central Executive

Working Memory Subtests, Associated Memory Components, and Reliability Coefficients*

Digit Recall—Phonological STM	.81
Word List Recall—Phonological STM	.80
Nonword List Recall—Phonological STM	.68
Word List Matching—Phonological STM	.45
Block Recall—Visuospatial STM	.63
Mazes Memory—Visuospatial STM	.68
Listening Recall—Executive WM	.83
Counting Recall—Executive WM	.74
Backward Digit Recall—Executive WM	.53

*Based on a sample of children ranging from 64–96 months in age.

subtests, test-retest reliability coefficients were higher for younger children than for older children. Exploratory and confirmatory factor analyses resulted in a factor structure mostly supportive of the tripartite model the test is based upon. Similar to other cognitive scales, the WMTB-C factor structure changes with development. With increasing age, the executive factor becomes more closely related with the phonological loop while the association with the visuo spatial component declines. Furthermore, the separation between the phonological loop and the visuospatial sketchpad increases with age. Even prior to the battery's publication, Gathercole and Pickering (2000b) reported that their central executive and phonological loop measures have high construct validity, as well as strong predictive validity for vocabulary development, literacy, and arithmetic test performance. The WMTB-C manual (Pickering & Gathercole, 2001b) reports that children's level of attainment on England's National Curriculum test is closely associated with their performance on the WMTB-C.

In regards to students with learning problems, their performance on the WMTB-C is consistent with the evidence-based relationships working memory has with academic learning. According to research reported in the manual, children with dyslexia perform poorly on the phonological and executive components while obtaining average visuospatial scores. Moreover, there is strong evidence that the WMTB-C can be a very useful tool for diagnosing learning disabilities. Using a weighted combination of scores from a preliminary version of the WMTB-C, Pickering and Gathercole (2001b) were able to correctly classify the special education status of 81% of a sample of 52 7-year-old children. Central executive measures were the best predictors of academic failure and success, with poor performance on the Backward Digit Recall subtest score being the single best predictor of special education status.

Descriptions of Subtests

Given that the WMTB-C is based on the predominant theory of working memory, its subtests will not be realigned, as has been the case with other scales reviewed in this text. Upon examination, all of the subtests seem to be measuring the short-term or working memory factor to which they were assigned by the battery's authors (see Table 8.7). Three of the four phonological loop subtests use a serial recall method in which the examinee must repeat spoken items in the original order, whereas the fourth subtest consists of a matching activity. These widely used measurement paradigms appear to call upon both components of the phonological loop—storage and subvocal rehearsal. All of the three central executive subtests require simultaneous storage and processing. Each of the executive measures consists of a complex-span procedure, including the classic listening span task originally developed by Daneman and Carpenter (1980). The stimuli involve spoken sentences, dot displays, and digit names. The predominantly verbal nature of the executive subtests means that performance on all three of the executive tasks is likely to be verbally mediated. Thus, the central executive composite score may be heavily influenced by the phonological loop and verbal abilities. For its part, the visuospatial composite may be heavily mediated by executive processes, as research has established that the visuospatial sketchpad places significant demands on central executive resources. Because older children tend to recode visual information into names, the WMTB-C visuospatial stimuli were selected on the basis of being very difficult to recode verbally, thereby reducing the influence of verbal working memory. Additional details about the WMTB-C battery and subtests can be found in Pickering (2006), Pickering and Gathercole (2001b), and Savage et al. (2006).

Digit Recall

This is a variation of the classic digits forward task, with digits spoken by the examiner at the rate of one per second. The length of the first span administered is determined by the greatest span (one to three digits) the examinee correctly responds to during the practice trial. Examinees must correctly complete four of six trials per span in order to continue to a higher span.

Word List Recall

Word List Recall is administered in exactly the same manner as Digit Recall, with the only difference being that words are used instead of digits and the maximum span is seven. The items are monosyllabic words with a consonant-vowel-consonant structure, and no word is used more than once.

Nonword List Recall

Nonword List Recall is the same as Word List Recall, except that pseudowords are used and the highest span is six. Interestingly, the nonsense words were created from the same pool of phonemes as the words used in Word List Recall. Again, the stimuli are monosyllabic with a consonant-vowel-consonant structure and no item is used more than once. In the case of nonwords, there is minimal lexical support from long-term memory, making this subtest a highly sensitive measure of phonological short-term memory.

Word List Matching

For this task, examinees are required to judge whether a word list is presented in the same or different order as the original presentation. For instance, "cat, house" is presented and followed by "house, cat." Determination of the start point, the presentation rate, and continuation rule are the same as the Digit Recall subtest. Because it involves matching, instead of repetition, this subtest removes the influence of articulatory output skills that are often deficient in young children.

Block Recall

This classic Corsi block task requires examinees to reproduce the exact sequence of block tapping presented by the examiner. A board with nine randomly attached blocks is used, and the general procedures are the same as for the Digit Recall subtest, beginning with the tapping of a single block.

Mazes Memory

On each trial, the examinee views a two-dimensional maze with a red path drawn through it. In view of the child, the examiner traces the red line with her or his finger. The maze without the line is then shown to the child who must correctly draw the line in pencil. Rather than simply solving the maze by finding a route out, the examinee must recall the exact route traced by the examiner. Each wall of a maze has two openings. Maze complexity is increased by adding more walls to the maze.

Listening Recall

The examiner says a series of short, 1- to 2-second sentences, only some of which make sense. The examinee must then immediately state whether the sentence is true or false. After hearing all the sentences in a trial (1–6 sentences), the examinee is asked to recall the final word of each sentence in the order they were presented. This task, often referred to as listening span in the experimental literature, is a type of complex-span task because it requires processing along with recall of information. The additional processing requirement necessitates the involvement of the central executive.

Counting Recall

This task involves simultaneous processing and maintenance of information because it requires the examinee to count red dots on cards and then recall the number of dots on each card in the order they were presented. The number of red dots per array ranges from three to six and the examinee must say each total number aloud.

Backward Digit Recall

This classic digits backward task is administered in exactly the same way as the Digit Recall subtest, except the examinee must recall the sequence in reverse.

Interpretation

The WMTB-C manual (Pickering & Gathercole, 2001b) does not contain any statistical tables, such as critical values for discrepancies, that can be used in conducting a profile analysis. Consequently, clinicians should proceed directly to the structured *Working Memory Analysis Worksheet* found in Appendix C. With the WMTB-C, there is no need to compute clinical factor scores because the three WMTB-C factors match the structure and definitions of the Integrated Model. For instance, the WMTB-C's Phonological Loop Component score should be entered as the Phonological Short-Term Memory "Component Mean." If no additional testing has been completed, the three component scores should be averaged and that amount entered in the "Composite or Mean" column. For the remainder of the profile analysis, including pairwise comparisons, follow the directions on the worksheet. Given its theoretical foundation, comprehensive measurement of working memory, and sound structure, the WMTB-C results should be analyzed alone. If additional memory or processing testing has been conducted, a separate cross-battery analysis should be conducted and WMTB-C scores can be included in that.

In addition to the usual profile analysis, a "within" component analysis is warranted with the WMTB-C. For each working memory component, compute the mean of the subtest scores and then compare each subtest score to that mean. For example, the subtest scores of the four phonological loop subtests should be averaged and then each subtest score compared to that mean. (The WMTB-C subtest scores have a mean of 100 and a standard deviation of 15.) A difference of one standard deviation is indicative of a significant discrepancy. Pairwise comparisons can also be conducted at the subtest level. When considering hypotheses, implications, and recommendations, there are some unique WMTB-C subtest properties to keep in mind: (a) poor performance on Backward Digit Recall is especially predictive of academic learning problems; (b) Word List Matching is a purer measure of the phonological loop, as performance is less influenced by long-term memory representations and speech production difficulties; (c) Block Recall is regarded as a test of "spatial" working memory; (d) Mazes Memory involves both visual and spatial information; and (e) performance on Counting Recall, Digit Recall, and Backward Digit Recall may be influenced by poorly developed arithmetic skills. In addition to scaled scores for each subtest, the WMTB-C provides standardized data on Span scores. Span scores denote the number of sequential items that can be held in working memory; for example, if the examinee successfully completes a span of three digits on Digit Recall, his or her Span score for Digit Recall is 3. The highest attainable spans range from six to nine. Age-divided tables provide the percentage of children who obtain each Span score.

Strengths and Weaknesses As a Working Memory Measure

The WMTB-C has much to offer: (a) it facilitates interpretation because of its theoretical foundation; (b) its structure is supported through factor analysis and other validity studies; and (c) it provides in-depth sampling for three short-term memory and working memory components. Weaknesses include: (a) the test is based on a small sample in England; (b) Baddeley's episodic component is not included; and (c) no discrepancy data are available in the manual.

Automated Working Memory Assessment (AWMA)

The AWMA (Alloway, 2007; Alloway et al., 2006, 2004; see Table 8.8) is a computer-based assessment of working memory skills that was developed in the United Kingdom. Its main purpose is to identify significant working memory problems in individuals between 4 and 22 years of age. Most of the AWMA's subtests are modifications of WMTB-C subtests. However, the structure of AWMA is different from the WMTB-C and the AWMA includes several unique subtests. The administration, scoring, and interpretation are fully automated. Because only minimal training is required for its use, teachers are able to use the screening version of the AWMA. In addition to a two-subtest screener, there is a short-form with four subtests and a long form with 12 subtests. The long form takes up to 40 minutes to complete. The AWMA is available in 10 languages, including Spanish and Mandarin. A standardized version of the AWMA was released in October of 2007.

Of the currently available memory batteries, the AWMA most closely approximates the Integrated Model of Working Memory proposed in this text. Alloway (2007) has taken Baddeley's theory another step further by abandoning the domain-general notion of working memory and its "central executive" label. Instead, Alloway has divided working memory into verbal working memory and visuospatial working memory. Although nearly all memory scales assess visuospatial short-term memory in depth, the AWMA is the first scale that attempts to separately measure visuospatial working memory, distinguishing the subtests from their short-term memory

Table 8.8

Automated Working Memory Assessment (AWMA)

Author: Tracy P. Alloway
Publisher: Harcourt Assessment (London)
Publication Date: 2007
Age Range: 4–22

Memory Composites
   Verbal Short-Term Memory
   Verbal Working Memory
   Visuospatial Short-Term Memory
   Visuospatial Working Memory

Memory Subtests, Associated Memory Components, and Reliability Coefficients

Digit Recall—Phonological STM	.84
Word Recall—Phonological STM	.76
Nonword Recall—Phonological STM	.64
Listening Recall—Verbal WM, Executive WM	.81
Counting Recall—Verbal WM, Executive WM	.79
Backwards Digit—Verbal WM, Executive WM	.64
Dot Matrix—Visuospatial STM	.83
Mazes Memory—Visuospatial STM	.81
Block Recall—Visuospatial STM	.83
Odd-One-Out—Visuospatial WM	.81
Mr. X—Visuospatial WM	.77
Spatial Span—Visuospatial WM	.82

counterparts by incorporating additional processing tasks. Empirical support for the inclusion of a visuospatial working memory factor is reviewed by Alloway et al. (2006). According to Alloway et al., working memory was probably undivided in the past because nearly all measures of storage plus processing were verbal. The division of working memory into a visuospatial working memory factor and a verbal working memory factor is consistent with the Integrated Model of Working Memory advocated in this text.

Validity Evidence Regarding Working Memory

Despite the logical structure of the AWMA, confirmatory factor analysis (Alloway et al., 2006) resulted in more support for Baddeley's traditional three-factor model, with separate verbal and visuospatial factors at the short-term level and a third factor representing the shared variance between the verbal and visuospatial working memory tasks. This finding is in line with Baddeley's perspective that working memory consists of a domain-general processing factor that is primarily executive. In the Alloway et al. study, the visuospatial and verbal working memory components appear to be the same factor because they share 83% of the variance. Alloway et al. concluded that the dynamic formats of complex visuospatial tasks involve executive functions just like verbal tasks do. Despite the unclear findings, the AWMA structure omits the central executive and retains the two new working memory factors.

Memory Subtests and Tasks

All of the subtests begin with auditory directions presented while the computer screen is blank. For verbal tests, the computer presents the stimuli auditorily and the examinee speaks the response. The examiner then presses the left or right arrow keys to record whether the response was correct or incorrect.

Digit Recall, Word Recall, and Nonword Recall

These are the traditional measures of phonological short-term memory, with Digit Recall consisting only of forward digits.

Listening Recall, Counting Recall, and Backwards Digit

Alloway (2007) classifies these three subtests as measures of verbal working memory, but according to the scheme in this text they are also measuring executive working memory because all of them include a secondary processing task. Counting Recall, in particular, places heavy demands on executive working memory because it incorporates counting and visuospatial processing. See the WMBT-C section for details on the listening recall and counting recall paradigms.

Dot Matrix, Mazes Memory, and Block Recall

Mazes Memory and Block Recall are modifications of the WMBT-C subtests with the same names (see WMBT-C section for details). In Dot Matrix, a red dot in a 4×4 matrix is exposed for 2 seconds, then the examinee recalls the positions by tapping the appropriate squares on the computer screen. All three of these tasks are clearly measures of visuospatial short-term memory.

Odd-One-Out, Mr. X, and Spatial Span

In Odd-One-Out, the examinee views three shapes presented in a row of boxes and then identifies the odd-one-out shape. After a series of presentations, the examinee must recall the location of each odd-one-out in the correct order. In Mr. X, two cartoon characters, one wearing a blue hat and the other wearing a yellow hat, hold a ball in various positions. At the end of the sequence the examinee must recall the locations of the ball held by Mr. X with the blue hat by pointing to a picture with eight compass points. Complexity is created by rotating Mr. X with the blue hat. Spatial Span is similar to Mr. X in that the examinee must recall the correct locations of a red dot on one of two objects by pointing to a picture with three compass points.

Like the Mr. X subtest, a brief secondary processing task is also introduced. All three of these subtests can be considered complex visual span tasks that are more demanding than visuospatial short-term tasks but yet do not require extensive involvement from executive working memory. Thus, they seem to be appropriately categorized as visuospatial working memory measures. However, as indicated in the factor-analytic studies and suggested by Alloway et al. (2006), these subtests also tap executive working memory processes.

Interpretation

The AWMA software was unavailable as this book went to press. However, given the theory-based structure of the AWMA, it is recommended that clinicians base their interpretation primarily on the AWMA's computerized analysis. The only suggested deviation from the battery's analysis is that the Verbal Working Memory score should also be considered as representative of executive working memory. Otherwise, there is no need to realign any of the subtests. As always, there is the option of combining AWMA component scores with other test results in a cross-battery fashion (see Appendix C).

Strengths and Weaknesses As a Working Memory Measure

The AWMA is a major step forward in the delineation of short-term memory and working memory components. In particular, it supports the idea that working memory functions should be separated, instead of grouping all of them under an executive construct. In addition, it explicitly discriminates between short-term memory components and working memory components. Also, the AWMA facilitates the assessment of working memory, making it feasible to screen large numbers of children for working memory weaknesses.

Swanson Cognitive Processing Test (S-CPT)

The S-CPT (Swanson, 1995; see Table 8.9) is a norm-referenced processing test that was standardized on a United States sample of 1,630 subjects, ranging in age from 4.5 to 78.6 years. Although not indicated by the title, the test appears to be designed mainly for in-depth assessment of working memory. While not explicitly divided into factors that align with Baddeley's model, the S-CPT is consistent with Baddeley's theory in that all of the tasks require simultaneous processing and storage of information (Swanson & Berninger, 1995). Accordingly, each of the 11 subtests interjects processing (interference) between stimulus presentation and recall. The distracter, referred to as a *process* question, is introduced to induce simultaneous processing. Consequently, all of the subtests tap executive working memory. Many of the S-CPT's working memory tasks are related to the Sentence Span measure originally developed by Daneman and Carpenter (1980). Daneman and Carpenter's goal was

Table 8.9

Swanson Cognitive Processing Test (S-CPT)

Author: H. Lee Swanson
Publisher: PRO-ED
Publication Date: 1995
Age Range: 4:5–78:6

Memory Composites
  Total
  Semantic
  Episodic
  Auditory
  Visual
  Prospective
  Retrospective
  Strategy Efficiency Index
  Processing Difference Index
  Instructional Efficiency Index
  Stability Index

Memory Subtests and Associated Memory Components
  Rhyming Words—Executive WM, Verbal WM
  Visual Matrix—Executive WM, Visuospatial WM
  Auditory Digital Sequence—Executive WM, Verbal WM
  Mapping and Directions—Executive WM, Visuospatial WM
  Story Retelling—Executive WM, Verbal WM
  Picture Sequence—Executive WM, Visuospatial WM
  Phrase Sequence—Executive WM, Verbal WM
  Spatial Organization—Executive WM, Visuospatial WM
  Semantic Association—Executive WM, Verbal WM
  Semantic Categorization—Executive WM, Verbal WM
  Nonverbal Sequencing—Executive WM, Visuospatial WM

to develop complex measures of memory span, a goal that Swanson has operationalized in depth.

Unique Features

Although traditional "static" testing can be conducted with the S-CPT, Swanson (2006b) promotes its use as a "dynamic" measure. Swanson defines *dynamic assessment* as the examiner modifying test procedures, much like testing of the limits, in an effort to understand learning potential. Dynamic administration follows a test-teach-test format that yields three types of scores: *initial, gain*, and *maintenance*. The initial scores result from traditional, static testing procedures that allow no feedback or prompting. The dynamic round is accomplished by the examiner providing prompts, called probes, whenever the examinee fails an item. Several hints or cues are then provided, with general hints given first and then more explicit hints if needed. The highest score obtained under probing conditions, referred to as the *gain* score, is taken as an indication of the examinee's potential, and the number of hints necessary to achieve it is considered an indication of the examinee's responsiveness to instruction. It seems that Swanson (2006b) interprets responsiveness to probes as an indication of a performance deficit and an indication that the examinee would benefit from strategy instruction. The maintenance scores are derived from retesting (after about a 30 minute interval) in which no assistance is provided. Swanson (2006b) argues that the dynamic testing gain scores are better predictors of reading and mathematics achievement than the S-CPT's static (initial) scores or IQ scores from other batteries.

Perhaps the most unique contribution of the S-CPT to working memory assessment is Swanson's (1995) attempt to measure the influence of strategy knowledge and use. Several of the subtests present the examinee with four strategies for remembering information and require him or her to select a strategy for use during the subtest. However, there is no attempt to teach any strategies. The specific strategies offered depend on the subtest's content; they are different for each subtest. The S-CPT is also unique in that it samples a broad array of memory processes: verbal and visuospatial; semantic and episodic; and prospective and retrospective retrieval conditions.

Validity Evidence Regarding Working Memory

Regarding technical properties, the reliability coefficients of the composite and subtest scores are within acceptable limits. Swanson (1995) reported that internal consistency reliability estimates for the subtests range from .72 to .92, and composite score reliability coefficients range from .82 to .95. Swanson (1992, 1995) also found high intercorrelations among these working memory subtests, indicating that a general working memory factor transcends the type of processing (e.g., verbal or visuospatial) required. Factor analysis actually revealed two primary factors—semantic memory and episodic memory—with a second-order factor—executive processing—reflecting the shared variance between the two. Additional validity evidence for the S-CPT consists of correlations ranging from .50 to .86 between S-CPT subtests and Daneman and Carpenter's (1980) reading and listening span tasks (Swanson, 1995). The S-CPT initial scores also have moderate correlations with traditional intellectual measures (e.g., .80 with the K-ABC). Regarding students with learning disabilities, they demonstrate less improvement under the dynamic testing conditions than do their average-achieving peers. More details on the S-CPT, as well as research conducted with it, can be found in Swanson (1992, 1995, 1996).

Memory Subtests and Tasks

Because each of the S-CPT subtests introduces an interference task, all of them are measures of executive working memory, even those that are modality specific. Nonetheless, each subtest could also be categorized by its content and labeled as verbal working memory or visuospatial working memory (see Table 8.9). Certainly, none of the subtests should be considered measures of short-term memory because all of them are complex-span paradigms. Administration of the entire battery takes approximately 2 hours, but there are abbreviated administration options.

Rhyming Words

The purpose of the Rhyming Words task is to assess the examinee's ability to recall acoustically similar words. Rhyming sets of words (e.g., *ship-blip-clip*) are presented at the rate of 2 seconds per word. There are nine word sets that range from 2 to 14 monosyllabic words. Before recalling the words, the examinee is asked whether a particular word was included in the set. The examinee must then recall the previously presented words in order. In addition to executive working memory, this task taps verbal working memory.

Visual Matrix

The purpose of this task is to assess the examinee's ability to remember visual sequences within a matrix. The examinee studies a matrix containing a series of dots for 5 seconds. After the matrix is removed, the examinee is asked a process question, such as "Were there any dots in the first column?" Then the examinee is directed to draw the dots in the correct boxes on the blank matrix. The matrices range in difficulty from 4 squares and 2 dots to 45 squares and 12 dots. In addition to executive working memory, this task measures visuospatial working memory.

Auditory Digital Sequence

This subtest assesses the examinee's ability to remember numbers embedded in a short sentence, such as, "Now suppose somebody wanted to have you take them to the hospital at 1802 Main Street?" Prior to stimulus presentation, the examinee is shown a figure depicting four strategies for recalling numeric information: rehearsal, chunking, association, and elaboration. After the strategies have been explained, the examinee is presented with a sentence that has embedded numbers. The examiner then asks a process question about nonnumerical information in the sentence. Examinees are then told that they will have to recall the numbers in order after pointing to the figure of the strategy they will attempt to use. They are allowed 10 seconds to select a strategy. Finally, examinees are required to recall the numbers in order. The range of difficulty is from 3 to 14 digits. This task primarily measures executive and verbal working memory.

Mapping and Directions

The purpose of this task is to determine whether the examinee can remember a sequence of directions on a map that is devoid of any written labeling. For 10 seconds, the examinee views a street map containing lines connected to dots that illustrate the path of a bicycle through a city. Then the examinee must answer a process question, such as, "Were there any dots in the first street?" Then the examinee is shown pictures of recall strategies and asked to select one he or she will use (same procedure as in Auditory Digital Sequence). Finally, examinees are asked to reproduce the lines and dots on a blank map. The number of dots presented ranges from 4 to 19. This task essentially measures executive and visuospatial working memory.

Story Retelling

The purpose of this recall task is to assess the examinee's ability to remember a series of episodes from a paragraph read by the examiner. The paragraph is a 12-sentence story, and each sentence contains 8 to 11 words and two idea units. After being asked a process question about the content, the examinee is directed to recall all the events that occurred. For a sentence to be recalled correctly, it must include the two idea units in the correct order. The subtest measures executive and verbal working memory.

Picture Sequence

This subtest assesses the examinee's ability to remember a sequence of shapes of increasing spatial complexity. Pictures of shapes are presented on a series of cards, a process question is presented, cards are gathered and shuffled, and then the examinee is directed to arrange the cards in the correct sequence. The set size varies from 3 to 15 cards. In addition to executive working memory, this task measures visuospatial working memory.

Phrase Sequence

The purpose of this subtest is to assess the examinee's ability to recall isolated phrases (e.g., "a barking dog," "a rolling ball"). After each presentation, there is a process question and the same strategy selection procedure as in Auditory Digital Sequence. The number of phrases ranges from 2 to 12. This subtest measures executive working memory, as well as verbal working memory.

Spatial Organization

The purpose of this task is to determine the examinee's ability to remember the spatial organization of cards that have pictures of various shapes. The examinee is allowed 30 seconds to examine a set of eight cards arranged in a row-by-row, top-down fashion. After a process question and the same strategy selection procedure as in Auditory Digital Sequence, the examinee must rearrange the now shuffled up cards in the correct order. The raw score is the number of rows correctly recalled. In addition to tapping executive working memory, this task also assesses visuospatial working memory.

Semantic Association

The purpose of this task is to assess the examinee's ability to organize sequences of words into abstract categories. The examinee is first presented with a set of words (one every 2 seconds), such as: *coat, saw, pants, hammer, boots, wrench*. Then the examinee is required to answer a process question, such as "Which word, *saw* or *pliers*, was said in the list of words?" Then the examinee is directed to recall the words that go together (i.e., *coat, pants, boots*, and *saw, hammer, wrench*). The examinee may recall the words in any order within a particular category. The range of difficulty is two categories with two words each to five categories with four words each. In addition to executive working memory, this task taps verbal working memory.

Semantic Categorization

This task assesses the examinee's ability to remember words within categories. The examinee is given a category label and a list of words that goes with the category, for example, "*job*, teacher, doctor, plumber." There are two or three words within each category. After a process question and the same strategy selection procedure as in Auditory Digital Sequence, the examinee is asked to recall the category name first and then any words that went with that category. Because it taps semantic memory, this task involves verbal as well as executive working memory.

Nonverbal Sequencing

This subtest assesses the examinee's ability to sequence a series of cards depicting nonsense shapes. Given a series of mixed-up cards, the examinee is allowed 2 minutes to organize the cards in rows, with the first row having one card, the second row having two cards, and so on. The examinee then studies the arrangement for 30 seconds, before the examiner picks up the cards and shuffles them, inserting two distractor cards. After a process question and the same strategy selection procedure as in Auditory Digital Sequence, the examinee must reproduce the arrangement by each row. This subtest primarily measures executive and visuospatial working memory.

Interpretation

In the case of the S-CPT, use of the *Working Memory Analysis Worksheet* may be unnecessary, unless there is a desire to include S-CPT component scores in a broader cross-battery analysis involving other memory factors or related cognitive factors. The S-CPT's many unique scores require clinicians to follow the interpretative procedures recommended in the manual (Swanson, 1995). Standard scores are available for each testing condition—initial, gain, and maintenance—on each subtest and for all of the composites, except the indexes. There are also norm-referenced tables for: (a) the Processing Difference Index scores (the difference between the initial and gain score); (b) the Stability Index scores (the difference between the initial and maintenance score); (c) the Strategy Efficiency Index scores (how well the examinee chooses appropriate strategies); and (d) the Instructional Efficiency Index scores (the number of prompts necessary for a correct response). Certainly, the Auditory (verbal working memory) and Visual (visuospatial working memory) Components should be compared with the Total Composite and with each other, using a standard deviation of difference as an indication of significance. Clinicians who desire a thorough profile analysis may elect to compute the subtest mean for each of the domain-specific clusters, and compare each subtest to its respective mean. This procedure may be followed with subtest pairwise comparisons. In keeping with the test's design and stated objective, the Processing Difference Index scores (provided only for individual subtests) should be examined to determine how responsive the examinee is to cues and hints. Of course the Processing Index Difference scores need to be tempered by the Instructional Efficiency Index scores; that is, if gains required several prompts, then they are less meaningful. Stability Index scores for each subtest should also be examined. The Stability Index score is like a delayed-recall score in that it measures how well the examinee retains information for an interval of about 30 minutes.

Although the intended meaning and implications of each score are explained in-depth, the manual's advice on the computation and interpretation of scores is a little confusing. Furthermore, interpreting S-CPT results is particularly challenging because some data and technical properties necessary for reliable statistical analysis are lacking. Among the technical deficiencies are: (a) all of the composite scores are derived from one conversion table, instead of separate norms for each composite; (b) there are separate tables for each subtest but they are divided into only six age groups, with only four tables covering the age range from 4:11 to 19:11; and (c) there are no tables that identify critical values for discrepancies or the base rates for discrepancies.

Strengths and Weaknesses As a Working Memory Measure

One of the main advantages of S-CPT use is that the Total Composite Score may be the best representation of overall working memory functioning currently available because: (a) the Total Composite does not include any short-term memory measures; (b) all of the subtests involve a secondary processing task, thereby involving executive working memory, which is considered the essence of working memory; (c) there is a balance of verbal and visuospatial measures; (d) there is no attempt to prevent strategy use (it is encouraged); and (e) there are a total of 11 subtests tapping core working memory functions. Therefore, the Total Composite can be interpreted as a very valid representation of the examinee's overall working memory capacity. Moreover, the S-CPT makes several noteworthy contributions to the assessment of working memory. First, Swanson (1995) has selected and enhanced measures known to be strongly correlated with higher level memory processes and learning. Second, the S-CPT provides an opportunity to assess the impact of strategy use and prompting on performance. Third, the S-CPT certainly offers a broad and in-depth assessment of working memory.

Nevertheless, there are several concerns with the S-CPT, in addition to the interpretative challenges:

1. First, some test reviewers have expressed reservations about the S-CPT. In a *Mental Measurements Yearbook* review, Callahan (1998) was highly critical of the S-CPT. Callahan contended that the S-CPT: (a) has complex, confusing, and vague administration and scoring rules; (b) has a sample that was not carefully stratified; and (c) has only two composite scores that are supported by factor analysis. Because of these concerns, Callahan concluded that the S-CPT should be used only for research purposes.

2. From the title of the test and discussion in the manual, it appears as if Swanson (1995) believes the battery is a measure of broad cognitive processes, not just working memory. At times, he seems to consider the Total Composite Score as the equivalent of a FSIQ.

3. Suggested interpretations of the gain scores seem to be quite speculative, as there is no research linking this dynamic assessment measure to instructional approaches and interventions. Perhaps the safest interpretation of gain scores is that they reveal the effectiveness of simple feedback on the examinee's working memory performance.

4. Another potential concern related to dynamic testing and to encouraging examinees to use strategies during testing emerges from a recent investigation by St. Clair-Thompson (2007), who found that allowing examinees extra time to implement strategies does indeed result in higher span scores. However, St. Clair-Thompson concluded that extensive strategy use during testing eliminates the ability of the measure to predict higher level cognitive and academic skills. If the purpose of working memory assessment is to predict cognitive and academic performance, then results from dynamic testing may miss the mark.

Key Points

1. Although working memory batteries and broad memory scales tend to assess working memory components in more depth than cognitive instruments, the inclusion of subtests from additional batteries may still be necessary when a comprehensive assessment of short-term and working memory is required.

2. The categorization of subtests in broad memory scales is often at odds with contemporary theories of working memory and inconsistent with the Integrated Model of Working Memory. Thus, memory subtests often need to be realigned in order to assess performance on specific memory components. Realignment facilitates profile analysis (using the *Working Memory Analysis Worksheet*) and enhances interpretation.

3. When conducting a profile analysis, there are several options for the composite or mean that memory scores will be compared with: (a) a FSIQ or the equivalent; (b) a cognitive processing mean that may include memory scores; (c) a global memory score from a memory battery; and (d) a mean derived from all the memory subtests that were administered. Two of these routes should always be taken when analyzing results from a memory battery: (a) memory components should be compared to an IQ or cognitive processing mean, and (b) a "within memory" analysis should be conducted using either a global memory score or a calculated memory mean.

4. See Table 8.10 for additional memory scales not reviewed in this chapter.

Table 8.10 Other Scales that Measure Working Memory

Burns Brief Inventory of Communication and Cognition
Author: Martha S. Burns
Publisher: The Psychological Corporation
Publication Date: 1997
Age Range: 18+
Memory Composites
   Orientation to Factual Memory
   Auditory Attention and Memory
   Visual Attention and Memory

Working Memory Subtests
   Immediate Auditory Recall of Digits
   Immediate Auditory Recall of Digits with Distractions
   Immediate Auditory Recall of Functional Information
   Functional Short-Term Recognition
   Short-Term Recognition of Pictures
   Short-Term Recognition of Words

California Verbal Learning Test–Second Edition, Adult Version
Authors: Dean C. Delis, Joel H. Kramer, Edith Kaplan, and Beth A. Ober
Publisher: The Psychological Corporation
Publication Date: 2000
Age Range: 16–89

Memory Composites
   Immediate Recall
   Primacy-Recency Recall
   Short-Delay Free Recall
   Short-Delay Cued Recall
   Long-Delay Free Recall

Table 8.10 (Continued)

Other Scales that Measure Working Memory

    Long-Delay Free Recall-Retention
    Long-Delay Cued Recall

Working Memory Subtests
    List A Immediate Recall
    List A Short-Delay Free Recall
    List A Short-Delay Cued Recall
    List A Long-Delay Free Recall
    List A Long-Delay Cued Recall

California Verbal Learning Test–Children's Version
Authors: Dean C. Delis, Joel H. Kramer, Edith Kaplan, and Beth A. Ober
Publisher: The Psychological Corporation
Publication Date: 1994
Age Range: 5–16

Memory Composites
    None

Working Memory Subtests
    List A Trials 1–5
    List B Free-Recall Trial
    Short-Delay Free Recall
    Short-Delay Cued Recall

Children's Auditory Verbal Learning Test–Second Edition
Author: Jack L. Talley
Publisher: Psychological Assessment Resources, Inc.
Publication Date: 1993
Age Range: 6:6–17:11

Memory Composites
    Immediate Memory Span
    Level of Learning
    Interference Trial
    Immediate Recall
    Delayed Recall
    Recognition Accuracy
    Total Intrusions

Working Memory Subtests
    Trial 1
    Interference

(*Continued*)

Table 8.10   (Continued)

Other Scales that Measure Working Memory

Comprehensive Test of Phonological Processing (CTOPP)

Authors: Richard K. Wagner, Joseph K. Torgesen, and Carol A. Rashotte
Publisher: PRO-ED
Publication Date: 1999
Age Range: 5–24:11

Memory Composites
  Phonological Memory
  Rapid Naming

Working Memory Subtests
  Memory for Digits
  Nonword Repetition
  Rapid Color Naming
  Rapid Digit Naming
  Rapid Letter Naming
  Rapid Object Naming

Learning and Memory Battery (LAMB)

Authors: James P. Schmidt and Tom N. Tombaugh
Publisher: Multi-Health Systems Inc.
Publication Date: 1995
Age Range: 20–80

Memory Composites
  None

Working Memory Subtests
  Digit Span
  Supraspan Digit

Learning Efficiency Test–Second Edition

Author: Raymond E. Webster
Publisher: Academic Therapy Publications
Publication Date: 1992
Age Range: 5–75

Memory Composites
  Visual Ordered Recall
  Visual Unordered Recall
  Auditory Ordered Recall
  Auditory Unordered Recall
  Total Visual Memory

Table 8.10   (Continued)

Other Scales that Measure Working Memory

   Total Auditory Memory
   Global Memory

Working Memory Subtests
   Visual Ordered Immediate Recall
   Visual Ordered Short-Term Recall
   Visual Unordered Immediate Recall
   Visual Unordered Short-Term Recall
   Auditory Ordered Immediate Recall
   Auditory Ordered Short-Term Recall
   Auditory Unordered Immediate Recall
   Auditory Unordered Short-Term Recall

Memory Assessment Scales

Author: J. Michael Williams
Publisher: Psychological Assessment Resources, Inc.
Publication Date: 1991
Age Range: 18 and over

Memory Composites
   Global Memory
   Short-Term Memory Summary
   Verbal Memory Summary
   Visual Memory Summary

Working Memory Subtests
   List Learning
   Verbal Span
   Visual Span
   Prose Memory

The Word Memory Test

Author: Pat Green, Kevin Astner, and Lyle M. Allen
Publisher: CogniSyst, Inc.
Publication Date: 2000
Age Range: 18+

Memory Composites
   None

Working Memory Subtests
   Immediate Recognition
   Free Recall

CHAPTER 9

Working Memory Interventions

One unique characteristic of successful attempts to improve working memory performance is that we may never be able to determine the actual basis of the change. As implied by the controversies over capacity discussed in Chapter 2, improved performance may result from expanded capacity, increased efficiency, or growth in collateral processes. Because most psychologists believe that capacity is primarily innate, there is a great deal of skepticism about anyone's ability to actually increase working memory capacity. As such, direct remediation of impaired working memory functioning is usually considered unrealistic (Glisky & Glisky, 2002). Therefore, the consensus seems to be that improved working memory performance should mainly be attributed to more effective use of existing and generally immutable working memory capacity. This consensus is consistent with the research literature on interventions for processing and memory impairments—nearly all of the efficacious interventions consist of teaching individuals cognitive strategies and mnemonics designed to improve performance, mostly through more effective utilization of resources. A strategy is how an individual approaches a task; it includes such dimensions as planning, executing, and evaluating one's performance. Ironically, taking a behavioral perspective on this cognitive psychology dilemma seems appropriate. That is, let's not worry too much about *why* working memory performance improves. It is more important that we know *what works*.

We do know what works and we have for some time. Extensive laboratory and applied research (e.g., Ericsson & Kintsch, 1995) has documented many interventions that significantly increase the amount of information that can be stored and retrieved, both in the short and long term. Interventions for cognitive and working memory processing deficiencies have mostly been researched and developed within the fields of neuropsychology, cognitive psychology, educational psychology, and special education (for a review, see Dehn, 2007). After introducing the constructs of information processing and working memory, cognitive psychologists (e.g.,

Anderson, 1976; Gagne, 1974) were instrumental in promoting early research on compensatory strategies for working memory limitations. Educational psychologists and special educators followed with investigations into how strategic processing and effective teaching practices might enhance encoding and retrieval of information (e.g., Rosenshine & Stevens, 1986; Swanson & Hoskyn, 1998). More recently, neuroscientists have been using neuroimaging technology to reveal the various brain processes involved in learning (Berninger & Richards, 2002), and neuropsychologists have been developing new treatments for working memory deficits associated with ADHD (Klingberg et al., 2002) and acquired brain injury (Eslinger, 2002). Descriptions of various interventions, including details on training procedures and general training recommendations, are the subject of this chapter. The methods in this chapter are evidence-based procedures supported by extensive experimental and applied research.

Working memory interventions are appropriate for those with either normative or intraindividual weaknesses, but imperative for those with deficits. Whereas most learners spontaneously develop and utilize memory strategies, even generating their own when the need arises, students with learning disabilities are less adept at generating and utilizing effective memory strategies. Although they would benefit most individuals, the interventions discussed in this chapter are primarily intended for young children, students with learning disabilities, students with cognitive disabilities, students with acquired working memory loss, and individuals with poor working memory performance or poor academic performance. For those with a severe normative weakness but no intraindividual weakness, working memory interventions are still appropriate, but low functioning in related cognitive processes may limit improvement.

In the educational environment, acceptable interventions need to include the goal of optimizing academic learning outcomes, not just developing specific cognitive abilities, such as working memory. Fortunately, working memory is known to underlie nearly every aspect of academic learning. Thus, working memory interventions are very appropriate in an educational environment. Furthermore, most of the interventions discussed herein can be conducted by teachers and other school staff, with only minimal training or self-study. Keeping the strategies simple is not just for the benefit of teachers. Higher level, more involved strategies demand greater working memory resources to implement. For individuals with impaired working memory capacity, trying to use complex strategies can be self-defeating. Consequently, teachers and others who teach cognitive strategies need to appraise a student's working memory capacity prior to intervention and select strategies unlikely to further overload the student's working memory. Assessment should continue during intervention (see Chapter 6 for informal assessment recommendations) to evaluate the efficacy of the treatment. Educators should also base their final determination of effectiveness on measurement of related cognitive processes and academic skills, especially since academic improvement is a primary objective. For instance, some studies have found no postintervention improvement in working memory processes but have found improvement in related areas of achievement (Leasak, Hunt, & Randhawa, 1982).

Finally, readers may be surprised by some of the interventions recommended in this chapter, especially those not traditionally considered to be short-term memory or working memory interventions. Keep in mind the multiple reciprocal relationships working memory has with other memory systems, cognitive processes, and academic skills. Given these close and mutually interdependent relationships, interventions that enhance functioning in related cognitive processes and academic skills can produce subsequent improvement in working memory. Furthermore, there is interdependency among the subcomponents of short-term, long-term, and working memory. Thus, it should be assumed that an intervention directed toward one memory component will have crossover benefits for closely associated components, and that interventions that address one memory system may impact others. In particular, any and all interventions for long-term memory are recommended when the goal is to improve working memory performance. Even if the outcomes of long-term memory interventions are limited to long-term memory functioning, such improvement will either reduce demands on working memory or allow individuals to circumvent the capacity limitations of short-term and working memory (Ericsson & Kintsch, 1995). Therefore, strategies and mnemonics originally developed for long-term memory are very appropriate interventions for working memory.

To illustrate the potential effects of related interventions on working memory, consider the case of Joey, introduced in Chapter 5. Recall that Joey had reading and written language disabilities and that he had deficits in short-term and working memory, but his phonemic awareness was average. Over the course of 6 months, Joey received after-school tutoring in reading for 1 to 2 hours a week. The reading program emphasized a phonetic approach to reading decoding. No direct effort was made to improve Joey's short-term or working memory. When retested at the end of 6 months, Joey's standard score in basic reading skills had gone from an 84 to a 93, about a year's growth, and his score in reading comprehension had improved from an 82 to a 91, also a year's growth. However, the most significant improvement was in his working memory, the score climbing from 87 to 100 (a 12-point or greater change in standard scores is usually statistically significant), driven mainly by a 12-point improvement in a backward digits task. Keep in mind there was no instruction or practice directed toward working memory. A plausible explanation for the changes is that his improved reading decoding skills freed up more working memory resources, leading to enhanced working memory functioning during reading (as indicated by his improved reading comprehension) and possibly to improved working memory performance, in general.

General Approaches to Working Memory Interventions

Working memory, and other cognitive processing interventions, can be categorized as remedial, compensatory, or a combination of remedial and compensatory. Remedial interventions have the expressed goal of correcting a working memory deficit by directly addressing the area of weakness. Compensatory interventions emphasize using the individual's cognitive or memory strengths and assets, in an effort to bypass the deficit, thereby reducing its impact on learning and performance. Interestingly, the brain's response to innate and acquired impairments seems to be compensatory. Neurological investigations have discovered that the brain compensates for functional loss by using other brain regions to perform cognitive functions not normally associated with those regions (Berninger & Richards, 2002; Wilson, 1987). The fact that associated cognitive processes are sometimes able to perform the function of a damaged or poorly developed process is testimony to the plasticity of the brain (Shaywitz, 2003). It is also a compelling reason for attempting memory and cognitive processing interventions; that is, interventions classified as remedial may prompt the brain to compensate, thereby improving functioning. Finally, many interventions combine the remedial and compensatory approaches, utilizing the individual's strengths in effort to remedy his or her specific deficits.

Past attempts to address memory and other processing deficits through a remedial approach alone have generally been unsuccessful (Lee & Riccio, 2005). Although some recent studies (e.g., Olesen, Westerberg, & Klingberg, 2004) have suggested that some working memory processes can be improved through direct training (that does not include strategy training), the extent of this research is limited. This is not surprising, given that the capacities of various cognitive processes have traditionally been thought to be constant. Despite the limited success of remedial interventions, we should not assume that the brain's capacity for working memory is immutable. The neural systems on which working memory depends may have more plasticity than once thought. A recent study of interventions (Olesen et al.) designed to remediate executive working memory in adults with acquired brain injury has shown promising results. Not only did working memory performance improve, but, after training, there was increased brain activity in areas where working memory is housed.

Perhaps one reason for the failure of remedial interventions is that they have an exclusive emphasis on specific impairments while ignoring intact functions (Eslinger & Oliveri, 2002). In contrast, compensatory approaches entail methods that focus on strengths, bypassing the deficient processes (Glisky & Glisky, 2002). Compensatory approaches typically involve strategy training, but they may also include external aids, accommodations, or substitute methods of reaching the same goal. Compensatory methods also include practices that modify the learning environment, such as the effective instruction techniques that reduce demands on working memory. Given the complexity of working memory and involvement of several cognitive processes in any given academic learning task, compensatory interventions may succeed because they tend to be broad-based and focus on higher level processes. For example, a performance problem on a measure of working memory may be due to a specific impairment in phonological short-term memory. A broad-based treatment approach would include all working memory components, with an emphasis on executive working memory. Such an approach is more likely to promote generalization (Levine et al., 2000) and may also indirectly improve unidentified related processing deficits.

Combined Interventions

Interventions that address working memory limitations may be both remedial and compensatory, with the general goals of improving performance in a deficient area while increasing the efficiency of the individual's normal working memory processes. Most effective interventions reported in the literature are multidimensional, and most psychologists and educators agree that a combined approach, with the potential of additive effects from multiple methods, has the best chance of success (Work & Choi, 2005). For example, when there is a documented shortcoming in phonological short-term memory, a combined approach would be to target a normal executive working memory along with an intervention for phonological short-term memory. The result might be an improvement in the individual's ability to use executive working memory strengths to compensate for the deficit in phonological short-term memory. With the combined approach, the goal of focusing on a deficient process is not so much to increase capacity, but rather to optimize its use (Lee & Riccio, 2005). In addition, individuals are taught strategies that further enhance the functioning of a strong working memory component. The overall goal of the combined approach is more efficient use of existing working memory resources.

Strategy Interventions

Many of the evidence-based interventions discussed in this chapter involve the teaching of strategies. In and of themselves, the strategies are neither remedial nor compensatory; how they are classified depends on how they are used. For example, if the purpose of implementing a strategy is solely to improve an impaired working memory component, it is considered a remedial strategy. Whether a strategy will be used in a remedial or compensatory manner is important for the trainer or teacher to consider when selecting interventions. Nonetheless, because the intent of most strategies is to increase efficiency, they are, by their nature, more compensatory than remedial. Thus, the primary focus of this chapter will be on evidence-based compensatory interventions, generally classified as strategies. Strategy training can be incorporated into classroom instruction or conducted with individual students. Furthermore, the emphasis on strategic interventions is based on the assumption that strategies can improve working memory performance, whether the origin of the poor performance is restricted capacity or a lack of strategy knowledge and strategy use (Kar et al., 1993).

General Strategy Training Procedures

In general, strategy training should be explicit and intensive over an extended period of time until strategy use becomes automatic. In contrast to other educational interventions, successful strategy training requires more than the teaching of procedural knowledge. Post-intervention maintenance also depends on the trainee knowing why, when, and how to use the strategy. Deshler and Schumaker (1993), Mastropieri and Scruggs (1998), Pressley and Woloshyn (1995), and Pressley, Johnson, and Symons (1987) all provide suggestions for strategy training procedures. Ultimately, the success of memory strategy training depends on adherence to the following training procedures:

1. Conduct training during one-on-one brief, focused sessions, held at least a couple times weekly over a period of several weeks.

2. Precede memory strategy training by informing the student of her or his memory strengths and weakness so that the student acquires metamemory and begins to recognize the personal need for adopting strategies.

3. Teach only one memory strategy at a time, at least until the student is familiar with the idea of strategy use.

4. Inform the student about the purpose and rationale for the strategy, including when, where, why, and how to use the strategy. Explain the benefits and how use will result in better memory performance. Without this knowledge, the student will have difficulty selecting the most appropriate strategy for the task at hand.

5. When introducing a strategy, model all steps and components of the strategy while thinking aloud. Use different examples when modeling and demonstrate how your thinking progresses while implementing a strategy.

6. Explain, demonstrate, and teach in detail each step in the strategy procedures, with special attention paid to aspects of strategy use that generally are not well understood.

7. Provide plenty of relevant practice, first with external guidance, then with the student thinking aloud, and finally while encouraging the student to internalize the strategy, such as having the student whisper the steps while enacting them.

8. Provide multiple practice sessions that permit the strategy to be learned, over-learned, and automatized. During practice provide corrective feedback on strategy usage.

9. To facilitate recall of strategy procedures, it is helpful to teach students a cuing system, such as an acronym.

10. Give the student positive reinforcement for using the new strategy. Also, provide data on the success of the strategy so that the student understands the personal efficacy of strategy use.

11. Encourage the student to monitor and evaluate strategy use and to attribute his or her success to strategy use.

12. Encourage generalization by discussing applications of the strategy and practicing the strategy with different materials and under different situations.

Good Strategy Users

Following effective training procedures will not guarantee that trainees will generalize strategies or continue to use the strategies they have learned. Training procedures can encourage generalization and maintenance, and metacognitive training can increase the likelihood of continued use (see the later section on metacognition), but only some trainees will persist over the long-term. Trainees who continue to use the new strategy are most likely those who have been called *good strategy users* by Pressley et al. (1987). If this is true, an overall objective of any strategy training should be to help the trainee develop into a better strategy user. In regards to working memory, a good strategy user:

1. Possesses numerous strategies for accomplishing a variety of working memory goals.

2. Is aware of her or his memory strengths and weaknesses.

3. Knows when and where memory strategies are applicable.

4. Knows how to modify techniques for specific situations and materials.

5. Can coordinate a number of goal-specific strategies.

6. Knows how to select a memory strategy that will be effective for the task at hand.

7. Monitors strategy use and task performance to determine if the goal is being accomplished.

8. Attributes successful performance to strategic memory processing.

9. Has developed memory strategies that are efficient, automatic, and flexible.

10. Has a repertoire of several memory strategies that can enhance working memory performance.

When Interventions Fail

There are a variety of reasons for intervention failure when training has been provided in evidence-based strategies. When troubleshooting to identify potential causes of the failure, consider the following causes and remedies:

1. The trainer has not followed the training procedures with integrity. If interventions are to succeed, the trainer needs to adhere to general training guidelines (see earlier section) and the specific training steps for each strategy.

2. The trainee may be a poor strategy user. This is often the case with students who have learning disabilities. Consider the characteristics of *good strategy users*

described in the previous section and incorporate training procedures that will help the trainee to develop into a good strategy user.

3. There is a failure to generalize and apply the strategy to different situations and materials. Whereas most students are capable of generalizing and transferring memory strategies they have been taught (Lange & Pierce, 1992), students with cognitive and learning disabilities often have difficulty generalizing. Nonetheless, failure to generalize may not be a student problem but may be due to insufficient generalization training. For example, training should include specific generalization procedures, such as conducting the training with a variety of materials and in a variety of settings.

4. The trainee's working memory performance becomes worse during or after training. Learning and using a new strategy will itself put increased demands on working memory, resulting in even less capacity leftover for storage. Complex strategies, in particular, overload working memory further because they are essentially introducing a secondary task. Consequently, it is important to provide scaffolding during memory strategy training. For example, trainers and teachers might aide the learner's short-term storage by repeating the information as many times as necessary so that the learner can focus on the new process. Also, the trainer should provide overt guidance as the learner progresses through the steps. Extensive practice is important; the demands on working memory will be reduced once the strategy has become automatized. One way to prevent a decline in working memory performance is to start with teaching a simple strategy and progress to more challenging strategies while closely monitoring their impact.

5. There is a decline in performance of nonmemory tasks that rely heavily on working memory. The explanation is the same as in number 4. Involved strategies, such as elaboration, may overtax an already limited working memory, resulting in even poorer performance on a task such as reading comprehension.

6. Deficiencies in related cognitive processes may reduce the effectiveness of the memory strategy. For instance, very slow processing speed or limited fluid reasoning ability may make it difficult to utilize some complex or higher level strategies. In such cases, it may be necessary to address these deficiencies first or determine approaches that will circumvent them.

7. The student is not taking the training seriously. For students to be motivated they must become convinced of the strategy's personal efficacy. The best approach is to demonstrate the efficacy of the strategy; show the student the data that document his or her improvement.

8. Not every memory strategy will work with every individual. Despite the best efforts to carefully assess memory strengths and weaknesses, other undetected variables may be influencing working memory performance. Furthermore, not

all students respond well to the usual training techniques, or the strategy may be a mismatch with the unique manner in which the trainee processes information. In such instances, try teaching another strategy or adapt the training methods to match the trainee's learning style.

Overall, students with low working memory spans can be expected to benefit the most from training in working memory strategies, even though they are slower to learn the strategies than trainees with high working memory spans (Turley-Ames & Whitfield, 2003). This is not surprising, given that those with high spans are most likely strategy-wise and efficiently utilizing their capacity already. Despite the finding that learning higher level strategies, such as semantic strategies, leads to superior performance over the learning of simple strategies, such as rehearsal (McNamara & Scott, 2001), those with low spans may not benefit as much from more involved strategies. This most likely results from the fact that learning and applying complex strategies consumes even more of the limited working memory resources of those with low spans. For example, learning a new imagery strategy may conjure up interfering thoughts that working memory must then inhibit.

Selection of Interventions

In general, success is not guaranteed, even with well-established, evidence-based interventions and faithful adherence to training procedures. Another determinant of success is how well an intervention matches the needs of the learner, the academic task, and the environmental demands. Interventions for working memory problems should be closely tailored to the cognitive or neurodevelopmental profile of the student, thereby increasing the likelihood of positive outcomes (Feifer & DeFina, 2000). Moreover, selecting an intervention that focuses on an isolated short-term or working memory process may not be the most appropriate choice, given the interactive nature of memory components during cognitive activity (Swanson, Hoskyn, & Lee, 1999). It is also frequently the case that a student has impairments in several cognitive processes. Thus, broad-based, higher level processing interventions have the best chance of success.

There should be a match between a student's needs, areas targeted for improvement, and intervention method selected. Appropriate matching depends on the teacher or trainer being knowledgeable of working memory components and their interaction, as well as the individual student's working memory strengths and weaknesses. For example, if there is a phonological short-term deficit and the goal is to increase sequential phonological memory span, then the intervention should be purely auditory. That is, using visual stimuli for practice may increase performance during training but may not carry over to situations where the stimuli are auditory only. On the other hand, cross-modal or cross-component interventions are probably a good idea, especially when the goal is to increase overall working memory performance.

The Importance of Early Interventions

Education's renewed emphasis on early interventions is consistent with the brain-based research on early development and the ability of the brain to adapt to impairments. Similar to academic interventions, some working memory and related interventions are more effective at earlier ages; for example, there are diminishing returns on phonological processing interventions as students progress through elementary school (National Reading Panel, 2000). Memory interventions, especially those of a remedial nature, need to occur before the maturing of the specific brain regions where the process of concern is located. The key to successfully educating and retraining the brain is enrichment and treatment at critical developmental stages (Feifer & DeFina, 2000). Change is more difficult once neural structures are established and myelination is complete. The windows of opportunity for most memory processes are in early childhood and early elementary years; however, higher level cognitive processes that involve executive functions continue to develop throughout adolescence. Another reason for early intervention is that working memory underlies so many types of learning. For example, phonological short-term memory development creates a critical foundation for language learning, as well as for literacy development.

Metacognitive Training

Even when individuals with learning disabilities and working memory deficits possess a repertoire of cognitive and memory strategies, they seldom select and apply an effective strategy when the situation warrants its use (Pressley & Woloshyn, 1995). One reason this occurs is that these individuals are deficient in metacognition, a prominent aspect of executive processing (Wynn-Dancy & Gillam, 1997). The conscious use of executive control processes is referred to as *metacognition* (Livingston, 2003). Metacognition consists of two aspects: self-awareness and self-control. Self-awareness consists of knowledge of one's skills and cognitive abilities, understanding how one's skills and abilities match up with task requirements, and knowing which processes and strategies will lead to successful goal attainment. Self-control is comprised of the ability to consciously monitor, manage, control, and evaluate one's cognitive activities; it also includes strategy selection and usage. For example, recognizing the need for a strategy and selecting an appropriate one are metacognitive acts. For most individuals, metacognition develops naturally, without instruction or intervention. Poorly developed metacognition is often the cause of inefficient executive functioning. The level of metacognition is highly correlated with success on complex cognitive tasks, such as reading comprehension (Gersten et al., 2001). Despite its importance, special efforts to teach metacognition are usually unnecessary, as metacognitive thinking and control are embedded in most cognitive strategies, including working memory strategies. When they are not, teachers and trainers need only adhere to the general procedures for strategy training (see previous section) to incorporate metacognitive training. Nevertheless, there are times when the awareness component of metacognition and metamemory (see following section) needs to be addressed prior to the strategy training. In conclusion, the effective use of working memory resources and strategies significantly depends on metacognition and metamemory.

Interventions designed to improve metacognitive functioning go back more than 30 years (e.g., Meichenbaum & Goodman, 1971). Metacognitive strategy training typically involves the teaching of strategies relating to a specific cognitive, behavioral, or academic task (Graham & Harris, 1989; Loarer, 2003); for example, poor readers are often taught metacognitive strategies concerning reading comprehension. Key aspects of metacognitive interventions include teaching the individual: to become aware of his or her processing deficits and strengths; to select an appropriate strategy for the task at hand; to self-monitor progress toward an objective; to revise or change strategies when necessary; and to self-evaluate. Isolated metacognitive strategies, such as self-monitoring, can also be taught and typically result in significantly improved metacognitive functioning and cognitive strategy use and performance (Moreno & Saldana, 2005; Swanson, 2001; Wynn-Dancy & Gillam, 1997). Training in self-instruction, which has consistently been supported in the literature (Cicerone, 2002), is another form of metacognitive training. To develop internalization of self-regulatory behavior, three stages of self-instruction training are involved: the student first learns to verbalize or think aloud; the student then whispers to herself or himself while engaging in self-regulatory behavior; and finally the student talks silently to himself or herself before and during actual task performance. Self-instruction training is often paired with learning a problem-solving algorithm, such as goal-management training (Levine et al., 2000).

Metacognitive or executive strategy training is often selected even when there is no evidence of a metacognitive or executive processing deficit. This is because higher level strategic thinking permits more effective use of underutilized or impaired processes. Educators might also select executive strategy training when students fail to spontaneously use or maintain strategies they have learned (Lawson & Rice, 1989). When executive or metacognitive processing is itself the underdeveloped process, then the intervention should include self-instruction training because self-regulation depends on internal self-talk.

Metamemory Training

Essentially, metamemory is metacognition as it applies to memory. Adequate metamemory is an essential prerequisite for memory strategy training because successful self-directed strategy use depends on self-awareness. Since the regulation of memory functioning is already relegated to general metacognition, the construct of metamemory is restricted to: self-awareness of memory strengths and weaknesses; an understanding of how memory functions; and memory strategy knowledge, including the self-efficacy of various mnemonics (Bunnell, Baken, & Richards-Ward, 1999). Young children and those with learning disabilities have limited metamemory.

Poorly developed metamemory is one reason individuals may not allocate sufficient resources or select an adequate strategy, given a demanding memory task. An indication of poorly developed metamemory is when individuals underestimate or overestimate their memory performance before, during, and after a memory task. Another way to assess metamemory is through an interview or self-report, including asking the individual to self-appraise memory strengths and weaknesses. Given its importance, metamemory instruction should precede strategy training or be embedded in strategy training. The crucial elements of metamemory training are:

1. Using age-appropriate language and concepts, teach the learner about how memory works. Include descriptions of short-term, long-term, and working memory, with an emphasis on how everyone experiences an overloaded working memory and how this leads to forgetting. Also discuss how learning depends on efficient use of our memory systems. Finally, explain to the child that we have control over our memory systems; for example, consciously organizing information helps us remember it better.

2. Educate the learner about his or her memory strengths and weaknesses. Begin by explaining memory assessment results in language the child can comprehend. Once the learner understands his or her memory functioning and how it relates to the task at hand, he or she will be able to accurately appraise the situation and select appropriate strategies.

3. Discuss the rationale for making an effort to use memory strategies. Explain that learning the procedures in a strategy is not enough; we also need to learn the when, where, why, and how of strategy use.

4. Conduct some simple memory exercises and ask the learner how he or she tried to remember the information. Provide feedback on the effectiveness of the strategy that was used and talk with the learner about how to self-evaluate effectiveness. In discussing effectiveness, attribute success to skill and effort (not luck or ability) and to the faithful implementation of the strategy.

5. Once the learner has acquired rudimentary metamemory, including awareness of which strategies work for him or her, encourage the learner to self-advocate for accommodations and methods that minimize load on working memory. Self-advocacy may strengthen metamemory and reinforce the use of strategies.

Working Memory Interventions

The majority of the memory interventions reviewed in this chapter are appropriate educational interventions that do not require special training to implement. Educational staff, including special education teachers, school psychologists, other educational consultants, and pupil services providers are capable of training students in most of these procedures. In addition to independent study of the training methods involved, the trainers need to have basic background knowledge of working memory and related processes, such as is provided in this text. Faithful adherence to the procedural details recommended in the research literature is the other prerequisite. Practitioners also need to keep in mind that the interventions reviewed in this chapter are primarily intended for those students who have learning challenges or who are already identified as having a learning disability or a working memory impairment. However, even successful students may benefit from exposure to these interventions. Most of the interventions can be adapted for individual, group, or classroom use.

Traditionally, working memory interventions have had the express purpose of increasing capacity for short-term retention of information. Nevertheless, there has always been the implicit goal of increasing the amount of information encoded into long-term memory, based on the presumption that a longer interval in short-term storage increases the likelihood of long-term storage. Given this implicit goal and the fact that a primary function of working memory is to facilitate learning, the success of working memory interventions should ultimately be judged as much by long-term retention, as by short-term retention. Consequently, the working memory interventions described in this chapter consist of strategies designed to improve short-term memory, working memory, and long-term memory. Strategies that have customarily been categorized as long-term memory (see later section on long-term memory interventions) methods are included because they improve the performance of working memory. Furthermore, interventions designed for related cognitive processes and skills, such as phonological processing and reading comprehension, are included because they also influence working memory performance. Therefore, this text broadens the scope of working memory interventions and emphasizes increased learning, not just short-term retention, as an indicator of working memory improvement.

Interventions for short-term and working memory typically involve the teaching of a strategy or mnemonic. Most individuals acquire several short-term memory and working memory strategies over the course of development, but some do not or they do not use strategies consistently. The benefits of strategy use are evident; strategic individuals recall more information than individuals who are nonstrategic (McNamara & Scott, 2001). Many investigations have confirmed that working memory capacity, especially working memory span, can be increased through strategy training (Comblain, 1994; McNamara & Scott, 2001; Minear & Shah, 2006) and that the improvement often generalizes to untrained working memory tasks and related cognitive processes, such as reasoning (Klingberg et al., 2002). Also, Olesen et al. (2004) found that brain activity related to working memory increases after working memory training. Strategy use is the result of experience and practice and is usually domain specific (Ericsson & Chase, 1982). So, unless the trainee is encouraged to apply the strategy to different situations, generalization of strategy use seldom occurs. Continued strategy use may also depend on the individual's awareness of its benefits. Working memory strategies can be divided into two basic types: rote and relational. Rote strategies involve reproducing information in the same form in which it was encountered. Relational strategies transform information through recoding, organizing, or reconstructing (Levin & Levin, 1990).

Rote Strategies

Rote strategies consist mainly of basic rehearsal strategies, such as simple repetition, that serve the primary purpose of maintaining items in phonological short-term memory. Rote strategies have the advantage of being simple to learn and apply because they do not involve any higher level processing that attaches meaning to the stimuli. They also place minimal demands on working memory resources, especially after they become routine and automatized. Several studies (see later section on rehearsal strategies) have reported significant improvement in short-term memory and working memory performance after subjects learn to use rote strategies. However, the teaching and use of rote strategies has been heavily criticized because rote strategies are usually less efficient and effective than higher level strategies that are meaning based.

At first glance, rote repetition may seem efficient and effective. A process that requires minimal attention and no comprehension is efficient in the sense that it requires little involvement by working memory. And rote repetition can be deemed effective because it certainly preserves information for the short term. Nevertheless, if long-term retention is the goal, rote memory strategies fall short. The amount of learning resulting from merely repeating an item is typically small and dependent on the type of material. The assumption that simply holding verbal information in short-term memory for a longer period of time leads to more learning and retention appears to be fallacious (Baddeley, 1990; Shiffrin, 1999). It seems that rote rehearsal of information does not necessarily enhance transfer to long-term storage (Estes, 1999). When it comes to learning, simple rehearsal-based strategies are sometimes inferior to no strategy at all (Scruggs & Mastropieri, 1990).

The actual amount and durability of information transferred to long-term memory is thought to depend on whether the information is just being passively rehearsed or is being more actively and consciously manipulated. There is little evidence to suggest that simply holding information in short-term passive storage facilitates learning. Rather, the degree of learning depends on the manner in which the information is processed in working memory (Baddeley, 2006). Similar to the levels-of-processing model advocated by Craig and Lockhart (1972), deeper processing of the information seems to lead to better long-term retention than superficial processing, such as rote repetition. In essence, rote strategies are inferior to relational strategies that attach meaning to the information to be learned. Another drawback to rote strategies is that they do little to increase the overall processing efficiency and capacity of working memory (Parente & Herrmann, 1996). Despite the disadvantages, for some individuals, especially those with low cognitive abilities and constricted working memory capacity, training in rote strategies may be very beneficial and necessary before higher level strategies can be taught.

Relational Strategies

In contrast to rote strategies, extended higher level working memory processing does increase the probability of long-term storage. Higher level processes, classified as relational strategies, make the information more meaningful, thereby increasing the probability of retaining information over the long term. When related schemas are available, relational processing can occur automatically; when a developed schema is absent, effortful relational strategies can create relationships where none existed previously. Nearly all mnemonics, especially those involving imagery, can be considered relational strategies. The learning principle underlying the effectiveness of relational strategies is that meaningfulness strongly influences learning; attaching meaning to information makes it more memorable.

Phonological Short-Term Memory Interventions

Most phonological short-term memory interventions involve rehearsal training. The interventions are mainly intended for children who demonstrate an actual deficit in the phonological store (e.g., substandard scores on a digits forward or memory for words task). Rehearsal training may also be provided to children who are not using a rehearsal strategy, are using one infrequently, or would benefit from a more sophisticated rehearsal strategy. Children with phonological processing delays should also be considered for rehearsal training. Developmentally, children begin to employ rehearsal strategies as early as 5 years of age. Thus, with school-aged children, it is never too early to start; for instance, there is empirical evidence that even 5-year-old children can be trained to use verbal rehearsal and that this improves their recall (Henry & Millar, 1993). To determine if a child is using rehearsal, observe for indicators, such as moving lips, or ask the individual what she or he is doing to remember the information.

Rehearsal Strategies

Rehearsal, simply saying the material over and over to oneself, is the first and most basic memory strategy acquired, and it usually develops without any explicit instruction or training. The development of subvocal rehearsal strategies is thought to be at least partially responsible for increased verbal working memory span as children develop (Minear & Shah, 2006). Although children may begin using a simple rehearsal strategy as early as 5 or 6 years of age, rehearsal is not a widespread strategy until the age of 10 (Gill et al., 2003). Rehearsal, a serial repetitive process, allows information to be maintained in working memory for a longer period of time (Gathercole, 1999), thus enhancing short-term recall and facilitating long-term storage encoding. In older children and adults, rehearsal can be carried out semiautomatically without a very concentrated use of attention or working memory resources (Cowan, 2005). Children with disabilities often fail to develop or use verbal rehearsal strategies.

Numerous studies have found explicit rehearsal training to significantly improve short-term memory span, as well as the working memory performance of children, with and without disabilities (Comblain, 1994; Conners et al., 2001; Klingberg et al., 2002; Olesen et al., 2003). Also, Minear and Shah (2006) cite several studies in which explicit rehearsal training resulted in significantly improved working memory performance. Teaching rehearsal strategies may be particularly beneficial for students with learning or intellectual disabilities. Hulme and Mackenzie (1992) reviewed research that improved short-term recall in subjects with moderate learning difficulties to the same level as that of age-matched normal control subjects. Other inquiries have reported that rehearsal training can improve working memory in individuals with Down's syndrome. In one rehearsal training study (Conners et al., 2001), the digit span of subjects with Down's syndrome improved by a whole digit (from 1.8 to 2.8). In another study of children to adults with Down's syndrome (Comblain, 1994), verbal memory span was increased from two to three words after 8 weeks of training. None of the subjects showed signs of rehearsal prior to training but all of them were using the rehearsal strategy by the time training ended. As expected, strategy use declined after training. Nevertheless, subjects still had a half-word gain when retested 6 months later, even though they no longer displayed signs of rehearsal.

Even normally developing students may benefit from rehearsal training. For instance, Ornstein, Naus, and Stone (1977) found that second-graders, who were already rehearsing one or two items together, were able to learn to rehearse more items together and, when they did, their recall became similar to that of sixth graders. Adults with low working memory spans have also shown improvement after training in simple rote rehearsal strategies (McNamara & Scott, 2001; Turley-Ames & Whitfield, 2003). Many other investigations (reviewed in Ornstein et al., 1977) have demonstrated that children and adults can improve short-term verbal memory span by learning more active and effective rehearsal strategies. Moreover, there is evidence of improvement in nontrained memory activities (Olesen et al., 2003) and evidence for the maintenance and durability of rehearsal training, especially when extensive practice and overlearning are provided during the initial training phase (Broadley, MacDonald, & Buckley, 1994). At least in regards to short-term retention, rehearsal strategies have often been shown to be more effective than more elaborate memory strategies (Turley-Ames & Whitfield). Perhaps this is because their simplicity is less demanding of already limited working memory resources or because more complicated strategies introduce interference.

Despite their effectiveness, rehearsal strategies are not a panacea for working memory limitations. For instance, rehearsal training of students with learning disabilities does not always eliminate their intraindividual working memory weaknesses. It also appears that the benefits of training are highly task specific; generalization seldom occurs. Furthermore, although there are strong indications that subvocal rehearsal extends phonological short-term memory span, it appears to have less impact on maintaining or increasing complex verbal working memory span or long-term learning (Engle et al., 1992). Perhaps this is because subvocal rehearsal consists of phonetically based encoding whereas higher level processing and encoding of information is semantically oriented.

Rehearsal Training Procedures

The task involves training children to name the first item after it is presented, then the first and second items together after the second item is presented, and so on until all items in the series have been presented and rehearsed. For example, the subject (S) is taught to overtly repeat successively longer sequences as each word is spoken by the instructor (I) (e.g., I-foot, S-foot; I-bird, S-foot, bird; I-house, S-foot, bird, house; and so on). In the overt cumulative approach, participants receive one new list item at a time and each time they hear a new item they repeat the entire list from the beginning. An alternative is to repeat the list as many times as possible while waiting for another item to be added. With this option, the trainer instructs the learner to say the to-be-remembered words aloud as many times as possible between presentation of items and to keep adding new items to the list as they are presented (Turley-Ames & Whitfield, 2003). At first, students should be directed to say the stimuli aloud to make sure they are rehearsing correctly, but as the intervention progresses they should whisper the words and eventually subvocalize.

For children with normal cognitive ability, lists constructed of randomly chosen similar and dissimilar words should be used. Continue practicing until the trainee is visibly failing to concentrate or fails six times at a given span length. For those with a very low memory span, start with words from the same semantic category, and stop adding words to the list when the first failure occurs. As training progresses, the difficulty level can be adjusted by increasing the number of words. Verbal rehearsal may also be supplemented by providing pictures of the words as they are presented. If digits or letters are used for rehearsal practice, construction of training materials is relatively easy. Students may benefit from rehearsal training sessions of only 10 minutes per day over a period of 10 days, but daily training over a period of several weeks may produce better long-term change.

Other Interventions

Besides training children in rote repetition, a few other interventions have been proposed for preschool-aged children with poor phonological short-term memory. For instance, Mann (1984) suggested naming letters and objects, repeating spoken sentences, and listening to stories and nursery rhymes. Nursery rhymes are thought to be particularly beneficial because they highlight the phonological structure of language. Rhyming games may also enhance phonemic awareness and the ability to store phonological information. In one rhyming game (Montgomery, 1996), the adult tells the child that she or he is thinking of a word that begins with a particular sound. After each incorrect guess the adult provides the next sound in the word.

Verbal Working Memory Interventions

Elaborative Rehearsal

Some variations of rehearsal go beyond rote repetition by associating meaning with the stimuli. These types of rehearsal, which have been shown to be very effective, are designed to directly improve verbal working memory, not phonological short-term memory. One of these, elaborative rehearsal (Banikowski & Mehring, 1999), involves associating the new information with related prior knowledge. The association helps keep the information active in working memory without repetition and also facilitates moving the information into long-term memory (for details on elaboration training see the long-term memory interventions section later in this chapter). The more an individual chooses to code and retrieve items according to their common category membership, the greater her or his recall. Children as young as 4 to 5 years of age show evidence of using conceptual knowledge to identify and retrieve items from memory (Davies, 1980).

Semantic Rehearsal

Semantic rehearsal is another option, similar to elaborative rehearsal. In this condition, students are directed to create a brief sentence using the to-be-remembered word (Turley-Ames & Whitfield, 2003). After they create the sentence, have them say it aloud and then keep repeating it until the next item is presented. A potentially more powerful technique is to present all of the words at once. Then have the learner create a story with all of the stimulus words embedded sequentially. This approach should be more effective than trying to remember a sequence of unrelated sentences.

Chunking

Chunking refers to the pairing, clustering, grouping, or association of different items into units that are processed and remembered as a whole, thereby facilitating short-term retention and encoding into long-term storage. For example, instead of separately remembering the digits 8 and 6 it is easier to recall them grouped as the multi-digit number 86. Like subvocal rehearsal, most children acquire basic chunking strategies without any specific training. Automated skills, such as reading decoding, depend heavily on chunking (e.g., the three phonemes in *cat* become one unit instead of three). There are simple surface chunks, such as temporarily linking together two or three digits that follow each other, and then there are more elaborate chunks that correspond to representations stored in long-term memory. The development of chunking may be a prerequisite for the formation of complex representations and schemas. During working memory processing, preexisting chunks, which usually consist of associations (Cowan, 2005), are retrieved from long-term storage. Once in working memory, chunks may be rapidly amended or enlarged as new information is considered. In addition to leading to more efficient encoding and retrieval, the development of chunking is crucial for efficient working memory functioning in general. Capacity expands as working memory operates on chunks, instead of discrete, indivisible units.

To explicitly train students to use a basic chunking strategy, follow these steps (recommended by Parente & Herrmann, 1996):

1. Using digits or words, require the student to group single items into a larger unit.

2. Require the student to group a longer list of items into multiple units.

3. Continue training with commonly used words or numbers, such as phone numbers, for practice.

4. Continue practicing until the chunking is performed consistently and automatically.

5. Convince the student that the strategy is effective by reporting baseline and postintervention data. Higher level clustering of information can be encouraged by having learners group words by semantic categories.

Paraphrasing

Paraphrasing is a strategy that builds off of both rehearsal and chunking. Having students restate information in their own words requires that they reorganize and condense a large amount of linguistic information into smaller, well-integrated, and more personally meaningful units (Donahue & Pidek, 1993). To train students, begin with short, single sentences, and emphasize that students should use their own words, not simply repeat what they hear. The paraphrased statement should convey the same meaning as the original sentence. Once students can successfully paraphrase a sentence, increase the length of the information by one sentence at a time. Paraphrasing that preserves the meaning of the message should be allowed during the practice of rehearsal strategies, whenever verbatim recall is unnecessary. For students who have difficulty remembering directions, have students repeat paraphrased instructions until they have completed the task (Gill et al., 2003). Paraphrasing may improve comprehension and retention through more effective utilization of verbal working memory resources.

Visuospatial Working Memory Interventions

For individuals with severe limitations in verbal working memory, such as those with language and literacy disabilities, training them to more effectively utilize their typically normal visuospatial working memory may prove extremely beneficial (Gathercole & Baddeley, 1993). Visuospatial interventions primarily consist of time-tested visual mnemonics, several of which are described in the visual mnemonics section found later in this chapter. Visual mnemonics training has been found to be highly effective in normal and disabled populations. Younger children may actually be more amenable to training in advanced visual strategies, as they more fully utilize visual storage than older children and adults (Hitch, 1990).

For normal individuals, the natural developmental progression in childhood is to increasingly rely on verbal rehearsal strategies for visually presented information. Young children who have not yet adopted recoding of visuospatial material into a verbal code can be trained to do so (Gathercole & Baddeley, 1993). In this type of training, children should be directed to verbalize what they see. For example, if a picture of ball, bat, and glove is presented, the child should say "ball, bat, and glove" and keep repeating this until the task is complete. This type of training might particularly benefit those with low visuospatial and executive working memory.

However, for individuals with severe verbal working memory deficits, transforming visuospatial input into verbal storage may not be a viable option; in such instances, visual mnemonics is recommended. Essentially, visual mnemonics recode verbal information into visuospatial information. For example, students can be trained to mentally create a visual image of a to-be-remembered word or words. When conducting this training, allow students ample time to create an image and then ask them to describe it. After they have described the image in detail, tell them to keep thinking of it for as long as they can. For children who have difficulty generating helpful images, suggest images. For those who have difficulty recalling the images later, have them draw a picture of each image they create.

Executive Working Memory Interventions

There is very little research on training designed specifically for executive working memory, although many of the interventions for other working memory components may also benefit the executive component. Moreover, training designed to improve attentional processes and general executive processing (Dawson & Guare, 2004) may produce transfer effects. For example, training designed to maintain the focus of attention and inhibit irrelevant information should have a positive impact on executive working memory performance. Above all, executive working memory should profit most from training programs designed to improve self-regulation and general strategic processing, such as those described in the metacognitive section at the beginning of this chapter.

An example of a comprehensive intervention designed to specifically improve executive working memory was reported by Cicerone (2000). Using subjects who had suffered mild traumatic brain injuries at least 3 months prior to the intervention, the goal was to teach compensatory strategies that would allow more efficient use of remaining working memory capacity. The treatment went beyond rote practice with strategies by emphasizing the conscious and deliberate use of strategies to effectively allocate attentional resources. Using a deck of cards and variations of the *n*-back procedure (see Chapter 5), subjects were directed to continuously remember previously exposed numbers while conducting a secondary processing task, such as random generation. Other real-world intrusive tasks, individually tailored for each subject, were also introduced, forcing the participants to effectively allocate their reduced resources if they were to cope with the situation. Verbal mediation, rehearsal, and self-pacing strategies were introduced. After 30 to 40 minutes of training each week, 20 to 30 minutes were devoted to feedback and discussion of the participant's performance, including dealing with their frustration and how to improve their strategies. There was also emphasis on the subjects' self-appraisal and application of the strategies to their everyday challenges. Significant clinical improvement in executive working memory resulted—specifically the ability to maintain information during concurrent processing tasks. Participants also demonstrated improved ability to effectively allocate their attentional resources.

Dual Encoding

Any strategies that involve visuospatial and verbal processing in conjunction involve executive working memory, as coordination among different components is one of its primary roles. Strategies that involve concurrent visual and verbal encoding, referred to as *dual encoding*, are thought to be more powerful than isolated verbal or visual encoding. Some dual encoding occurs naturally, such as when we are reading. However, individuals usually must consciously elect to engage in dual encoding. The long-term memory benefits of dual encoding have been known ever since Pavio and Csapo (1969) demonstrated that concepts presented once in verbal form and once in visual form were remembered better than concepts presented twice in one mode or the other. The logic behind dual encoding is that retention and recall are more likely when the learner creates multiple retrieval routes to the same information. In learning environments, dual encoding should be encouraged whenever possible. If the material presented is verbal, visual imagery should be added, and when the material is visual, a verbal mnemonic should be employed (Cook, 1989).

Combining verbal rehearsal and visualization is one example of dual encoding. Once a learner spontaneously uses a verbal rehearsal strategy, they can be taught to visualize instructions as an additional way of keeping the information active. To train children to visualize the application of verbal instructions, begin by presenting them with multistep instructions (Gill et al., 2003). With young children, have the objects necessary for the task within view and then ask them to look at the objects as they imagine completing the tasks. As training progresses, some objects are removed so that the student is required to visualize them. Children should be encouraged to keep on verbally rehearsing the instructions as they imagine themselves carrying out the instructions. This type of strategy may be particularly helpful for children with a language impairment who typically have difficulty remembering verbal instructions. The approach has been found to be more effective and enduring with language disordered children than using verbal rehearsal alone (Clark & Klecan-Aker, 1992). The concurrent use of visual imagery may tap the strength of a child with a language disability, as suggested by the discovery in the Gill et al. study that these children quickly learned to use and maintain the visualization strategy. Gill and colleagues concluded that adding a visualization component to a verbal rehearsal strategy increased its effectiveness and long-term application.

Organizational Strategies

One of the key principles of learning is that organized material is easier to remember, especially when the learner recognizes the organization or reorganizes the information in a more meaningful way (Carlson et al., 1990; Davies, 1980). When an individual organizes information, he or she does so by associating items that at first appear to be unrelated. Unlike methods that rely on recoding of the information, organizational strategies usually do not require the transformation of the information, but simply fitting the existing information into an organized structure. There are several evidence-based organizational strategies known to enhance the encoding and retrieval functions of working memory. The principle that binds them together is the linking of new information to existing, related concepts. One method of organizing input is to group items by category, usually by semantic category. Subsequent retrieval of the new information is then facilitated by drawing on the semantic network to which the material was related. Structuring and organizing information reduces the processing load on working memory, thereby allowing more efficient encoding of material into long-term storage. Organizing information prior to encoding also facilitates the association of the new information with related schemas already activated in long-term memory. Essentially, organizing information involves rehearsal and the processing of information at a deeper level. It also extends the interval that information is kept active in working memory. All of these variables contribute to more efficient use of working memory capacity and a consequent improvement in learning.

Not only are organizational strategies easy to teach but they can also be used to demonstrate the efficacy of memory strategies to a skeptical student. Before teaching an organizational strategy, collect data on the student's performance. Collect data again after the strategy is learned and compare it with baseline. When the student acknowledges the improved performance, he or she is likely to accept the importance of using strategies. Here is how to demonstrate the effectiveness of an organizational memory strategy:

1. Present the student with a list of about 20 randomly arranged words that comprise four concrete categories, such as food, clothing, and so on. Direct the student to memorize these words and allow 2 minutes to do so.

2. Remove the list and interject 10 minutes or more of interfering processing, such as having the student complete some other academic work. Then have the student write down as many words as he or she can recall.

3. Together with the student, tally the number correct and compute the percentage. Ask the student what strategies he or she used to memorize the list. Some students will say they noticed some categories but did not have time to organize them.

4. Then have the student examine the list and ask if he or she notices any way the items can be grouped. Explain that grouping the items by category will improve learning and recall. Also, explain that this method will be even more effective if he or she also tries to remember the number of categories, the name of each category, and the number of items that are in each category.

5. Then introduce a list of 20 new words comprising four to five categories. This time the words are grouped by category, with the category name at the top of the list. Direct the student to memorize the words, by first memorizing the category names and the number of items in each category. Allow the student 2 minutes to study the words.

6. After an interval of 10 minutes or more, test the student's recall, compute the percentage correct, and compare it with the percentage obtained in the first trial. In almost all cases, the second score will be significantly higher than the first.

7. Emphasize the dramatic improvement with the student, attributing the difference to the organization of the material. Point out that, in the future, the student will need to organize the information into categories and that this step will further enhance memory.

Most students will now believe in the efficacy of the method and will be more willing to practice and apply it. In subsequent sessions, apply the method to course content the student needs to learn. For example, facts in a history chapter can be grouped by category (e.g., people, dates, locations) before attempting to commit them to memory. When using this method, stress the importance of rehearsing the category names first instead of the individual items. Subsequent recall of each category will serve to cue the individual items, which are then easily recognized. Also, the number of categories should be limited to three to five. Furthermore, it is vital that the student learn to focus on the organization rather than rehearsing individual elements (Parente & Herrmann, 1996).

Mnemonics

Mnemonics are a subtype of memory strategies that enhance the meaningfulness of the material to be remembered, thereby facilitating learning. Mnemonics, which go back to the days of the ancient Greeks and have been used in schools for over 250 years, are strategies for associating relatively meaningless input with more meaningful images or words already stored in long-term memory. Mnemonics facilitate both encoding and retrieval by supplying structure, meaning, integration, and cues where none naturally exist (Cook, 1989). Oddly, many mnemonic devices use memory representations that bear little or no relation to the conceptual content of the material being committed to memory (Bellezza, 1981). Nonetheless, mnemonics improve retention and recall because they encode information in ways that make retrieval easier. Over the past 30 years, an abundance of empirical evidence has supported the finding that the use of mnemonic strategies improves memory and learning (Eslinger, 2002; Levin, 1993; Mastropieri & Scruggs, 1991). In a meta-analysis of 34 studies involving the use of mnemonic strategies with students who have learning disabilities, the overall effect size was a very strong 1.62 (Mastropieri, Sweda, & Scruggs, 2000).

Mnemonics are based on the principle that the way we encode information determines subsequent retrieval (Mastropieri & Scruggs, 1998). So, if new information is related to something that is firmly locked in long-term memory, such as images of everyday objects, retrieval will be easier. The methods include: recoding or transformation of the information; additions to or elaborations of the material; and a systematic retrieval component (Mastropieri, Scruggs, & Levin, 1985). Essentially, the encoding operations create cognitive cuing structures, usually in the form of visual images, sentences, or rhymes. The cuing structures, which are intended for later use by the learner, act as mediators between the recall signal and the information to be remembered. Successful recall depends on the quality and uniqueness of the cuing structure. The cognitive cue is recalled first, and this in turn leads to recall of the desired information. The characteristics that make mnemonic structures successful include meaningfulness, organization, association, visualization, and interest. Mnemonics also improve retention and retrieval through creating additional memory codes, such as construction of a visual image to associate with auditory information. Thus, mnemonics work because they connect unrelated information into a unique representation that is more easily retrieved. Although mnemonics are generally considered as long-term memory interventions, they are appropriate interventions for students with working memory weaknesses because mnemonics involve encoding, and encoding is a working memory function.

Mnemonics are needed most when the learner does not possess a schema that allows for easy assimilation of unfamiliar information. In such instances, mnemonic devices create an artificial schema, which typically results in better learning than rote rehearsal. Rescarch has indicated that mnemonics function like a temporary bridge to long-term learning. Each time the information is retrieved, new associations with related schema are formed, eventually obviating the need for the mnemonic aide. For example, students may initially depend on the acronym *HOMES* to recall the names of the Great Lakes, but after numerous associations have been made, the use of the mnemonic declines (Bellezza, 1981). In fact, overreliance on a mnemonic may make it difficult to relate the new information to an appropriate schema. Thus, mnemonics are particularly beneficial when they are used to associate meaning with information that initially has little meaning for the learner.

Some researchers and educators have expressed the concern that mnemonic strategies add to the total amount of information to be remembered, possibly overloading working memory and creating confusion in the minds of learners. This concern does not seem warranted, as those with the least available working memory, such as children with cognitive disabilities, improve the most when they are taught how to use mnemonic strategies. However, trainers need to consider whether learning a mnemonic device is worth the effort. It may not be worthwhile if the learner will be unable to apply it to different types of content. Because mnemonics typically involve multiple steps and procedures, the consistent, correct, and effective use of a mnemonic usually requires systematic training and practice. Connecting the new material with an appropriate mnemonic may require considerable time and effort. Young students and those with disabilities may find it too difficult to discover an appropriate mnemonic image or device, requiring the teacher to create one for them. Although teacher-created mnemonics are effective, it is generally better for the learner to generate his or her own mnemonic. Also, when using mnemonics, instructors are advised not to teach more content at a faster pace than they otherwise would. For readers who desire more details than those offered in this chapter, guidelines for developing mnemonic strategies are commercially available (Mastropieri & Scruggs, 1991).

Imagery

Visual imagery, which often involves transforming verbal content into visual information, is a visual mnemonic that can be used in a variety of ways. It is especially beneficial with students who have language disorders or deficits in verbal working memory. Such students tend to possess strong visuospatial working memory that can capitalize on imagery. With normal students, visuospatial strategies may be particularly valuable in mathematics (McLean & Hitch, 1999). The method creates associations between unrelated words and objects, thereby instilling meaning into these arbitrary relationships and prompting recall of the verbal information. There are several types of effective visual mnemonics that involve imagery. Whichever is selected, it is important to first demonstrate the power of a visual image by having the student try to recall a list of words through rote memorization and then directing the student to form a visual image of each word and comparing recall with that of rote memorization. When training imagery, begin with concrete images, as they are easier to recall than abstract images. For example, begin with a list of concrete words and have the learners close their eyes and form a mental image of what the item looks like. Images are most effective when they are created by the student and when parts of the image interact, the image has personal meaning, and the image is unique, funny, or bizarre (Ritchie & Karge, 1996).

Pegwords

An example of a visual imagery mnemonic is the rhyming pegword method, whereby the numbers from one to ten are associated with easily pictured rhyming words (e.g., "one-bun," "two-shoe"). The first item to be memorized is visually linked with a bun, the second with a shoe, and so on (Wilson, 1987). The teacher or learner creates an image that pairs each item to be learned with the predetermined images associated with particular numbers. For example, to remember that insects have six legs, create a picture of insects on sticks (sticks being a possible pegword for six). The pegword method is ideal for remembering numerical information or material that needs to be recalled sequentially.

Loci

Loci is a visual mnemonic that goes back to the days when Roman orators memorized their speeches. The first step is to memorize the serial order of a large number of rooms that are found in some public building, or perhaps one's house, if it contains enough rooms for the purpose. Content to be learned is then associated with visual images which are then placed in rooms that are arranged sequentially. During recall, the individual imagines himself or herself walking from one room to the next and recalling the image that was placed in each room. Visualizing the room prompts recall of the image associated with the room, and the image, in turn, prompts retrieval of the desired information. For example, a student who must memorize the order of early U.S. presidents can use the loci technique. To construct the mnemonic, the student should visualize a painting of Washington in the first room, Adams in the second, and so on. When a new series of information needs to be memorized, the same set of loci (rooms) can be used again by inserting new images.

The Keyword Method

The keyword method, a mnemonic that incorporates visual imagery, can be used when learning a variety of material, but is especially effective when learning new vocabulary words, such as when learning a second language. Of all the mnemonic strategies, the keyword method is the most researched and the most effective; consistently high effect sizes have been reported (Mastropieri & Scruggs, 1998). For instance, Scruggs and Mastropieri (1990) reported that students with a learning disability who learn and apply the keyword mnemonic consistently outperform untrained students and those who receive direct instruction only.

Essentially, the keyword method is a mnemonic that combines verbal information with visual imagery. The process of forming and retrieving a keyword mnemonic consists of several stages:

1. During the first stage, the acoustical link stage, the learner selects or is given a concrete word (the keyword) that sounds like the stimulus word. For example, in learning the French word *cochon* (pig), the learner decides that it reminds him or her of the English keyword *cushion*. With longer words, only the first part of the stimulus word needs to be matched with a keyword; for example, *sack* could be the keyword for *Sacramento*.

2. In the second stage, the learner is provided with or creates an image of the keyword interacting with the appropriate definition or response. To remember that *cochon* means pig, the teacher or student creates an image pairing the keyword *cushion* with the meaning of the word; for example, an image of a pig lying on a cushion. When teachers are creating images, they should show an actual picture, instead of just describing the image. Younger children should be encouraged to draw a picture; with older children, it is usually sufficient to have them visualize the image.

3. When retrieving, students are directed to think of the keyword first (e.g., cochon sounds like the keyword, cushion). Then try to recall images containing the keyword. When the image is retrieved, the association in the image should lead directly to recall of the correct response (Mather & Wendling, 2005).

The keyword method can be used to learn more than vocabulary. The keyword technique has also been successfully used to memorize social studies facts, such as associating the names of historical figures with their accomplishments, cities with their products, and capitals with their states. For some material, it is necessary to create two keywords and then bind them together in one image. For example, here are the steps involved in creating and retrieving a mnemonic that will allow a student to remember that Sacramento is the capital of California:

1. Create the keyword for the state; *California* sounds like *cauliflower*.
2. Create the keyword for the capital; *Sacramento* can be recoded as *sack*.
3. Create a picture of a worker putting cauliflower into a large sack.
4. When retrieving ask, "What is the keyword for the state, California?"
5. Direct the student to remember the image with the keyword (*cauliflower*) in it.
6. Direct the student to focus on what is happening in the picture. This should lead to the other keyword, *sack*.
7. Ask the student what *sack* is the keyword for, and the student should retrieve Sacramento.
8. Practice steps 4 through 7 several times until the student proceeds through the steps without prompting and responses are quick and firm.

Mastropieri and Scruggs (1998) emphasize how well students with cognitive disabilities can remember state capitals when the keyword method is used. Different variations of the keyword approach exist; Bulgren, Hock, Schumaker, and Deshler (1995) expanded the keyword method into a comprehensive strategy referred to as Paired Associates Strategy (PAS) and provided empirical evidence for its use. In addition to keyword pairing and mental imagery, the PAS method has students put the informational pairs on study cards, draw the visual image, and do a self-test. Also, the keyword method can be combined with other strategies, such as the *pegword* approach. When combining keyword and pegword, a similar sounding word is selected before being paired with a number-related image.

The keyword method, like most mnemonics, is most necessary and effective when the learner does not have sufficient background knowledge or a schema to which the new material can be linked. In such instances, the keyword strategy allows the creation of a meaningful proxy that indirectly ties the stimulus (e.g., a word) with the response (Scruggs & Mastropieri, 1990). The more unique, ridiculous, personal, and interactive the images, the easier they are to recall. With young children and those who have learning difficulties or working memory deficits, the teacher should provide the keywords and images. While young children and students with learning disabilities can effectively generate their own keywords and interactive images, their retrieval is better when they are provided with the keywords and interactive mnemonic pictures.

Chaining

Chaining is another mnemonic that can be used when items must be remembered in serial order. In the visual variation of chaining, the learner creates a visual image associating the first and second word in the list, then another image to link the second and third word, and so on. The cuing structure that results is a series of overlapping visual images. In the verbal variation of chaining, visual imagery is unnecessary; the cuing structure is primarily verbal. Participants are trained to remember up to 15 words from a list by incorporating each successive item into a story that the learner creates. The emphasis is on creating simple stories with interrelated sentences, and syntactic and semantic errors are ignored. When the story is recalled, the learner usually has no difficulty distinguishing the stimulus words form words used to create the story (Bellezza, 1981). When using this approach, the trainer or teacher should provide each participant with feedback on how well his or her story matches word order. McNamara and Scott (2001) investigated verbal chaining with children and found that verbal working memory span increased significantly as a result of training.

First-Letter Mnemonics

There are several other popular mnemonic techniques, many of which are quite familiar to teachers and students. The so-called *first-letter mnemonics,* which include acrostics and acronyms, make use of first-letter cuing and seem to be helpful when it is necessary to recall already known material in the correct order (Wilson, 1987). For instance, the well-worn acronym *HOMES* may help to remember the names of the Great Lakes. When acronyms cannot be created, then it may be possible to form an acrostic. For example, the colors of the rainbow can be remembered by the acrostic "*R*ichard *O*f *Y*ork *G*ives *B*attle *I*n *V*ain." Unfortunately, popularity does not equal effectiveness. According to Levin (1993), first-letter mnemonics are not supported empirically despite their popularity. They are probably ineffective because single letters make poor retrieval cues. They are also unlikely to be effective with those who have phonological short-term or verbal working memory deficits.

Long-Term Memory Interventions

With the contemporary emphasis on the role of working memory in long-term memory functioning, interventions classified as long-term memory interventions are very appropriate when the goal is to improve working memory. There are several justifications for employing long-term interventions when the goal is enhancement of working memory. First, primary processes, especially effortful encoding and retrieval, once considered long-term memory functions, are now ascribed to working memory. Second, regardless of theoretical orientation, it is difficult to draw the line between long-term and working memory. Consequently, methods that are effective for one system will likely benefit the other as well. Third, if learning is the overall goal of increasing working memory efficiency, then it makes even more sense to incorporate long-term strategies. Finally, for educators and psychologists who believe working memory primarily serves short-term memory and who desire interventions specific to short-term and working memory, consider the significant impact related systems have on working memory. In particular, poor and indistinct long-term memory representations result in reduced working memory efficiency and capacity. Conversely, well-established structures and firm associations in long-term memory facilitate automatic retrieval and responding, thereby freeing up more cognitive resources for working memory. Therefore, using long-term memory strategies to strengthen long-term representations reduces subsequent demands on working memory, effectively increasing working memory efficiency and short-term memory performance. In summary, long-term memory interventions may produce collateral improvement in working memory, due to the integral relationship between long-term memory and working memory.

Most long-term memory strategies are designed to facilitate retrieval by attaching effective cues or to provide a more efficient and more meaningful way of encoding information, such as associating it with existing knowledge. Long-term memory interventions can be classified under four general categories: rehearsal (repetition), organization, elaboration, and visualization. In long-term memory interventions, rehearsal includes practice techniques, such as distributed practice and frequent review, not just immediate repetition. Organizational strategies support and align with the structure of semantic long-term memory, which is thought to be organized into hierarchical schemas (Gagne et al., 1993). Elaboration is a process of enhancing meaningfulness by relating the new information to existing schemas. And visualization involves connecting auditory or verbal input with a visual image that will cue the correct verbal response. The choice of memory strategy should depend on the learner's profile and the learning requirements of the task; for example, if a memory deficit is confined to the auditory or verbal domain, then visual strategies are most likely to be effective (Glisky & Glisky, 2002). Similarly, children with a specific language impairment are known to have difficulty encoding and retrieving auditory or verbal information. Consequently, the use of visual imagery may tap the strength of the child with a language impairment (Gill et al., 2003). Substantial literature documents the efficacy and benefits of long-term memory interventions, especially with normal populations and with individuals who have mild to moderate memory impairments (Glisky & Glisky, 2002). Several of the methods already discussed in this chapter, such as mnemonics, are usually considered long-term memory interventions.

Rehearsal

Rehearsal, commonly referred to as *repetition*, is the first approach most individuals will attempt when memorization is required. The main distinction between short-term memory rehearsal strategies and long-term memory rehearsal strategies is that short-term versions tend to be subvocal and are limited to a short list. In contrast, long-term rehearsal strategies are intended for more content, can include alternate modes (such as copying the items over and over), and can be conducted on an intermittent basis (such as daily reviews). Studies have shown that even children in the first grade can be taught to use sophisticated rehearsal strategies (Rafoth, Leal, & DeFabo, 1993). Although repetition is a rote strategy that does not promote meaningful processing of information, it does result in learning information required for basic academics. However, training in long-term rehearsal strategies seldom improves working memory functioning (Glisky & Glisky, 2002). Nevertheless, basic rehearsal is a crucial step because without rehearsal it would not be possible to maintain information in working memory long enough to encode it into long-term memory (Parente & Herrmann, 1996).

Practice and Review Techniques

Distributed practice, in which several short intervals of instruction or self-study are separated by other activities, has been found to result in greater long-term retention of skills and knowledge than massed practice. The positive effects of distributed practice have been demonstrated with a variety of academic subjects, settings, and tasks, as well as with learners with various special needs (Crawford & Baine, 1992; Swanson, 2001). Spaced retrieval, a distributed practice technique in which there are gradually increasing intervals between rehearsal, has even been found to be effective for severely memory-impaired individuals (Eslinger, 2002). In the classroom, distributed practice requires a teacher to periodically review previously taught material, with a gradual increase in the intervening intervals. Distributed practice is consistent with the literature on effective teaching, and it is incorporated into structured methodologies, such as direct instruction (see later section on classroom instruction).

Organizational Methods

Another class of long-term memory strategies involves the organization of information into natural groupings or categories. These methods are particularly relevant for encoding information into and retrieving information from semantic memory, such as when studying an advanced academic subject. For instance, when learning a list of items, it is worthwhile to group the items into categories and then later try to recall them by category (see details on organizational techniques under the previous section on working memory strategies). During classroom instruction, effective teachers can facilitate long-term encoding and retrieval through organized presentations and by grouping information items categorically (see later section on classroom instruction).

Elaboration

Elaboration occurs whenever a person thinks about a specific piece of information and constructs a link between it and related information already stored in long-term memory (Ritchie & Karge, 1996). Elaboration can be classified as a meaning-based or relational memory strategy. The process of making information meaningful is accomplished by integrating new information with already stored information (Gagne et al., 1993). Elaboration occurs when a learner brings associated or related knowledge from long-term semantic memory into working memory and constructs a verbal or visual memory link between that knowledge and the information to be learned (Ritchie & Karge). If conducted correctly, elaboration actually adds to the incoming information, and it improves retrieval through storing related facts and concepts together. The elaboration process can also facilitate retrieval directly—thinking about what you know about a general topic often leads to recall of the specific information needed. From a working memory perspective, elaboration is a higher level form of encoding information into long-term memory. Thus, elaboration is not so much a strategy for increasing working capacity as for increasing the effectiveness of its encoding function. Even incomplete elaboration may improve working memory efficiency and learning. The initial step, thinking about related information, serves to activate related schema, bringing them into the pool of readily accessible long-term memory structures. Once accessible, automatic encoding processes may correctly associate related concepts without any further elaborative thinking on the part of the learner. Cognitive psychologists (e.g., Anderson, 1983) believe that elaboration increases the probability that information will be retained in long-term memory. In addition to long-term storage and retrieval, elaboration improves comprehension and learning (Levin & Levin, 1990).

For many successful learners, an explicit elaboration process is unnecessary. For example, appropriate memory representations or cognitive schema are often automatically activated during learning. If the new information relates to the activated schema, it is often assimilated without conscious effort (Bellezza, 1981). For students with cognitive and learning disabilities, elaboration may not be an automatic process or a strategy of which they are aware. Because children do not spontaneously elaborate until about 11 years of age, elementary-aged children—especially those with learning difficulties or working memory deficits—will benefit from training in elaboration. In fact, it is this author's experience that many successful high school and college students are unaware of conscious elaboration strategies and how these impact learning and memory. On the other hand, elaboration is so endemic in education that teachers and students may not recognize it as the process underlying so many successful teaching and learning strategies. For example, paraphrasing, summarizing, drawing inferences, semantic mapping, and generating questions all involve elaborative processes (Ritchie & Karge, 1996).

In general, effective teaching practices, such as providing advance organizers, support elaborative thinking. Without explicitly training the strategy, instructors may further facilitate elaboration by prompting students to do it and by allowing time for it. Prompts include directions to paraphrase, summarize, draw inferences, or generate questions (Ritchie & Karge, 1996). Teachers may also suggest specific links between new information and prior knowledge. A critical factor in the utilization of elaborations is that they need to be as precise as possible (Pressley et al., 1987); vague or general elaborations are less effective. When training students to use an elaboration strategy, follow these steps:

1. Explain what elaboration is and why it helps learning and memory, as well as when to use it.

2. Model the strategy by thinking aloud, using material the students are familiar with.

3. Given new material, instruct students to think about what they already know about it.

4. Direct students to think about how the new information and the prior knowledge are related. Proceed with having them create and verbalize a new meaningful link, such as an inference. One way to prompt a new link is to ask, "Why does this new information make sense?" Encourage specific links, as opposed to general or vague links.

5. For young children and students with learning and memory difficulties, the teacher may remind students of related knowledge they already know. Then allow students time to create a meaningful link. If they are unable to create precise links, the teacher should assist with the process.

6. Provide plenty of practice completing Steps 3 and 4 until students can complete the process without prompting. Encourage students to think aloud as they elaborate. If they are unable or unwilling to think aloud, have them write down what they already know and how the new information is related.

7. Illustrate how elaborations improve learning and retention. Direct students to think about the general subject and identify the new information they have learned.

8. Encourage students to use the strategy whenever they study independently or are listening to instruction in the classroom. Encourage the students' teachers to allow time for elaboration during instruction.

Cues

Successful retrieval from long-term storage is achieved by using retrieval cues. Many mnemonic strategies enhance retrieval because they are methods of attaching effective cues to the information to be remembered. In situations where no cues were deliberately attached, students should be taught to use self-cuing strategies, such as running through the alphabet when trying to remember someone's name. For those who struggle with semantic learning and retrieval, recall of episodic memories may cue retrieval of semantic information. Episodic memories include elements of the context (temporal, spatial, sensory) that occurred during learning (Estes, 1999). Thus, partial reinstatement of the learning context may cue recall of the appropriate representation. When students cannot recall factual details, direct them to think about when and where they learned something about that content. For example, if a science principle was learned during a laboratory exercise, visualizing the scene and recalling the events may augment retrieval of the semantic information.

Phonological Processing Interventions

As discussed in Chapter 4, phonological processes underlie the functioning of phonological short-term memory; in part, phonological short-term memory performance is a manifestation of phonological processing. Speech input is processed phonologically as it is fed directly and automatically into the phonological short-term store (Hitch, 1990). The verbal working memory system depends on the ability to gain access to phonological structure and use it briefly to acquire access to higher level linguistic information (Crain et al., 1990). Consequently, poor development of phonological processing not only constrains phonological short-term memory but also adversely impacts higher level working memory processes, such as reading and language comprehension. For individuals who have deficits in both phonological short-term memory and phonological processing, direct attempts to ameliorate phonological memory span may prove futile. It makes more sense to address the likely underlying problem—the phonological processing deficit. Through phonemic awareness training, phonological processing deficiencies can be ameliorated (Hurford et al., 1994), potentially leading to improved functioning of phonological short-term memory.

Of all the evidence-based processing interventions related to academic learning, phonemic awareness training has the most consistent track record of success.

Phonemic awareness interventions have been shown to be highly effective with younger children (National Reading Panel, 2000). In addition to improving phonological processing, numerous studies have also unequivocally shown that explicit phonological processing or phonemic awareness training has significant positive transfer effects on reading, spelling, and other linguistic processes (Bus & Van Ijzendoorn, 1999; for a review, see Snider, 1995). Of the phonemic awareness studies reviewed by the National Reading Panel (2000), the overall effect sizes were .86 for phonemic awareness outcomes, .53 for reading outcomes, and .59 for spelling outcomes. As the ability to detect and manipulate phonemes increases, children more effectively chunk phonemes. Chunking further alleviates the load on a limited-capacity phonological short-term memory and facilitates cuing and storage of phoneme chunks in long-term memory (Gathercole & Baddeley, 1993).

The teaching of phonemic awareness skills is often incorporated into early reading programs. However, for students with phonological deficiencies, more intensive training may be needed, and it should precede the introduction of reading. Educators can select from several commercially available phonemic awareness training programs intended for classroom use (e.g., Adams et al., 1998), including computer software designed for this purpose (Moore, Rosenberg, & Coleman, 2004). Or, educators may construct their own materials. When teaching phonemic awareness skills without a structured curriculum, following the developmental sequence of phonemic awareness is important. Children become aware of larger sound units (words and syllables) before they become aware of phonemes. That is, syllable awareness precedes phonemic awareness. Thus, training techniques, such as blending and segmenting, should begin with whole words, such as *horseshoe*, then progress to syllable manipulation before working with phonemes, the smallest units. Phoneme segmentation should be delayed until syllable segmentation is mastered. Snider (1995) recommends that blending activities should precede segmenting, and that manipulation procedures, such as deleting a specific sound, should be taught last. Finally, oral phonemic awareness training should precede its application to written material, but it is not necessary to wait until all phonemic abilities are mastered before introducing the alphabet and embedding phonemic awareness techniques, such as blending and segmenting, within oral reading practice. A major difference among phonemic awareness programs is whether or not they include a linkage with written letters and words. Programs that directly connect phonological processing with reading are generally more effective (Bus & Van Ijzendoorn, 1999).

Teachers who wish to create their own phonemic awareness training materials should include the following key activities.

1. Rhyming with familiar words increases awareness of the different sounds in words.

2. Alliteration, generating words that begin with the same sound, is another way of increasing awareness of sounds in words.

3. Isolating and identifying phonemes, such as having children identify the three phonemes in "cat," are crucial first steps in phoneme manipulation.

4. Blending begins with blending syllables and then progresses to phonemes. The teacher says words one syllable or phoneme at a time and the students put all the word parts together into a smoothly pronounced word.

5. After blending is mastered, children are ready for segmentation. Again, students should practice dividing words into syllables before saying them phoneme by phoneme. Because the ability to segment words into phonemic units is the hallmark of phonological awareness, it should be the focus of any phonemic awareness training. Nonetheless, combined segmenting and blending tasks are more effective than either segmenting or blending alone (Snider, 1995).

6. The most advanced stage is the manipulation of phonemes, such as replacing phonemes to form different words or deleting phonemes at the beginning, middle, or end of a word.

Reading Comprehension Strategies

Because reading comprehension can be very demanding of working memory resources, the teaching of reading comprehension strategies is important, especially with students who have working memory deficits. It has been hypothesized that working memory and reading comprehension have a reciprocal relationship (Cain, 2006). Thus, it may be possible to strengthen working memory capacity through the teaching of strategies that improve reading comprehension. At the very least, teaching readers more effective ways to process text and read strategically may circumvent working memory impairments (Cain et al., 2004; Paris, Cross, & Lipson, 1984). Conversely, working memory strategies can also significantly improve reading comprehension.

There are several evidence-based reading comprehension strategies that have been shown to increase comprehension, learning, and retention of information (e.g., Gersten et al., 2001; Salembier, 1999). Presumably, most of these strategies work because they promote more effective utilization of working memory resources. The element these strategies have in common is that they all increase active processing of the text. Unlike mnemonics and other working memory strategies that can be used in isolation, the simultaneous use of multiple comprehension strategies may be necessary for successful reading comprehension. Therefore, several evidence-based strategies, such as those discussed in the following sections, should be taught, following the general guidelines for the teaching of strategies that are discussed at the beginning of this chapter.

Monitoring

The successful application of reading comprehension skills begins with the monitoring of reading comprehension. Monitoring of ongoing comprehension is a critical reading function often found to be lacking in students with reading disabilities. For example, a reader who is not monitoring comprehension seems unaware of deliberately introduced textual errors and nonsense (Dehn, 1997). Increasing monitoring requires making students aware of the state of their comprehension. Begin training by modeling monitoring processes aloud. Then, have the student read orally and stop the student after each sentence or paragraph to ask, "Did everything in that sentence or paragraph make sense?" Then encourage the reader to constantly stop and ask if the material is making sense. Have them do this aloud at first, and then look for signs that it has been internalized. Continue to assist monitoring by stopping the reader whenever you suspect a comprehension failure, such as when a critical word is mispronounced. Another crucial step in developing monitoring skills is to teach the student to figure out what is causing the comprehension difficulty, and then discuss what should be done to correct the problem. For instance, if unknown vocabulary is the cause, looking up the definition in a dictionary would be an appropriate strategy.

Look-backs

When there has been a comprehension failure, for most readers the natural inclination is to reread the confusing portion of the text. In most instances, this will solve the comprehension problem. For students with working memory deficits, the comprehension failure may have resulted from overloading of working memory, not a text processing problem per se. In such instances, rereading the text, referred to as a *look-back,* is a primary and usually effective remedy. The effectiveness of look-backs has been documented by Burton and Daneman (2007), who found that metacognitively mature low verbal span readers effectively spent time rereading unfamiliar text information. This process reinstates the difficult but important information into working memory, thereby increasing the odds that it will be comprehended. Interestingly, less skilled readers and those with a disability will often try to compensate for low working memory capacity by rereading text (Linderholm & Van Den Broek, 2002), without any previous strategy instruction. They also tend to favor look-backs over higher level reading comprehension strategies, probably because the look-back strategy does not itself add load to an already stressed working memory. Teaching the basic look-back strategy is simple. Once monitoring is occurring, direct students to reread any text that contains information not initially comprehended.

Verbal Rehearsal

In a study by Rose, Cundick, and Higbee (1983), children with learning disabilities were taught verbal rehearsal strategies to more effectively utilize their working memory resources and facilitate reading comprehension. Some children were taught a verbal rehearsal strategy in which they paused after reading a few sentences and talked to themselves aloud about what they were reading. This verbal rehearsal approach appeared to be effective, as it significantly increased reading comprehension and retention of the information.

Visualization

It has been reported that while children with a learning disability are reading they do not generate images of the text as well as normal readers (Torgesen & Goldman, 1977). When this appears to be the case, readers should be taught to pause after reading a few sentences and "make mental pictures or a movie" about what they have read. Rose et al. (1983) found learning to visualize while reading significantly improved comprehension and retention of the information.

Previewing

Previewing is a prereading strategy that activates attention and prior knowledge, thereby facilitating comprehension and association of new information with related schemas. From a contemporary perspective of working memory, previewing serves to bring related memory units into the activated pool, making them readily accessible for processing, thereby increasing working memory efficiency. Most texts on reading comprehension (e.g., Blachowicz & Ogle, 2001) describe the components of previewing, which essentially involves looking at and reading everything except the regular printed text. In other words, previewing consists of reading titles, subtitles, captions, and chapter review questions, as well as looking at graphics and pictures.

Concerns

Teachers and trainers should monitor the impact of new strategies on reading comprehension because with some learners the use of new strategies may actually add to working memory load without enhancing comprehension. For example, most students quickly become adept at finding and underlining main ideas. But for some students, this procedure, even after it appears automated, does not seem to produce any improvement in comprehension. In effect, underlining main ideas may be increasing processing load as a secondary task, further reducing storage and processing of the information itself. Also, trying to enact several comprehension strategies simultaneously is likely to overload a limited-capacity working memory system. For those with deficits, the alternative may be to use the strategies sequentially or focus on only one while reading. For readers with severe working memory limitations, external assistance may be necessary, such as stopping the reader after each paragraph and asking, "What is the main idea of that paragraph?" The other challenge with teaching reading comprehension strategies is that extensive guided practice may be necessary if any generalization and maintenance is to occur (Gersten et al., 2001).

Academic Skills and Automaticity

Because of identified reciprocal relationships between academic skills acquisition and working memory (Brown & Hulme, 1996), academic skills interventions have at least an indirect impact on working memory functioning. Any teaching or interventions that improve student mastery of basic skills increase automaticity, and automaticity reduces load on working memory, thereby allowing working memory to operate more efficiently. Automatized processes can operate in the background without drawing on working memory resources, and automaticity increases the speed of task completion. More information can be processed and retained when it is processed quickly. As stated previously, the development of automaticity may be the great equalizer. With automaticity, those with working memory deficits can focus on critical higher level information processing. The importance of automaticity has been discussed previously in this text; see Chapters 4 and 5 for more details on the impact of automaticity on working memory.

Working Memory Training in Children With ADHD

Working memory is a core cognitive deficit in children with ADHD. Attempts to ameliorate working memory problems with this population are important because improved working memory might reduce some of the symptoms of and associated behavior problems in ADHD (Klingberg et al., 2002). Most working memory interventions for individuals with ADHD have been conducted in clinical settings but many of the methods could be applied in a school environment. The most unique aspect of working memory interventions for children with ADHD is that the interventions are usually computer mediated. In a study involving seven children with ADHD, Klingberg et al. found a significant treatment effect for a reasoning task and a nonpracticed visuospatial working memory task, as well as significant increases in working memory capacity for trained tasks. The computerized training consisted of tasks that are usually reserved for working memory assessment, such as the Corsi block tapping task. While still preliminary and in need of replication, the results of these initial investigations are promising, given the lack of success in training attention.

Medication

In the future, it is possible that medication will be used as a treatment for working memory deficits. Although not currently recommended as treatment for working memory impairments, some empirical investigations have discovered that medication can improve working memory performance. A number of studies (reviewed in

Bedard et al., 2004; Minear & Shah, 2006; Tannock, Ickowicz, & Schachar, 1995) have reported that stimulant medications, such as methylphenidate (i.e., Ritalin), may improve certain aspects of working memory function in normal adults and in children with ADHD. Stimulant medication has led to improved performance in verbal, visuospatial, and executive working memory tasks in children with ADHD. For instance, Bedard et al. found stimulants to improve visuospatial working memory storage capacity in children with ADHD. However, there was no increase in strategy use or improvement in visuospatial planning and problem solving. Metha, Owen, Sahakian, Mavaddat, Pickard, and Robbins (2000) also found that methylphenidate enhances visuospatial working memory, with subjects having lower working memory demonstrating the greatest improvement. Medication is thought to enhance working memory performance by suppressing distracting, irrelevant information and by increasing the efficiency of working memory. Perhaps the reason stimulant medications improve the academic performance of students with ADHD is that the medications affect working memory, not just attention per se. Moreover, drug therapies used to treat Schizophrenia (reviewed in Minear & Shah)—especially neuroleptics, such as risperidone, that increase dopaminergic activity—have been found to enhance working memory performance.

Computerized Working Memory Training

The forefront of working memory training consists of software that has been adapted from treatment programs initially developed for individuals with ADHD. Computerized interventions for ADHD have focused on basic attentional components, such as sustained, divided, and shifting attention. While such training has carryover to executive working memory, software designed specifically for working memory may be more beneficial. Studies have found computerized working memory training to increase working memory capacity and bring about changes in associated brain activity (Klingberg et al., 2002; Klingberg et al., 2005; Olesen et al., 2004). Recently, Westerberg et al. (2007) piloted software for working memory training with young-adult stroke victims who were past the stage of spontaneous recovery. Using various auditory and visual formats, their computerized tasks involved: simultaneous maintenance of multiple stimuli; short delays during which stimuli must be held in working memory; and changing the sequencing of stimuli in each trial. The training consisted of about 40 minutes a day, 5 days a week, for 5 weeks. Compared to the controls, the treated subjects improved significantly on nontrained measures of working memory. For instance, their digit span improved from a mean of 5.8 to 7.3, an effect size of 1.58. Furthermore, results from a self-report measure (an effect size of .80) indicated that the improvements had generalized to daily life.

Based on the research of Klingberg et al. (2005), Martinussen et al. (2005), and Olesen et al. (2004), commercial intervention software has been developed and is now marketed in the United States under the registered trademark *RoboMemo*. The software is intended to improve the working memory span and attention span of children who have working memory deficits, especially those who are diagnosed with ADHD. As reported by COGMED, the U.S. distributor, preliminary research indicates that approximately 80% of children who complete the training show measurable improvement in attention and complex reasoning skills. Of those who benefit from training, 79% still demonstrate benefits a year later, according to parent report. The internet-based training program consists of a daily session of 1 hour or less, 5 days a week, for 5 weeks. Children complete the training sessions at home under the supervision of parents. Each training session consists of several short visuospatial and verbal activities, or some combination thereof. Most of the activities are based on traditional psychometric or research paradigms. For example, there are digits reversed tasks, letter span tasks, and Corsi blocks tasks. The computer program automatically adjusts difficulty level as the child progresses. The child's compliance and performance are monitored through the internet by a "coach" who has a weekly phone conversation with the parent and child. Given the computerized medium, the training is more visuospatially loaded than verbally loaded, including visual items that rotate after the sequence is provided. This emphasis seems to be a particularly good match for children with ADHD who are typically more deficient in visuospatial working memory than verbal working memory. The training essentially entails the practice of memory span activities, many of which can be classified as complex-span tasks, thereby involving executive working memory to some extent. The trainee is given corrective feedback on every item, as well as access to cumulative data that illustrate progress.

Computerized interventions have the advantage of eliminating the need for human trainers to deliver and monitor the interventions, as well as increasing the flexibility of training times and locations. Another advantage of computerized training is that it can be programmed to automatically adjust the difficulty level, on a trial-by-trial basis, to closely match the working memory capacity of the participant. In contrast, computerized interventions do not provide any strategy training or any metacognitive information that might ensure maintenance and transfer.

Classroom Instruction that Supports Working Memory

Of all the environments humans function in, the learning environment is the most notorious for the continual overloading of working memory. Regardless of the learner's working memory capacity, the structure and instructional practices in the typical classroom overwhelm the learner's working memory capacity many times each day. For those with working memory deficiencies, the continual loss of information before it can be processed or stored permanently must be very frustrating. The first step in encouraging teachers to adopt more practices that support working memory is to promote more teacher awareness of the working memory loads created by classroom activities and instruction. Awareness can be increased by helping teachers understand how various learning activities and instructional practices impact working memory. Essentially, working memory overload is created by the absence of the practices recommended in this section; for example, there is loss of information whenever a secondary processing task is required while trying to retain and encode information. The second step is to help teachers realize that some very basic effective instructional strategies, many of which they are already practice, can reduce student working memory load and ameliorate learning problems associated with working memory impairments (Gathercole & Alloway, 2004). Arguably, the main reason effective instructional methods produce better academic learning outcomes is because they support limited short-term storage and limited working memory processes.

General Principles for Reducing Working Memory Load in the Classroom

1. Working memory strategies and mnemonics that are effective with individuals can be taught successfully in the classroom.

2. The comprehension and retention of verbal material will be enhanced if the input is simple, structured, and redundant.

3. Learners will have difficulty remembering information while they are engaged in another activity that is demanding their attention.

4. Students with impaired working memory can learn effectively if they have ample exposure to material while demands on working memory are minimal.

5. Many teaching practices recommended for children with ADHD (see Rief, 1993) are effective with students who have working memory deficits.

6. More learning occurs when students are allowed sufficient time to process new information—in particular, when they have enough time to rehearse and apply working memory strategies.

7. Most teaching practices identified as *effective* or as *direct instruction* support the storage and capacity limitations of working memory.

Specific Techniques

The techniques described in the following have been supported in educational and psychological research. For additional evidence-based suggestions, see Mastropieri and Scruggs (1998, 2007).

Simple Verbalizations

The style of language used in teaching determines how much demand is placed on working memory. All verbal communication—for example, directions, instruction, and explanations—should be linguistically simple, brief, and concise. The use of short sentences, which omit unnecessary information, will reduce the demands on working memory. For students with phonological short-term memory weaknesses, simple directions and instruction are important. For example, task instructions should be syntactically simple; sentences should be redundant; wording should be precise; and vocabulary should be highly familiar.

Simple, Isolated Procedures

As the complexity of a task increases, so do the challenges for working memory. Working memory is challenged by complex classroom activities, such as listening to a speaker while taking notes. Working memory load can be diminished considerably by providing more structure, such as a template for note taking, or by helping the learner structure the task into simple steps. The best approach to managing complexity is to avoid tasks that require secondary processing. Dual-task research confirms that additional processing tasks slow down and impair working memory performance. For example, asking a student with low working memory capacity to listen attentively to a lecture and take notes at the same time is likely to result in poorly recorded notes, minimal comprehension of the orally presented material, or both. Even the simplest interfering activities can capture attention and reduce complex cognitive and academic performance (Lepine et al., 2005). Also, teachers should avoid activities that require extensive shifting, such as from instructor's instructions, to blackboard, and to paper. In general, teachers should try to minimize competing inputs, to request only one process or operation at a time, and to help the student focus on one step at a time.

Lots of Repetition

Because it is a well-known fact that frequent review and practice help students learn and remember information better, the structure of many learning activities provides many opportunities for repetition. Nonetheless, with struggling learners there can never be too much repetition. Directions and instructions should be repeated frequently, and students should be required to repeat information also. Distributed practice, instead of massed practice, is also known to be effective.

Allow Time for Rehearsal and Processing

All research stresses the crucial role of rehearsal in short-term item retention and subsequent processing and learning. If an item is lost from short-term storage, it cannot be processed further in working memory or encoded in long-term memory. Thus, opportunities for rehearsal, processing, and other strategies during instruction are crucial (Banikowski & Mehring, 1999). Teachers should not only allow enough time for rehearsal, but also teach the strategies and encourage their use. Also, teachers should remember that the primary goal is to encode the information into long-term storage; they should not assume that immediate recall will result in long-term encoding.

Promote Higher Level Processing

Although opportunities for simple strategies are helpful, they are insufficient for higher level learning. Consequently, teachers should promote active reasoning and thinking about the material, rather than just repetition. For example, teachers should ask students why the new concept makes sense and teach them elaborative strategies (see long-term memory section). Also, teachers should promote active manipulation of the material, rather than just having students listen to a presentation.

External Memory Aides

Dawson and Guare (2004) suggest that children with working memory weaknesses may benefit from external support systems—for example, visual cues, checklists, and prompts that help them remember specific goals and procedures. There are numerous external memory aides that reduce working memory load; for example, a number line or notes on step-by-step procedures. For students with disabilities, teachers should provide external memory supports wherever possible. Similar to strategy use, a memory aide may itself increase working memory load. Thus, it is important that students practice using external aides under low load conditions.

Quiet Learning Environment

Background speech is known to reduce verbal working memory span by interfering with the rehearsal function of phonological short-term memory (Gathercole & Baddeley, 1993). Thus, a quiet learning environment is essential for those with verbal working memory limitations. It is not sound intensity that disrupts working memory processes, but rather phonological similarity. For example, a child trying to memorize arithmetic facts in one corner of a classroom while the rest of the class is receiving arithmetic instruction will likely find the class instruction disruptive, whereas instrumental music playing in the background will be only minimally disruptive.

Organized Presentations

There is neuroscientific evidence that presenting related information in an integrated and organized manner can reduce the load on working memory. For example, Prabhakaran et al. (2000) found that the volume of brain area activated by unintegrated information was more than twice that activated by integrated information. Organized presentations enhance academic learning because they reduce the processing load on working memory, specifically because they activate and maintain the focus on relevant long-term representations, thereby facilitating additions and alterations to those representations.

Scaffolding

Scaffolding is another general classroom strategy that can enhance working memory functioning. The practice of scaffolding involves providing struggling learners with graduated learning supports until the supports are no longer needed. For example, the teacher tailors the material and difficulty level to the student's level, models the skill, guides the learning, and provides feedback. Advance organizers are a type of scaffolding that provide a framework to which learners can attach forthcoming facts.

Activating Relevant Information

Teachers can prepare students for effective meaning-based memory encoding by helping students activate relevant schema. A structured manner of doing this is to use advance organizers. Advance organizers activate relevant knowledge prior to presentation of the new material; they also provide a structure for adding new information. Advance organizers include such things as metaphors, analogies, diagrams, models, and idea maps. Their effectiveness as a teaching strategy is well documented in educational research. Most likely, advance organizers facilitate learning by enhancing the effectiveness of working memory encoding and long-term memory organization. Other methods of pulling relevant schema into the activated pool include: identifying and emphasizing main ideas; providing examples that illustrate connections between ideas; directly relating the new material to prior knowledge; and drawing parallels to the students' own lives.

Effective Teaching Practices

Most of the instructional techniques recommended for reducing working memory load have been identified as effective teaching practices. One reason effective instructional practices are successful with students who have learning problems is that the practices include methods that reduce the load on working memory (Rosenshine, 1997). For example, teaching information in small steps followed by guided practice supports a limited-capacity working memory. Research on effective teaching principles has identified an evidence-based model of effective teaching that primarily consists of fundamental direct instruction methods (Rosenshine, 1995, 1997; Rosenshine & Stevens, 1986). Although not their explicit intent, nearly all of these procedures seemed to be designed for the purpose of supporting working memory limitations. The six main components of the effective instruction model are:

1. Daily review and checking of homework, along with review of relevant past learning and reteaching when necessary.

2. Rapid-paced presentations that are clear and structured, with lots of demonstrations, examples, and questions. Presentations begin with objectives and an overview, then proceed in small steps. Main points are highlighted and detailed, redundant instruction is provided as necessary.

3. Initial, teacher-guided practice until a success rate of 80% is reached. Questions are asked to check for student understanding, and additional explanation is provided where necessary. All students are given a chance to respond and receive feedback. Prompts are provided as practice progresses.

4. Guided practice and immediate corrective feedback continues until students can perform the new skill independently. Students are monitored for errors and in-depth reteaching is conducted as necessary.

5. Independent practice continues until responses are firm, quick, and automatic, with a 95% accuracy rate. Students are actively supervised and held accountable for their independent work.

6. Weekly and monthly reviews are conducted that include systematic review of previously learned material. This includes frequent tests that are followed by reteaching of material missed in tests.

Clearly, one of the main reasons these teaching practices are effective with students who have impaired working memory capacity is the ongoing repetition and the emphasis on developing automaticity.

Direct Instruction

Many educators use the term *direct instruction* to refer to any form of explicit teaching. However, *direct instruction* specifically refers to a structured curriculum that incorporates effective teaching techniques in a scripted fashion. Direct instruction involves small-group instruction; explicit teaching; fast-paced instruction; well-sequenced and focused lessons; modeling and shaping of correct responses; reinforcement of appropriate responses; systematic procedures for corrective feedback; continuous assessment of performance; lots of repetition and frequent review of material; and an emphasis on mastery at each step in the learning process (Gersten, 1985; Swanson, 1999a).

Direct instruction has proven to be an extremely effective teaching approach, especially with children who need it most: younger children, slow learners, at-risk children, and those with learning disabilities (Gersten & Keating, 1987). In a meta-analysis of 25 studies comparing different instructional methods (White, 1988), direct instruction, with a very significant effect size of .84, emerged as the most effective instructional method for students in special education. Another meta-analysis of 37 studies by Adams and Engelmann (1996) found that 87% of the studies favored direct instruction programs over other methods. A meta-analysis of 12 direct instruction math programs (Przychodzin, Marchand-Martella, & Martella, 2004) reached the conclusion that they are effective at improving math skills in a variety of settings with a variety of students. The application of direct instruction methods is not limited to formally identified direct instruction curricula. Direct instruction methodology is embedded in many effective curricula, and the general principles of direct instruction can be applied to the teaching of nearly every academic skill and subject. Most direct instruction curricula focus on basic academic skills in reading, math, and written expression, but the model has also been applied to higher level learning, such as problem solving.

The primary reason for direct instruction's documented success may be that it successfully addresses students' working memory shortcomings. Direct instruction characteristics that reduce working memory load (Rosenshine & Stevens, 1986) include: (a) frequent repetition of new material; (b) practice until a high level of mastery is reached (mastery is a prerequisite for automatization); (c) systematic strengthening of long-term memory representations; and (d) keeping students actively engaged by having them all respond in unison. In conclusion, direct instruction is considered one of the most effective instructional methodologies for students with working memory deficiencies.

Mnemonic Strategy Instruction

Despite the strong empirical evidence supporting the effectiveness of direct instruction, mnemonic strategy instruction appears to be even more efficacious at improving learning and memory (Gathercole, Alloway, Willis, & Adams, 2006; Mastropieri et al., 1985; Scruggs & Mastropieri, 1990, 2000; Swanson, 1999a). Essentially, mnemonic strategy instruction entails classroom-wide teaching of the strategies and mnemonics detailed earlier in this chapter. For example, a classroom instructor might teach young children how to better remember directions by combining a verbal rehearsal strategy and a visual mnemonic. Examining the differences between direct instruction and mnemonic strategy instruction illuminates why strategy instruction is more effective. Whereas direct instruction emphasizes student mastery of specific academic skills and subskills, mnemonic instruction focuses more on developing cognitive processes and rule-based global skills that can be applied to nearly all types of academic learning. This distinction leads to the characterization of direct instruction as a *bottom-up* instructional approach and strategy training as a *top-down* approach (Swanson, 1999a). The metacognitive training embedded in mnemonic instruction—learning why, how, and when to use a strategy—is a unique aspect of mnemonic instruction that accounts for better generalization. In fact, the fast pace of direct instruction, much like an experimental interference task, may actually prevent student use of working memory strategies (Mastropieri et al., 1985).

Over the past 30 years, mnemonic strategy instruction has proven to be highly effective with students who have learning problems, as well as with normally achieving students (Mastropieri et al., 2000). In a meta-analysis of 34 studies involving the use of mnemonic strategies with students with learning disabilities, Scruggs and Mastropieri (1990) discovered a formidable effect size of 1.62 across a variety of content areas and instructional settings. Scruggs and Mastropieri contend that mnemonic strategies in the classroom are the most effective strategies ever experimentally investigated in special education. Educators who are skeptical of mnemonic-based instruction and the teaching of strategies in the classroom should consider some classroom data reported by Scruggs and Mastropieri: Students with learning disabilities correctly recalled 79% of content taught mnemonically versus only 27.9% correct recall for nonmnemonically presented material. In another applied study, the classroom teacher reported that her special education students scored only 36.7% correct on content taught nonmnemonically, but they had 75% correct on material taught mnemonically, using the keyword method (Mastropieri et al., 2000). Given such impressive findings, every teacher should consider adopting mnemonic strategy instruction, especially whenever memory for content is important. Mnemonic strategy instruction, exemplified by the keyword method discussed earlier in this chapter, can benefit all students, not just learners in need of memory intervention.

Implementing mnemonic strategy instruction in the classroom will require extra work from the teacher, at least initially. Teachers who are concerned about the additional time should remember that the investment can reap huge dividends for students and teachers alike. For instance, in the Gill et al. (2003) study only 3 hours of training were needed to improve the direction-following ability of children, a change that was still in existence 8 months later. Enlisting assistance from students can reduce teacher preparation time. For example, when using the keyword method, teachers can have students develop keyword mnemonics in groups, or they can require students to generate their own links and images individually. Although less effective than teacher-provided images, students who self-generate keywords and interactive images still significantly outperform their nonmnemonic peers (Scruggs & Mastropieri, 1990). Another advantage of student-generated images and associations is that the images and links will have more personal relevance, a factor that will increase retention. For teachers creating images themselves, an efficient method is to include several related pieces of information in a single mnemonic picture.

Teaching students to use the keyword method to memorize facts in courses such as social studies is only one aspect of classroom strategy instruction. In a strategy focused classroom, several other mnemonics and working memory strategies, such as elaboration, should be taught. Furthermore, the encouragement of strategy use should be continuous, with the teacher providing frequent prompts and reminders to use strategies, as well as documenting the benefits of their use. With widespread and ongoing strategy instruction and applications, related processes and skills, such as reading comprehension, may also show improvement. Research has documented that mnemonic instruction not only leads to improved retention of information, but it can also facilitate student performance on higher order tasks (Levin & Levin, 1990). Finally, strategy instruction meshes well with several effective instructional practices, including direct instruction. As Swanson (1999a) discovered, combining effective instructional methods can provide greater support for working memory limitations. After completing a meta-analysis of 180 intervention studies, Swanson (1999a) concluded that a combined direct instruction and strategy instruction model is the most effective at remediating academic learning difficulties. The mean effect size for the combined model was .84, whereas the effect sizes for direct instruction alone and strategy instruction alone were .68 and .72, respectively.

In conclusion, there are many instructional practices with documented effectiveness that not only serve to minimize the working memory load of learners, but also enhance the learning functions of working memory. Although these methods are most effective with students who have learning problems, the approaches seem to benefit all students. Unfortunately, this text may not be read by very many educators. It is, therefore, incumbent on readers who work in educational environments to share this valuable information whenever they are consulting with teachers.

Key Points

1. Extensive research in psychology and education has documented many memory interventions and strategies that can significantly increase the retention and retrieval of information.

2. Given the close and mutually interdependent relationships among memory systems, cognitive processes, and academic skills, interventions that enhance functioning in related areas may produce collateral improvement in working memory.

3. Compensatory interventions, or interventions that combine compensatory and remedial approaches, are likely to be more effective than remedial methods alone.

4. Given that a primary function of working memory is to facilitate learning, the success of working memory interventions should ultimately be judged as much by long-term retention as by short-term retention. Consequently, effective working memory interventions should also improve long-term memory functioning.

5. Interventions traditionally designated as long-term memory interventions are appropriate interventions for working memory deficits.

6. The durability of information transferred to long-term memory is a function of how much working memory actively manipulates the information. There is little evidence to suggest that simply holding information in short-term passive storage facilitates learning.

7. Most interventions for working memory consist of strategies, such as mnemonics. With appropriate self-study and adherence to strategy training guidelines, teachers can provide strategy training.

8. Attaching meaning to information makes it more memorable.

9. Learning and using a new strategy will itself put increased demands on working memory, resulting in even less capacity leftover for storage. This is a

particular concern for individuals who have impaired working memory capacity. In such instances, simple strategies should be taught first.

10. For individuals who are lacking in self-awareness and self-regulation, explicit training in metacognitive strategies and metamemory awareness should precede strategy training.

11. Organized material is easier to remember, especially when the learner recognizes the organization or reorganizes the information in a more meaningful way.

12. Working memory interventions and strategies that are effective with individuals can be taught successfully on a classroom-wide basis.

13. Students with impaired working memory can learn effectively if they have ample exposure to material while demands on working memory are minimal.

14. Most of the instructional techniques recommended for reducing working memory load have been identified as effective teaching practices.

15. The main reasons effective instructional methods produce better academic learning outcomes is that they support the functioning of working memory and address working memory limitations by minimizing the demands placed on working memory resources.

CHAPTER 10

Case Studies, Reporting Results, and Recommendations

A substantial amount of psychological and educational research has supported the working memory construct and its relationship with academic learning. One goal of this book has been to "translate" the scientific literature so that practitioners can see the relevance and applications to real-world environments. The book has also attempted to make the case for including working memory testing whenever learning disability evaluations are conducted. Obviously, not every learning problem is due to a working memory deficiency, and not all students with working memory weaknesses have a learning disability. Nonetheless, the incidence rate of working memory weaknesses is much higher among students with learning disabilities than among normal students, and students with a working memory weakness are very much at risk for learning problems (Pickering & Gathercole, 2001b). Consequently, working memory testing is a valuable assessment component that can enhance the identification of students with learning disabilities and demonstrate the need for appropriate interventions and accommodations. In this final chapter, actual assessment data will be used to bolster the arguments for more screening, testing, and interventions.

Applied Research Study

Subjects and Method

The students in this applied study were assessed at a private learning center (located in the Midwest) as they began receiving tutoring for academic learning problems. These children and adolescents were enrolled in tutoring by their concerned parents, although some parents enrolled their children at the urging of school personnel. All 74 of the students were either deficient in academic skills or performing poorly in school, and all had a history of learning problems or academic performance problems. At the time of testing, only a minority (19%) had an official disability diagnosis. Of the sample, 46% were female and 54% were male. The mean age was 12.79 years and the mean grade placement was 6.99. Most of the students required tutoring in reading, mathematics, or study skills. All 74 of the students were assessed with the Woodcock-Johnson III Tests of Achievement (WJ III ACH) and Woodcock-Johnson III Tests of Cognitive Abilities (WJ III COG). Along with other cognitive clusters, the Short-Term Memory and Working Memory clusters from the WJ III COG (see Chapter 7 for details) were administered to most of the students (70 completed the Short-Term Memory cluster and 64 completed the Working Memory Cluster). The Short-Term Memory cluster consists of Numbers Reversed and Memory for Words, whereas the Working Memory cluster is comprised of Numbers Reversed and Auditory Working Memory. The short-term memory subtests measure a combination of executive working memory and phonological short-term memory. Both of the working memory subtests primarily tap executive working memory.

Results and Discussion

The cluster and subtest means were in the average range for all of the cognitive and achievement areas tested (see Table 10.1). Curiously, there was an 8.52 point difference between the two working memory subtests—Numbers Reversed and Auditory Working Memory—both of which tap executive working memory. The lower mean was on the digits backward task (Numbers Reversed), a long-established marker for learning problems. Perhaps the level of mathematics calculation skills had some influence on Numbers Reversed performance (the means were nearly identical). Or perhaps Numbers Reversed is a more reliable and valid measure of executive working memory than is the WJ III COG Auditory Working Memory subtest. Correlations among various clusters and subtests were calculated to determine the strength of relations among the variables and the extent of consistency with published research. With related cognitive processes (see Table 10.2), correlations were generally as predicted, except for the lack of a significant relationship between the Short-Term Memory and Phonemic Awareness clusters. The extremely high correlations both memory factors have with the General Intellectual Ability (GIA) cluster is concordant with reported findings in the experimental literature. The significant relations with the Long-Term Retrieval and Processing Speed clusters are also consistent with evidence that these processes are closely connected with short-term and working memory. Table 10.3 displays the correlations between memory and achievement clusters. Most of the correlations are moderately strong, just as they are in the research literature. The lack of a significant correlation between Reading Comprehension and Auditory Working Memory is surprising, but nonsignificant correlations in the Mathematics Calculation column are not. As would be predicted from previous findings,

Table 10.1 W J III Means and Standard Deviations*

Cluster	Mean	Standard Deviation
General Intellectual Ability	98.44	11.08
Long-Term Retrieval	95.54	11.36
Processing Speed	95.87	12.26
Short-Term Memory	96.11	13.66
Phonemic Awareness	103.30	11.65
Working Memory	97.69	13.81
Basic Reading Skills	93.18	8.47
Reading Comprehension	95.29	7.91
Math Calculation Skills	95.33	11.03
Math Reasoning	95.72	10.12
Basic Writing Skills	94.37	10.13
Written Expression	98.98	9.69
Subtest		
Visual-Auditory Learning	95.24	11.69
Numbers Reversed	95.23	12.58
Auditory Working Memory	103.75	12.81
Retrieval Fluency	99.77	11.94
Memory for Words	99.83	13.64

*The WJ III standard scores have a mean of 100 and a standard deviation of 15.

Phonological Short-Term Memory and Verbal Working Memory are not significantly related with Mathematics Calculation.

Incidence of Memory Weaknesses

A second analysis of the assessment data divided the students into two groups: normal students who had no previous diagnosis or did not obtain a significant

Table 10.2 W J III Memory Correlations with Cognitive Clusters

	Working Memory	Short-Term Memory	General Intellectual Ability	Long-Term Retrieval	Processing Speed	Phonemic Awareness
Working Memory	1.00	.779*	.622*	.352*	.332*	.195
Short-Term Memory		1.00	.754*	.306*	.238**	.240

*Correlation is significant at the .01 level.

**Correlation is significant at the .05 level.

Table 10.3 W J III Memory Correlations with Achievement Clusters

	Basic Reading Skills	Reading Comp.	Math Calculation Skills	Math Reasoning	Basic Writing Skills	Written Expression
Short-Term Memory	.427*	.529*	.322**	.486*	.443*	.499*
Working Memory	.475*	.462*	.428*	.556*	.391*	.447*
Numbers Reversed	.459*	.421*	.407*	.426*	.420*	.454*
Auditory Working Memory	.302**	.226	.269	.523**	.257	.351**
Memory for Words	.280**	.450*	.207	.440*	.346**	.392*

*Correlation is significant at the .01 level.

**Correlation is significant at the .05 level.

ability–achievement discrepancy ($n = 46$), and students with a significant ability–achievement discrepancy or a previous disability diagnosis ($n = 28$). The criterion for a significant discrepancy was set at a -1.00 standard deviation difference between predicted achievement and actual achievement, using the *Intellectual Ability/ Achievement Discrepancies* table from the WJ III Compuscore report. Each individual's short-term memory and working memory scores were examined, and the percentage of cases with memory scores more than one standard deviation below the mean (below a score of 85) was determined for each group (see Table 10.4). The Numbers Reversed subtest (a measure of executive working memory) was the best marker for a disability/discrepancy. More than 42% of the disabled/discrepant group had a normative weakness (a standard score below 85) in Numbers Reversed, compared with only 6.5% of the normal group.

When the 14 subjects with diagnosed disabilities (ADHD, LD, and Traumatic Brain Injury) were singled out, their low Numbers Reversed scores indicated that 42.8% of them had a deficit (both a normative and ipsative weakness) in executive

Table 10.4 Percentage of Cases with Normative Memory Weaknesses

WJ III COG Cluster/Subtest	Normal	Disabled/Discrepant
Short-Term Memory	10.8	42.8
Working Memory	6.5	29.1
Numbers Reversed	6.5	42.8
Auditory Working Memory	.02	17.9
Memory for Words	10.8	32.1

working memory. In contrast, none of those with a significant ability-achievement discrepancy but no disability diagnosis ($n = 14$) had a deficit in Numbers Reversed (although 42.8% of them had a normative weakness). And only 4.3% of students who had neither a diagnosis nor a significant discrepancy had a deficit. However, 19.5% of the normal students (who were nevertheless struggling academically) had an ipsative weakness in Numbers Reversed performance. The apparent reason their ipsative weakness was not associated with a disability is that their executive working memory performance was still within the average range (and thus not a normative weakness). These findings and the results reported in Table 10.4 support the claim that students with disabilities have a much higher incidence rate of working memory normative weaknesses, ipsative weaknesses, and deficits. Clearly, performance on short-term memory and working memory measures differentiates between normal and disabled/discrepant students. In particular, the extent of the working memory weakness is related to the severity of the learning problems. For example, in this study discrepant subjects with a normative working memory weakness but not an ipsative weakness were less likely to have a learning disability diagnosis than those who had both a normative and an ipsative weakness. In conclusion, it appears that a deficit in working memory is much more predictive of a learning disability than a normative weakness or ipsative weakness alone.

Case Studies

Adolescent with a Reading Disability

Hoping to gain admittance to a reputable college, a 17-year-old female with a reading disability requested a re-evaluation. She had been diagnosed in early elementary school and had received special education support services and classroom accommodations throughout her elementary years. Since middle school she had been successful in regular education classes at a private school. Although this young person was succeeding in high school, her reading disability was evident when she read orally. In spite of her difficulty decoding words, her reading comprehension seemed average. She was assessed with the WJ III COG and WJ III ACH, and the *Working Memory Analysis Worksheet* (see Table 10.5) was used to analyze her cognitive and memory scores. Due to the realignment of some of the WJ III COG memory subtests (see Appendix A), her WJ III COG Short-Term Memory cluster score was not used, but her Working Memory Cluster score was used to represent executive working memory. Her relevant achievement scores were Basic Reading Skills—82, Reading Comprehension—100, Math Calculation Skills—84, and Math Reasoning—92.

Her profile analysis (see Table 10.5) revealed an individual strength in phonemic awareness and an asset in auditory processing. However, both memory components in the verbal domain—phonological short-term memory and verbal

Table 10.5 Working Memory Analysis Worksheet

Examinee's Name: Adolescent Reading Disability   DOB: _____   Age: 17 Grade: _____   Dates of Testing: _____

Memory Component	Battery Name	Subtest/ Factor Name	Subtest Score	Component Mean	Composite or Mean	Difference	Normative S or W	Ipsative S or W	Deficit or Asset
Phonological STM	WJ III COG	Memory for Words	80	80	WJ III GIA—89	−9	W	—	—
Visuospatial STM	WJ III COG	Picture Recognition	97	97	89	+8	Avg.	—	—
Verbal WM	WJ III COG	Auditory Working Memory	79	79	89	−10	W	—	—
Executive WM	WJ III COG	Working Memory	74	74	89	−15	W	W	Deficit
Long-Term Retrieval	WJ III COG	Retrieval Fluency	96	96	89	+7	Avg.	W	—
Visual Processing	WJ III COG	Visual-Spatial Thinking	98	98	89	+9	Avg.	—	—

(*Continued*)

Table 10.5 (Continued)

Memory Component	Battery Name	Subtest/ Factor Name	Subtest Score	Component Mean	Composite or Mean	Difference	Normative S or W	Ipsative S or W	Deficit or Asset
Phonological Processing	WJ III COG	Phonemic Awareness	106	106	89	+17	Avg.	S	—
Fluid Reasoning	WJ III COG	Fluid Reasoning	89	89	89	0	W	—	—
Processing Speed	WJ III COG	Processing Speed	86	86	89	−3	W	—	—
Auditory Processing	WJ III COG	Auditory Processing	117	117	89	+28	S	S	Asset

Subtest or Clinical Factor Score	Subtest or Clinical Factor Score	Discrepancy	Significant: Y/N
Phonological STM (80)	Visuospatial STM (97)	17	Y
Phonological STM (80)	Phonological Processing (106)	26	Y
Verbal WM (79)	Auditory Processing (117)	38	Y
Executive WM (74)	Long-Term Retrieval (96)	22	Y

313

working memory—were normative weaknesses. Her deficit in executive working memory, at the fourth percentile, seemed to be the main problem. These phonological, verbal, and executive working memory weaknesses could certainly account for her basic reading skills disability. Fortunately, she had some relative memory strengths that she must have been using effectively. First, her visuospatial short-term memory was a strength relative to her phonological short-term memory. Second, her long-term retrieval was a strength relative to her executive working memory. From her test scores, it did not appear that related cognitive processes were helping her compensate for memory shortcomings. Her Processing Speed cluster score was an 86 and the Fluid Reasoning cluster was an 89. Yet her reading comprehension and knowledge scores were average, as was her academic performance.

Given her significant weaknesses in short-term memory and working memory components, as well as some below average related processes, how did she succeed as a learner? Some hypotheses are: (a) She must have acquired academic knowledge under "low load" learning conditions that allowed time for rehearsal, repetition, processing, and encoding; (b) she had developed strategies for efficient utilization of her memory resources, perhaps by capitalizing on her visuospatial strengths; (c) she had developed successful reading comprehension strategies; and (d) her long-term memory knowledge-base, along with average long-term retrieval, helped to compensate for her short-term memory and working memory deficiencies (except in basic reading skills). A couple months after the evaluation, this student took the ACT college entrance examination with extended time and obtained a composite score of 23, and shortly thereafter she was admitted to the college of her choice.

Child with a Traumatic Brain Injury (TBI)

As this manuscript was nearing completion, concerned parents brought a 9-year-old female in for summer tutoring. Because of her TBI the student had been receiving special education services and speech and language therapy. At 12 months of age the child had suffered a right parietal skull fracture from parental abuse. She was immediately removed from her biological parents and soon thereafter adopted by her current parents. Six months after her traumatic brain injury, her neurosurgeon stated that there should not be any lasting effects from the brain trauma. In spite of this assertion, the child's history was replete with behaviors and difficulties indicative of significant language and memory deficiencies. Among the recorded concerns were word retrieval problems; language processing problems; delayed language development; limited use of words; difficulty organizing and expressing thoughts; and difficulty sequencing words. Despite the several "red flags," her school records did not contain any record of comprehensive memory testing.

A brief assessment of this child's short-term memory and working memory components, as well as related processes, was conducted with the WJ III COG. The student's scores were analyzed with the *Working Memory Analysis Worksheet*, with the mean of 91 (see Table 10.6) obtained by computing the average of all the processing and memory components involved. None of her scores were discrepant enough from the mean to meet the criterion for an ipsative weakness, but she did display normative weaknesses in phonological short-term memory, long-term retrieval, and learning. In contrast, her verbal and executive working memory scores were in the average range. (Her visuospatial memory components were not tested because prior evaluations had documented mid-average visuospatial abilities.) The child's memory problems seemed to lie primarily with phonological short-term memory and verbal long-term memory, not working memory capacity. The short-term and long-term retrieval difficulties were corroborated by the parents who provided several examples of memory problems observed in the home environment. Although long-term retrieval problems can often be attributed to slow retrieval speed, in this case the retrieval difficulties appeared to be at least partially a function of poorly formed long-term memory structures. The child's poorly formed memory representations could have been the result of inefficient encoding or insufficient time for encoding, hypotheses supported by her relatively low Visual-Auditory Learning score (an indication of her encoding and learning efficiency) and her short phonological memory span. Further support for the hypothesis that her difficulty originated with weak long-term representations, instead of slow long-term retrieval alone, was provided by her mid-average processing speed score (processing speed and retrieval speed are often related).

After reviewing the assessment results with the parents, it was decided that the student would receive individual tutoring for 3 hours a week over 10 weeks. Two hours per week would focus on improving academic skills, primarily reading comprehension and mathematics reasoning, while 1 hour per week would be invested in memory strategy training. Over the summer, the 10 hours dedicated to memory interventions consisted of the following:

1. The training began with the metamemory approach described in Chapter 9. This 9-year old child already knew that she had memory problems, and she had a strong desire to overcome them. She was comfortable learning about her memory strengths and weaknesses and very interested in how memory works. She reported that she was unaware of strategies, such as rehearsal, but wanted to learn so that she could improve her memory and learning.

2. Next, the child was taught a basic verbal rehearsal strategy (see Chapter 9) in which she practiced saying the material over and over to herself. It began with having her say the information aloud, then whispering it, and then finally repeating it subvocally. After she was comfortable using the strategy with word lists, it was applied to remembering simple step-by-step instructions. The objective was not just to help her retain information for immediate use but to extend the interval for encoding information into long-term storage.

Table 10.6 Working Memory Analysis Worksheet

Examinee's Name: Traumatic Brain Injury DOB:_____ Age: 9 Grade:____ Dates of Testing:_____

Memory or Processing Component	Battery Name	Subtest/Factor Name	Subtest Score	Component Mean	Composite or Mean	Difference	Normative S or W	Ipsative S or W	Deficit or Asset
Phonological STM	WJ III COG	Memory for Words	82	82	91	−9	W	—	—
Verbal WM	WJ III COG	Auditory Working Memory	94	94	91	+3	Avg.	—	—
Executive WM	WJ III COG	Working Memory	92	92	91	+1	Avg.	—	—
Long-Term Retrieval	WJ III COG	Retrieval Fluency	82	82	91	−9	W	—	—
Phonological Processing	WJ III COG	Phonemic Awareness	95	95	91	+4	Avg.	—	—
Fluid Reasoning	WJ III COG	Fluid Reasoning	83	83	91	−8	W	—	—
Processing Speed	WJ III COG	Processing Speed	101	101	91	+10	Avg.	—	—
Auditory Processing	WJ III COG	Auditory Processing	100	100	91	+9	Avg.	—	—
Learning	WJ III COG	Visual-Auditory Learning	85	85	91	−6	W	—	—

Subtest or Clinical Factor Score	Subtest or Clinical Factor Score	Discrepancy	Significant: Y/N
Processing Speed (101)	Long-Term Retrieval (82)	19	Y
Phonological Processing (95)	Phonological STM (82)	13	N

3. During several sessions, the child was taught to use an organizational strategy when trying to commit information to memory. The strategy consisted of grouping items by category, both with word lists and with actual objects. The goal was to improve the effectiveness of her semantic encoding. As suggested in Chapter 9, adoption of this strategy produced an immediate improvement in long-term retention that impressed and pleased the child. For example, during one session she was able to recall nearly every one of 50 objects she had sorted by category.

4. Finally, the student was taught how to utilize her visuospatial processing strength by learning some basic visual mnemonics. This consisted primarily of having her associate visual images with words and other verbal information that she was trying to remember. The goal was to facilitate retrieval by having her attach additional cues to the stored information. Recoding the verbal information into a visual mode would also provide an alternative retrieval route.

When the interventions ended, the child was retested with the WJ III COG (about 4 months had elapsed since the initial testing). Although the improvements in her standard scores could be due to measurement error, the differences were certainly approaching significance. The largest gain, 12 points, was in Visual-Auditory Learning, a learning task that depends heavily on efficient encoding of novel information. This change was particularly encouraging, given that there was no change in her retrieval speed (as measured by the Retrieval Fluency subtest). The improvement in learning was probably associated with an apparent increase in phonological short-term memory (as indicated by a 10-point improvement in Memory for Words). Interestingly, there was no change in working memory, as the Working Memory cluster score remained the same.

After the new school year began, there was a follow-up consultation meeting with the student's teachers and parents. Teachers reported that the student seemed more confident and sought out assistance when she needed it. The teachers were also very accepting of the memory interventions that had been implemented over the summer and reported using similar strategies that were embedded in the special education curriculum they were using. The teachers also agreed to more modifications that addressed the student's long-term retrieval problems, including providing prompts and cues when the child's retrieval efforts were unsuccessful.

Written Interpretation of Working Memory Test Results

When writing educational evaluation reports or psychological reports about working memory assessment results, some unique structuring and detailed explanations will allow readers to grasp the intended meaning, especially when memory subtests have been realigned (see Appendices A and E) or when a cross-battery analysis has been completed. Some of the suggestions found in the oral interpretation section later in this chapter also can be applied to the written format. Here are a few important suggestions for structuring the test-results interpretation section of a report.

1. If an IQ score or an equivalent score, such as a memory composite, is available, that score should be interpreted first.

2. Proceed with an explanation of why and how the selective, cross-battery assessment was conducted. Begin by identifying the batteries, factors, and subtests that were used, followed by an explanation of how the scores were realigned and analyzed. In particular, explain how the cross-battery mean was derived and how clinical factor scores were calculated.

3. The remainder of the interpretative section should be organized by memory components and cognitive processes, not by test battery. For example, if two subtests used to measure verbal working memory were drawn from two different scales, the subtests should be combined into a clinical factor that is then interpreted as representing verbal working memory. Begin each of these subsections with a definition of the memory component. After interpreting scores, integrate corroborating data from other sources and methods.

4. When reporting memory strengths and weaknesses, always specify whether they are normative, ipsative, or both. When reporting the results of an ipsative analysis, state which of the following the strength or weakness is relative to: (a) a full intellectual or cognitive composite; (b) the mean of the memory components; (c) an overall processing mean that includes memory and nonmemory factors; or (d) another memory or processing score in a pairwise comparison.

Illustrative Report

Those who evaluate children are quite familiar with the traditional format of a psychological report. Thus, the report example provided in this section is limited to the test-results interpretative section that might be written when there has been a cross-battery assessment of working memory and related processes. The following illustrative written report section is about Joey, the case that has been discussed in previous chapters (see Table 6.7).

This evaluation was initiated by Joey's parents who are very concerned about Joey's lack of progress in basic reading skills. The parents are seeking supplemental instruction for Joey so that he stops falling farther behind his peers in reading. As previous evaluations have not reported any memory testing, it was decided to include the testing of short-term and working memory in the current evaluation because short-term and working memory are known to be highly related to the

Table 10.7 Joey's Test Results

Memory or Processing Component	Component Score	WJ III GIA	Difference	Normative Strength or Weakness	Intra-Individual Strength or Weakness	Deficit or Asset
Phonological STM	106	106	0	Avg.	—	—
Visuospatial STM	85	106	−21	W	W	Deficit
Verbal WM	101	106	−5	Avg.	—	—
Visuospatial WM	95	106	−11	Avg.	—	—
Executive WM	89	106	−17	W	W	Deficit
Long-Term Retrieval	91	106	−15	Avg.	W	—
Phonemic Awareness	128	106	+22	S	S	Asset
Fluid Reasoning	95	106	−11	Avg.	—	—
Processing Speed	107	106	+1	Avg.	—	—

development of reading skills. *Working memory* is a term used to describe the processing of information from either short-term or long-term memory. Other cognitive processes that support the development of basic reading skills and reading comprehension also were tested: phonological processing (phonemic awareness), processing speed, and fluid reasoning.

When Joey is compared to other students the same age, his overall level of cognitive functioning appears to be in the mid-average range. On the Woodcock-Johnson III Tests of Cognitive Abilities (WJ III COG), Joey obtained a General Intellectual Ability (GIA) score of 106. The accompanying percentile rank of 66 reveals that Joey's GIA score is higher than 66% of his same-aged peers. If Joey were retested with the WJ III, there is a 95% chance he would obtain a score within the range of 101 to 112. Joey's GIA score is essentially an average of the various cognitive abilities that were tested. However, in Joey's case, the GIA score does not accurately depict all of his cognitive abilities. As will be discussed in more detail later in this report, some of Joey's cognitive processing abilities are average, whereas others are above average or below average.

In order to broaden the assessment of Joey's memory systems, two different cognitive test batteries were administered: portions of the WJ III COG and a couple of subtests from the Wechsler Intelligence Scale for Children–Fourth Edition, Integrated (WISC-IV Integrated). Test scores from the two batteries were combined in a cross-battery analysis (see Table 10.7), in which Joey's GIA score of 106 was used to determine his intraindividual strengths and weaknesses in memory and related processes. Each of Joey's memory and related processing scores were compared with his GIA. Scores that are 12 or more points lower than his GIA score are indicative of intraindividual weaknesses. Some pairs of related memory and cognitive processes were also compared, with a discrepancy of 15 or more points considered significant.

Phonological Processing and Phonological Short-Term Memory

For someone with a severe reading disability, Joey demonstrates a surprising strength in phonemic awareness. Phonemic awareness skills involve awareness and manipulation of the sound units that form words. Joey's Phonemic Awareness score of 128 is in the high average range when Joey is compared to same-aged peers. For Joey, phonemic awareness is also an individual strength, compared to his overall level of cognitive functioning. Consistent with his exceptionally strong phonemic awareness skills is Joey's mid-average performance in phonological short-term memory. This memory component involves the short-term sequential retention of simple verbal information, such as recalling a series of letters. Although Joey's ability in phonological short-term memory is mid-average, it is neither an individual nor a normative (compared to the performance of same-aged peers) strength for him. Joey's strengths in the phonological domain are consistent with his reading decoding; for example, he is more successful at decoding words that are spelled phonetically.

Visuospatial Short-Term Memory

This type of short-term memory involves memory for objects and their location. The Spatial-Span Forward subtest from the WISC-IV Integrated was used to measure Joey's development of this type of memory. Based on his score of 85, it appears that visuospatial short-term memory is both a normative and an individual weakness for Joey. Thus, there is a strong possibility that this deficit may be accounting for some of Joey's difficulties in reading. For example, when Joey reads, he often loses track of his place in the sentence or paragraph. This type of tracking is a function of visuospatial short-term memory.

Verbal Working Memory

Verbal working memory involves the processing and retention of verbal information, such as remembering a sentence. Joey's verbal working memory was assessed with the Auditory-Working Memory subtest from the WJ III COG. During this subtest the task is to transform information without forgetting any of it. Joey's mid-average score of 101 indicates that his verbal working memory capacity is similar to that of his phonological short-term memory, which also involves the retention of verbal information. Joey's average ability for recalling verbal information is also consistent with his average abilities in verbal expression, reasoning, and comprehension. His high verbal working memory score is also concordant with observations. For instance, Joey is extremely talkative; oral expression is one of his strengths.

Visuospatial Working Memory

Visuospatial working memory is similar to visuospatial short-term memory, the main difference being that the working memory dimension processes and retains more complex visuospatial information. Joey's visuospatial working memory ability was measured with the Spatial Span Backward subtest from the WISC-IV Integrated. Joey's visuospatial working memory score is in the average range and somewhat higher than his visuospatial short-term memory score; however, the difference between the two scores is not statistically significant. The higher score on the visuospatial working memory component is unexpected. Perhaps more in-depth testing of Joey's visuospatial memory components is needed.

Executive Working Memory

Executive working memory coordinates the storage and processing of information, including the coordination of verbal and visuospatial memory processes. Executive working memory is called on whenever students must multitask while trying to remember or learn information. Joey's executive working memory functioning appears to be deficient; his score on Numbers Reversed, one of the subtests used to measure executive working memory, was at the seventh percentile. In addition to his executive working memory performance being below average, it is also a significant intraindividual weakness when compared to his GIA. Limited capacity or inefficient utilization of executive working memory could account for some of the difficulties Joey is experiencing in basic reading skills, reading comprehension, and written expression.

Long-Term Retrieval

In the model of working memory used to organize this evaluation, long-term retrieval is restricted to conscious, effortful retrieval, instead of automatic, instantaneous retrieval. Conscious, effortful retrieval is considered a function of working memory. Two subtests from the WJ III COG were used to assess Joey's long-term retrieval, and then the scores were averaged to obtain an estimate of his functioning level. Although Joey's long-term retrieval is within the average range, for Joey it is an intraindividual weakness. This finding is consistent with teacher reports that Joey has difficulty remembering new words from one day to the next.

Processing Speed

Like memory, processing speed plays an important role in all types of learning. Faster processing speed allows more information to be processed in working memory before it is forgotten. With a percentile rank of 67, Joey's processing speed appears to be solidly average. Thus, it is not a contributing factor to the learning problems he is experiencing.

Fluid Reasoning

Fluid reasoning, which is inductive and deductive reasoning with novel material, is strongly related with the ability to comprehend. Joey's average Fluid Reasoning score of 95 indicates that his reading comprehension weakness cannot be attributed to a deficiency in fluid reasoning.

Summary

Joey demonstrates average abilities in phonological short-term memory, verbal working memory, visuospatial working memory, long-term retrieval, fluid reasoning, and processing speed. He also displays a significant normative and intraindividual strength in phonological processing. Based on his test performance, he appears to have deficits in visuospatial short-term memory and executive working memory. In addition, he has an intraindividual weakness in long-term retrieval. The integrated functioning of memory systems is essential for effective learning and memory. Joey's weak executive working memory, which is responsible for coordinating memory functions, may be preventing him from effectively applying his normal phonological and verbal memory resources during reading decoding. His weak visuospatial short-term memory may also be interfering with the reading decoding process.

Oral Interpretation of Working Memory Test Results

Working memory test results should be explained in a manner that students, parents, teachers, and related professionals can understand. The oral interpretation of test results can be a challenging task, even when the evaluator has expertise in testing and has in-depth knowledge of working memory and the problems associated with working memory weaknesses and deficits. The main challenge is to explain the results in language that all involved parties can understand. The interpretation needs to be focused and simple, yet provide enough information so that participants gain some new insights into the student's cognitive functioning and learning difficulties. When working memory weaknesses or deficits exist, the overriding goal is to help participants recognize the student's needs. Subsequent consultation may lead to appropriate accommodations and the implementation of effective interventions. Here are sequentially ordered suggestions for oral interpretation at a postevaluation meeting.

1. Begin by reviewing the academic learning concerns that led to the referral and evaluation. Explain that the purpose of the evaluation and testing is to gain a better understanding of *why* the student is experiencing these learning problems so that appropriate accommodations and interventions can be provided if needed. Explain that memory testing was included because of the important role that all types of memory play in learning. (Although the examiner may have planned the assessment around referral hypotheses, discussing these is introducing more complexity than needed.)

2. Proceed with a summary of relevant nontest information gathered during the evaluation. Begin with reviewing history, reporting indications of memory problems discovered in records or previous evaluation reports. Continue with a summary of observations, focusing on student behaviors that denote memory problems (see Table 6.6). Remind participants of memory-related information they reported during interviews. Conclude these introductory comments by asking participants if they agree with the summaries and if they have anything to add. (It is a good strategy to get students and parents involved in the meeting before proceeding with test results.)

3. When the short-term memory and working memory test results are discussed, begin by defining working memory. A basic explanation might be something like: "Working memory is the *active* part of memory; we are using working memory whenever we are making an effort to remember something for a short or long period of time; working memory helps transfer information from short-term memory to long-term memory; working memory is limited in everyone; working memory easily becomes overloaded and when it does we miss information, forget it quickly, or do not get it stored in our long-term memory; working memory is extremely important for learning; and students

with learning problems often have working memory problems." Then provide some examples of when we are using working memory, such as in doing mental arithmetic; trying to memorize something; trying to recall something that we do not immediately remember; listening and taking notes at the same time; and expressing ideas in writing.

4. Before reporting test performance for each short-term memory and working memory component, take a few moments to explain the main functions of each component and how each component relates to specific areas of learning. For example, you might define *phonological short-term memory* as "the verbal aspect of short-term memory that is important for language development and learning to read."

5. When reviewing test performance, keep the focus on the individual and his or her functioning in specific memory components, not on the test scores. For example, it is better to say, "the student appears to have below average capacity in verbal working memory" than to say, "the test score on Memory for Sentences is below average."

6. When reporting test results, factor scores (including clinical factor scores) should take precedence over subtest scores. Factor scores (the combination of two or more subtests) more reliably represent capacity and levels of functioning. Subtest performance should only be discussed when there is only one subtest score representing a memory component, or when the subtest scores that comprise the factor differ by more than 1.5 standard deviations.

7. Always use a graph when reporting test scores. (It is very difficult for nearly everyone to visualize test performance from a verbal description.) When memory subtests have been realigned (see Appendices A and E) or when a cross-battery assessment has been completed, it will be necessary to create a graph (this is easily accomplished with computer software programs). Use the names of the memory components and related cognitive processes (see the first column in Appendix A) instead of the names of subtests and composites. On the graph, draw lines at 90 and 109 and state that this is the average range of performance.

8. On the graph, it is best to represent performance with confidence intervals instead of the standard score alone. Confidence intervals for subtest and composite scores are always available in test manuals; 90% or 95% are usually the options. When a clinical factor score has been computed, the best estimate of a 95% confidence interval is to add and subtract 10 points to the score. For example, if the clinical factor score is 90, a band ranging from 80 to 100 should be drawn on the graph. The confidence intervals are particularly helpful when comparing pairs of memory components. When the differences are

severe, the confidence bands will not overlap, making it easy for parents and other participants to actually see that the components are different from each other. For example, in Joey's case (see Table 6.7) it will be evident that his visuospatial short-term memory is significantly weaker than his phonological short-term memory because the two confidence bands will be separated.

9. Interpret each score from a normative and ipsative perspective. Use the graph to illustrate how each of the student's memory components compare with the average range. An appropriate descriptive statement might be, "the student appears to have a weakness in visuospatial short-term memory compared to the performance of average students his age." When identifying an intraindividual weakness, always clarify that it is a within-child weakness and specify what the component is being compared to, such as "compared to the student's overall cognitive processing ability, this type of memory is a weakness for him." When the student has both a normative and ipsative weakness (a deficit), emphasize that this is unusual and that it is very likely connected with the learning problems the student is experiencing.

10. After the student's performance on each component has been reviewed, cite supporting assessment information; for example, you might report that you observed signs of the weakness or deficit during a classroom observation. Conclude the discussion of each memory component by pointing out the educational implications of any weaknesses or deficits; for example, you might explain that research tells us that students with deficits in executive working memory are likely to have broad-based learning problems.

11. Remember to include a discussion of strengths, particularly intraindividual strengths. The emphasis should be on how the student might capitalize on these strengths when trying to compensate for his or her weaknesses and how interventions should incorporate these strengths.

12. Conclude the oral interpretation with a summary of the student's strengths and weaknesses, and at this point put the pieces back together so that participants can understand the functioning of the working memory system. For example, in Joey's case (see Table 6.7), you might say, "Joey demonstrates strengths in phonological processing and in phonological short-term memory. In contrast, he has weaknesses in visuospatial short-term memory and executive working memory. Because executive working memory has responsibility for the coordinating verbal and visuospatial memory components, his executive deficit has important consequences. For example, the executive working memory deficit might make it difficult for Joey to discover how to use his relatively strong verbal memory abilities to support his weaker visuospatial memory abilities."

Recommendations for Future Working Memory Tests

Although there are several cognitive and memory batteries that contain reliable and valid measures of various short-term memory and working memory components, there is certainly room for improvement. The primary recommendation is that memory subtests be designed to have high specificity (i.e., they should be designed to measure mainly one aspect of memory). Too many "working memory" subtests measure a combination of short-term memory and working memory components; for example, some subtests measure both phonological short-term memory and executive working memory. The best way to narrow down subtest measurement is to limit the subtest to a single task; changing the activity during the subtest confounds the measurement and makes interpretation difficult. Some elements that need more separation in most cognitive and memory batteries are short-term storage versus complex working memory processes; short-term storage versus learning; and verbal working memory versus executive working memory. Cleaner separation of memory components would allow evaluators to better discriminate between the examinee's storage capacity and processing capacity. In addition to higher subtest specificity, higher factor specificity would also be helpful. For example, only subtests that measure the same short-term memory or working memory component should be aggregated. Furthermore, factor scores representing separable memory components should be combined into composites that represent the overall functioning of the three memory systems: short-term, long-term, and working memory. A global memory score that includes all memory systems would increase the validity of intraindividual analysis.

Other test-development suggestions that might lead to improved measurement of working memory and related memory systems include:

1. A standardized checklist of behaviors to observe for during subtest administration. Behaviors that denote storage and processing problems should be included, along with behaviors indicative of strategy use. The selected behaviors should vary by subtest, depending on the modality, the structure of the activity, and the strategies typically employed.

2. Activities designed to measure the use of memory strategies, the effectiveness of current strategies, and the examinee's ability to learn and apply a strategy during a controlled learning activity.

3. As attempted by Swanson (1995), more measures that allow the differentiation of capacity versus efficiency.

4. More working memory subtests that are complex enough to tap real-world working memory functioning. Such measures are needed because some students perform well on simple-span measures but have impairments in the working memory functions of daily life.

5. More verbal working memory subtests, such as story retelling, that avoid the introduction of interference. These tasks should be complex enough to require more than phonological short-term memory while being basic enough to avoid extensive involvement from executive working memory.

6. Tasks that attempt to measure how effectively working memory encodes semantic information into long-term memory.

7. More tasks that measure conscious, effortful retrieval of specific information from long-term memory.

8. Activities that attempt to measure the capacity of the activated pool of long-term memory items.

9. Fewer tasks that introduce interference designed to prevent strategy use. Although this classic paradigm makes sense in the experimental laboratory, it makes less sense when trying to measure real-world functioning.

10. Attempts to more directly measure executive working memory functions. All of the current executive working memory subtests continue to measure span. One function that could be measured directly is the ability to inhibit information that has become irrelevant.

11. More age-appropriate early childhood short-term memory and working memory measures that can be used to screen preschoolers and to determine who is at risk for language and literacy development problems.

12. A self-report (self-rating) scale focused on working memory functions and strategies, similar to self-report scales used to assess attention problems. A self-report instrument would allow an efficient and norm-based assessment of the development and use of strategies.

13. More visuospatial measures that are strictly nonverbal. That is, the presentation is nonverbal and the response is nonverbal. Too many "visuospatial" subtests mix modalities by requiring a verbal response to a visual presentation.

14. Verbal short-term memory and working memory measures are needed in more languages. Translations of verbal memory tests are mostly invalid due to change in length of utterance and words that do not translate well.

15. More theory-based working memory measures. Adherence to a central theory would increase the consistency of measurement across scales and facilitate the interpretation of results.

APPENDIX A

Working Memory Subtests in Cognitive Scales

Memory Component	WISC-IV	WISC-IV Integrated	WAIS-III	SB-5	DAS-II	WJ III Cognitive	KABC-II	CAS	UNIT
Phonological STM	Digit Span Forward	Letter Span Rhyming; Letter Span Nonrhyming	Digit Span Forward		Recall of Digits Forward	Memory for Words	Number Recall	Word Series	
Visuospatial STM		Visual Digit Span; Spatial Span Forward		Delayed Response (Part of Nonverbal WM subtest)	Recall of Designs; Recognition of Pictures	Picture Recognition	Hand Movements; Face Recognition	Figure Memory	Symbolic Memory; Spatial Memory; Object Memory
Verbal WM	Letter-Number Sequencing	Letter-Number Sequencing PA	Letter-Number Sequencing	Memory for Sentences (Part of Verbal WM subtest)		Auditory Working Memory		Sentence Repetition; Sentence Questions	
Visuospatial WM		Spatial Span Backward		Block Span (Part of Nonverbal WM subtest)					

Executive WM	Digit Span Backward; Letter-Number Sequencing; Arithmetic	Spatial Span Backward; Letter Number Sequencing PA; Arithmetic PA Part A and B	Digit Span Backward; Letter-Number Sequencing; Arithmetic	Last Word (Part of Verbal WM subtest)	Recall of Digits Backward; Recall of Sequential Order	Numbers Reversed; Auditory Working Memory	Word Order	Sentence Questions
Long-Term Retrieval					Rapid Naming	Retrieval Fluency; Rapid Picture Naming		

WISC-IV = Wechsler Intelligence Scale for Children–Fourth Edition; WAIS-III = Wechsler Adult Intelligence Scale–Third Edition; SB-5 = Stanford-Binet Intelligence Scales–Fifth Edition; DAS-II = Differential Ability Scales–Second Edition; W3 Cognitive = Woodcock Johnson Cognitive; KABC-II = Kaufman Assessment Battery for Children–Second Edition; CAS = Cognitive Assessment System; UNIT = Universal Nonverbal Intelligence Test.

APPENDIX B

Working Memory Assessment Plan

Examinee's Name: _____ DOB: _____ Age: _____ Grade: _____ Assessment Dates: _____

Referral Concerns	Memory or Processing Hypotheses	Memory Factors or Subtests	Observations	Interviews	Other Methods

Directions: Under Memory Factors or Subtests, specify the name of the battery, factor, and/or subtest that will be used. Under Observations, specify when and where. Under Interviews, specify with whom.

APPENDIX C

Working Memory Analysis Worksheet

Examinee's Name: _____ **DOB:** _____ **Age:** _____ **Grade:** _____ **Dates of Testing:** _____

Memory Component	Battery Name	Subtest/Factor Name	Subtest Score	Component Mean	Composite or Mean	Difference	Normative S or W	Ipsative S or W	Deficit or Asset
Phonological STM									
Visuospatial STM									
Verbal WM									
Visuospatial WM									
Executive WM									
Long-Term Retrieval									
Related Process									
Related Process									

Subtest or Clinical Factor Score	Subtest or Clinical Factor Score	Discrepancy	Significant: Y/N

Directions: (1) Convert all subtest scores to standard scores with a mean of 100 and an SD of 15. (2) For each component, compute the mean of the subtest scores and round to the nearest whole number. (3) Enter a cognitive composite, such as a FSIQ, or compute the mean of all available memory components. (4) Subtract the composite or mean from each component mean and enter amount in Difference column. (5) Indicate whether the component mean is a normative weakness or strength (90–109 is average). (6) Using a criterion of 12 points, determine intraindividual strengths and weaknesses. (7) Determine deficits and assets. A deficit is both a normative and intraindividual weakness; an asset is both a normative and intraindividual strength. (8) Determine which components are nonunitary. Components are nonunitary when the range between the highest and lowest subtest scores exceeds 1.5 standard deviations. Nonunitary components should be interpreted cautiously and should not be used in pairwise comparisons. (9) Compare logical pairs of components, using a 15-point difference as an indication of a significant discrepancy.

APPENDIX D

Working Memory Interpretative Summary

Examinee's Name: _____ DOB: _____ Age: _____ Grade: _____ Assessment Dates: _____

Memory Component	Memory and Processing Hypotheses	Cognitive/ Memory Test Results	Achievement Test Results	Observations	Interviews	Records	Conclusion
Phonological STM							
Visuospatial STM							
Verbal WM							
Visuospatial WM							
Executive WM							
Long-Term Retrieval							
Related Process							
Related Process							
Related Process							

Directions: Transfer the memory and processing hypotheses from the Working Memory Assessment Plan. After reviewing all data, write a summary statement in each applicable cell. In the Conclusion column indicate whether the hypothesis is supported or not supported.

338

APPENDIX E

Working Memory Subtests in Memory Scales

Memory Component	WMTB-C	S-CPT	WMS-III	CMS	TOMAL-2	WRAML2	AWMA
Phonological STM	Digit Recall; Word List Recall; Nonword List Recall; Word List Matching		Digit Span Forward	Numbers (Forward)	Digits Forward; Letters Forward	Number/Letter	Digit Recall; Word Recall; Nonword Recall
Visuospatial STM	Block Recall; Mazes Memory		Faces I; Family Pictures I; Visual Reproduction I; Spatial Span Forward	Faces; Family Pictures; Picture Locations	Facial Memory; Abstract Visual Memory; Memory for Location; Manual Imitation	Design Memory; Finger Windows	Dot Matrix; Mazes Memory; Block Recall
Verbal WM		Rhyming Words; Auditory Digital Sequence; Story Retelling; Phrase Sequence; Semantic Association; Semantic Categorization	Logical Memory I; Letter-Number Sequencing	Stories	Memory for Stories	Story Memory; Sentence Memory	Listening Recall; Counting Recall; Backwards Digit

Construct	WMTB-C	SCP-T	WMS-III	CMS	TOMAL-2	WRAML2	AWMA
Visuospatial WM		Visual Matrix; Mapping and Directions; Picture Sequence; Spatial Organization; Nonverbal Sequencing	Spatial Span Backward			Picture Memory	Odd-One-Out; Mr. X; Spatial Span
Executive WM	Listening Recall; Counting Recall; Backward Digit Recall	All S-CPT subtests are also measures of Executive WM	Letter-Number Sequencing; Mental Control; Digit Span Backward	Numbers (Backward); Sequences	Digits Backward; Letters Backward	Verbal Working Memory; Symbolic Working Memory	Listening Recall; Counting Recall; Backwards Digit
Long-Term Retrieval			Mental Control	Sequences			

WMTB-C = Working Memory Test Battery for Children; SCP-T = Swanson Cognitive Processing Test; WMS-III = Wechsler Memory Scale–Third Edition; CMS = Children's Memory Scale; TOMAL-2 = Test of Memory and Learning–Second Edition; WRAML2 = Wide Range Assessment of Memory and Learning–Second Edition; AWMA = Automated Working Memory Assessment.

APPENDIX F

Conversion Table: Scaled Scores to Standard Scores

Scaled Score (M = 10; SD = 3)	Standard Score (M = 100; SD = 15)
19	145
18	140
17	135
16	130
15	125
14	120
13	115
12	110
11	105
10	100
9	95
8	90
7	85
6	80
5	75
4	70
3	65
2	60
1	55

APPENDIX G

Related Processing Subtests in Cognitive Scales

Process	WISC-IV	WISC-IV Integrated	WAIS-III	SB-5	DAS-II	WJ III Cognitive	KABC-II	UNIT
Fluid Reasoning	Matrix Reasoning; Picture Concepts	Elithorn Mazes	Matrix Reasoning	Verbal Fluid Reasoning; Nonverbal Fluid Reasoning	Matrices; Sequential and Quantitative Reasoning	Concept Formation; Analysis-Synthesis	Story Completion; Pattern Reasoning	Cube Design; Analogic Reasoning; Mazes
Phonological Processing					Phonological Processing	Sound Blending; Incomplete Words		
Processing Speed	Coding; Symbol Search	Coding Recall; Coding Copy	Digit Symbol-Coding; Symbol Search		Speed of Information Processing; Rapid Naming	Visual Matching; Decision Speed		
Visual Processing	Block Design; Picture Completion	Block Design Multiple Choice; Block Design Process Approach	Block Design; Object Assembly	Verbal Visual-Spatial Processing; Nonverbal Visual-Spatial Processing	Pattern Construction; Recall of Designs	Spatial Relations; Picture Recognition	Rover; Triangles; Block Counting	

WISC-IV = Wechsler Intelligence Scale for Children–Fourth Edition; WAIS-III = Wechsler Adult Intelligence Scale–Third Edition; SB-5 = Stanford-Binet Intelligence Scales–Fifth Edition; DAS-II = Differential Ability Scales–Second Edition; WJ III Cognitive = Woodcock Johnson Cognitive; KABC-II = Kaufman Assessment Battery for Children–Second Edition; CAS = Cognitive Assessment System; UNIT = Universal Nonverbal Intelligence Test.

REFERENCES

Ackerman, P. L., Beier, M. E., & Boyle, M. O. (2002a). Individual differences in working memory within a nomological network of cognitive and perceptual speed abilities. *Journal of Experimental Psychology: General, 131*, 567–589.

Ackerman, P. L., Beier, M. E., & Boyle, M. O. (2002b). Working memory and intelligence: The same or different constructs? *Psychological Bulletin, 131*, 30–60.

Adams, G., & Engelmann, S. (1996). *Research on Direct Instruction 25 years beyond DISTAR.* Seattle, WA: Educational Achievement Systems.

Adams, J. A., Foorman, B. R., Lundberg, I., & Beeler, T. (1998). *Phonemic awareness in young children: A classroom curriculum.* Baltimore: Brookes.

Adams, W., & Sheslow, W. (2003). *Wide Range Assessment of Memory and Learning–second edition.* Wilmington, DE: Wide Range.

Alloway, T. P. (2007). *Automated Working Memory Assessment.* London: Harcourt Assessment.

Alloway, T. P., Gathercole, S. E., Adams, A. M., & Willis, C. (2005). Working memory abilities in children with special educational needs. *Educational & Child Psychology, 22*, 56–67.

Alloway, T. P., Gathercole, S. E., & Pickering, S. J. (2006). Verbal and visuo-spatial short-term and working memory in children: Are they separable? *Child Development, 77*, 1698–1716.

Alloway, T. P., Gathercole, S. E., Willis, C., & Adams, A. M. (2004). A structural analysis of working memory and related cognitive skills in young children. *Journal of Experimental Child Psychology, 87*, 85–106.

Anderson, J. R. (1976). *Language, memory, and thought.* Hillsdale, NJ: Lawrence Erlbaum Associates.

Anderson, J. R. (1983). *The architecture of cognition.* Cambridge, MA: Harvard University Press.

Andersson, U., & Lyxell, B. (2007). Working memory deficit in children with mathematical disabilities: A general or specific deficit? *Journal of Experimental Child Psychology, 96*, 197–228.

Atkinson, R. C., & Shiffrin, R. M. (1968). Human memory: A proposed system and its control processes. In K. W. Spence (Ed.), *The psychology of learning and motivation: Advances in research and theory* (Vol. 2, pp. 89–195). New York: Academic Press.

Awh, E., & Jonides, J. (2001). Overlapping mechanisms of attention and spatial working memory. *Trends in Cognitive Sciences, 5*, 119–126.

Baars, B. J., & Franklin, S. (2003). How conscious experience and working memory interact. *Trends in Cognitive Sciences, 7*, 166–172.

Baddeley, A. D. (1986). *Working memory*. New York: Oxford University Press.

Baddeley, A. D. (1990). The development of the concept of working memory: Implications and contributions of neuropsychology. In G. Vallar & J. Shallice (Eds.), *Neuropsychological impairments of short-term memory* (pp. 54–73). New York: Cambridge University Press.

Baddeley, A. D. (1996a). The concept of working memory. In S. E. Gathercole (Ed.), *Models of short-term memory* (pp. 1–27). East Sussex, UK: Lawrence Erlbaum.

Baddeley, A. D. (1996b). Exploring the central executive. *The Quarterly Journal of Experimental Psychology, 49A*, 5–28.

Baddeley, A. D. (2000). The episodic buffer: A new component in working memory? *Trends in Cognitive Sciences, 4*, 417–423.

Baddeley, A. D. (2003a). Working memory and language: An overview. *Journal of Communication Disorders, 36*, 189–208.

Baddeley, A. D. (2003b). Working memory: Looking back and looking forward. *Nature Reviews: Neuroscience, 4*, 829–839.

Baddeley, A. D. (2006). Working memory: An overview. In S. J. Pickering (Ed.), *Working memory and education* (pp. 1–31). Burlington, MA: Academic Press.

Baddeley, A., Gathercole, S., & Papagno, C. (1998). The phonological loop as a language learning device. *Psychological Review, 105*, 158–173.

Baddeley, A. D., & Hitch, G. J. (1974). Working memory. In G. A. Bower (Ed.), *Recent advances in learning and motivation* (Vol. 8, pp. 47–89). New York: Academic Press.

Baldo, J. V., & Dronkers, N. F. (2006). The role of inferior parietal and inferior frontal cortex in working memory. *Neuropsychology, 20*, 529–538.

Banikowski, A. K., & Mehring, T. A. (1999). Strategies to enhance memory based on brain-research. *Focus on Exceptional Children, 32*, 1–16.

Barkley, R. A. (1997a). *ADHD and the nature of self-control*. New York: Guilford.

Barkley, R. A. (1997b). Behavioral inhibition, sustained attention and executive functions: Constructing a unifying theory of ADHD. *Psychological Bulletin, 121*, 65–94.

Barrouillet, P., Bernardin, S., Portrat, S., Vergauwe, E., & Camos, V. (2007). Time and cognitive load in working memory. *Journal of Experimental Psychology: Learning, Memory, & Cognition, 33*, 570–585.

Barrouillet, P., & Camos, V. (2001). Developmental increase in working memory span: Resource sharing or temporal decay? *Journal of Memory and Language, 45*, 1–20.

Barrouillet, P., & Lepine, R. (2005). Working memory and children's use of retrieval to solve addition problems. *Journal of Experimental Child Psychology, 91*, 183–204.

Bayliss, D. M., Jarrold, C., Baddeley, A. D., & Gunn, D. M. (2003). The complexities of complex span: Explaining individual differences in working memory in children and adults. *Journal of Experimental Psychology: General, 132,* 71–92.

Bayliss, D. M., Jarrold, C., Baddeley, A. D., & Gunn, D. M. (2005). The relationship between short-term memory and working memory: Complex span made simple? *Memory, 13,* 414–421.

Bayliss, D. M., Jarrold, C., Baddeley, A. D., Gunn, D. M., & Leigh, E. (2005). Mapping the developmental constraints on working memory span performance. *Developmental Psychology, 41,* 579–597.

Bedard, A-C., Martinussen, R., Ickowicz, A., & Tannock, R. (2004). Methylphenidate improves visual-spatial memory in children with attention-deficit/hyperactivity disorder. *Journal of the American Academy of Child and Adolescent Psychiatry, 43,* 260–280.

Bellezza, F. S. (1981). Mnemonic devices: Classification, characteristics, and criteria. *Review of Educational Research, 51,* 247–275.

Berninger, V. W., & Richards, T. L. (2002). *Brain literacy for educators and psychologists.* San Diego: Academic Press.

Bishop, D. V. M., North, T., & Donlan, C. (1996). Nonword repetition as a phenotypic marker for inherited language impairment: Evidence from a twin study. *Journal of Child Psychology and Child Psychiatry, 37,* 391–404.

Blachowicz, C., & Ogle, D. (2001). *Reading comprehension: Strategies for independent learners.* New York: Guilford.

Bracken, B. A., & McCallum, R. S. (1998). *Universal Nonverbal Intelligence Test.* Itasca, IL: Riverside.

Brainerd, C. J. (1978). *Piaget's theory of intelligence.* Englewood Cliffs, NJ: Prentice Hall.

Brainerd, C. J. (1983). Young children's mental arithmetic errors: A working-memory analysis. *Child Development, 54,* 812–830.

Broadbent, D. E. (1958). *Perception and communication.* New York: Pergamon Press.

Broadbent, D. E. (1971). *Decision and stress.* London: Academic Press.

Broadley, I., MacDonald, J., & Buckley, S. (1994). Are children with Down's syndrome able to maintain skills learned from a short-term memory training programme? *Down Syndrome: Research and Practice, 2,* 116–122.

Brown, D. A., & Hulme, C. (1996). Nonword repetition, STM, and word age-of-acquisition: A computational model. A model and a method. In S. E. Gathercole (Ed.), *Models of short-term memory* (pp. 129–148). East Sussex, UK: Lawrence Erlbaum.

Brown, T. E., Reichel, P. C., & Quinlan, D. M. (2007). *117 high-IQ youths with ADHD:* Cognitive impairments and unique risks. Poster session presented at the annual meeting of the American Psychological Association, San Francisco, CA.

Buehner, M., Krumm, S., Ziegler, M., & Pluecken, T. (2006). Cognitive abilities and their interplay: Reasoning, crystallized intelligence, working memory components, and sustained attention. *Journal of Individual Differences, 27,* 57–72.

Buehner, M., Mangels, M., Krumm, S., & Ziegler, M. (2005). Are working memory and attention related constructs? *Journal of Individual Differences, 26,* 121–131.

Bulgren, J. A., Hock, M. F., Schumaker, J. B., & Deshler, D. D. (1995). The effects of instruction in a paired associate strategy on information mastery performance of students with learning disabilities. *Learning Disabilities Research & Practice, 10,* 22–37.

Bull, R., & Espy, K. A. (2006). Working memory, executive functioning, and children's mathematics. In S. J. Pickering (Ed.), *Working memory and education* (pp. 93–123). Burlington, MA: Academic Press.

Bull, R., & Johnston, R. S. (1997). Children's arithmetic difficulties: Contributions from processing speed, item identification, and short-term memory. *Journal of Experimental Child Psychology, 65*, 1–24.

Bunnell, J. K., Baken, D. M., & Richards-Ward, L. A. (1999). The effect of age on metamemory for working memory. *New Zealand Journal of Psychology, 28*, 23–29.

Burton, C., & Daneman, M. (2007). Compensating for a limited working memory capacity during reading: Evidence from eye movements. *Reading Psychology, 28*, 163–186.

Bus, A., & Van Ijzendoorn, M. (1999). Phonological awareness and early reading: A meta-analysis of experimental training studies. *Journal of Educational Psychology, 91*, 403–414.

Cain, K. (2006). Children's reading comprehension: The role of working memory in normal and impaired development. In S. J. Pickering (Ed.), *Working memory and education* (pp. 61–91). Burlington, MA: Academic Press.

Cain, K., Oakhill, J., & Bryant, P. (2004). Children's reading comprehension ability: Concurrent prediction by working memory, verbal ability, and component skills. *Journal of Educational Psychology, 96*, 31–42.

Callahan, C. M. (1998). Review of the Swanson-Cognitive Processing Test. In J. C. Impara & B. S. Plake (Eds.), *Mental measurements yearbook* (Vol. 13, pp. 990–991). Lincoln, NE: Buros Institute for Mental Measurements.

Cantor, J., & Engle, R. W. (1993). Working-memory capacity as long-term memory activation: An individual differences approach. *Journal of Experimental Psychology: Learning, Memory, and Cognition, 19*, 1101–1114.

Carlson, R. A., Khoo, B. H., Yaure, R. G., & Schneider, W. (1990). Acquisition of a problem-solving skill: Levels of organization and use of working memory. *Journal of Experimental Psychology: General, 119*, 194–214.

Carroll, J. B. (1993). *Human cognitive abilities: A survey of factor-analytic studies*. Cambridge: Cambridge University Press.

Case, R., Kurland, D. M., & Goldberg, J. (1982). Operational efficiency and the growth of short-term memory span. *Journal of Experimental Child Psychology, 33*, 386–404.

Cicerone, K. D. (2000). Remediation of "working attention" in mild traumatic brain injury. *Brain Injury, 16*, 185–195.

Cicerone, K. D. (2002). The enigma of executive functioning. In P. J. Eslinger (Ed.), *Neuropsychological interventions: Clinical research and practice* (pp. 3–15). New York: Guilford.

Clark, J., & Klecan-Aker, J. (1992). Therapeutic strategies for language disordered children: The impact of visual imagery on verbal encoding in vocabulary instruction. *Journal of Childhood Communication Disorders, 14*, 129–145.

Cohen, J. (1997). *Children's Memory Scale*. San Antonio: The Psychological Corporation.

Cohen-Mimran, R., & Sapir, S. (2007). Deficits in working memory in young adults with reading disabilities. *Journal of Communication Disorders, 40*, 168–183.

Colom, R., Rebollo, I., Palacios, A., Juan-Espinosa, M., & Kyllonen, P. C. (2004). Working memory is (almost) perfectly predicted by g. *Intelligence, 32*, 277–296.

Comblain, A. (1994). Working memory in Down's syndrome: Training the rehearsal strategy. *Down Syndrome: Research and Practice, 2*, 123–126.

Conlin, J. A., & Gathercole, S. E. (2006). Lexicality and interference in working memory in children and adults. *Journal of Memory and Language, 55*, 363–380.

Conlin, J. A., Gathercole, S. E., & Adams, J. W. (2005). Children's working memory: Investigating performance limitations in complex span tasks. *Journal of Experimental Child Psychology, 90*, 303–317.

Conners, F. A., Rosenquist, C. J., & Taylor, L. A. (2001). Memory training for children with Down syndrome. *Down Syndrome: Research and Practice, 7*, 25–33.

Conway, A. R. A., Cowan, N., & Bunting, M. F. (2001). The cocktail party revisited: The importance of working memory capacity. *Psychonomic Bulletin & Review, 8*, 331–335.

Conway, A. R. A., Cowan, N., Bunting, M. F., Therriault, D. J., & Minkoff, S. R. B. (2002). A latent variable analysis of working memory capacity, short-term memory capacity, processing speed, and general fluid intelligence. *Intelligence, 30*, 163–183.

Conway, A. R. A., & Engle, R. W. (1994). Working memory and retrieval: A resource-dependent inhibition model. *Journal of Experimental Psychology: General, 123*, 354–373.

Conway, A. R. A., & Engle, R. W. (1996). Individual differences in working memory capacity: More evidence for a general capacity theory. *Memory, 4*, 577–590.

Conway, A. R. A., Kane, M. J., & Engle, R. W. (2003). Working memory capacity and its relation to general intelligence. *Trends in Cognitive Sciences, 7*, 547–552.

Cook, N. M. (1989). The applicability of verbal mnemonics for different populations: A review. *Applied Cognitive Psychology, 3*, 3–22.

Cornish, K., Wilding, J., & Grant, C. (2006). Deconstructing working memory in developmental disorders of attention. In S. J. Pickering (Ed.), *Working memory and education* (pp. 157–188). Burlington, MA: Academic Press.

Cowan, N. (1993). Activation, attention, and short-term memory. *Memory & Cognition, 21*, 162–167.

Cowan, N. (1995). *Attention and memory: An integrated framework*. Oxford Psychology Series, #26. New York: Oxford University Press.

Cowan, N. (1999). An embedded-process model of working memory. In A. Miyake & P. Shah (Eds.), *Models of working memory: Mechanisms of active maintenance and executive control* (pp. 62–101). Cambridge, UK: Cambridge University Press.

Cowan, N. (2001). The magical number 4 in short-term memory: A reconsideration of mental storage capacity. *Behavioral and Brain Sciences, 24*, 87–185.

Cowan, N. (2005). *Working memory capacity*. New York: Lawrence Erlbaum.

Cowan, N., Nugent, L. D., Elliot, E. M., Ponomarev, I., & Saults, J. S. (1999). The role of attention in the development of short-term memory: Age differences in verbal span of apprehension. *Child Development, 70*, 1082–1097.

Cowan, N., Saults, J. S., & Morey, C. C. (2006). Development of working memory for verbal-spatial relations. *Journal of Memory and Language, 55*, 274–289.

Cowan, N., Wood, N. L., Wood, P. K., Keller, T. A., Nugent, L. D., & Keller, C. V. (1998). Two separate verbal processing rates contributing to short-term memory span. *Journal of Experimental Psychology: General, 127*, 141–160.

Craig, F. I. M., & Lockhart, R. S. (1972). Levels of processing: A framework for memory research. *Journal of Verbal Learning and Verbal Behavior, 11*, 671–684.

Crain, S., Shankweiler, D., Macaruso, P., & Bar-Shalom, E. (1990). Working memory and comprehension of spoken sentences: Investigations of children with reading disorder.

In G. Vallar & J. Shallice (Eds.), *Neuropsychological impairments of short-term memory* (pp. 477–509). New York: Cambridge University Press.

Crawford, S. A. S., & Baine, D. (1992). Making learning memorable: Distributed practice and long-term retention by special needs students. *Canadian Journal of Special Education, 8,* 118–128.

Daneman, M., & Carpenter, P. A. (1980). Individual differences in working memory and reading. *Journal of Verbal Learning and Verbal Behavior, 19,* 450–466.

Daneman, M., & Merikle, P. M. (1996). Working memory and language comprehension: A meta-analysis. *Psychonomic Bulletin and Review, 3,* 422–433.

Daneman, M., & Tardiff, T. (1987). Working memory and reading skill reexamined. In M. Coltheart (Ed.), *Attention and performance XII: The psychology of reading* (pp. 491–508). Hove, UK: Erlbaum.

Davies, G. M. (1980). Can memory be educated? *Educational Studies, 6,* 155–161.

Dawson, P., & Guare, R. (2004). *Executive skills in children and adolescents.* New York: Guilford.

De Beni, R., Borella, E., & Carretti, B. (2007). Reading comprehension in aging: The role of working memory and metacomprehension. *Aging, Neuropsychology, and Cognition, 14,* 189–212.

De Beni, R., & Palladino, P. (2000). Intrusion errors in working memory tasks: Are they related to reading comprehension ability. *Learning and Individual Differences, 12,* 131–145.

De Beni, R., Pazzaglia, F., Meneghetti, C., & Mondoloni, A. (2007). Working memory components and imagery instructions in the elaboration of a spatial mental model. *Psychological Research, 71,* 373–382.

Dehn, M. J. (1997). *The effects of informed strategy training and computer mediated text on comprehension monitoring and reading comprehension.* (ERIC Document Reproduction Service No. ED 402 545).

Dehn, M. J. (2006). *Essentials of processing assessment.* Hoboken, NJ: Wiley.

Dehn, M. J. (2007). Cognitive processing deficits. In R. J. Morris & N. Mather (Eds.), *Evidence-based interventions for students with learning and behavioral challenges* (pp. 258–287). Mahwah, NJ: Lawrence Erlbaum.

De Jong, P. F. (1998). Working memory deficits of reading disabled children. *Journal of Experimental Child Psychology, 70,* 75–96.

De Jong, P. F. (2006). Understanding normal and impaired reading development: A working memory perspective. In S. J. Pickering (Ed.), *Working memory and education* (pp. 33–60). Burlington, MA: Academic Press.

Denckla, M. B. (1996). Biological correlates of learning and attention: What is relevant to learning disability and attention-deficit hyperactivity disorder? *Journal of Developmental and Behavioral Pediatrics, 17,* 114–119.

Deshler, D. D., & Schumaker, J. B. (1993). Strategy mastery by at-risk students: Not a simple matter. *The Elementary School Journal, 94,* 153–167.

D'Esposito, M., Detre, J. A., Alsop, D. C., Shin, R. K., Atlas, S., & Grossman, M. (1995). The neural basis of the central executive system of working memory. *Nature, 378,* 279–281.

Dixon, P., LeFevre, J., & Twilley, L. C. (1988). Word knowledge and working memory as predictors of reading skill. *Journal of Educational Psychology, 80,* 465–472.

Donahue, M., & Pidek, C. (1993). Listening comprehension and paraphrasing in content-area classrooms. *Journal of Childhood Communication Disorders, 15*, 35–42.

Duff, S. C., & Logie, R. H. (2001). Processing and storage in working memory span. *The Quarterly Journal of Experimental Psychology, 54A*, 31–48.

Elliott, C. D. (2006). *Differential Ability Scales–second edition.* San Antonio, TX: PsychCorp.

Ellis, N. C., & Hennelley, R. A. (1980). A bilingual word-length effect: Implications for intelligence testing and the relative ease of mental calculation in Welsh and English. *British Journal of Psychology, 71*, 43–52.

Engle, R. W. (1996). Working memory and retrieval: An inhibition-resource approach. In J. T. E. Richardson, R. W. Engle, L. Hasher, R. H. Logie, E. R. Stoltzfus, & R. T. Zacks (Eds.), *Working memory and human cognition* (pp. 89–119). New York: Oxford University Press.

Engle, R. W. (2002). Working memory capacity as executive attention. *Current Directions in Psychological Science, 11*(1), 19–23.

Engle, R. W., Cantor, J. J., & Carullo, J. J. (1992). Individual differences in working memory and comprehension: A test of four hypotheses. *Journal of Experimental Psychology: Learning, Memory, and Cognition, 18*, 972–992.

Engle, R. W., Carullo, J. J., & Collins, K. W. (1991). Individual differences in working memory for comprehension and following directions. *Journal of Educational Research, 84*, 253–262.

Engle, R. W., Kane, M. J., & Tuholski, S. W. (1999). Individual differences in working memory capacity and what they tell us about controlled attention, general fluid intelligence and functions of the prefrontal cortex. In A. Miyake & P. Shah (Eds.), *Models of working memory: Mechanisms of active maintenance and executive control* (pp. 102–134). Cambridge, UK: Cambridge University Press.

Engle, R. W., Tuholski, S. W., Laughlin, J. E., & Conway, A. R. A. (1999). Working memory, short-term memory, and general fluid intelligence: A latent-variable approach. *Journal of Experimental Psychology: General, 128*, 309–331.

Ericsson, K. A., & Chase, W. G. (1982). Exceptional memory. *American Scientist, 70*, 607–615.

Ericsson, K. A., & Kintsch, W. (1995). Long-term working memory. *Psychological Review, 102*, 211–245.

Erlenmeyer-Kimling, L., Rock, D. R., Roberts, S. A., Janal, M., Kestenbaum, C., Cornblatt, B., et al. (2000). Attention, memory, and motor skills as childhood predictors of schizophrenia-related psychosis: The New York high-risk project. *American Journal of Psychiatry, 157*, 1416–1422.

Eslinger, P. J. (Ed.). (2002). *Neuropsychological interventions: Clinical research and practice.* New York: Guilford.

Eslinger, P. J., & Oliveri, M. V. (2002). Approaching interventions clinically and scientifically. In P. J. Eslinger (Ed.), *Neuropsychological interventions: Clinical research and practice* (pp. 3–15). New York: Guilford.

Espy, K. A., McDiarmid, M. D., Cwik, M. F., Stalets, M. M., Hamby, A., & Senn, T. E. (2004). The contribution of executive functions to emergent mathematics skills in preschool children. *Developmental Neuropsychology, 26*, 465–486.

Estes, W. K. (1999). Models of human memory: A 30-year retrospective. In C. Izawa (Ed.), *On human memory: Evolution, progress, and reflections on the 30th anniversary of the Atkinson-Shiffrin model* (pp. 59–86). Mahwah, NJ: Lawrence Erlbaum.

Evans, J. J., Floyd, R. G., McGrew, K. S., & Leforgee, M. H. (2002). The relations between measures of Cattell-Horn-Carroll (CHC) cognitive abilities and reading achievement during childhood and adolescence. *School Psychology Review, 31* (2), 246–262.

Feifer, S. G., & DeFina, P. D. (2000). *The neuropsychology of reading disorders: Diagnosis and intervention workbook.* Middletown, MD: School Neuropsych Press.

Fiez, J. A. (1996). A positron emission tomography study of the short-term maintenance of verbal information. *Journal of Neuroscience, 16,* 808–822.

Flanagan, D. P., & Ortiz, S. (2001). *Essentials of cross-battery assessment.* New York: Wiley.

Flanagan, D. P., & Ortiz, S. (2007). *Essentials of cross-battery assessment* (2nd ed.). New York: Wiley.

Frick, R. W. (1988). Issues of representation and limited capacity in the auditory short-term store. *British Journal of Psychology, 79,* 213–240.

Fry, A. F., & Hale, S. (1996). Processing speed, working memory, and fluid intelligence: Evidence for a developmental cascade. *Psychological Science, 7,* 237–241.

Fuchs, L. S., Fuchs, D., Compton, D. L., Powell, S. R., Seethaler, P. M., Capizzi, A. M., et al. (2006). The cognitive correlates of third-grade skills in arithmetic, algorithmic computation, and arithmetic word problems. *Journal of Educational Psychology, 98,* 29–43.

Gagne, R. M. (1974). *Essentials of learning for instruction.* New York: Holt, Rinehart, and Winston.

Gagne, E. D., Yekovich, C. W., & Yekovich, F. R. (1993). *The cognitive psychology of school learning* (2nd ed.). New York: HarperCollins College.

Gathercole, S. E. (1999). Cognitive approaches to the development of short-term memory. *Trends in Cognitive Sciences, 3,* 410–419.

Gathercole, S. E., & Adams, A-M. (1993). Phonological working memory in very young children. *Developmental Psychology, 29,* 770–778.

Gathercole, S. E., & Alloway, T. P. (2004). Working memory and classroom learning. *Dyslexia Review, 15,* 4–9.

Gathercole, S. E., Alloway, T. P., Willis, C., & Adams, A-M. (2006). Working memory in children with reading disabilities. *Journal of Experimental Child Psychology, 93,* 265–281.

Gathercole, S. E., & Baddeley, A. D. (1989). Evaluation of the role of phonological STM in the development of vocabulary in children: A longitudinal study. *Journal of Memory and Language, 28,* 200–213.

Gathercole, S. E., & Baddeley, A. D. (1990). The role of phonological memory in vocabulary acquisition: A study of young children learning new names. *British Journal of Psychology, 81,* 439–454.

Gathercole, S. E., & Baddeley, A. D. (1993). *Working memory and language.* East Sussex, UK: Lawrence Erlbaum.

Gathercole, S. E., Brown, L., & Pickering, S. J. (2003). Working memory assessments at school entry as longitudinal predictors of National Curriculum attainment levels. *Educational and Child Psychology, 20,* 109–122.

Gathercole, S. E., Lamont, E., & Alloway, T. P. (2006). Working memory in the classroom. In S. J. Pickering (Ed.), *Working memory and education* (pp. 219–240). Burlington, MA: Academic Press.

Gathercole, S. E., & Martin, A. J. (1996). Interactive processes in phonological memory. A model and a method. In S. E. Gathercole (Ed.), *Models of short-term memory* (pp. 73–100). East Sussex, UK: Lawrence Erlbaum.

Gathercole, S. E., & Pickering, S. J. (2000a). Assessment of working memory in six- and seven-year-old children. *Journal of Educational Psychology, 92,* 377–390.

Gathercole, S. E., & Pickering, S. J. (2000b). Working memory deficits in children with low achievements in the National Curriculum at seven years of age. *British Journal of Educational Psychology, 70,* 177–194.

Gathercole, S. E., & Pickering, S. J. (2001). Working memory deficits in children with special educational needs. *British Journal of Special Education, 28,* 89–97.

Gathercole, S. E., Pickering, S. J., Ambridge, B., & Wearing, H. (2004). The structure of working memory from 4-15 years of age. *Developmental Psychology, 40,* 177–190.

Gathercole, S. E., Tiffany, C., Briscoe, J., & Thorn, A. (2005). Developmental consequences of poor phonological short-term memory function in childhood. *Journal of Child Psychology and Psychiatry, 46,* 598–611.

Geary, D. C., Hoard, M. K., Byrd-Craven, J., & DeSoto, M. C. (2004). Strategy choices in simple and complex addition: Contributions of working memory and counting knowledge for children with mathematical disability. *Journal of Experimental Child Psychology, 88,* 121–151.

Gersten, R. (1985). Direct instruction with special education students: A review of evaluation research. *The Journal of Special Education, 19,* 41–58.

Gersten, R., Fuchs, L. S., Williams, J. P., & Baker, S. (2001). Teaching reading comprehension strategies to students with learning disabilities: A review of the research. *Review of Educational Research, 71,* 279–320.

Gersten, R., & Keating, T. (1987). Long-term benefits from direct instruction. *Educational Leadership, 44,* 28–29.

Gill, C. B., Klecan-Aker, J., Roberts, T., & Fredenburg, K. A. (2003). Following directions: Rehearsal and visualization strategies for children with specific language impairment. *Child Language Teaching & Therapy, 19,* 85–104.

Gilliam, R. B., & vanKleeck, A. (1996). Phonological awareness training and short-term working memory: Clinical implications. *Topics in Language Disorders, 17,* 72–81.

Glisky, E. L., & Glisky, M. L. (2002). Learning and memory impairments. In P. J. Eslinger (Ed.), *Neuropsychological interventions: Clinical research and practice* (pp. 137–162). New York: Guilford.

Glutting, J. J., McDermott, P. A., & Konold, T. R. (1997). Ontology, structure, and diagnostic benefits of a normative subtest taxonomy from the WISC-III standardization sample. In D. P. Flanagan, J. L. Genshaft, & P. L. Harrison (Eds.), *Contemporary intellectual assessment: Theories, tests, and issues* (pp. 340–372). New York: Guilford.

Gobet, F. (2000). Some shortcomings of long-term working memory. *British Journal of Psychology, 91,* 551–570.

Gobet, F., & Clarkson, G. (2004). Chunks in expert memory: Evidence for the magical number four . . . or is it two? *Memory, 12,* 732–747.

Goff, D. A., Pratt, C., & Ong, B. (2005). The relations between children's reading comprehension, working memory, language skills and components of reading decoding in a normal sample. *Reading and Writing, 18,* 583–616.

Goldman-Rakic, P. S. (1992). Working memory and the mind. *Scientific American, 267* (3), 111–117.

Goldman-Rakic, P. S. (1995). Architecture of the prefrontal cortex and the central executive. In J. Grafman, K. J. Holyoak, & F. Boller (Eds.), *Structure and functions of the human prefrontal cortex: Vol. 769. Annals of the New York Academy of the Sciences* (pp. 71–83). New York: New York Academy of Sciences.

Graham, S., & Harris, K. R. (1989). Component analysis of cognitive strategy instruction: Effects on learning disabled students' compositions and self-efficacy. *Journal of Educational Psychology, 81,* 353–361.

Gutierrez-Clellen, V. F., Calderon, J., & Weismer, S. E. (2004). Verbal working memory in bilingual children. *Journal of Speech, Language, and Hearing Research, 47,* 863–876.

Hale, J. B., & Fiorello, C. A. (2004). *School neuropsychology: A practitioner's handbook.* New York: Guilford.

Halford, G. S., Wilson, W. H., & Phillips, S. (2001). Processing capacity limits are not explained by storage limits. *Behavioral and Brain Sciences, 24,* 123–124.

Hartsuiker, R. J., & Barkuysen, P. N. (2006). Language production and working memory: The case of subject-verb agreement. *Language and Cognitive Processes, 21,* 181–204.

Harvey, P. D., Reichenberg, A., Romero, M., & Granholm, E. (2006). Dual-task information processing in schizotypal personality disorder: Evidence of impaired processing capacity. *Neuropsychology, 20,* 453–460.

Hasher, L., & Zacks, R. T. (1988). Working memory, comprehension, and aging: A review and a new view. In G. H. Bower (Ed.), *The psychology of learning and motivation* (Vol. 22, pp. 193–225). San Diego, CA: Academic Press.

Hebb, D. O. (1949). *Organization of behavior.* Wiley: New York.

Hedden, T., & Yoon, C. (2006). Individual differences in executive processing predict susceptibility to interference in verbal working memory. *Neuropsychology, 20,* 511–528.

Henry, L. A. (2001). How does the severity of a learning disability affect working memory performance? *Memory, 9,* 233–247.

Henry, L. A., & MacLean, M. (2002). Working memory performance in children with and without intellectual disabilities. *American Journal on Mental Retardation, 107,* 421–432.

Henry, L. A., & Millar, S. (1993). Why does memory span improve with age? A review of the evidence for two current hypotheses. *European Journal of Cognitive Psychology, 5,* 241–287.

Hester, R., & Garavan, H. (2005). Working memory and executive function: The influence of content and load on the control of attention. *Memory & Cognition, 33,* 221–233.

Hitch, G. J. (1990). Developmental fractionation of working memory. In G. Vallar & J. Shallice (Eds.), *Neuropsychological impairments of short-term memory* (pp. 221–246). New York: Cambridge University Press.

Hitch, G. J., Halliday, S., Schaafstal, A. M., & Schraagen, M. C. (1988). Visual working memory in young children. *Memory & Cognition, 16,* 120–132.

Hitch, G. J., Towse, J. N., & Hutton, U. (2001). What limits children's working memory capacity? Theoretical accounts and applications for scholastic development. *Journal of Experimental Psychology: General, 130,* 183–198.

Holmes, J., & Adams, J. W. (2006). Working memory and children's mathematical skills: Implications for mathematical development and mathematics curricula. *Educational Psychology, 26,* 339–366.

Horn, J. L., & Blankson, N. (2005). Foundations for better understanding of cognitive abilities. In D. P. Flanagan & P. L. Harrison (Eds.), *Contemporary intellectual assessment: Theories, tests, and issues* (2nd ed., pp. 41–68). New York: Guilford.

Hurford, D., Johnston, M., Nepote, P., Hampton, S., Moore, S., Neal, J., et al. (1994). Early identification and remediation of phonological-processing deficits in first-grade children at risk for reading disabilities. *Journal of Learning Disabilities, 27,* 647–659.

Hulme, C., & Mackenzie, S. (1992). *Working memory and severe learning difficulties.* East Sussex, UK: Lawrence Erlbaum.

Hutton, U. M. Z., & Towse, J. N. (2001). Short-term memory and working memory as indices of children's cognitive skills. *Memory, 9,* 383–394.

Imbo, I., & Vandierendonck, A. (2007). The development of strategy use in elementary school children: Working memory and individual differences. *Journal of Experimental Child Psychology, 96,* 284–309.

Imbo, I., Vandierendonck, A., & Vergauwe, E. (2007). The role of working memory in carrying and borrowing. *Psychological Research, 71,* 467–483.

James, W. (1890). *The principles of psychology.* New York: Henry Holt.

Jeffries, S., & Everatt, J. (2004). Working memory: Its role in dyslexia and other specific learning disabilities. *Dyslexia, 10,* 196–214.

Johnston, R. S., & Anderson, M. (1998). Memory span, naming speed, and memory strategies in normal and poor readers. *Memory, 6,* 143–164.

Jonides, J., Smith, E. E., Marshuetz, C., & Koeppe, R. A. (1998). Inhibition in verbal working memory revealed by brain activation. *Proceedings of the National Academy of Sciences, U.S.A., 95,* 8410–8413.

Just, M. A., & Carpenter, P. A. (1992). A capacity theory of comprehension: Individual differences in working memory. *Psychological Review, 99,* 122–149.

Kail, R. (2007). Longitudinal evidence that increases in processing speed and working memory enhance children's reasoning. *Psychological Science, 18,* 312–313.

Kail, R., & Hall, L. K. (2001). Distinguishing short-term memory from working memory. *Memory & Cognition, 29,* 1–9.

Kamhi, A. G., & Pollock, K. E. (2005). *Phonological disorders in children: Clinical decision making in assessment and intervention.* Baltimore: Brookes.

Kane, M. J., Conway, A. R. A., Bleckley, M. K., & Engle, R. W. (2001). A controlled-attention view of working memory capacity. *Journal of Experimental Psychology: General, 130,* 169–183.

Kane, M. J., Conway, A. R. A., Miura, T. K., & Colfiesh, G. J. H. (2007). Working memory, attention control, and the n-back task: A question of construct validity. *Journal of Experimental Psychology: Learning, Memory, & Cognition, 33,* 615–622.

Kane, M. J., & Engle, R. W. (2000). Working-memory capacity, proactive interference, and divided attention: Limits on long-term memory retrieval. *Journal of Experimental Psychology: Learning, Memory, and Cognition, 26,* 336–358.

Kane, M. J., & Engle, R. W. (2002). The role of prefrontal cortex in working-memory capacity, executive attention, and general fluid intelligence: An individual-differences perspective. *Psychonomic Bulletin and Review, 9,* 637–671.

Kane, M. J., Hambrick, D. Z., Tuholski, S. W., Wilhelm, O., Payne, T. W., & Engle, R. W. (2004). The generality of working memory capacity: A latent-variable approach to verbal and visuospatial memory span and reasoning. *Journal of Experimental Psychology: General, 133*, 189–217.

Kar, B. C., Dash, U. N., Das, J. P., & Carlson, J. (1993). Two experiments on the dynamic assessment of planning. *Learning and Individual Differences, 5*, 13–29.

Kaufman, A. S., & Kaufman, N. L. (2004a). *Kaufman Assessment Battery for Children–second edition*. Circle Pines, MN: AGS Publishing.

Kaufman, A. S., & Kaufman, N. L. (2004b). *Kaufman Test of Educational Achievement–second edition*. Circle Pines, MN: AGS Publishing.

Kaufman, A. S., Lichtenberger, E. O., Fletcher-Janzen, E., & Kaufman, N. (2005). *Essentials of KABC-II assessment*. Hoboken, NJ: Wiley.

Keeler, M. L., & Swanson, H. L. (2001). Does strategy knowledge influence working memory in children with mathematical disabilities? *Journal of Learning Disabilities, 34*, 418–434.

Keith, T. Z., Fine, J. G., Taub, G. E., Reynolds, M. R., & Kranzler, J. H. (2006). Higher order, multisample, confirmatory factor analysis of the Wechsler Intelligence Scale for Children–fourth edition: What does it measure? *School Psychology Review, 35*, 108–127.

Keith, T. Z., Kranzler, J. H., Flanagan, D. P. (2001). Joint CFA of the CAS and WJ III. *School Psychology Review, 29*, 203–207.

Kellogg, R. T. (1996). A model of working memory in writing. In C. M. Levy, & S. E. Ransdell (Eds.), *The science of writing* (pp. 57–71). Mahwah, NJ: Erlbaum.

Kellogg, R. T., Olive, T., & Piolat, A. (2007). Verbal, visual, and spatial working memory in written language production. *Acta Psychologica, 124*, 382–297.

Kemp, S., Kirk, U., & Korkman, M. (2001). *Essentials of NEPSY assessment*. New York: Wiley.

Kemps, E. (1999). Effects of complexity on visuo-spatial working memory. *European Journal of Cognitive Psychology, 11*, 335–356.

Klein, K., & Boals, A. (2001). Expressive writing can increase working memory capacity. *Journal of Experimental Psychology: General, 130*, 520–523.

Klingberg, T., Fernell, E., Olesen, P., Johnston, M., Gustafsson, P., Dahlstrom, K., et al. (2005). Computerized training of working memory in children with ADHD—a controlled, randomized, double-blind trial. *Journal of the American Academy of Child and Adolescent Psychiatry, 44*, 177–186.

Klingberg, T., Forssberg, H., & Westerberg, H. (2002). Training of working memory in children with ADHD. *Journal of Clinical and Experimental Neuropsychology, 24*, 781–791.

Korkman, M., Kirk, U., & Kemp, S. (1998). *NEPSY: A developmental neuropsychological assessment*. San Antonio, TX: The Psychological Corporation.

Korkman, M., Kirk, U., & Kemp, S. (2007). *NEPSY-II: A developmental neuropsychological assessment*. San Antonio, TX: The Psychological Corporation.

Kyllonen, P. C. (1996). Is working memory capacity Spearman's g? In I. Dennis & P. Tapsfield (Eds.), *Human abilities: Their nature and measurement* (pp. 49–76). Mahwah, NJ: Erlbaum.

Kyllonen, P. C., & Christal, R. E. (1990). Reasoning ability is (little more than) working-memory capacity?! *Intelligence, 14*, 389–433.

Lange, G., & Pierce, S. H. (1992). Memory-strategy learning and maintenance in preschool children. *Developmental Psychology, 28*, 453–462.

Lawson, M. J., & Rice, D. N. (1989). Effects of training in use of executive strategies on a verbal memory problem resulting from a closed head injury. *Journal of Clinical and Experimental Neuropsychology, 11*, 842–854.

Leahey, T. H., & Harris, R. J. (1989). *Human learning* (2nd ed.). Englewood Cliffs, NJ: Prentice-Hall.

Leasak, J., Hunt, D., & Randhawa, B. S. (1982). Cognitive processing, intervention, and achievement. *The Alberta Journal of Educational Research, 28*, 257–266.

Leather, C. V., & Henry, L. A. (1994). Working memory span and phonological awareness tasks as predictors of early reading ability. *Journal of Experimental Child Psychology, 58*, 88–111.

LeBlanc, M. D., & Weber-Russell, S. (1996). Text integration and mathematical connections: A computer model of arithmetic word problem solving. *Cognitive Science, 20*, 357–407.

Lee, D., & Riccio, C. A. (2005). Understanding and implementing cognitive neuropsychological retraining. In R. C. D'Amato, E. Fletcher-Janzen, & C. R. Reynolds (Eds.), *Handbook of school neuropsychology* (pp. 701–720). Hoboken, NJ: Wiley.

Leonard, L. B., Weismer, S. E., Miller, C. A., Francis, D. J., Tomblin, J. B., & Kail, R. V. (2007). Speed of processing, working memory, and language impairment in children. *Journal of Speech, Language, and Hearing Research, 50*, 408–428.

Lepine, R., Barrouillet, P., & Camos, V. (2005). What makes working memory spans so predictive of high-level cognition. *Psychonomic Bulletin and Review, 12*(1), 165–170.

Levin, H. S., Hanten, G., Zhang, L., Swank, P. R., Ewing-Cobbs, L., Dennis, M., et al. (2004). Changes in working memory after traumatic brain injury in children. *Neuropsychology, 18*, 240–247.

Levin, J. R. (1993). Mnemonic strategies and classroom learning: A twenty-year report card. *The Elementary School Journal, 94*, 235–244.

Levin, M. E., & Levin, J. R. (1990). Scientific mnemonics: Methods for maximizing more than memory. *American Educational Research Journal, 27*, 301–321.

Levine, B., Robertson, I. H., Clare, L., Carter, G., Hong, J., Wilson, B. A., et al. (2000). Rehabilitation of executive functioning: An experimental-clinical validation of goal management training. *Journal of the International Neuropsychological Society, 6*, 299–312.

Lichtenberger, E. O., Kaufman, A. S., & Lai, Z. C. (2002). *Essentials of WMS-III assessment.* New York: Wiley.

Linden, D. E. J. (2007). The working memory networks of the human brain. *The Neuroscientist, 13*, 257–267.

Linderholm, T., & Van Den Broek, P. (2002). The effects of reading purpose and working memory capacity on the processing of expository text. *Journal of Educational Psychology, 94*, 778–784.

Livingston, J. A. (2003). *Metacognition: An overview.* (ERIC Document Reproduction Service No. ED474273)

Loarer, E. (2003). Cognitive training for individuals with deficits. In R. J. Sternberg, J. Lautrey, & T. I. Lubart (Eds.), *Models of intelligence: International perspectives* (pp. 243–260). Washington, DC: American Psychological Association.

Locke, J. (1690). *An essay concerning humane understanding.* London: Thomas Bassett.

Logie, R. H. (1996). The seven ages of working memory. In J. T. E. Richardson, R. W. Engle, L. Hasher, R. H. Logie, E. R. Stoltzfus, & R. T. Zacks (Eds.), *Working memory and human cognition* (pp. 31–65). New York: Oxford University Press.

Luciana, M., Conklin, H. M., Hooper, C. J., & Yarger, R. S. (2005). The development of nonverbal working memory and executive control processes in adolescents. *Child Development, 76*, 697–712.

Luria, A. R. (1970). The functional organization of the brain. *Scientific American, 222*, 66–78.

MacDonald, M. C., & Christiansen, M. H. (2002). Reassessing working memory: Comment on Just and Carpenter (1992) and Waters and Caplan (1996). *Psychological Review, 109*, 35–54.

Mann, V. (1984). Longitudinal prediction and prevention of early reading difficulty. *Annals of Dyslexia, 34*, 117–136.

Martinussen, R., Hayden, J., Hogg-Johnson, S., & Tannock, R. (2005). A meta-analysis of working memory impairments in children with attention-deficit/hyperactivity disorder. *Journal of the American Academy of Child and Adolescent Psychiatry, 44*, 377–384.

Martinussen, R., & Tannock, R. (2006). Working memory impairments in children with attention-deficit hyperactivity disorder with and without comorbid language learning disorders. *Journal of Clinical and Experimental Neuropsychology, 28*, 1073–1094.

Masoura, E. V. (2006). Establishing the link between working memory function and learning disabilities. *Learning Disabilities: A Contemporary Journal, 4*, 29–41.

Mastropieri, M. A., & Scruggs, T. E. (1991). *Teaching students ways to remember: Strategies for learning mnemonically.* Cambridge, MA: Brookline Books.

Mastropieri, M. A., & Scruggs, T. E. (1998). Enhancing school success with mnemonic strategies. *Intervention in School and Clinic, 33*, 201–208.

Mastropieri, M. A., & Scruggs, T. E. (2007). The inclusive classroom: Strategies for effective instruction. Columbus, OH: Pearson.

Mastropieri, M. A., Scruggs, T. E., & Levin, J. R. (1985). Maximizing what exceptional students can learn: A review of research on the keyword method and related mnemonic techniques. *Remedial and Special Education, 6*, 39–45.

Mastropieri, M. A., Sweda, J., & Scruggs, T. E. (2000). Putting mnemonic strategies to work in an inclusive classroom. *Learning Disabilities Research & Practice, 15*, 69–74.

Mather, N., & Wendling, B. J. (2005). Linking cognitive assessment results to academic interventions for students with learning disabilities. In D. P. Flanagan & P. L. Harrison (Eds.), *Contemporary intellectual assessment: Theories, tests, and issues* (2nd ed., pp. 269–298). New York: Guilford.

McCallum, R. S., Bell, S. M., Wood, M. S., Below, J. L., Choate, S. M., & McCane, S. J. (2006). What is the role of working memory in reading relative to the big three processing variables (orthography, phonology, and rapid naming)? *Journal of Psychoeducational Assessment, 24*, 243–259.

McElree, B. (1998). Attended and non-attended states in working memory: Accessing categorized structures. *Journal of Memory and Language, 38*, 225–252.

McGrew, K. S. (2005). The Cattell-Horn-Carroll theory of cognitive abilities. In D. P. Flanagan & P. L. Harrison (Eds.), *Contemporary intellectual assessment: Theories, tests, and issues* (2nd ed., pp. 136–181). New York: Guilford.

McGrew, K. S., & Woodcock, R. W. (2001). *Woodcock-Johnson III technical manual.* Itasca, IL: Riverside Publishing.

McLean, J. F., & Hitch, G. J. (1999). Working memory impairments in children with specific arithmetic learning difficulties. *Journal of Experimental Child Psychology, 74*, 240–260.

McNamara, D. S., & Kintsch, W. (1996). Working memory in text comprehension: Interrupting difficult text. In G. W. Cottrell (Ed.), *Proceedings of the Eighteenth Annual Meeting of the Cognitive Science Society* (pp. 104–109). Hillsdale, NJ: Erlbaum.

McNamara, D. S., & Scott, J. L. (2001). Working memory capacity and strategy use. *Memory & Cognition, 29*, 10–17.

Meichenbaum, D., & Goodman, J. (1971). Training impulsive children to talk to themselves: A means of developing self-control. *Journal of Abnormal Psychology, 77*, 115–126.

Metha, M. A., Owen, A. M., Sahakian, B. J., Mavaddat, N., Pickard, J. D., & Robbins, T. W. (2000). Methylphenidate enhances working memory by modulating discrete frontal and parietal lobe regions in the human brain. *The Journal of Neuroscience, 20*(6), 1–6.

Miller, G. A. (1956). The magical number seven, plus or minus two: Some limits on our capacity for processing information. *Psychological Review, 63*, 81–97.

Minear, M., & Shah, P. (2006). Sources of working memory deficits in children and possibilities for remediation. In S. J. Pickering (Ed.), *Working memory and education* (pp. 273–307). Burlington, MA: Academic Press.

Miyake, A., Friedman, N. P., Emerson, M. J., Witzki, A. H., & Howerter, A. (2000). The unity and diversity of executive functions and their contributions to complex "frontal lobe" tasks: A latent variable analysis. *Cognitive Psychology, 41*, 49–100.

Montgomery, J. W. (1996). Sentence comprehension and working memory in children with specific language impairment. *Topics in Language Disorders, 17*, 19–32.

Moore, D. R., Rosenberg, J. F., & Coleman, J. S. (2004). Discrimination training of phonemic contrasts enhances phonological processing in mainstream school children. *Brain and Language, 94*, 72–85.

Moreno, J., & Saldana, D. (2004). Use of a computer-assisted program to improve meta-cognition in persons with severe intellectual disabilities. *Research in Developmental Disabilities, 26*, 341–357.

Morris, R. D. (1996). Relationships and distinctions among the concepts of attention, memory and executive function: A developmental perspective. In G. R. Lyon & N. A. Krasnegor (Eds.), *Attention, memory, and executive function* (pp. 11–16). Baltimore: Paul H. Brookes.

Moser, D. D., Fridriksson, J., & Healy, E. W. (2007). Sentence comprehension and general working memory. *Clinical Linguistics & Phonetics, 21*, 147–156.

Naglieri, J. A. (1999). *Essentials of CAS assessment.* Hoboken, NJ: Wiley.

Naglieri, J. A., & Das, J. P. (1997). *Cognitive Assessment System.* Itasca, IL: Riverside Publishing.

Nairne, J. S. (2002). Remembering over the short-term: The case against the standard model. *Annual Review of Psychology, 53*, 53–81.

Nation, K., Adams, J. W., Bowyer-Crane, C. A., & Snowling, M. J. (1999). Working memory impairments in poor comprehenders reflect underlying language impairments. *Journal of Experimental Child Psychology, 73*, 139–158.

National Reading Panel. (2000). *Teaching children to read: An evidence-based assessment of the scientific literature on reading and its applications for reading instruction.* Washington, DC: National Institute of Child Health and Human Development (NICHD).

Nelson, D. L., & Goodmon, L. B. (2003). Disrupting attention: The need for retrieval cues in working memory theories. *Memory & Cognition, 31*, 65–76.

Norman, D. A., & Shallice, T. (1980). *Attention to action: Willed and automatic control of behavior.* University of California, San Diego, CHIP Report 99.

Oberauer, K. (2002). Access to information in working memory: Exploring the focus of attention. *Journal of Experimental Psychology: Learning, Memory, and Cognition, 28*, 411–421.

Oberauer, K., Sub, H.-M., Schulze, R., Wilhelm, O., & Wittman, W. W. (2000). Working memory capacity—facets of a cognitive ability construct. *Personality and Individual Differences, 29*, 1017–1045.

Oberauer, K., Sub, H.-M., Wilhelm, O., & Wittman, W. W. (2003). The multiple faces of working memory: Storage, processing, supervision, and coordination. *Intelligence, 31*, 167–193.

Olesen, P. J., Westerberg, H., & Klingberg, T. (2004). Increased prefrontal and parietal activity after training of working memory. *Nature Neuroscience, 7*, 75–79.

Olive, T. (2004). Working memory in writing: Empirical evidence from the dual-task technique. *European Psychologist, 9*, 32–42.

Olivers, C. N. L., Meijer, F., & Theeuwes, J. (2006). Feature-based memory-driven attentional closure: Visual working memory content affects visual attention. *Journal of Experimental Psychology, 32*, 1243–1265.

Ornstein, P. A., Naus, M. J., & Stone, B. P. (1977). Rehearsal training and developmental differences in children's memory. *Child Development, 46*, 818–830.

O'Shaughnessy, T., & Swanson, H. L. (1998). Do immediate memory deficits in students with learning disabilities in reading reflect a developmental lag or deficit? *Learning Disability Quarterly, 21*, 123–148.

Palmer, S. (2000). Phonological recoding deficit in working memory of dyslexic teenagers. *Journal of Research in Reading, 23*, 28–40.

Parente, R., & Herrmann, D. (1996). Retraining memory strategies. *Topics in Language Disorders, 17*, 45–57.

Paris, S. G., Cross, D. R., & Lipson, M. Y. (1984). Informed strategies for learning: A program to improve children's reading awareness and comprehension. *Journal of Educational Psychology, 76*, 1239–1252.

Pascual-Leone, J. (2001). If the magical number is 4, how does one account for operations within working memory? *Behavioral and Brain Sciences, 24*, 136–138.

Passolunghi, M. C., & Siegel, L. S. (2001). Short-term memory, working memory, and inhibitory control in children with difficulties in arithmetic problem-solving. *Journal of Experimental Child Psychology, 80*, 44–57.

Passolunghi, M. C., & Siegel, L. S. (2004). Working memory and access to numerical information in children with disability in mathematics. *Journal of Experimental Child Psychology, 88*, 348–367.

Pavio, A., & Csapo, K. I. (1969). Concrete-image and verbal memory codes. *Journal of Experimental Psychology, 80*, 279–285.

Pearson, D. G., Logie, R. H., & Gilhooly, K. J. (1999). Verbal representations and spatial manipulation during mental synthesis. *European Journal of Cognitive Psychology, 11*, 295–314.

Pennington, B. F., Bennetto, L., McAleer, O., & Roberts, R. J. (1996). Executive functions and working memory: Theoretical and measurement issues. In G. R. Lyon & N. A. Krasnegor (Eds.), *Attention, memory, and executive function* (pp. 327–348). Baltimore: Paul H. Brookes.

Pickering, S. J. (2006). Assessment of working memory in children. In S. J. Pickering (Ed.), *Working memory and education* (pp. 241–271). Burlington, MA: Academic Press.

Pickering, S. J., & Gathercole, S. E. (2001a). *Working Memory Test Battery for Children.* London: Psychological Corporation Europe.

Pickering, S. J., & Gathercole, S. E. (2001b). *Working Memory Test Battery for Children (WMTB-C) manual.* London: Psychological Corporation Europe.

Pickering, S. J., & Gathercole, S. E. (2004). Distinctive working memory profiles in children with special educational needs. *Educational Psychology, 24,* 393–408.

Pickering, S. J., Gathercole, S. E., Hall, M., & Lloyd, S. A. (2001). Development of memory for pattern and path: Further evidence for the fractionation of visuo-spatial memory. *Quarterly Journal of Experimental Psychology, 54A,* 397–420.

Prabhakaran, V., Narayanan, K., Zhao, Z., & Gabrieli, J. D. E. (2000). Integration of diverse information in working memory within the frontal lobe. *Nature Neuroscience, 3,* 85–90.

Pressley, M., Johnson, C. J., & Symons, S. (1987). Elaborating to learn and learning to elaborate. *Journal of Learning Disabilities, 20,* 76–91.

Pressley, M., & Woloshyn, V. (1995). *Cognitive strategy instruction that really improves children's academic instruction* (2nd ed.). Cambridge, MA: Brookline Books.

Przychodzin, A. M., Marchand-Martella, N. E., & Martella, R. C. (2004). Direct instruction mathematics programs: An overview and research summary. *Journal of Direct Instruction, 4,* 53–84.

Quinlan, D. M., & Brown, T. E. (2003). Assessment of short-term verbal memory impairments in adolescents and adults with ADHD. *Journal of Attention Disorders, 6,* 143–152.

Radvansky, G. A., & Copeland, D. E. (2006). Memory retrieval and interference: Working memory issues. *Journal of Memory and Language, 55,* 33–46.

Rafoth, M. A., Leal, L., & DeFabo, L. (1993). *Strategies for learning and remembering: Study skills across the curriculum.* Washington, DC: National Education Association.

Raine, A., Hulme, C., Chadderton, H., & Bailey, P. (1991). Verbal short-term memory span in speech disordered children: Implications for articulatory coding in short-term memory. *Child Development, 62,* 415–423.

Ranganath, C., Johnson, M. K., & D'Esposito, M. (2003). Prefrontal activity associated with working memory and episodic long-term memory. *Neuropsychologia, 41,* 378–389.

Rasmussen, C., & Bisanz, J. (2005). Representation and working memory in early arithmetic. *Journal of Experimental Child Psychology, 91,* 137–157.

Reber, P. J., & Kotovksy, K. (1997). Implicit learning in problem solving: The role of working memory capacity. *Journal of Experimental Psychology: General, 126,* 178–203.

Reynolds, C. R., & Bigler, E. D. (1994). *Test of Memory and Learning.* Austin: TX: PRO-ED.

Reynolds, C. R., & Voress, J. K. (2007). *Test of Memory and Learning–second edition.* Austin: TX: PRO-ED.

Richardson, J. T. E. (1996a). Evolving concepts of working memory. In J. T. E. Richardson, R. W. Engle, L. Hasher, R. H. Logie, E. R. Stoltzfus, & R. T. Zacks (Eds.), *Working memory and human cognition* (pp. 3–30). New York: Oxford University Press.

Richardson, J. T. E. (1996b). Evolving issues in working memory. In J. T. E. Richardson, R. W. Engle, L. Hasher, R. H. Logie, E. R. Stoltzfus, & R. T. Zacks (Eds.), *Working memory and human cognition* (pp. 120–154). New York: Oxford University Press.

Rief, S. F. (1993). *How to reach and teach ADD/ADHD children.* West Nyack, NY: Center for Applied Research in Education.

Riggs, K. J., McTaggart, J., Simpson, A., & Freeman, R. P. J. (2006). Changes in the capacity of visual working memory in 5- to 10-year-olds. *Journal of Experimental Child Psychology, 95,* 18–26.

Ritchie, D., & Karge, B. D. (1996). Making information memorable: Enhanced knowledge retention and recall through the elaboration process. *Preventing School Failure, 41*, 28–33.

Roberts, R. J., & Pennington, B. F. (1996). An interactive framework for examining prefrontal cognitive processes. *Developmental Neuropsychology, 12*, 105–126.

Roid, G. H. (2003). *Stanford-Binet Intelligence Scales–fifth edition*. Itasca, IL: Riverside Publishing.

Roid, G. H., & Barram, R. A. (2004). *Essentials of Stanford-Binet Intelligence Scales (SB5) assessment*. Hoboken, NJ: Wiley.

Rose, M. C., Cundick, B. P., & Higbee, K. L. (1983). Verbal rehearsal and visual imagery: Mnemonic aids for learning-disabled children. *Journal of Learning Disabilities, 16*, 352–354.

Rosen, V. M., & Engle, R. W. (1997). The role of working memory capacity in retrieval. *Journal of Experimental Psychology: General, 126*, 211–227.

Rosenshine, B. (1995). Advances in research on instruction. *Journal of Educational Research, 88*, 262–268.

Rosenshine, B. (1997). Advances in research on instruction. In J. W. Lloyd, E. J. Kameanue, & D. Chard (Eds.), *Issues in educating students with disabilities*. (pp. 197–221). Mahwah, NJ: Erlbaum.

Rosenshine, B., & Stevens, R. (1986). Teaching functions. In M. C. Wittrock (Ed.), *Handbook of research on teaching* (3rd ed., pp. 376–391). Washington, DC: American Educational Research Association.

Rudner, M., Fransson, P., Ingvar, M., Nyberg, L., & Ronnberg, J. (2007). Neural representation of binding lexical signs and words in the episodic buffer of working memory. *Neuropsychologia, 45*, 2258–2276.

Rypma, B., & D'Esposito, M. (1999). The roles of prefrontal brain regions in components of working memory: Effects of memory load and individual differences. *Proceedings of the National Academy of Sciences, 96*, 6558–6563.

Rypma, B., & D'Esposito, M. (2000). Isolating the neural mechanisms of age-related changes in human working memory. *Nature Neuroscience, 3*, 509–515.

Salembier, G. B. (1999). SCAN and RUN: A reading comprehension strategy that works. *Journal of Adolescent and Adult Literacy, 42*, 386–394.

Savage, R., Cornish, K., Manly, T., & Hollis, C. (2006). Cognitive processes in children's reading and attention: The role of working memory, divided attention, and response inhibition. *British Journal of Psychology, 97*, 365–385.

Savage, R., Lavers, N., & Pillay, V. (2007). Working memory and reading difficulties: What we know and what we don't know about the relationship. *Educational Psychology Review 19*, 185–221.

Schrank, F. A. (2006). Specification of the cognitive processes involved in performance on the Woodcock-Johnson III. *Woodcock-Johnson III assessment service bulletin number 7*. Itasca, IL: Riverside Publishing.

Scruggs, T. E., & Mastropieri, M. A. (1990). The case for mnemonic instruction: From laboratory research to classroom applications. *The Journal of Special Education, 24*, 7–32.

Scruggs, T. E., & Mastropieri, M. A. (2000). The effectiveness of mnemonic instruction for students with learning and behavior problems: An update and research synthesis. *Journal of Behavioral Education, 10*, 163–173.

Seigneuric, A., & Ehrlich, M. (2005). Contribution of working memory capacity to children's reading comprehension: A longitudinal investigation. *Reading and Writing, 18*, 617–656.

Seigneuric, A., Ehrlich, M., Oakhill, J. V., & Yuill, N. M. (2000). Working memory resources and children's reading comprehension. *Reading and Writing: An Interdisciplinary Journal, 13*, 81–103.

Service, E. (1992). Phonology, working memory, and foreign language learning. *The Quarterly Journal of Experimental Psychology, 45A*, 21–50.

Shaywitz, S. E. (2003). *Overcoming dyslexia: A new and complete science-based program for overcoming reading problems at any level.* New York: Knopf.

Shiffrin, R. M. (1999). 30 years of memory. In C. Izawa (Ed.), *On human memory: Evolution, progress, and reflections on the 30th anniversary of the Atkinson-Shiffrin model* (pp. 17–33). Mahwah, NJ: Lawrence Erlbaum.

Siegel, L. S., & Ryan, E. B. (1989). The development of working memory in normally achieving and subtypes of learning disabilities. *Child Development, 60*, 973–980.

Smith, E. E., & Jonides, J. (1997). Working memory: A view from neuroimaging. *Cognitive Psychology, 33*, 5–42.

Smith-Spark, J. H., & Fisk, J. E. (2007). Working memory functioning in developmental dyslexia. *Memory, 15*, 34–56.

Smyth, M. M., & Scholey, K. A. (1994). Interference in immediate spatial memory. *Memory & Cognition, 22*, 1–13.

Snider, V. E. (1995). A primer on phonemic awareness: What it is, why it's important, and how to teach it. *School Psychology Review, 24*, 443–455.

Soto, D., Heinke, D., Humphreys, G. W., & Blanco, M. J. (2005). Early involuntary top-down guidance of attention from working memory. *Journal of Experimental Psychology: Human Perception and Performance, 31*, 248–261.

Speece, D. L. (1987). Information subtypes of learning disabled readers. *Learning Disabilities Research, 2*, 91–102.

St.Clair-Thompson, H. L. (2007). The influence of strategies upon relationships between working memory and cognitive skills. *Memory, 15*, 353–365.

Steele, S. D., Minshew, N. J., Luna, B., & Sweeney, J. A. (2007). Spatial working memory deficits in autism. *Journal of Autism and Developmental Disorders, 37*, 605–612.

Stephane, M., & Pellizzer, G. (2007). The dynamic architecture of working memory in schizophrenia. *Schizophrenia Research, 92*, 160–167.

Stoltzfus, E. R., Hasher, L., & Zacks, R. T. (1996). Working memory and retrieval: An inhibition-resource approach. In J. T. E. Richardson, R. W. Engle, L. Hasher, R. H. Logie, E. R. Stoltzfus, & R. T. Zacks (Eds.), *Working memory and human cognition* (pp. 66–88). New York: Oxford University Press.

Strauss, E., Sherman, E. M. S., & Spreen, O. (2006). *A compendium of neuropsychological tests.* New York: Oxford University Press.

Sub, H. M., Oberauer, K., Wittmann, W. W., Wilhelm, O., & Schulze, R. (2002). Working-memory capacity explains reasoning ability—and a little bit more. *Intelligence, 30*, 261–288.

Swanson, H. L. (1987). Verbal coding deficit in learning disabled readers: Remembering pictures and words. *Advances in Learning and Behavioral Disabilities, Supplement 2*, 263–304.

Swanson, H. L. (1992). Generality and modifiability of working memory among skilled and less skilled readers. *Journal of Educational Psychology, 84*, 473–488.

Swanson, H. L. (1993). Working memory in learning disability subgroups. *Journal of Experimental Child Psychology, 56,* 87–114.

Swanson, H. L. (1994). Short-term and working memory: Do both contribute to our understanding of academic achievement in children and adults with learning disabilities? *Journal of Learning Disabilities, 27,* 34–50.

Swanson, H. L. (1995). *Swanson Cognitive Processing Test (S-CPT): A dynamic assessment measure.* Austin, TX: PRO-ED.

Swanson, H. L. (1996). Individual and age-related differences in children's working memory. *Memory & Cognition, 24,* 70–82.

Swanson, H. L. (1999a). Instructional components that predict treatment outcomes for students with learning disabilities: Support for a combined strategy and direct instruction model. *Learning Disabilities Research, 14,* 129–140.

Swanson, H. L. (1999b). Reading comprehension and working memory in learning-disabled readers: Is the phonological loop more important that the executive system? *Journal of Experimental Child Psychology, 72,* 1–31.

Swanson, H. L. (2000). Are working memory deficits in readers with learning disabilities hard to change? *Journal of Learning Disabilities, 33,* 551–566.

Swanson, H. L. (2001). Research on interventions for adolescents with learning disabilities: A meta-analysis of outcomes related to higher-order processing. *Elementary School Journal, 101,* 331–348.

Swanson, H. L. (2006a). Cross-sectional and incremental changes in working memory and mathematical problem solving. *Journal of Educational Psychology, 98,* 265–281.

Swanson, H. L. (2006b). Working memory and dynamic testing in children with learning disabilities. In S. J. Pickering (Ed.), *Working memory and education* (pp. 125–156). Burlington, MA: Academic Press.

Swanson, H. L., & Alexander, J. (1997). Cognitive processes as predictors of word recognition and reading comprehension in learning disabled and skilled readers: Revisiting the specificity hypothesis. *Journal of Educational Psychology, 89,* 128–158.

Swanson, H. L., & Beebe-Frankenberger, M. (2004). The relationship between working memory and mathematical problem solving in children at risk and not at risk for serious math difficulties. *Journal of Educational Psychology, 96,* 471–491.

Swanson, H. L., & Berninger, V. W. (1995). The role of working memory in skilled and less skilled readers' comprehension. *Intelligence, 21,* 83–108.

Swanson, H. L., & Berninger, V. W. (1996). Individual differences in children's working memory and writing skill. *Journal of Experimental Child Psychology, 63,* 358–385.

Swanson, H. L., Cochran, K. F., & Ewers, C. A. (1990). Can learning disabilities be determined from working memory performance? *Journal of Learning Disabilities, 23,* 59–67.

Swanson, H. L., & Hoskyn, M. (1998). A synthesis of experimental intervention literature for students with learning disabilities: A meta-analysis of treatment outcomes. *Review of Educational Research, 68,* 277–321.

Swanson, H. L., Hoskyn, M., & Lee, C. (1999). *Interventions for students with learning disabilities: A meta-analysis of treatment outcomes.* New York: Guilford.

Swanson, H. L., Howard, C. B., & Saez, L. (2006). Do different components of working memory underlie different subgroups of reading disabilities? *Journal of Learning Disabilities, 39,* 252–269.

Swanson, H. L., & Howell, M. (2001). Working memory, short-term memory, and speech rate as predictors of children's reading. *Journal of Educational Psychology, 93*, 720–734.

Swanson, H. L., & Jerman, O. (2007). The influence of working memory on reading growth in subgroups of children with disabilities. *Journal of Experimental Child Psychology, 96*, 249–283.

Swanson, H. L., & Sachse-Lee, C. (2001). Mathematical problem solving and working memory in children with learning disabilities: Both executive and phonological processes are important. *Journal of Experimental Child Psychology, 79*, 294–321.

Swanson, H. L., & Siegel, L. (2001). Learning disabilities as a working memory deficit. *Issues in Education: Contributions from Educational Psychology, 7*, 1–48.

Tannock, R., Ickowicz, A., & Schachar, R. (1995). Differential effects of methylphenidate on working memory in ADHD children with and without comorbid anxiety. *Journal of the American Academy of Child and Adolescent Psychiatry, 34*, 886–896.

Thorndike, E. L. (1910). The relation between memory for words and memory for numbers, and the relation between memory over short and long intervals. *American Journal of Psychology, 21*, 487–488.

Torgesen, J. K. (1996). Model of memory from an information processing perspective: The special case of phonological memory. In G. R. Lyon & N. A. Krasnegor (Eds.), *Attention, memory, and executive function* (pp. 157–184). Baltimore: Paul H. Brookes.

Torgesen, J. K. (2001). Learning disabilities as a working memory deficit: The important next questions. *Issues in Education, 7*, 93–102.

Torgesen, J. K., & Goldman, T. (1977). Rehearsal and short-term memory in reading disabled children. *Child Development, 48*, 56–60.

Towse, J. N., & Hitch, G. J. (1995). Is there a relationship between task demand and storage space in tests of working memory capacity? *Quarterly Journal of Experimental Psychology, 48*, 108–124.

Towse, J. N., Hitch, G. J., & Hutton, U. (1998). A reevaluation of working memory capacity in children. *Journal of Memory and Language, 39*, 195–217.

Towse, J. N., Hitch, G. J., & Hutton, U. (2002). On the nature of the relationship between processing activity and item retention in children. *Journal of Experimental Child Psychology, 82*, 156–184.

Trbovich, P. L., & LeFevre, J. -A. (2003). Phonological and visual working memory in mental addition. *Memory & Cognition, 31*, 738–745.

Tronsky, L. N. (2005). Strategy use, the development of automaticity, and working memory involvement in complex multiplication. *Memory & Cognition, 33*, 927–940.

Turley-Ames, K. J., & Whitfield, M. M. (2003). Strategy training and working memory task performance. *Journal of Memory and Language, 49*, 446–468.

Turner, M. L., & Engle, R. W. (1989). Is working memory capacity task dependent? *Journal of Memory and Language, 28*, 127–154.

Turner, J. E., Henry, L. A., & Smith, P. T. (2000). The development of the use of long-term knowledge to assist short-term recall. *Quarterly Journal of Experimental Psychology, 53A*, 457–478.

Unsworth, N., & Engle, R. W. (2007). The nature of individual differences in working memory capacity: Active maintenance in primary memory and controlled search from secondary memory. *Psychological Review, 114*, 104–132.

U.S. Department of Education, Office of Special Education and Rehabilitative Services. (2006). *Twenty-sixth annual report to congress on the implementation of the Individuals with Disabilities Education Act.* Washington, DC: Author.

Van Der Sluis, S., Van Der Leij, A., & De Jong, P. F. (2005). Working memory in Dutch children with reading-and arithmetic-related LD. *Journal of Learning Disabilities, 38,* 207–221.

Van Snellenberg, J. X., Torres, I. J., & Thornton, A. E. (2006). Functional neuroimaging of working memory in schizophrenia: Task performance as a moderating variable. *Neuropsychology, 20,* 497–510.

Verhaeghen, P., Cerella, J., & Basak, C. (2004). A working-memory workout: How to expand the focus of serial attention from one to four items, in ten hours or less. *Journal of Experimental Psychology: Learning, Memory, and Cognition, 30,* 1322–1337.

Wagner, R. K. (1996). From simple structure to complex function: Major trends in the development of theories, models, and measurements of memory. In G. R. Lyon & N. A. Krasnegor (Eds.), *Attention, memory, and executive function* (pp. 139–156). Baltimore: Paul H. Brookes.

Was, C. A., & Woltz, D. J. (2006). Reexamining the relationship between working memory and comprehension: The role of available long-term memory. *Journal of Memory and Language, 56,* 86–102.

Waters, G. S., & Caplan, D. (1996). Processing resource capacity and the comprehension of garden path sentences. *Memory and Cognition, 24,* 342–355.

Wechsler, D. (1997a). *Wechsler Adult Intelligence Scale—third edition.* San Antonio: The Psychological Corporation.

Wechsler, D. (1997b). *Wechsler Memory Scale—third edition.* San Antonio: The Psychological Corporation.

Wechsler, D. (2002). *Wechsler Preschool and Primary Scale of Intelligence—third edition.* San Antonio: The Psychological Corporation.

Wechsler, D. (2003). *Wechsler Intelligence Scale for Children—fourth edition.* San Antonio: The Psychological Corporation.

Wechsler, D., Kaplan, E., Fein, D., Kramer, J., Morris, R., Delis, D., & Maerlender, A. (2004a). *Wechsler Intelligence Scale for Children Fourth Edition—Integrated.* San Antonio: The Psychological Corporation.

Wechsler, D., Kaplan, E., Fein, D., Kramer, J., Morris, R., Delis, D., & Maerlender, A. (2004b). *Wechsler Intelligence Scale for Children Fourth Edition—Integrated: Technical and interpretative manual.* San Antonio: The Psychological Corporation.

Westerberg, H., Jacobaeus, H., Hirvikoski, T., Clevberger, M. -L., Ostensson, A., Bartfai, A., et al. (2007). Computerized working memory training after stroke—a pilot study. *Brain Injury, 21,* 21–29.

White, W. A. T. (1988). A meta-analysis of the effects of direct instruction in special education. *Education and Treatment of Children, 11,* 364–374.

Williams, D. L., Goldstein, G., Carpenter, P. A., & Minshew, N. J. (2005). Verbal and spatial working memory in autism. *Journal of Autism and Developmental Disorders, 35,* 747–756.

Wilson, B. A. (1987). *Rehabilitation of memory.* New York: Guilford.

Wilson, K. M., & Swanson, H. L. (2001). Are mathematics disabilities due to a domain-general or a domain-specific working memory deficit? *Journal of Learning Disabilities, 34*, 237–248.

Woodcock, R. W., McGrew, K. S., & Mather, N. (2001a). *Woodcock-Johnson III Tests of Achievement*. Itasca, IL: Riverside Publishing.

Woodcock, R. W., McGrew, K. S., & Mather, N. (2001b). *Woodcock-Johnson III Tests of Cognitive Abilities*. Itasca, IL: Riverside Publishing.

Work, P. H. L., & Choi, H. (2005). Developing classroom and group interventions based on a neuropsychological paradigm. In R. K. D'Amato, E. Fletcher-Janzen, & C. R. Reynolds (Eds.), *Handbook of school neuropsychology* (pp. 663–683). Hoboken, NJ: Wiley.

Wu, K. K., Anderson, V., & Castiello, U. (2006). Attention-deficit/hyperactivity disorder and working memory: A task switching paradigm. *Journal of Clinical and Experimental Neuropsychology, 28*, 1288–1306.

Wynn-Dancy, M. L., & Gillam, R. B. (1997). Accessing long-term memory: Metacognitive strategies and strategic action in adolescents. *Topics in Language Disorders, 18*, 32–44.

INDEX